Branches & Byways
Cornwall

Branches & Byways
Cornwall

John Vaughan

OPC
Oxford Publishing Co

Half title:
In addition to three important early narrow gauge plateways/railways, *Branches and Byways: Cornwall* includes all recognised standard gauge Cornish branch lines that were connected to the erstwhile British Railways (GWR/SR) network. With the 'Cornish Railways' insignia visible on the front end, Class 37 diesel locomotive No 37207 *William Cookworthy* runs 'light engine' past Coombe Junction on the Looe branch, on its way to Moorswater to collect some china clay wagons on 9 June 1986. *JV*

Title page:
A picturesque and still extant Cornish byway is the St Ives branch in the west of the county. With an incoming tide in the estuary of the River Hayle, two-car diesel multiple-unit (DMU) set No T304 approaches Lelant station on 24 September 1993 forming the 10.55 St Ives to St Erth service. This was the last Cornish branch line worked by these first-generation diesel units before their withdrawal later in the decade. Various DMU classes were the mainstay of Cornish branch line operations for over 30 years. *JV*

Below:
One of the many British Railways (BR) corporate organisational experiments was the creation in 1983 of a 'west of Plymouth' subdivision called 'Cornish Railways'. Many operational and financial aspects of the railway business were delegated to local management, based at St Blazey depot. However, total independence was not possible and the arrangements came to an end within a couple of years. This was the subdivision's chosen insignia. *JV*

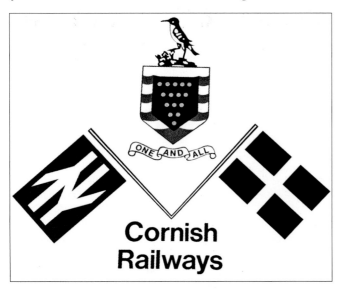

Cornish Railways

First published 2002

ISBN 0 86093 566 3

© John Vaughan 2002

Published by Oxford Publishing Co

an imprint of Ian Allan Publishing Ltd, Hersham, Surrey KT12 4RG.
Printed by Ian Allan Printing Ltd, Hersham, Surrey KT12 4RG.

Code 0207/A2

Contents

Introduction

This book incorporates every standard gauge Cornish branch line and byway that was connected to the erstwhile British Railways (GWR/SR) network as well as three historically important narrow gauge lines. It was agreed with the publisher that without detracting in any way from dedicated and definitive histories of certain Cornish branches, many of which are included in the Bibliography, to have an all-in-one illustrated reference book would be novel and serve a really useful purpose. Of the branches featured, three quarters have closed while the others have either partly closed or, at the time of writing, remain open. Although all branches and byways, as defined above, have been included, it must be remembered that in industrial areas of Cornwall just about every works, quarry and mine had some form of rail or wagonway for the transportation of materials and minerals. In fact it was reported that the Happy Union mine near Pentewan had a complete underground tramroad back in 1783! There were hundreds of lines ranging in length from a few dozen yards to a couple of miles or more. The layout of these normally narrow gauge lines changed daily and it would not therefore be possible to include them, even in a book of this size.

It is difficult to define precisely a railway 'branch' line or 'byway'. The classic image is that of a normally single line railway leaving a nearby main line at a junction to serve either a town or industry not located on the main line route. A byway is perhaps a very minor branch, or perhaps a long siding, or maybe a railway line built to serve a particular industrial installation. By dictionary definition a branch is 'a limb, an extension, subdivision, offshoot, something that divides into two'. A byway is 'of secondary importance, a by-road, a sidetrack or off the beaten track'. Whatever the definition, certain Cornish branches effectively changed their status on Summer Saturdays when through trains or coaches from London, the Midlands, the North and even Scotland worked along them with trainloads of holidaymakers. Newquay, Falmouth, Perranporth and St Ives all had through workings, as did the Southern Railway lines to Bude and Padstow. Now only Newquay experiences this temporary change of status on a few days in summer, with travellers for other surviving branch destinations having to change at junction stations in time-honoured tradition.

This book deals very specifically with branches and byways west of the Tamar. Where branches straddle the Devon/Cornwall boundary only the Cornish sections are dealt with in any detail; these include Bude, Launceston (GWR), Callington and the North Cornwall Railway. Within Cornwall there has been the most wonderful mix of Great Western Railway (GWR), London & South Western Railway (LSWR) and minor private and public lines of broad, standard and narrow gauges. Some were mere tramways or plateways, some never carried passengers, and some used horses for motive power. Many of these minor lines had relatively short lives.

The topography, geology, history and industrial archaeology of Cornwall are fascinating. The way that mining changed parts of the landscape in the 18th and 19th centuries with winding gear and engine houses, cluttering the previously rural and agricultural landscape, was dramatic. The needs of the industry resulted in significant improvements in what had been a primitive transport infrastructure and the change was radical. A rural community engaged in agriculture and fishing soon relied on mining and mineral extraction for its prosperity. Mining also brought sociological changes with fortunes being won and lost. As the fortunes of the mines and pits fluctuated, so the workers were either in employment or on the breadline. The boom and bust of the mining industry in the 19th and early 20th centuries saw thousands of Cornishmen emigrate to the Americas and the colonies in search of a better standard of living. The mid-19th century saw the coming of the railway linking Cornwall with the rest of England and the start of a tourist industry that would also have a substantial impact on Cornwall, especially its coastal resorts. Many of these 'rise and fall' developments are chronicled within these pages.

As regards topography and geology, the Cornish countryside is hugely varied with rolling farmland, deep valleys, sandy bays, steep cliffs, bleak moorland, deciduous and coniferous woodland, and tiny harbours, and I hope that some of the illustrations within the pages of this book do credit to the beauty and fascination of Kernow. The scenery in Cornwall is a delight to contend with, but often the weather is not, as 'southwesters' bring wind and rain across the landscape. From early Celtic times Cornwall has had a fascinating history, which is full of legend and folklore. The county also has its own language, although little used, which to some extent sets it apart from the rest of England. The other great divider is the mighty River Tamar, which for almost its entire length is the boundary between Cornwall and Devon.

The history of wagonways and byways in Cornwall goes back many years. As the industrial revolution got under way there was an unprecedented demand for a number of raw materials, which included lead, copper, tin, arsenic, china clay and a number of secondary minerals that were all mined in Cornwall. There was no railway connecting Cornwall to the rest of England until 1859, and until that time, and for many years after, all of the products of the mines had to be transported to various ports for loading on to ships. As mine output and customer demand increased, the speed, efficiency and capacity of what was then a horse-and-cart operation came under pressure. Metalled roads were an exception and, especially in winter, routes became heavily rutted, wagons got bogged down in mud and routes became almost impassable. At one time wagons with tyres not less than 6in wide were stipulated, but the problem was not resolved.

There was a two-way problem in that to feed the hundreds of greedy coal-powered steam-driven pumping engines that kept many of Cornwall's deep mines free from water, which appeared in Cornwall from about 1720, and the coal-fired china clay driers or other industrial machinery, huge volumes of coal were required. Coal was therefore the mineral that many wagons carried on a

Above:
No book could include every Cornish railway, tramway, plateway and wagonway because the majority of mines, pits, quarries and other industrial sites had some sort of internal system for transporting minerals. At one time or another over the past 200 years there have been literally thousands of minor tracks with human, horse, cable, gravity, steam, diesel, petrol and electric forms of motive power. This turn-of-the-century view of a tramway deep in Dolcoath mine shows a typical example of tramming, in dark, hot and unpleasant conditions.
P. Q. Treloar collection

also been considered, but the terrain was not really conducive to that mode of transport. By 1818 there were many other abortive schemes for tramways, but it was not until 1823 that notice was given in the *West Briton* newspaper of the intention to build a line from the Redruth area to the quay at Devoran on the Fal estuary. The 4ft gauge line opened in parts from 1825, and throughout in 1826. Until 1854 all traffic was horse-drawn, with sometimes teams of up to six horses hauling up to six wagons. The Redruth & Chasewater was to be the first 'proper' railway in Cornwall (See Chapter 2).

These early railways catered for the needs of the mines, but in 1829 the 'slightly' narrow 4ft 6in gauge Pentewan Railway opened between St Austell and Pentewan Harbour for the conveyance of china clay and many other commodities. The line was horse-powered until 1872 when steam locomotives arrived and a change of gauge to 2ft 6in took place. However, remoteness from its payloads' point of origin and a harbour prone to silting up were eventually to see its downfall. Most of these early railways were built without passengers in mind, but, as with the Pentewan Railway, many arranged excursions whereby locals travelled in goods wagons. Many other lines eventually performed a dual freight and passenger function.

By the early 1830s many other lines were under active consideration. The first standard gauge line was to be the Bodmin & Wadebridge Railway, which ran from Wadebridge to Bodmin and Wenford Bridge. Except for the aforementioned occasional excursions, the line was initially freight only and it was the first in Cornwall to employ steam locomotives for haulage. It opened between Wadebridge and Dunmere Junction in July 1834 and to Wenford Bridge in September of that year.

In the same year Royal Assent was given for the incorporation of the Hayle Railway. This line in West Cornwall was to provide a service for many mines in the Redruth and Camborne areas and to link them with the already important harbour at Hayle. The line was to terminate at Tresavean, but with many branches along the route. A further Act of 1836 enabled the company to build an alternative branch to Portreath (see Chapter 22). Unlike the Redruth & Chasewater, the line was to employ steam locomotives over much of its length. It was opened from Hayle Foundry to Pool and Portreath just before Christmas in 1837.

Another major milestone was the opening in 1841 of a section of the Treffry Tramway from Ponts Mill to Colcerrow Quarry, near Luxulyan. This was the first stage of a network of lines and byways that served the china clay industry around Bugle, north of the Hensbarrow Downs area. Tramway building also started at Newquay Harbour, reaching St Dennis and East Wheal Rose in 1849; all traffic was horse-drawn. In 1874, under the auspices of the Treffry Tramway's successor, the Cornwall Minerals Railway, Fowey and Par on Cornwall's south coast were connected with Newquay on the north coast. Some route realignment was necessary and locomotives replaced horses. Passenger trains were introduced in 1876.

In 1843 the standard gauge Liskeard & Caradon Railway was incorporated. The line linked the mines and quarries around Caradon Hill with the terminus of an 1828-built canal that ran from Moorswater to the coast near Looe. The line was opened to South Caradon by 1844 and to the Cheesewring by 1846. In 1860 the Liskeard & Looe Railway built a railway line up from Looe to meet the Caradon line, with locomotives replacing horses on the L&CR in 1862. Passengers were carried from 1879 and the line was linked to the (by then) GWR's main line in 1901.

Although not all branch line developments were linked to the following events, the completion of the West Cornwall standard gauge line from Penzance to Truro in 1852 and, more significantly, the opening of the Cornwall Railway line from Plymouth to Truro in 1859 resulted in a substantial expansion of the Cornish railway map. In 1855 the line to Newham (Truro) was opened, and this was followed by Falmouth in 1863, the GWR line to Launceston in 1865, Drinnick Mill and Fowey from

back-run from the ports, and this added to the wear on the primitive highways. Several wooden-railed tramways or 'rayle-ways' were in use in the UK as long ago as the 17th century, and were replaced by the end of the 18th century by cast-iron rails. In the early 19th century even more use was being made of plateways using mainly horse power drawing carts and running on a form of rail used in the collieries of South Wales as well as in the North of England. It was the early 1800s when wealthy land and mine owners proposed a tramroad from the mines near Scorrier to the north coast at Portreath. The wagons would be horse-drawn and would run on L-shaped cast-iron plates attached to granite blocks or sleepers. In 1812 part of this approximately 4ft gauge line opened (see Chapter 1, Poldice Tramway).

The Poldice tramroad was an immediate financial success and this resulted in other mine owners and entrepreneurs giving consideration to the construction of other tramroads. Canals had

Lostwithiel in 1869, the East Cornwall Mineral Railway from Calstock to Callington (Kelly Bray) in 1872, St Ives in 1877, Bodmin General in 1887 and on to Boscarne in 1888, Helston also in 1887, Goonbarrow in 1893, the North Cornwall Railway to Wadebridge in 1895 and on to Padstow in 1899, the Cornish part of the Bude branch in 1898, Chasewater to Newquay in 1903, the Callington branch in 1908, an extension to the Retew branch in 1912, and the Trenance Valley line, west of St Austell, in 1920.

By the time some of these branches had opened many of the early lines and tramways had already disappeared. Full details appear in the relevant chapters, but by 1852 part of the original Hayle Railway closed (upon the opening of the West Cornwall Railway). In 1856 the original Poldice Tramway was little used and by 1865 it had virtually closed, its primary mine having become exhausted. The Gravel Hill extension to the Treamble branch was gone by 1888 following the closure of a nearby Iron Mine, and after being in the Receiver's hands for decades the Redruth & Chasewater Railway was closed in 1915. In 1917 the line down from Caradon Hill to Moorswater was lifted to assist the war effort and a year later it was the narrow gauge Pentewan Railway that closed.

As in many other parts of the country the coming of omnibuses and lorries had a detrimental effect on the railways. The line from Fowey to Par closed to passengers (except for a workman's train) in 1925, and the Newquay Harbour branch was defunct by 1926. By about 1930 the little Gothers Tramway had closed, and in 1933 it was the turn of the line to Ruthern Bridge to see its last goods wagon. There were many other line and siding closures between the 1930s and the 1960s, but it was the advent of the so-called 'Beeching era' and the railways 're-shaping' plan of the 1960s that brought carnage to the branches and byways of Cornwall.

To be fair, some of the branches cited in the report, which was produced for government by Dr Beeching, were hopelessly unremunerative for a variety of reasons. These included local apathy, seasonal traffic, small populations near intermediate stations, badly sited stations, increased motor car ownership, poor service, industrial disputes, high fares, a lack of marketing, and declining freight traffic. The 1960s saw the closure of the branches to Bude, Launceston (WR), Callington (part), Bodmin General (to passengers) and North, Padstow, the North Cornwall line, Lostwithiel to Fowey (to passengers), Chasewater to Newquay, and Helston. However, there were some surprising

Right:
Cornwall is littered with the remains of old mine buildings, and these wonderful edifices are reminders of its past when copper, tin, lead, arsenic and other minerals were mined in many parts of the county. The products from the mines were mostly exported, while coal to feed the greedy steam pumping engines housed in engine houses such as that seen here, near Carnkie, needed to be imported. This resulted in the creation of early tramways and plateways, which connected the mining areas with various ports. *JV*

survivors amongst other branches that were scheduled for closure, including Looe, St Ives, Falmouth, Gunnislake and Newquay. These lines became political footballs as closure policies changed with almost every general election.

Just as the steam locomotive replaced the horse, diesel traction replaced steam. In many cases the arrival of economical-to-run diesel units failed to save branch closures. However, a downturn in the goods/freight business between the 1960s and 1990s accounted for many other branch and byway closures. Lines to Retew, Carbean (Goonbarrow branch), Wenford Bridge, Fowey (from Par), Lansalson (Trenance Valley), Newham, Carbis Wharf, Ponts Mill and Wheal Rose (on the Newquay branch), and Moorswater (later reopened) all closed during this period, and the majority of these developments are recorded and illustrated within these pages. The railway map of Cornwall has changed radically during the last 200 years and one thing is for sure — it will never be the same again!

The operation of all of these branches and byways has been in the hands of many diverse organisations over the years. In the early days it was wealthy land and mine owners who ruled the roost. There were a number of locally supported railway companies, which often sold out to larger companies, especially when they ran into financial difficulties or needed more capital for infrastructure expenditure. The GWR later absorbed the larger Cornish railway companies and had enormous influence on the development of railways in Cornwall, although it did not quite have it all its own way, as incursions from a northerly direction by the London & South Western Railway were a constant threat. By 1889 the Cornwall Railway had been sold to the GWR, and in 1892 the GWR broad gauge main line was converted to standard gauge.

The railway Grouping took place in 1923 and nationalisation was introduced in 1948, when British Railways, divided into various regions, took over the national war-torn railway network, including both Great Western and Southern Railway lines in Cornwall. Some lines in Cornwall were subjected to a tennis match of control, with first the Southern Region and then the Western Region assuming control. For a short period between 1983 and 1986 Cornwall was given certain delegated responsibilities for running its railways, a precursor to the division of BR into business sectors. The Railfreight side of the business gave rise to such names as,

Below:
In the construction of many local tramways, plateways and railways use was made of local materials. Granite was readily available from quarries in many parts of Cornwall and it was used to support rails, effectively in the capacity of sleepers, on many lines. These examples were photographed in 1990 at the southern end of the original Treffry Tramway route from Ponts Mill to Par Harbour. St Blazey depot is to the left and a signal on the Par to St Blazey spur can just be seen in the background. Granite blocks such as these can still be seen in many parts of Cornwall. *JV*

Above:
An interesting Cornish tramway that is worth a mention although outside of the general scope of this book is the Camborne & Redruth Tramway. This 3ft 6in gauge system, 3 miles 4 chains long, opened in November 1902 and carried passengers in street tramcars between the towns incorporated in its title. From November 1903 the system was also used to convey tin ore, which was mined at East Pool and Wheal Agar and conveyed in small wooden and steel bin wagons with a 3-ton capacity to the crushing stamps at Tolvaddon. Two small locomotives powered by two 25hp electric motors hauled three or four wagons at a time, taking power from an overhead line via a trolley pole. Here, in Edwardian times, No 2 leaves East Pool for Tolvaddon. Such workings ceased in 1934, passenger services having succumbed to bus competition seven years earlier.
JV collection

inter alia, Transrail, Loadhaul, Construction, Mainline and Railfreight Distribution. The effective privatisation of the railways followed in 1996 with the part-American-owned English, Welsh & Scottish Railway handling freight in Cornwall and First Great Western, Virgin Rail and Wales & West running passenger services, with Railtrack owning the permanent way and railway infrastructure. In the future railway operation will depend on a periodic bidding process with finance and efficiency being some of the criteria used before contracts are awarded to private railway companies. The long-term future of Railtrack has not been determined.

It is difficult to predict the future for the surviving branch lines and byways. There seems to be political conflict between the use of 'environmentally friendly' modes of transport and public expenditure on what are undoubtedly unremunerative branch lines. Anybody who has witnessed loadings on the Newquay branch during our long winter months will quickly realise that the line has little hope of ever making a profit. Other Cornish branches are in a similar position. From a railway romantic perspective it is hoped that they will survive for ever, but in the real commercial world this cannot be

guaranteed. As regards freight, many of the old commodities from the mines, the collieries and the fields are no longer transported by rail. Cornwall has always had a number of one-off payloads that in recent times have ranged from beer and fertilizer to seaweed, from fish and pipes to light fittings, and from slate dust to oil. However, the freight operators do not presently regard most of these as financially viable. But china clay in all its various forms is, by far, the most important commodity conveyed by rail freight. The industry has declined in recent years but many millions of tonnes are still conveyed to a wide range of destinations. However, in future years even china clay will be subjected to annual negotiations over the cost and speed of transportation.

The railway infrastructure has also changed significantly over the past couple of centuries. The old wooden-topped viaducts were mostly replaced before the last century, but other changes have been the same as in other parts of Britain. The removal of crossing gates, buildings at wayside halts, station awnings and overbridges, semaphore signals and signalboxes and almost anything ornamental, ranging from lamps to carefully maintained station gardens, has been widespread. Track has been rationalised and a large number of lines and sidings have closed completely. The railway is now impersonal, and although it is not their fault, railway staff have, to some extent, become mobile corporate employees. Happily some of the photographs show the days when you could have a chat with a signalman, crossing-keeper or porter at the local station.

On a more positive note, at the time of writing there are still some aesthetically pleasing sights remaining on Cornish branches, in addition to the scenery. For example, the passing loop, signalbox and semaphore signals at Goonbarrow Junction on the Newquay branch have survived, as have the signalbox and signals at St Blazey. The Looe branch line station at Liskeard is still attractive and the intermediate halts have been tastefully refurbished. The crossing gates on the way from St Blazey to Par Harbour are still manually operated. Although under threat, manually operated semaphore signals for the Fowey branch (and the main line) at Lostwithiel, the down signals to the Falmouth branch at Truro, and the St Ives branch signals at St Erth are presently extant. Stations at Roche and Lelant still have some charm, and Liskeard, Par, Truro and St Erth are still very much traditional junction stations.

In addition, the preservation movement is alive and well in Cornwall. The Bodmin & Wenford Railway runs standard gauge services from Bodmin Parkway (formerly Road) to Bodmin General and Boscarne Junction. Miniature railways run on part of the old Chacewater to Newquay branch (the Lappa Valley Railway) and also at Launceston, and there are many others, such as those at Dobwalls and Newquay Zoo, but in terms of a detailed description they are outside the scope of this book.

It is a pleasure and a privilege to again be associated, in literary terms, with the railways of Cornwall. It was in 1968 that Ian Allan published my first part-book, and since then 29 other books have appeared in print, four of them dedicated to some aspect of railways in Cornwall. My paternal great, great grandmother, Eliza Carne, was born at Kenwyn, Truro, in Cornwall in 1823, but other than that my only association with the county has come from some 100 visits over a period of 33 years. These years have given

much pleasure in both recording on film the Cornish railway scene, whether it was main line, branch line or 'bramble bashing' on a long-closed line, and in meeting a wide range of Cornish folk plus the odd Devonian!

Wherever possible I have tried to use photographs that have not been published before. However, it must be recognised that where a photograph is a classic view, or where something unusual is shown, or when a photograph is the only known view of a scene or event, such as the accident at Higher Carnon Bridge on the Redruth & Chasewater Railway in 1899, I have not hesitated to use the photograph(s) again. I have tried to balance ancient and modern to illustrate not only what has gone but also to demonstrate that there are still some active branches and byways to explore in Cornwall!

This book could not possibly have been undertaken without the help of many individuals and organisations. The authors of various line histories and contributing photographers are at the top of the list for special mention, and they are recognised in the Acknowledgements and Bibliography. Selected maps, track diagrams and timetable extracts have been included in addition to more than 380 photographs. My primary objective has been to produce an attractive book of reference that gives the reader as much pleasure as it has given me in its compilation. My secondary objective has been to create a sense of nostalgia about the way that things once were, whatever the era. For some this may well be some prewar grass-covered mineral line, for others it will be a pre-nationalisation steam-hauled branch train, while for many it will be the sight of a now withdrawn Class 37 diesel on a line that has closed for ever. Whatever your recollections, or indeed if you never witnessed this remarkable subject, I sincerely hope that you enjoy *Branches and Byways: Cornwall*.

John A. M. Vaughan
Goring by Sea
West Sussex

Above and left:
Three Cornish branch line nameboards still in use in the 1960s and early 1970s. The Bere Alston (in Devon) sign was photographed in 1970, four years after Callington to Gunnislake was closed. Happily, we can still change at Liskeard for Looe, but the Goods Office at Wenford Bridge is but a happy memory. *JV*

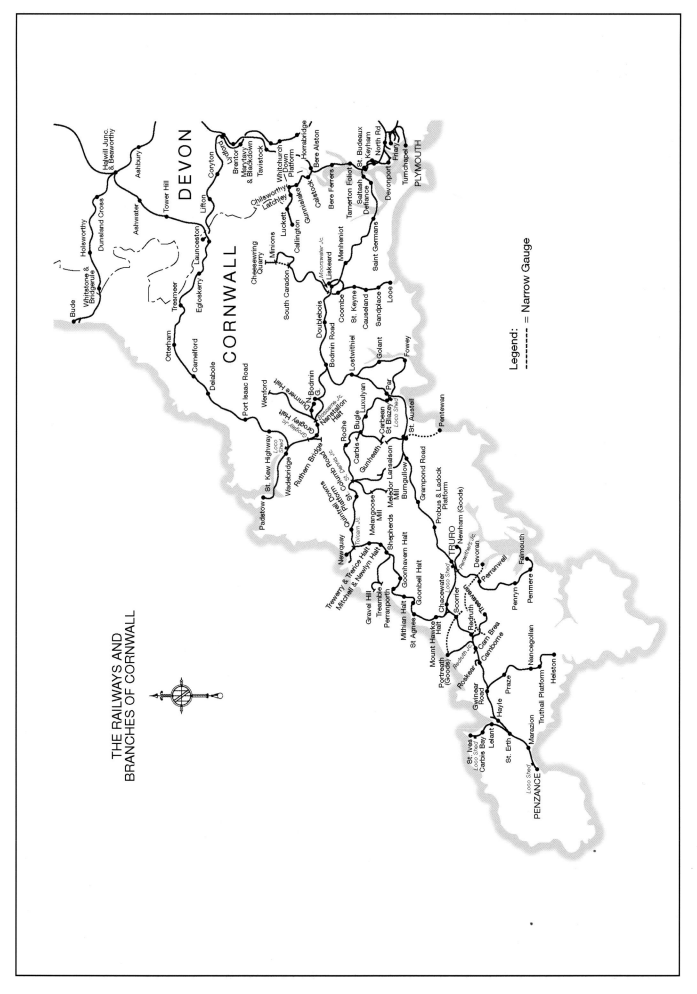

THE RAILWAYS AND
BRANCHES OF CORNWALL

Legend:
------- = Narrow Gauge

1. Poldice Tramway

Although there were minor wagonways within a number of mines and works in the county of Cornwall by the 18th century, it is generally accepted that railways in Cornwall commenced with the construction of the Poldice Tramway in 1809-10. This was a private railway, the first public one being the Redruth & Chasewater of 1824.

As briefly mentioned in the Introduction, the Cornish mines became a victim of their own success when it came to transportation. Tin mining preceded copper mining by many years, but by 1800 the output of the copper mines far exceeded that of tin. Throughout the 19th century there were chronic peaks and troughs in output, based on world demand and commodity prices, but until the early 1860s copper ore production was at its zenith. Millions upon millions of tons of ore were raised and Cornwall dominated copper production worldwide. The problem was getting the ore from the mines to the ships that waited at tiny harbours around Cornwall's coasts.

For over a century the mine owners had to make do with first packhorses and later wagons. One of the reasons why copper smelting never became established in Cornwall, except at Copperhouse, near Hayle, was that 18 times as much fuel, in the form of coal, was required to produce each ton of finished metal. Thus it was easier to export the ore to South Wales than to bring in coal from the Welsh pits. However, horse-powered transport by road struggled to cope, even without the smelting activity. As the steam beam/pumping engines multiplied, so the need for coal increased. Eventually there were thousands of mine machinery units to feed with coal and large tonnages of ore to carry to the harbours, resulting in a high number of journeys along primitive roads. These roads were badly 'cut up' and were sometimes impassable in winter.

On the north coast between Hayle and Newquay a small artificial harbour at Portreath, also known as Basset's Cove, had been carved out of the rock. It was owned by the Basset family, who had huge mining interests, and they leased the port to an operating company part owned by the enormously wealthy and influential Fox family of Falmouth, the Williams family of Scorrier House and others. Together they totally controlled all activities at Portreath Harbour. The owners had business connections in South Wales where 150 miles of tramways were already part of the colliery and general industrial scene. After a canal project had been dismissed, and a plan for a tramway from Dalcoath to Portreath had failed to materialise, it had been decided that a 5.42-mile tramway from Portreath to Poldice was the answer to the transportation problems in the area.

Lord de Dunstanville, a local dignitary, laid the first rail in October 1809. The horse-worked line was laid to very

Right:
The first railway of any distance in the county of Cornwall was the Poldice Tramway. A group of wealthy mine owners were anxious to connect their increasingly productive mines south of Scorrier to Portreath, a small privately owned harbour on Cornwall's north coast (see map page 229 and caption page 221). The first rail was laid in 1809 and part of the approximately 4ft gauge horse-operated line opened in 1812. The track comprised short L-shaped cast-iron sections attached to granite block sleepers. This rare close-up shows the narrow wheels that ran inside the flange of the L-shaped track.
Cornwall Record Office

approximate 4ft gauge and comprised short L-shaped cast-iron plates attached to roughly square granite blocks or 'sleepers'. At the time of opening it was reported that 'The wheels of the carriages run on cast iron, which facilitates in an extraordinary manner the progress of the vehicles and greatly lessens the force of animal exertion.' From Portreath the line ran in an easterly then southeasterly direction, via Bridge, Cambrose and Mawla to Scorrier House. A storage yard was built at North Downs. This section was opened by 1812 and was an immediate financial success. Copper mines around Scorrier, St Day and Treskerby were served, the latter by a branch line. By about 1816 the line was extended to St Day (Crofthandy) to serve the mining complexes of the colossal Poldice, Wheal Unity and Wheal Gorland mines. The cost of the tramway had been £20,000.

With the passing of time not much is known about the nature of the workings on the Poldice Tramway, but an unlikely survivor is an open four-wheeled carriage constructed of yellow pine and used by the owners of the line and certain officials. The cast-iron L-shaped sections of the plateway were very prone to fractures and breaks, and running repairs were a constant headache. It is likely that only two or three wagons could be hauled together, if the Redruth & Chasewater is anything to go by, that line having opened in 1824, giving mines access to the south coast port of Devoran. The Poldice to Portreath line was in operation from 1812 to about 1865, but Poldice mine had become exhausted by the late 1850s and was reported to be at a standstill, resulting in a much

reduced volume of traffic. A branch of the Hayle Railway (later West Cornwall Railway, then GWR) from near Carn Brea to Portreath was opened in December 1837 and this increased traffic so much that in 1846 an inner basin had to be built at Portreath, resulting in up to 20 vessels discharging or loading simultaneously (see Chapter 22)!

The Poldice Tramway had largely fallen out of use by 1865. The mines in the area and at Gwennap were all in decline, and were of necessity becoming deeper and more difficult to work, while competition from abroad was having a negative impact. There was a severe slump at the beginning of the 1860s that had serious social implications. The crash came in 1866 when Cornish copper production halved. In 1866-7 over 7,000 miners and their families were forced to emigrate or starve! Gradually the mines closed, and by 1884 it was said in the local press that the line had been much in use until the stoppage of Poldice (mine) in the 'sixties'. Some 70 years after opening, the track was removed for scrap and the only trace of the line today is a series of footpaths that follow its course together with a number of granite setts/blocks. The best section to trace is from Portreath to Wheal Rose (not to be confused with Wheal Rose near Bugle or East Wheal Rose near Newquay), beyond Scorrier House and below Unity Wood to Crofthandy, and from Unity Wood to Killifreth and Wheal Busy mines. At Portreath the Poldice Tramway can be traced between houses, but unfortunately housing development has impinged on the port itself.

2. Redruth & Chasewater Railway, and Basset Mines

Throughout this book readers could not be blamed for questioning the spelling of the name of the Cornish town Chacewater. The most common spelling in early days was with an 's', but in more recent times the spelling with a 'c' has been the accepted form. In this section only Chasewater will be used, as in the incorporated name of the railway company.

Although the first rails of the Poldice Tramway had been laid in 1809, the Redruth & Chasewater Railway was to be Cornwall's first public railway, thereby earning its place in the history books. The line was built to serve one of the greatest mining areas in the world, where tin, copper, lead and many other minerals were mined in large volumes. By about 1800 the output of copper far exceeded tin production, but, unlike tin, smelting copper in Cornwall was never successful because large volumes of coal had to be imported from South Wales for the process. As mentioned in Chapter 1, some 18 tons of coal were consumed to produce a single ton of copper, and it did not need a mathematician to deduce that it was far more economic to take the copper ore to the energy source for smelting. Except for that smelted at Copperhouse, near Hayle, all Cornish copper ore was therefore shipped to either Swansea or Llanelly (now Llanelli).

As the volumes of mined ore increased and the need for coal to fire the thousands of steam pumping engines also increased, the mine owners turned their attention to the subject of transportation. Volumes were so high that relying on packhorses and later horse-drawn wagons had certain limitations and, as mentioned in Chapter 1, tramways and railways were becoming viable alternatives. The Poldice Tramway was immediately profitable, not only reducing the costs and time of transportation, but also making a profit for the tramway itself, a sort of 'double whammy' for the mine, land and tramway owners. In about 1819 mining entrepreneur John Taylor had reopened the series of Consols mines in the Gwennap area, closed in 1811, and production boomed — he had opened up the largest copper lode in the world. In addition to Consols there were a large number of other mines in the parish of Gwennap, which resulted in long lines of packhorses carrying ore in sacks to and from minor ports in the River Fal estuary, including Newham, Roundwood, Pill, Point, Restronguet and Penryn.

Taylor further expanded and took over other mines above Lanner and near Redruth. Including Consols, the delightful names of his mines at this time were Wheal Virgin, Wheal Girl, West Wheal Virgin, Wheal Maid, Wheal Fortune & Cusvey, Wheal Buller, Wheal Beauchamp, Wheal Sparnon and Pednandrea, and, in 1824, the large United Mines group. In 1808 there had been a plan to build a canal from the Fal estuary to Bissoe. This was followed in 1818 by an advertisement in the *West Briton* newspaper for a tramroad over the same route but to Twelveheads. These efforts came to nothing, but in 1823 John Taylor took the bull by the horns and decided to seek Parliamentary powers to construct a tramway. A notice appeared in the *West Briton* on 5 September 1823 giving notice of his

intention to build a tramway from Redruth to Devoran Quay and Point Quay with branches to Wheal Buller, and from Nangiles to Twelveheads, or Twelveheads to Chasewater and Wheal Busy.

On 15 January 1824 a meeting was held in London attended by interested parties but presided over by Taylor, and without a murmur those present underwrote the capital requirement of £20,000. This was 'London money', venture capital provided by speculators and not by the great Cornish mine and landowners. The Williams family had objected to the line continuing all the way to Redruth and wanted it to end at Carharrack village. They had a substantial interest in the Poldice Tramway to Portreath and did not welcome potential opposition. Their objections were, however, ignored, and the Act received Royal Assent on 17 June 1824. The Act detailed the route, the branches (more than originally suggested) and the tolls to be charged for the various commodities. For example, manure was tuppence per ton mile, minerals threepence per ton mile, and grain and all other goods fourpence per ton mile. Milestones were to be provided along the tramway and the company was to be the toll-taker only, not the operator, in common with road and canal practice at that time.

Four-wheel wagons were restricted to an all-up weight of 3 tons. Use of the line was limited to between the hours of 5am and 10pm November to February, 4am to 10pm March, April, September and October, and 3am to 10pm during the remaining summer months. The Act specified that the Railway or Tram Road *(sic)* was to be called 'The Redruth Railway' (although '& Chasewater' was being used by the opening), and was full of detail, including wharves along Restronguet Creek and a floating harbour, which were never in fact built. Other detail stated that where the railway crossed the highway the track should not exceed three-quarters of an inch above the level of such road! The line was to be 9⅓ miles in length and the steepest gradient would be 1 in 35 between Wheal Buller and Wheal Beauchamp. The difference in altitude between Devoran and the summit of the line was 600ft. Construction was put in the hands of William Brunton, a London-based engineer who was born in Cornwall, and was straightforward except for a number of cuttings below Carharrack and a long embankment crossing from one side of the Carnon valley to the other below Nangiles.

There was no delay in starting construction work. The line was to be 4ft gauge, as commonly used in collieries in South Wales at the time. Wrought-iron rails were used, set in cast-iron chairs, which were bolted to granite sleeper blocks. Most important, however, and in contrast to the Poldice Tramway, edge rails were used with flanges on the wagon wheels themselves, as used in modern railway practice. The mine owners were so keen to make use of the line that it was probably in part use in 1825, before being completed throughout. The official opening ceremony of the Redruth & Chasewater Railway took place on 30 January 1826.

Although the railway was to be worked by horses, another means of propulsion was used on the opening day — gravity! At

Above:
Whereas the Poldice Tramway was the first significant private railway in Cornwall, the Redruth & Chasewater Railway, opened in 1825 (officially in 1826), was the first public railway. The line connected the busy mines in the Gwennap area with the port of Devoran on the estuary of the River Fal. At first only small-capacity sailing ships used the port, but later steam-powered coasters of up to 200 tons were used to export mined minerals and to import coal, mostly to and from South Wales. This view of SS *Greta*, a schooner, and a couple of railway wagons dates back nearly 100 years. *JV collection*

Right:
Miner, one of two 0-4-0 saddle tanks, was originally built by Messrs Neilson & Co of Glasgow. It was delivered in November 1853, and later a pair of trailing wheels was added to cure rough riding, making them 0-4-2Ts. After covering some 100,000 miles each, both locomotives were reboilered and rebuilt as 0-6-0 tanks at Devoran in 1869. In this 1900 view *Miner* is seen with railway staff at Devoran.
JV collection

the opening 'three covered wagons were provided for the accommodation of several of the proprietors and their friends who assembled at Wheal Buller Mine at eleven o'clock, and proceeding down the line to the New Quay in Restronguet Creek. As the carriages (each displaying a flag) moving briskly onward along the inclined plane, with no other impelling power than their own gravity, passed the different mines and villages in rapid succession, followed by a number of wagons loaded with copper ore from Wheal Buller, they exhibited a scene altogether novel and interesting, exciting expressions of surprise and approbation. The carriages arrived at the New Wharf at Narabo, a distance of nearly eight miles in 65 minutes without the aid of a horse. After inspecting the progress made in the formation of the quay, and the improvements of the navigation, the gentlemen again placed themselves in their carriages and were not a little surprised to find themselves conveyed up the railway, by a light horse, at a rate not greatly inferior to that which they had descended, and arrived at the summit of the line near Redruth, a distance of 7½ miles, in less than an hour and a half.' A dinner at Foss's Hotel in Redruth followed to round off the day in appropriate style.

At this time the line had not been completed at each end but otherwise traffic had exceeded all the preliminary estimates. Work had been done at Devoran so that 200-ton vessels could use the little port. This was to become the headquarters of the railway with warehouse, office, weighbridge, engine shed and tollhouse. There was no money to complete the branch to Chasewater, and in any event the nearby Wheal Busy had been abandoned in 1827 and the railway took the view that the other, smaller mines within the group would generate insufficient income. This caused some displeasure to Lord Falmouth over whose lands the branch would run and he instituted legal proceedings in 1828 to force the company to build the line as planned. He failed in his quest and the railway was not prepared to risk its money, even though a failure to serve Chasewater made a nonsense of the name of the railway! In 1827 the line was extended at the Redruth end and a further mile of line had been laid beyond Devoran to Point Quay. Horses always worked this section, even in the 'locomotive years'.

From the line's terminus at Redruth near Pednandrea Mine the line ran straight past Wheal Sparnon along the edge of Carn Marth to a dip between Lanner Hill and the Carnmenellis uplands to the west. Here it met a short but busy branch from Buller Downs, which was busier than the 'main' line and which crossed the Redruth to Penryn turnpike road by a level crossing. The junction was the highest point on the line. The line continued to follow the

contours of Carn Marth, running steeply past Pennance, with the great Tresavean Mine and Penstruthal Mine on the opposite side of the valley. It then ran below Wheal Damsel and near Ting Tang Mine and on to the population centre of Carharrack. This village had grown up with the surrounding mines and was home to the many horses employed on the railway. The line crossed the road into the village several times by gated crossings.

Below Carharrack the line ran between Wheal Jewel, Carharrack Mine and Wheal Maid to the north, and the vast Consolidated Mines to the south, with United Mines further south still. The last two mentioned were the mainstay of traffic and both were served by long branches and storage sidings over which wagons were always horse-drawn. There were several small sidings to coal yards serving individual pumping engines. The main line at the western end of Consols joined the valley that runs down from below Crofthandy to Twelveheads, running on a ledge cut into the valley side in a succession of sweeping curves. (Twelveheads was named after the twelve-headed stamps worked by a water wheel once used for ore crushing.) Here the line crossed from one side of the valley to the other past Wheal Andrew to a point below Nangiles Mine. As the line neared the Carnon Valley at Bissoe it levelled out and ran straight as far as the turnpike road at Carnon where the first Redruth & Chasewater wharves were built. The line passed through the many sidings to further wharves at Devoran, then through the trees and bushes that skirted Restronguet Creek to Point Quay. Horses were always used to shunt the quays at Devoran.

The railway was single track throughout but with plenty of passing loops, which were necessary if confusion and disputes amongst the independent carriers were to be avoided. Operating rules were drawn up, with descending wagons keeping to the left, as if on the highway. Any wagons left overnight had to be in a loop and not on the main branch. Trains meeting head-on on the single track had to decide by lots who was to reverse! There is evidence to show that while gravity operation was common, some carriers supplied horses up and down the line. Being a wagoner on the line was a dangerous occupation and deaths and injuries occurred five times in the first 15 years of operation.

The railway was a great success and transportation costs were halved, a real bonus to the mine owners. Although many commodities had been mentioned under 'tolls' in the Act, in reality the railway carried ore down to Devoran and coal back up. In 1830 the railway made a huge profit of £3,000 in hauling a total of 60,000 tons. To give some scale to the operations, Consolidated and United Mines employed over 3,000 persons at that time. Wheal Gorland, Wheal Unity, Poldice, Carharrack and Wheal

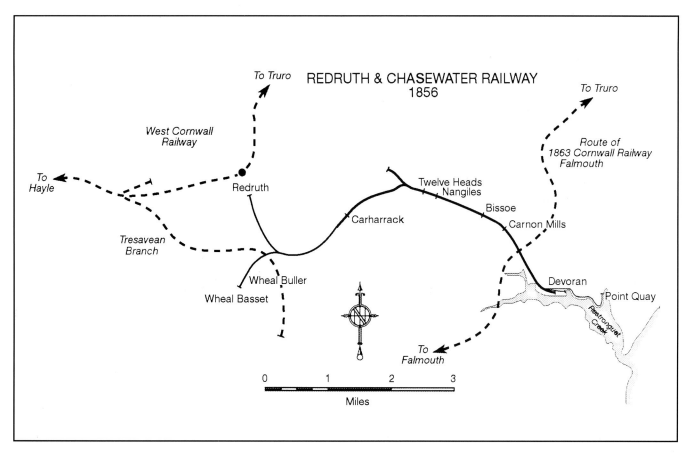

REDRUTH & CHASEWATER RAILWAY
1856

To Truro

West Cornwall
Railway

To Truro

Route of
1863 Cornwall Railway
Falmouth

To
Hayle

Redruth

Twelve Heads
Nangiles

Bissoe

Carharrack

Carnon Mills

Tresavean
Branch

Wheal Buller

Devoran

Point Quay

Wheal Basset

Restronguet Creek

To
Falmouth

N

0   1   2   3

Miles

Above:
Having run down from the mines of Gwennap with loads, *Miner* comes off its train at the bottom of Market Street, Devoran. The wagons in the background will be shunted down to the quay on the left (in the gap between the fences). In 1891, a typical year, some 36,000 tons of minerals were conveyed over the Redruth & Chasewater line. *JV collection*

In 1933, some 18 years after the closure of the line, its alignment along the Carnon Valley could be readily identified. Behind the old mine chimney on the left a two-coach Truro to Falmouth branch train can be seen crossing the valley on the 756ft-long, 96ft-high Carnon Viaduct. *JV collection*

Maid sent ores over the Poldice Tramway to Portreath, but most others used Devoran. The number of wagons in use by 1830 was about 40, and about 20 small vessels per week were leaving Devoran for South Wales. The great disadvantage of Devoran versus Portreath was that vessels from Devoran had to travel all the way around Lizard Point and Land's End to reach the Welsh smelters, adding over 50 miles to the journey. It was also a dangerous journey in the days of sail.

At this time Devoran was the busiest port serving the mining industry, mainly because Hayle was not yet rail-connected, while Portreath was at this time served only by the Poldice Tramway and vessels could not call there in bad weather. In the early 1830s Devoran was an unbelievably busy place with small vessels lined up side by side and workers loading and unloading ore, coal and, later, timber. Ship chandlers, warehouses, limekilns and shipbuilders all grew up around the port, and three inns helped to quench the thirst of sailors and port workers alike!

By 1831 the Redruth & Chasewater had become so busy that rail renewal was necessary in places. In the wet winters the horse track between the sleepers deteriorated, causing many minor delays. Taylor had stated that the railway would remain prosperous as long as the mines that it served remained prosperous. The 1830s were positive for the railway and it had certainly fulfilled the function for which it had been built. However, in 1838 competition arrived on the scene with the coming of the standard gauge Hayle Railway. This extended from Hayle to Redruth with branches down to the harbour at Portreath and up to the mining district around Tresavean. The latter line actually crossed the Redruth & Chasewater at right angles on the summit of Lanner Hill, although there was never any interchange of traffic.

Taylor had leased many of the mines he operated, including Consols, and it became clear towards the end of the 1830s that,

because he had done so well in the previous 20 years or so, the owners would not renew his lease. Therefore in 1838 he set about extracting the maximum he could from Consols in the time he had remaining. His successors soon realised that the best pickings had gone, and between 1840 and 1850 tonnages were down, and by the 1850s Consols was making losses. As far as the Redruth & Chasewater was concerned, the Hayle Railway offered to haul the Consols' ore at less than cost price, undeterred that its terminus was a mile from the mine. This resulted in the R&CR reducing its prices. Competition began to bite in other ways and by 1840 there was a 20% fall in the railway's profits.

More trouble came in 1841 as severe winter weather with frost and heavy rain loosened sleeper blocks and caused minor subsidences in several cuttings. Worse still, silting alongside the wharves at Devoran became a serious problem, leading eventually to the company forming a new deeper navigation channel. In 1844 the Hayle Railway proposed the amalgamation of the two lines, including an extension of locomotive working on to the Redruth & Chasewater. No decision was taken by the R&CR, possibly being influenced by increasing traffic during a boom for United Mines. In 1847 the company purchased a steam tug for use at Devoran, which would prevent delays caused by sailing vessels waiting for the right conditions before they docked. The cost of food for the horses that worked the line increased and forced up the carriers' charges, then the harbour-master absconded with a large amount of recently collected toll money! In a black period for the railway the steam tug regularly broke down and, to cap it all, collided with another vessel in the creek and sank! She was later raised from the shallow water and repaired.

By the end of the 1840s many of the mines in the Gwennap area had already seen their best days, but Wheal Buller was in good shape and the Directors of the R&CR decided to purchase the

Above:
One needs a great deal of imagination in tracing old railway lines, but now and then one is rewarded by the discovery of an original building. One of the survivors of the R&CR, which closed nearly 90 years ago, is the old wagon weighbridge building located a short distance from Devoran, seen here in June 1998. *JV*

Below:
The quaint-looking *Miner*, with its tall chimney and lack of cab, worked hard over the years, clocking up about 11,000 miles per year for several decades. Four round trip workings per day over the line was the norm until the downturn in the mining industry in 1866. *Miner* had the distinction of hauling the very last train over the line in September 1915, and a demolition train in 1918. *JV collection*

short extension to its branch that had been paid for by the adventurers who owned the mine. The price tag was a bargain at £85, and it helped to ensure that the R&CR would be the only large-scale carrier of Wheal Buller ore. Taylor was succeeded by his son in 1850, a time when coal was becoming more important than ore as a revenue-earner for the railway. By this time some of the track needed re-laying to a more substantial standard, perhaps with a view to employing locomotives. However, the output from Consols and United was in decline and the railway had to lower its rates to help the mines survive. Also 10,000 people in the parish depended on the mines for their existence. Wheal Buller continued to thrive, and by 1852 the railway had made total profits of £70,000 in 28 years, but no reserve fund or financial contingency had been made.

In September 1852 consideration was given to employing locomotives on the line, and later in the year a new survey was undertaken of the long-proposed Chasewater branch. Also some of the carriers were not giving an adequate service to some of the mines, resulting for the first time in the R&CR purchasing its own horses. At a meeting the railway company resolved to apply for an Act giving it powers to modify and extend the line, as well as to permit the use of steam traction, for which an increased capital of £18,000 would be needed. It was decided to proceed with the 'Chasewater' branch, but only to Poldice, even though the plans showed a branch of 2 miles 10 chains through to Wheal Busy. This would be on a completely different alignment from that proposed way back in 1824, the gradient would be 1 in 85/65, and minor curve easing by realignment was necessary at certain points. The Act was passed on 9 May 1853 and work started in earnest. The Wheal Buller branch was also to be extended by 69 chains following the contours of the hillside above Carnkie to serve the extremely productive Wheal Basset, West Basset and South Frances mines. That year, 1853, was the railway's busiest ever, with 97,764 tons being carried, but ominously copper tonnage was lower than at any time between 1828 and 1846.

Below:
By 1859 the small 0-4-2T locomotives needed frequent repairs and the company identified a need for a larger locomotive. Accordingly, in 1859 a larger 20-ton 0-6-0T from the Neilson stable was delivered, named *Spitfire*, and put to use on the steeper section of line above Nangiles. This photograph, taken in March 1899, shows the scene of a fatal accident involving *Spitfire*, which had been descending towards Devoran with four empty wagons in front of it and three loaded and five empty wagons behind. At Higher Carnon Bridge road crossing the rail flanges had been filled with chippings from road works and the leading wagons derailed, killing Stephen Gay, the brakeman who had been standing on one of the leading wagons. Some locals look at the resulting wreck. *JV collection*

Above:
With the leading four empty wagons being smashed in the wreck at Higher Carnon Bridge, 0-6-0T *Spitfire* waits for the debris to be cleared. The line never used brake-vans; brakemen, such as the fatally injured Stephen Gay, sat on the wagons pinning down and picking up the wagon brakes on the move. Wagon uncoupling was done by foot! Note the building behind the locomotive, which is featured in the next photograph. *JV collection*

In November 1853 two small 0-4-0 saddle tanks from Neilson & Co of Glasgow were unloaded at Devoran. They were named *Miner* and *Smelter*. New wagons were also ordered, and over a period of time a total of 120 would be delivered. Many lasted until the line closed in 1915, and each had a capacity of 4 to 5 tons. Work was slow on the branch due to construction difficulties and bad weather in the winter of 1854. Trials with the steam locomotives were successful and showed that eight loaded wagons could be taken up to the Wheal Fortune loop above Twelveheads, or six wagons through to Carharrack. A round trip took 1½ hours and six trains per day were planned.

In 1855 both locomotives were in daily use, with *Miner* running over 8,000 miles and *Smelter* over 7,000 miles, but despite carrying a large tonnage the railway lost £548 for the year. The locomotives were rough riding, causing excessive track wear, and a pair of trailing wheels was added. The locomotives were still not working above Ting Tang, but this was remedied in 1857 when heavier rails were laid all the way to Redruth. This resulted in a large increase in locomotive mileage, with both *Miner* and *Smelter* covering over 11,000 miles each. In 1857 Consolidated Mines closed and with a few notable exceptions the mining industry in the Gwennap area was in decline. Mine owners were

Right:
This is the same scene at Higher Carnon Bridge crossing a century after the March 1899 accident. The road in the foreground is on the precise alignment of the old railway. The line was in operation for 90 years and at the time of the 1899 accident employed 23 staff and nine crossing keepers; within 16 years they would all be redundant. *JV*

Above:
In this delightfully posed 1905 photograph on one of the many road crossings, *Spitfire* is seen at the head of a Redruth-bound train. *JV collection*

needing to mine deeper and this affected output. Traffic to Redruth and Wheal Buller was, however, still buoyant, leading to an annual profit of £658 for 1858. By 1859 the small locomotives needed frequent repairs and a larger 20-ton six-coupled locomotive was ordered and delivered to Devoran in September 1859, bearing the name *Spitfire*. It was usual for the small 0-4-2Ts to work from Devoran to Nangiles, where the larger 0-6-0ST would take over for the steeper part of the line. The primary loads were still copper ore down and coal up, although transportation of a substance called mundic (iron pyrites) from mine waste and used in chemical manufacture added 10,000 tons to the railway's coffers.

Devoran continued to become silted up and in 1863 nearly 9,000 tons of sand were dredged from the shipping channel. Taylor died in 1863 and was succeeded by his sons, who hived off the tug business and a more powerful vessel was obtained. Also in 1863 the wooden engine shed at Devoran was destroyed by fire. Two locomotives were in the shed at the time but damage was, luckily, superficial. A new stone-built shed was built, but there was never a turntable on the line. In the same year the Redruth & Chasewater moved several thousand tons of stone and timber up the Carnon Valley for the construction of the Cornwall Railway's viaduct over the valley on the route of its Falmouth branch. The 1864 statistics showed the locomotives covering over 23,000 miles on over 1,100 trains (in each direction). Both of the original locomotives were reboilered and rebuilt as 0-6-0Ts in 1868-69, after covering well in excess of 100,000 miles.

In the meantime the Poldice Tramway to Portreath had closed in about 1865, its track unusable and overgrown — an omen for the Redruth & Chasewater? Towards the end of 1866 there was a serious downturn in the mining industry. Copper prices fell worldwide, banks failed and mines closed with great rapidity. Carharrack, Lanner, Gwennap and St Day villages were badly affected and the great emigration rush started, mainly to the USA, South America and Australia. The railway was able to continue

due to the incoming coal traffic, but outgoing ore volumes dropped significantly. The last Gwennap mine closed in 1870, resulting in 1,400 redundancies. The railway lost 'at a stroke' 7,000 tons of copper ore and 14,000 tons of coal. After cutting its manpower it made just £402 in 1871. From that year the railway only steamed one locomotive each day, that being entirely adequate for the traffic conveyed in just two daily trains. The most important mines for the company at this time were Wheal Basset and the other tin mines near Carnkie, and track was relaid to them in 1872, over a section that had been lifted a few years before. A few minor sources of traffic such as stone and brick emerged, and by 1877 the annual traffic volume was 36,000 tons and net profit amounted to £72!

With the problems in the mines and further silting at Devoran, the R&C decided on 31 December 1877 to go into receivership, but it was July 1879 before this was executed. The railway continued operations, but sometimes only one train per day was run. In 1891 the tonnage for the year was a typical 34,000 tons, 76% of which was coal.

At that time the railway employed 23 staff plus nine crossing keepers. There were just a few signals on the line controlled by single levers, the last survivor being near the main road down at Devoran. In March 1899 there was a fatal accident at Higher Carnon Bridge road crossing. *Spitfire* was descending the line with four empty wagons in front of it and three loaded and five empty wagons behind. The train slowed to pick up an empty wagon that had been left on the 'main' line beyond the crossing, but the road had been relaid with chippings that had not been cleared out of the rail flange ways and the leading wagons derailed. In the resulting smash the brakesman Stephen Gay, who had been standing on one of leading wagons, received fatal injuries. The line never used brake-vans and the brakemen sat on the wagons, pinning down and picking up brakes on the move. Uncoupling was often done by foot, a dangerous occupation!

After 1900 traffic slowly declined, as did the quality of the track, but the company could not afford to pay for renewals. More mines closed, including Nangiles in 1908, which had a further negative impact on the railway's finances. A further disaster occurred in 1912 when St Day brickworks closed; it had sent one million bricks via the R&CR in 1907. By this time the Basset Mines group was the mainstay of the railborne traffic. The mine's nine engines were still using 15-16,000 tons of coal per annum, but elsewhere all the engine houses were silent. There were short periods of boom when prolonged gales resulted in Hayle and Portreath being inaccessible to shipping, and then coal from the store at Devoran would be in demand. Such an event occurred in 1911, when nearly 5,000 tons of coal were carried in a single month, the busiest for 40 years. Road chippings for new road construction around Redruth were another welcome source of new traffic.

By 1914 debenture interest had accrued to the sum of £8,000, no payments having been made since 1896. The company had been in receivership for 30 years and the future looked grim, even though over 22,000 tons of traffic had been hauled in 1914. The final nail in the coffin occurred in 1915 when under a new deal Basset Mines bought coal actually delivered to them at the colliery's expense rather than charged from the pithead. Tonnage fell disastrously and in the first six months of 1915 only 6,491 tons were carried. The decision was taken to close the line completely from 25 September 1915, by which time just about everything on the railway was worn out. The sad honour of working the last train down to Devoran fell to *Miner*. In 1918 a statutory certificate of abandonment was granted by the Board of Trade and the company's frugal assets were sold by tender at the Royal Courts of Justice. *Miner* was again steamed to work trains of lifted rail, but when her job was complete she, in common with the other locomotives, was cut up at Devoran. The company went into liquidation in 1920.

Without the railway Devoran's future as a small port was doomed. In fact the last schooner of coal berthed in the summer of 1916. After this the port silted up, the long line of quays fell into disuse and were soon overgrown. Nowadays there are a couple of ex-railway buildings and the occasional granite sleeper block to be seen at Devoran, but other than one of the crossing gates buried in the hedge on the main A39 Truro to Falmouth road at the Devoran turn-off on Restronguet Creek, not much remains in the area. The trackbed can be traced over much of its length, but a helicopter rather than walking boots might be the better option at some points. There is a splendid iron pedestrian bridge over the railway at Carharrack, and at Nangiles there are plenty of granite sleeper blocks along a dirt-road-cum-footpath. There are also some blocks at the Redruth terminus. The R&CR survived the great copper depression of the 1860s and the tin depression of the 1890s but life had been a struggle for more than half of its 90-year life, with its two most profitable years having been in 1834 and 1845, back in the days of horse-drawn trains. Its closure date now seems very distant, but the quaint old line undoubtedly deserves a place in the Hall of Fame of Cornish railways.

Right:
In this pleasant early Edwardian scene there appears to be some permanent way maintenance going on at the crossing below Carharrack Chapel (just to the left of the crossing keeper's cabin). Behind the fence is the 'main' line while the primitive gate in the foreground protects a short siding. By this time traffic was in steep decline and the line had technically been in receivership for over 20 years!
JV collection

Lower right:
This is exactly the same scene at Carharrack in 1990, some 90 years later. The chapel top left and the house on the right can both be readily identified. In view of the many decades that have passed since closure it is only the vigilant observer who can trace sections of the Redruth & Chasewater. The car is parked in the delightfully named Wheal Damsel Road. *JV*

Left:
One of the R&CR's largest customers was the Wheal Basset/Wheal Buller complex, served by a short but busy branch. In addition, the mines had an extensive internal railway system that was of 18in gauge and ran between the mines and the stamps, a distance of over 1½ miles. This old postcard view shows Orenstein & Koppel 0-4-0T locomotive *Kimberley* at one of the Basset mines. The locomotive weighed about 8 tons and could haul a 100-ton trailing load. *JV collection*

Left:
There are still many remains of the mining era in the Wheal Basset/Wheal Buller area near Carnkie. This view shows some spectacular industrial archaeology on a wonderful spring day in March 1997. Although such edifices remain, all railways in the area have long been silent. *JV*

Left:
Between 1825 and 1854 wagons on the R&CR were either horse-drawn or moved by gravity. From 1854 locomotives were used, but it was 1857 before they ran through to Redruth, when heavier rails were laid. This 1990 view shows the R&CR terminus at Redruth, with much evidence visible of the old granite sleeper blocks. *JV*

3. Pentewan Railway

Anybody visiting Pentewan today will find a delightful little village tucked away from the St Austell to Mevagissey Road. The centrepiece is the small harbour, which initially gives the impression of a large village pond with a few ducks and seabirds strutting around the perimeter. Steeply banked houses, a shop or two and a public house overlook the tranquil scene. On closer inspection and armed with either an old Ordnance Survey map or local history book, it soon becomes apparent that this was once a thriving place of some importance in the history of transportation in Cornwall. The key to all this is the old abandoned lock gates, once used to control the amount of water in the harbour. Another fairly obvious clue is the loading quay to the south side of the harbour where there is evidence of a slightly elevated railway and loading chutes. Exploration of the jetty reveals some narrow gauge trackwork, but however romantic the notion might be, this is not the remains of the Pentewan Railway, but a later tramway used until 1965 by the Pentewan Dock & Concrete Company. What is clear from the channel and beach beyond the lock gates is that the entrance to the harbour is blocked by sand, which throughout the years was always a curse for ships using the facility.

Although for hundreds of years there had been tin mines at Polgooth and tin and copper mines in the local Pentewan area, it was the emerging china clay industry in the early part of the 19th

Above:
In addition to the Poldice Tramway and the R&CR, the other great railway pioneer in Cornwall was the Pentewan Railway (PR), which opened in part in 1829 and completely in 1830. Between 1829 and 1872 the approximately 4ft 6in gauge line was operated by horses, but in the 1873-4 period the line was converted to 2ft 6in gauge and the first steam locomotive was procured. Although always a 'freight only' line, the Pentewan became famous for its Sunday school and special outings when passengers were carried in the tiny china clay and freight wagons from St Austell to the seaside at Pentewan. In this remarkable Sunday excursion view from an old postcard, 0-6-2T *Canopus* pauses at Iron Bridge in about 1910 with one wagonload of bandsmen and many wagons full of the church-going public. *JV collection*

century that provided the focus for efficient transportation systems. Another source of mineral traffic in the area was the output from Pentewan Quarry, which was used in the construction of Par Harbour (see Chapter 12). The stone was loaded directly on to ships from the quarry, which was dug into cliffs. Between the well-populated centre of St Austell and Pentewan, some 4 miles to the south, runs the St Austell River, which gently meanders down the St Austell Valley. In the early days the spoil from mining found its way into the river and silted up the cove at Pentewan.

Historically Pentewan had been associated with the fishing industry, and while it always played 'second fiddle' to Mevagissey, in 1744 a basin had been built beside the mouth of the river at Pentewan to accommodate a growing number of fishing vessels. However, the waste from the tin mines continued to be a problem, and by the start of the 19th century the little harbour had become dilapidated and in a state of decay. It was owned by the Hawkins family, who were enormously influential, having under their ownership and control huge tracts of land and many mines throughout Cornwall. Sir Christopher Hawkins rebuilt Pentewan Harbour, not for the benefit of fishermen but for the aforementioned china clay industry. The 30 square miles that comprise the Hensbarrow Downs area to the northwest of St Austell had been producing small quantities of china clay and china stone for many years, but all the signs pointed to an increasingly burgeoning business.

Charles Rashleigh, another prominent landowner, had anticipated this growth in business in 1791 when he had built a harbour at West Polmear, which he named Charlestown, after himself. As mentioned later in chapters 12 and 13, Charlestown for many years had a monopoly on the shipment of china clay by sea, but it suffered from transportation problems in that all of the clay had to be hauled from the various clay works and through the narrow streets of St Austell to reach the harbour. Hawkins also owned several clay pits and recognised that a second port, to rival Charlestown, would be successful. As he already owned Pentewan, that was where his energies were directed. Topography was also on his side because the valley connecting St Austell with Pentewan provided a natural route for the transportation of china clay. However, the main obstacle to the development of Pentewan continued to be the silting up of the harbour with industrial waste coming down the river, mixing with sea sand that had been blown into the harbour by the frequent gales.

It was not until 1818 that Hawkins granted a 60-year lease to run the harbour to one John Stanley of London, acting on behalf of the newly formed Pentewan Harbour Company. The old basin

and the harbour entrance were deepened, new quays and sea gates were built, and the entire entrance was to be protected by a new pier. Cranes and a reservoir to flush out the harbour were also provided. The new harbour was ready for use in 1820, but it seems that much work still needed to be done and it had cost five times its original estimate. Debts accumulated and the share price dropped, but Hawkins bought the cheap shares and eventually acquired the entire concern. Records show that in 1824 two ships used the harbour in April, two in June and 13 in July. The vessels were small, averaging about 65 tons each. The new basin had 1,132ft of wharfage, which was protected by a single pair of gates 26ft wide. Hawkins developed the area around the harbour and between 1826 and 1851 the village grew from 29 houses to 71, and a population of 350 persons.

Hawkins was aware of the Poldice Tramway and the Redruth & Chasewater Railway in the Scorrier/Redruth area, and it was obvious to him that a railway from 'Pentuan to St Austle' *(sic)* was vital if Pentewan was to prosper as a port, so in 1826 he employed an engineer to report on the feasibility of such a venture. He planned a railway from the harbour to a terminus at St Austell beside West Bridge on the Truro Road, closely following the course of the river on its eastern bank. Hawkins approached the few landowners affected and they had a meeting in the White Hart Inn in St Austell. He told them a positive tale and estimated that annual tonnage over the proposed railway would be 10-15,000 tons. He encountered little opposition. A prospectus was issued in 1827 giving details of the advantages, such as a halving of transport costs to exporters and forecasting an 8% return on investment. Landowners would get easy access to coal, lime and timber. However, the money was not forthcoming as confidence in Pentewan as a viable harbour was low.

Hawkins decided to proceed on his own, but progress was still slow. He was by then 71 years of age, and in 1829 he died without seeing his enterprise completed. His 9-year-old nephew, another Christopher (Henry Thomas) Hawkins, inherited the total estates and assets and he was to own the railway and the harbour for the next 74 years. Hawkins senior had left many debts and his affairs were in the hands of a Receiver, but nevertheless the family carried on, completing the line in 1829 but incurring the wrath of the Receiver. With a whole range of 'finishing touches', some of them substantial, the railway was completed in all respects in 1830 at a final cost of £5,732. Its precise gauge remains uncertain to this day, but the consensus is that it was 4ft 6in, the same as the Plymouth & Dartmoor Railway. Initially the stock amounted to only six wagons, which were horse-drawn, although there was some gravity working at the St Austell end of the line. The rails

Above:
Photographs of steam trains in action (as distinct from still 'poses') on the PR are uncommon. Steaming through King's Wood and heading for Pentewan with loads is 0-6-2T *Canopus* during the last years of the line's life. Manning Wardle built the locomotive in 1901 and it had the sad distinction of hauling the demolition train over the line in 1918. *Canopus* was scrapped in 1924. *Cornwall Record Office*

were of an old cast-iron fish-bellied design, running on granite block chairs.

The Pentewan Railway continued to be blighted by the harbour regularly silting up and it suffered by ending in St Austell, which was still a considerable distance from the point at which the china clay was extracted. There were plans to extend the line into 'clay country' but the finance was never available. The silting was so bad that a 160ft wooden breakwater was built at the end of the pier, on the seaward side of the harbour gates, but just two years later it was reported that two men were discharging coals from the good ship *Merton* to get her into the harbour. In 1838 a violent storm blew the harbour gates into the air, breaking the massive hinges.

A number of intermediate installations were built on the railway, such as a gasworks siding in St Austell and a coal yard to supply Polgooth Mine near London Apprentice, and a wall was built around the harbour in 1839. However, traffic volumes at the harbour were hardly brisk, with 86 ships using the harbour in 1830 and 72 in 1831, but there was then an upturn, and by the end of 1831 it seemed that Pentewan had overtaken Charlestown as a port, shipping out one-third of all the china clay produced in Cornwall. Unfortunately one of the railway's major customers got into financial difficulty in 1833 and this had an adverse effect on traffic receipts. By 1838 only one-tenth of all china clay produced was shipped from Pentewan, and by 1842 traffic volumes reached an all-time low.

One of the problems seemed to be that Pentewan was at its busiest when the clay trade was booming and Charlestown, Par and, later, Fowey were working to capacity. When there was a recession Pentewan suffered very badly. Some of these problems

were compensated for by an increase in the transportation of limestone. Also, once St Austell gasworks was in full operation in 1832 coal imports increased significantly. There were a number of other commodities transported by rail, but they were insignificant compared to clay, stone and coal. A limited passenger service was in operation, but this was an irrelevant sideline and there were never any passenger coaches or timetabled services on the line. The company lurched from profit to loss and back again, averaging out between 1829 and 1843 at an annual profit of £91, not much of a return on the total investment.

In 1843 Hawkins junior at last managed to lease the railway and harbour for seven years to a group of mine and landowners, and as a result the Pentewan Harbour & Railway Company was formed. The lease was twice extended, only coming to an end in 1871. During that period the railway prospered, and in 1867 over 22,000 tons were hauled, increasing to an average of over 28,000 tons per annum from 1869 to 1871. Total shipments in league table terms in 1872 were Par 52,000 tons, Charlestown 36,000 tons and Pentewan 20,000 tons, from a total Cornish production of 189,000 tons. By comparison, the small harbour of Newquay was handling about 3,000 tons. Fowey would be rail-connected from 1869, but in 1872 Pentewan was still handling just over 10% of the total output.

There had been numerous plans to extend the Pentewan Railway and to build other lines into clay country, for example to Treviscoe, into the Gover valley and along the Trenance Valley.

Above:
The date of this photograph is probably 1917-18 because the line looks disused. The track was ripped up in 1918, within a month of closure, to assist the First World War effort. The line served a purpose for nearly 90 years but it never reached its full potential because the track never actually reached the source of its outgoing minerals or the final destination of most inbound tonnage *Cornwall Record Office*

However, other railways were being built such as the Newquay & Cornwall Junction Railway in 1867-69 and the Cornwall Minerals Railway in 1874. The earlier Treffry Tramway was already carrying large volumes of clay by rail. Although doing well, the Pentewan concern was not without its problems, and although it may sound repetitive, the silting up of the harbour and the reluctance of some skippers to use it continued. In 1866 ships were prevented from entering the port because of a sand bar, and at other times a steam tug was used to haul vessels into dock. In 1870 the harbour-master reported that only one ship had been able to enter the harbour in several weeks. The same year additional reservoirs were built up-river to 'flush out' the harbour at regular intervals, and the wooden breakwater was greatly extended by 320ft. Despite all this activity the Pentewan Railway produced an average annual profit between 1844 and 1868 of just £202!

By 1872 the Pentewan Railway, with its four-legged motive power, had become something of an anachronism. In February 1873 a new Pentewan Railway & Harbour Company Limited was formed with the objective of converting the railway to allow locomotive haulage. In March a tender from Manning Wardle & Co of Leeds was accepted for building a locomotive. Later that year the harbour was again in the news, for badly silting up and because the first trading steamer had arrived. However, due to inactivity at the harbour in removing material waiting to be dredged it was not until April 1874 that it was reopened to shipping. This period of closure caused real damage to the business and the only traffic carried by the railway was a little stock-piled coal. On the positive side the first locomotive, an 0-6-0 named *Pentewan*, arrived in the early part of 1874.

However, all was not well when the Bill for the works was before Parliament, for many objections were raised, especially about the line and the road running side by side with no protection being afforded to the public by way of a fence. Also arrangements at the St Austell terminus were not satisfactory and arguments with the Highways Board ensued. Nevertheless the Bill received Royal Assent on 7 August 1874. Extensions to the north of St Austell were approved, as was a branch to meet the Cornwall Railway (main line) at St Austell and the inauguration of passenger services. A contract was also signed for converting the line to 2ft 6in gauge, constructing a terminal building, and providing 15 wagons and a passenger carriage. The length of the relaid railway would be 3 miles 1,342yd, with half a mile of sidings.

A prospectus for the work was issued, but only about 15% of the required capital was ever forthcoming. There was insufficient capital to pay for the previously mentioned conversion or for the engine, wagons and carriage. As a consequence the revenue account was raided. By October the Engineer and Managing Director of the company had inspected the line and found the work completed and satisfactory. The trouble then was that there were insufficient funds in the revenue account to pay rents and this resulted, in April 1877, in creditors distraining the railway's assets. These assets were placed for auction on 3 April 1877, but the railway scraped together sufficient cash to avoid that indignity.

Other factors that adversely impacted on the railway were the downturn in the china clay industry in 1874-6 and the opening of the Cornwall Minerals Railway and all its branches in 1874. One can imagine a clay company choosing between its rail-connected works using the deep-water facilities at Fowey, or those at Par, rather than loading their product into wagons, hauling them south to St Austell and using the harbour at Pentewan, which as likely as not would be silted up, and could accommodate only small-capacity wooden vessels! The Pentewan Railway lowered its rates but with little impact on trade. It struggled on, but it finally failed in June 1879 when Hawkins entered the property of the railway and took possession of the equipment in lieu of unpaid rent, claiming the company to be utterly insolvent. This proved to be a turning point for the railway. With Hawkins in control and a boom in the china clay industry, traffic volumes picked up substantially.

The rejuvenated railway continued to prosper and by 1889 a record total of 45,270 tons was carried. This was a dramatic turnaround in the railway's fortunes in that it had regained its former position of transporting about 10% of all the china clay produced in Cornwall. It is unlikely that these volumes could have been achieved using horse-drawn wagons. From 1889 traffic over the Pentewan railway slowly but steadily declined, with the opening of the Goonbarrow branch by the CMR in 1893 having a negative impact. Even though china clay production totals were ever increasing, by 1900 the railway was carrying only 5% of Cornwall's output, and by 1904 this had slumped to 2%. As an interesting aside, just before the railway reverted to Hawkins in 1879, the first of a series of free Sunday school and non-conformist chapel excursions took place. These specials were comprised entirely of the little goods wagons, the only carriage being reserved for Hawkins's personal use. In photographs the wagons seem to be bursting at the seams! There was never an official passenger service on the line.

There were plenty of changes over the years. The original steam locomotive *Pentewan* was replaced by a similar engine called *Trewithen* in 1886. Officially horses still worked the line north of Iron Bridge, south of St Austell. The limekilns along the line had all closed by 1900 and mica works had sprung up. The various extensions were under the microscope again and as St Austell became the first town in Cornwall to have electric light there was a proposal to electrify the Gover valley extension (if ever built!). Again, despite an Act of Parliament receiving Royal Assent and support from local landowners, the lines never came to fruition. Hawkins died in 1903 aged 82, having owned the railway since its opening. The railway and harbour were taken over by relations, ending up in the hands of Mrs Josephine Johnstone. In 1918 she registered the private company as the St Austell & Pentewan Dock & Railway Company.

In 1908 a ship of 189 tons entered the harbour and in 1909 the wooden breakwater was replaced by a larger one built of stone blocks, which extended 260ft beyond the pier, but even this was not enough to prevent blockages. In 1911 a crane was permanently employed to keep the channel clear. *Trewithen* was replaced in 1901 by a larger 0-6-2T locomotive called *Canopus*. This Manning Wardle tank was joined in 1912 by 2-6-2ST *Pioneer*, which acted as standby. In 1908 locomotives were, at last, allowed to work into St Austell, saving about £170 per annum in horse hire. In 1907 the town of St Austell was expanding and this afforded the Pentewan Railway the opportunity to carry large quantities of sand from the harbour to the town — at last a commercial application had been found for the dreaded material! This traffic continued until World War 1, except for 1912, after the first Brick & Stone Company failed.

The clay traffic dwindled to just a trickle as the GWR and Fowey Docks continued to win the larger market share. In 1913 5,000 clay workers went on strike, protesting about their appalling pay of about £1 per week. They went back to work after 10 weeks but the damage had been done. The strike was followed in 1914 by the outbreak of World War 1, which took men off to battle and reduced the demand for clay. By 1917 Cornwall's output was half the level of 1912.

During the war there was always a danger to shipping from enemy action, a fact not lost on skippers. Only 90 vessels used Pentewan Harbour in 1915, 51 in 1916 and 34 in 1917; 1915 was a black year, as St Austell gasworks withdrew its custom and many clay pits stopped exporting their output. The deteriorating situation saw the last ever load of clay taken down the railway on 29 January 1918, and the last ship to use the dock, while the railway was still in operation, unloaded 65 tons of manure on 19 February. Other commodities had dwindled to virtually nothing; 50 tons of sand were transported to St Austell on 28 February and

Right:
**Pioneer was a 2-6-2T built in 1903
by the Yorkshire Engine Company
of Sheffield for use on the military
Lodge Hill & Upnor Railway and
it was purchased by the PR in
1912 as a spare for *Canopus*.
However, it was unsuccessful in
that the large driving wheels were
designed for speed and not power
and the narrow wheel treads did
not suit the PR's poor track,
resulting in many derailments.
Here on 14 August 1912 the
curious locomotive passes the
lower reservoir, probably while
Canopus was under repair.**
M. Dart collection

a small 8-ton load of sand was taken as far as London Apprentice on 2 March. This was the very last time that the Pentewan Railway was used and the quaint line passed into oblivion. The track, engines and rolling stock were all requisitioned for the war effort and dispersed to a number of War Department depots. The track was ripped up within a month of the last train running.

No sooner had Mrs Johnstone signed away the railway when she sold the harbour to Messrs W. T. Lamb & Sons. Lamb, with the support of the county council, tried to resuscitate interest in the railway and some surveying work took place on the prospect of a St Austell to Mevagissey railway. Unfortunately for Lamb the GWR opened a branch line to Lansalson along the Trenance Valley in 1920, some 80 years after a railway was first mooted. The sand and concrete business continued to flourish at Pentewan, but after a number of false starts any ideas of the railway returning were gone for ever. A last load of china clay was brought down to Pentewan by road in 1929, and was loaded into the good ship *Duchess*. Small vessels continued to call infrequently with cement

Above:
**This interesting view shows the basin at Pentewan and the schooner *Kinnaird* having its cargo of coal unloaded.
The former iron ore quay, on the right, was used for coal imports from the end of the 19th century. A rake of
five wagons can be seen with a shunting horse waiting for the next movement.** *JV collection*

or for concrete blocks, but the harbour's days were numbered. The last commercial vessel called at Pentewan in 1940. The harbour entrance soon silted up; it would never see shipping again.

The actual route of the Pentewan Railway was pleasantly rural without being spectacular. In fact, the line climbed a mere 127ft in just under 4 miles. At St Austell West Hill there were railway offices, a weighbridge, china clay storage cellars and a coal yard. St Austell gasworks, a major customer for many years, was adjacent to the site. Clay wagons arrived at the terminus by road behind a trio of horses normally hauling a 3-ton payload. The clay was transferred to railway wagons manually, using shovels. The line left the terminus on a falling gradient of 1 in 73. At Pondhu there was a short trailing siding to two limekilns and later a malthouse, then 200yd further on a pair of trailing sidings served a small clay store and later salt, coal and timber merchants. The gradient eased to 1 in 86, then to 1 in 123 before reaching another short siding to Trewhiddle mica works.

At Tregorrick the line crossed the St Austell to Mevagissey road and the St Austell River by the Iron Bridge, then kept to the eastern bank all the way to Pentewan. Just beyond the ungated road crossing was a run-round loop, this being the limit for locomotive working until 1908. At London Apprentice there was a limekiln and later mica works, which was served by a trailing siding. Beyond this point was Polgooth coal yard, originally used for Polgooth Mine but later as a domestic supply centre.

From this point the railway curved with the meanders in the river, and there was a point where, despite the railway running on a low embankment, the track was regularly flooded. The line continued to descend but at a modest 1 in 223 and 1 in 343 past a couple of early but minor deviations from the original route and a series of reservoirs used, *inter alia*, to flush out the harbour from time to time. Pentewan limekilns were passed, which was also the location of the line's weighbridge in the 1870s and 1880s. The line entered Pentewan by the only gated level crossing on the line, with the dock area immediately beyond. A stone wall separated the harbour from the village. The track layout in the harbour area was gradually enlarged over the years to serve all sides of the basin. The first siding on the north side was known as the 'iron ore quay'. There was always a siding on the south side, but from 1873 a 157yd-long trestle was built on the edge of the dock with three wooden china clay loading chutes. The line extended along the pier, below the dock gates. There was an engine shed and many old warehouses that dated back to 1819 when they were used as fish cellars.

At best there were three round trip workings on the railway per day. Horses were restricted to two wagons on the up run and four wagons on the down, while locomotives could haul up to nine loaded wagons. Traffic was totally predicated on the number of vessels using the harbour and the output from the pits. Accordingly the line was always busier in the summer months, when there were fewer gales to disrupt shipping and silt up the harbour. There was never any form of signalling on the line. It seems that passengers were carried from an early date but many were simply jumping the train and riding on top of the clay in the small wagons. The only passenger coach, acquired in 1873 for £200, was equipped to carry 16 passengers but was always used exclusively by Hawkins and his family; it was kept at the back of the engine shed. In about 1915 its wheels were 'borrowed' for a china clay wagon and, after use as a summer house, it was sold for £14 and ended its life as a hen house near St Columb. The only other passenger traffic was the aforementioned Sunday school outings, for which the china clay wagons were cleaned and fitted with benches.

There had for many years been sand and concrete activity on the south side of the harbour at Pentewan. In the 1950s the Dock & Concrete Company's plant beside the dock was connected to the sand dunes by a 2ft 6in gauge tramway, the short line crossing the St Austell River in the process. The tramway was worked by three small 20hp Ruston & Hornsby-built diesel locomotives, which hauled small tippler wagons loaded with sand to a sand hopper at the concrete plant. The line continued to an engine shed by the dock gates and along the old pier. Finished products were taken away by lorry. The tramway was last used in February 1965 but some of the old tracks can still be traced (see the accompanying photograph).

The Pentewan Railway was one of Cornwall's oldest lines. It had always been a struggle to keep the harbour clear of silt, and only ships of up to about 200 tons could be accommodated. The line was remote from the clay pits it served, it was always under pressure from competitors, and it failed to modernise. In retrospect it was surprising that it lasted as long as it did. The harbour area is still a fascinating place to roam and there remains a little evidence of the workings of yesteryear. But soon there will be no living person who remembers the halcyon days. There is a commemorative plaque on the only surviving Pentewan Railway building at the St Austell terminus site, courtesy of the Cornwall Archaeological Unit and the Co-op supermarket!

Left:
This is the view from the northwest of the basin looking out to sea. On the left can be seen the PR sidings serving the harbour basin, while on the right is the elevated section of railway with china clay loading chutes visible in the raised position. The harbour was always prone to silting up by mine spoil from the river and sand from the sea.
JV collection

Above:
A wonderful 1912 view of *Canopus* on the raised section of track, used primarily for unloading china clay directly into waiting vessels. The basin can be seen behind and to the right of the locomotive, but not in view are the lock gates. The driver is William John Drew (1859–1941), the PR's only engineer between 1887 and 1913.
LPC, P. Q. Treloar collection

Centre right:
In the 1950s a 2ft 6in gauge tramway was built in the Pentewan Harbour area for servicing the adjacent sand and concrete works. The line closed in 1965, but even today some fragments of track remain. This September 1998 view looking out towards Mevagissey Bay shows the old quayside engine shed, which once housed Ruston & Hornsby diesel locomotives, and some pointwork. *JV*

Lower right:
A plaque commemorates the only surviving Pentewan Railway building at the St Austell terminus site. *JV*

PENTEWAN RAILWAY CLAY CELLARS

THIS IS THE ONLY REMAINING BUILDING OF THE ONCE EXTENSIVE PENTEWAN RAILWAY TERMINUS WHICH OCCUPIED THIS AREA OF ST AUSTELL FROM 1829 UNTIL ITS CLOSURE IN 1918. THE BUILDING, NOW GREATLY REDUCED, WAS CONSTRUCTED CIRCA 1860 AND WAS ORIGINALLY 202 FEET LONG. IT ACTED AS A STORE FOR CHINA CLAY CARTED HERE BY HORSE-DRAWN WAGONS FROM THE HENSBARROW UPLANDS PRIOR TO ITS TRANSHIPMENT AND EXPORT FROM PENTEWAN HARBOUR. THE CLAY WAS UNLOADED ON THE HIGHER RIGHT HAND SIDE AND STORED UNDER COVER UNTIL SHIPS WERE AVAILABLE, THEN SHOVELLED INTO RAILWAY WAGONS FROM THE LOWER LEFT HAND SIDE, TO BE TRANSPORTED DOWN THE RAILWAY TO THE HARBOUR.

CO-OPERATIVE RETAIL SERVICES LTD   CORNWALL ARCHAEOLOGICAL UNIT

4. Bude Branch and Harbour

Bude, in Cornwall, is 228¾ miles from London by rail, 31 miles west of Okehampton, Devon, and 18½ miles from the junction at Halwill. Opened in 1898, Bude was the only station on the branch that was not located in Devon and accordingly, to adhere to the geographical area covered by this book, an outline of the history of the branch line is included in the text but only the Bude area itself is covered in detail. Until closure in 1966 Bude was the most northerly station in Cornwall.

Although nationally the town of Bude is better known than the nearby town of Stratton, the latter was by far the larger of the two before the turn of the 20th century. In census terms the two were linked and in 1901 the joint population was 2,308. Before the coming of the railway in 1898 Bude was a widely scattered and disjointed village, located about half a mile from the sea. From a population of about 800 at the opening of the railway it grew to over 5,000 by 1950. It could be argued that the town would have grown even more had the railway arrived earlier. However, the railway had enormous influence on the population of Bude in summer months when thousands of holidaymakers flooded to the north Cornish resort.

A popular guidebook dated 1890 was not very complimentary to Bude, stating that the town was 'alike lacking in historical, architectural or picturesque interest'! It went on to say, in a more positive tone, that 'its attractions are extreme healthiness and a fine coast'. There had been a small harbour at Bude for years, but the same book stated that 'the grandeur of the sea during storms can in few places be more impressive than at Bude and.... it is a common thing for vessels to be unable to quit or enter the haven for weeks together'. In addition to mentioning Bude Castle, it stated that hotels included the Falcon (where the coaches to Holsworthy started), the Bude and the Globe, the latter 'unpretending and of very humble character'!

The harbour and Bude Canal were in fact the primary features of transport interest during the 19th century. The canal, sometimes referred to as the Holsworthy & Bude Canal, was constructed between 1819 and 1826 mainly to transport sea sand, which was used as manure by the agricultural community. The canal was 33 miles in length, including several 'branches', and opened, in part, in 1823; at that time it was the most remarkable engineering work of its day. The canal had several rail-fitted inclined planes on which the canal boats were placed in order to change levels. Some 20 miles to the south one branch of the canal terminated at Druxton Bridge, just north of Launceston.

In 1822 Lord Stanhope suggested that a plateway be built from the beach at Bude to the canal basin for the transhipment of sand into canal tub-boats for distribution inland. One year later the plateway was duly built to a gauge of 4ft and the wagons were horse-drawn. As mentioned later, a branch line was built from the 'main line' just outside Bude station down to the canal basin at Bude Wharf. Gradually it was railway wagons that were filled with sand rather than canal boats, until the canal closed. The sand was tipped from the plateway tipplers and then loaded into standard gauge goods wagons for distribution inland. The 4ft gauge line lasted until 1923, when it was relaid to 2ft gauge using ordinary rails but with horses continuing to provide the motive power. The line fell into disuse about 1942, after which distribution was made by lorry direct to the farms.

In 1862 the Okehampton Railway was incorporated to build a standard gauge line from Coleford, on the North Devon Railway's Barnstaple line, to Okehampton. The following year the company made plans to extend the intended railway to Lydford on the broad gauge Launceston & South Devon Railway, with provision for a third rail, not for electrification but to allow through mixed gauge running to Plymouth! In 1865 the Okehampton Railway changed its name to the Devon & Cornwall Railway and increased its potential by seeking powers to build extensions to Bude and Torrington.

The London & South Western Railway absorbed the Devon & Cornwall Railway in 1872. In the meantime the line from Coleford to Okehampton had progressed slowly and in stages due to limited finances, but nevertheless Okehampton 'proper' was reached on 3 October 1871 and, for the record, Lydford some three years later. The 1865 powers to build a railway to Bude lapsed and subsequently, in 1873, an Act of Parliament was obtained to build a branch line as far as Holsworthy, Devon. This opened on 20 January 1879. Stations on the line from Okehampton were Maddaford Moor Halt (for Thorndon Cross, open from 1922 to 1938), Ashbury (for North Lew), Halwill Junction (for Beaworthy), and, specifically on the Bude branch, Dunsland Cross and Holsworthy, 20½ miles from Okehampton. From that date Holsworthy was the railhead for Bude, which was served by the LSWR's smart coach service. In 1890 the return fare from London to Bude by rail and coach was 70 shillings (£3.50) 1st Class, 52 shillings (£2.60) 2nd Class and 41s 3d (£2.06) 3rd Class.

Powers to build the line on to Bude were obtained by a local company but no progress was made and it was the LSWR that eventually built and ran the line, which was single track with passing loops at stations. The Cornish section was built along level marshes to the south of Bude. The entire line was opened on 10 August 1898, with the station terminus being located on the outskirts of the town, allegedly to keep the population of Stratton happy but also on cost grounds. The Bude terminus boasted refreshment rooms. There was one station between Holsworthy and Bude, Whitstone & Bridgerule, which opened on 1 November 1898. Interestingly Whitstone is in Cornwall but both Bridgerule and the station are in the county of Devon. By the time the railway arrived, Bude was already in decline as a port but growing as a leisure resort. It is said that had the railway arrived some 30 years earlier Bude would have become a top West Country holiday destination with a much larger population than it presently enjoys.

At Bude there was a single long platform and a shorter bay platform. Goods facilities were provided and there was a locomotive shed with turntable and relevant infrastructure,

Above:

The majority of the LSWR's Bude branch ran through the county of Devon, but photographically we are concerned only with the Bude branch terminus and the branch down to the canal basin, which were located in Cornwall. The terminus comprised one main and one bay platform. On 16 June 1962 Standard 2-6-2T No 82023 is about to reverse on to two Maunsell Southern Railway coaches and two postal vans before departing for Okehampton, 31 miles away.

R. C. Riley, The Transport Treasury

including a water tower, a 36-lever signalbox, run-round loop and sidings, coal dock, cattle dock and the aforementioned half-mile branch down to the wharf, shown as 'harbour' on old postcards. The wharf line was used for various commodities, such as fertilizers, animal feeds and coal, but these were destined for wharf-side merchants and not for interchange with commercial shipping. As mentioned previously, in years gone by the line had also been used for the transportation of sand, brought up to the railhead on the ancient 1823 plateway.

For its entire life the Bude line was little more than a rural branch. Its claim to fame was the town's dedicated portion of the famous 'Atlantic Coast Express', or ACE, which, at its best, conveyed passengers from London to Bude in a fraction over 5 hours at an average speed of just under 45mph. The number of trains serving Bude was remarkably consistent over the 68-year life of the branch. At the time of opening there were seven round trips per day and immediately prior to closure there were eight journeys per day. In some years the low season service amounted to only six trains per day each way. This is of course a simplistic view because in the summer there were normally at least two extra trains per day, and on summer Saturdays there were up to five extra trains, which included through coaches from London Waterloo. These summer expresses did not stop at minor intermediate stations on the route.

For most of the branch's lifetime there was at least one, and during certain periods two, weekday daily freight trains that trundled along to Bude, shunting such delightful installations as Whitstone Brick Siding. For example, in 1952 a freight and mail train that left Okehampton at 4.37am arrived at Bude at 6.14am. It returned at 9.45am, arriving at Okehampton at 2.14pm, after spending over 2 hours at Holsworthy! The second freight of the day was the 3.30am from Exmouth Junction, arriving at the seaside at 11.57am and departing Bude at 1.20pm. The maximum length of goods trains on the Bude branch was 40 wagons. The working timetable gave details of the precise formation required

for up freights: behind the locomotive the order was Nine Elms vacuum-fitted traffic, Nine Elms non-vacuum-fitted traffic, Exeter St Davids Road-box, Exeter St Davids, Halwill, Okehampton, Yeoford, Woking, Salisbury (including mineral traffic for Nine Elms), Exeter Central to Milborne Port inclusive, and the brake-van. Gradually freight petered out due to a malaise that was creeping throughout the British Railways system in the 1960s. Problems included everything from time delays, inflexibility, cost, industrial disputes and the cheaper door-to-door efficiency of road haulage. Goods facilities were withdrawn from the entire line from 7 September 1964.

Sunday services were at times non-existent, but for many years there was a single departure on Sunday evening that also carried the up mails. Depending on the time of year, between two and three times as many tickets were collected at Bude than were issued, which broadly reflected the traffic in incoming visitors. In prewar years there was an average annual total of 5,000 parcels forwarded from Bude and some 30,000 received. As regards total goods tonnage, for every ton of freight, including general goods, coal, minerals and livestock, dispatched from Bude approximately 3 tons was received. For many years top of the list of outgoing tonnage was mineral traffic, which included the sea sand.

Most of the popular LSWR, SR and BR steam locomotive classes associated with the West Country worked the Bude branch. In later years these included Classes O2 0-4-4T, M7 0-4-4T, T9 4-4-0, L11 4-4-0, N 2-6-0, LMS Ivatt 2-6-2T, Standard 3MT 2-6-2T and 4MT 2-6-4T. The Bulleid 4-6-2 light Pacifics did not normally work the branch because they were too long for the turntable at the terminus. It was normal for locomotives to work the branch chimney-first but photographs reveal that this was not always the case. Train lengths varied but two or three coaches was the norm with occasionally a van or two added. The last steam train to traverse the branch was an enthusiasts' special in September 1965, DMUs and single-coach 'bubble cars' having taken over the service in January 1965.

Right:
One of the classic 'T9' class 'Greyhounds', No 30710, heads the 3.15pm Bude to Okehampton train on 19 July 1957. These elegant 4-4-0s were a common sight on West Country branches and many ended their days in the South West. The main platform could hold 10 coaches but trains were rarely that long; although Bude was one of the destinations of the famous 'Atlantic Coast Express', it would see only a small portion of the train that left Waterloo. *JV collection*

Centre right:
At the start of World War 2, and particularly due to the subsequent Blitz in the Capital, many of London's children were evacuated to the countryside, and the Southern Railway sometimes ran special trains for the purpose. In this view there is much excitement as a consignment of youngsters and their minders walk away from the Bude terminus and make their way to their new temporary homes in Cornwall.
P. Q. Treloar collection

Below:
From Bude terminus a half-mile branch line ran down to the basin on the Bude Canal. This canal, opened in part as early as 1823, was used mainly to transport sea sand to inland farmers who used it as manure. There were many merchants beside the basin but little transfer of merchandise between railway wagons and sea-going vessels. Leaving the basin on 7 September 1956 is BR Class 3MT 2-6-2T No 82011 with three wagons. The line closed in September 1964 when all freight services at Bude were withdrawn. *M. R. Galley*

Right:
Back at Bude station this view shows the rather modest single-road engine shed and the 50ft turntable. Most locomotives on the Bude branch were turned on this turntable, thus ensuring that they would normally work 'chimney first'. On shed on 12 August 1963 is 'N' class 2-6-0 No 31836. These versatile Moguls worked to Bude regularly on both passenger and freight trains. The steam depot closed on 7 September 1964. *P. Paye*

Lower right:
The Bude branch and North Cornwall Railway timetable for January 1927.

Above:
This remarkable old postcard shows the main lock giving access to the sea at the end of the Bude Canal. This photograph, more than 100 years old, not only shows plenty of shipping but also, on the right, the original 1823 4ft gauge sand tramway. Horses drew wagons from the beach to the Bude Canal basin where the sand was loaded on to canal boats. In 1923 the little line was relaid to 2ft gauge but by then most of the sand was loaded into railway wagons at the basin siding. *JV collection*

Traffic on the branch was never substantial, especially outside the four months comprising the British summer. Records show that including season tickets, just over 16,000 tickets were issued at Bude booking office in 1928 and about 9,000 in 1936 or, put another way, about 51 and 29 per working day respectively, or about four or five passengers per train ex-Bude. Returning visitors would of course inflate these figures two or threefold but traffic could hardly be called heavy, particularly off-season. The line was losing money and like so many others it was a prime candidate for closure under the infamous Beeching Plan of the early 1960s.

Closure notices were posted and, after formalities had been summarily dispensed with, passenger services on the branch were withdrawn on 3 October 1966. The North Cornwall line closed the same day. During 1963 operation of the line had been transferred to the Western Region of BR and some railway journalists suggested that the Western Region had little interest in keeping open former Southern Region lines. Apparently this attitude dated back to pre-nationalisation days when the two companies were rivals, particularly in the West Country. But whatever prejudices existed, the line required a subsidy to stay open and it was alleged that buses could provide a cheaper replacement service.

The site of Bude station and associated buildings has long been razed and there is little trace of what for a few years had been a rural branch serving a somewhat remote community. Modern houses now cover the site of the railway, although the wharf branch is now a footpath. In terms of railway history the line was short-lived and, with closure occurring over 35 years ago, it is only photographs such as these that keep the memory alive or give an appreciation of what some may have missed.

Below left:
The same scene in 2001 shows the canal and lock on the left with the track of the 2ft gauge tramway, which fell into disuse in about 1942, still *in situ* **on the right. Commercial shipping has long since given way to small pleasure craft, fishing boats and holidaymakers.** *JV*

Below right:
The sand tramway is part of the Bude Heritage Trail and is celebrated by this sign beside the canal basin, just above the old rails, most of which have survived the ravages of time and weather. *JV*

LONDON, EXETER, YEOFORD, OKEHAMPTON, BUDE, WADEBRIDGE, and PADSTOW.

Miles	Down.	Week Days only. mrn	mrn		mrn	mrn	mrn	mrn		aft	aft	mrn (Atlantic Coast Express)	aft	aft	aft	aft
	LONDON (Waterloo) 179 dep.											11R0		1R0		3R0
83¾	**Salisbury 179** arr.											12 30		2 49		4 30
—	**Salisbury 170** dep.							8 13				12 34		2 54		4 34
171¼	**Exeter** (Queen St.) **170** arr.							1119				2R22		5R14		6R22
—	**Exeter** (Queen Street) dep						8 30	1140				2 38		5 22		6 40
172¼	" (St. David's) arr.						8 33	1143				2 41		5 25		6 43
	" (St. David's) dep.						8 38	1146				2 44		5 29		6 46
176¾	Newton St. Cyres						8 48	1155								
179	Crediton						8 55	12 3								6 57
183	Yeoford arr.						9 4	1212								7 6
	Yeoford dep.						9 10	1213								7 7
187¾	Bow						9 22	1224								
191	North Tawton						9 30	1232								
193¾	Sampford Courtenay						9 37	1239								
197¾	**Okehampton** arr.						9 46	1248				3 25		6 8		7 31
	Okehampton dep.						10 4	1 8				3 42		6 25		7 43
—	Maddaford Moor Halt **A**						1017	1 21				3 55				
206¼	Ashbury, for North Lew						1026	1 30				4 4		6 43		8 3
210½	Halwill, for Beaworthy arr.						1034	1 38				4 12		6 52		8 11
—	Halwill dep.				8 15		1043	1 44				4 20		6 54		8 17
213¾	Dunsland Cross				8 21		1051	1 52				4 28		7 2		8 25
218¼	Holsworthy				8 30		11 0	2 1				4 37		7 14		8 34
223	Whitstone and Bridgerule				8 40		1110	2 11				4 47		7 24		8 44
228¾	**Bude** arr.				8 50		1121	2 21				4 57		7 34		8 54
—	Halwill dep.						1037	1 40				4 15				8 12
215¼	Ashwater						1047	1 49				4 25				8 22
219	Tower Hill						1054	1 56				4 32				8 29
224	Launceston 60		7 45				11 3	2 5				4 41				8 38
228¼	Egloskerry		7 53				1115					4 52				8 48
231¾	Tresmeer		8 2				1123					5 0				8 56
236¼	Otterham **B**		8 12				1133					5 10				9 6
241¾	Camelford		8 21				1144					5 18				9 14
—	Camelford (By Coach or other conveyance) dep.											5 25				
245¾	**Boscastle** arr.											5 55				
—	Camelford (By Coach or other conveyance) dep.											5 25				
246¼	**Tintagel** arr.											6 0				
243¾	Delabole		8 27				1150					5 25				9 21
247¾	Port Isaac Road		8 35				1158					5 33				9 29
250½	St. Kew Highway		8 40				12 3					5 38				9 34
254¼	**Wadebridge** (*below*) arr.		8 48				1211					5 46				9 42
	Wadebridge dep.	7 53	8 52			9 45	1215			1 40	4 50	5 50	6 45		8 42	9 46
260	**Padstow** arr.	8 2	9 1			9 54	1224			1 54	5 4	5 59	6 54		8 51	9 54

A For Thorndon Cross.
B Station for Wilsey Down and Davidstow (2½ miles) and Crackington Haven (5 miles).
b Via Eastleigh.

R Restaurant Car Train.

For Local Trains BETWEEN Exeter and Okehampton........ PAGE 170

*** **For other Trains** BETWEEN Exeter and Yeoford........ PAGE 170, 176

5. North Cornwall Railway

In 1864 the Launceston, Bodmin & Wadebridge Junction Railway was incorporated, but just one year later it changed its name to the Cornwall Central Railway. In collaboration with the Devon & Cornwall Railway (previously the Okehampton Railway) the companies had aspirations to build a standard gauge railway not only from Okehampton to connect to the LSWR's then remote Bodmin & Wadebridge Railway, but also to Truro. Access could then be had to Penzance along the mixed gauge West Cornwall Railway's route. From 1866 the Devon & Cornwall Railway was treated as a subsidiary of the LSWR and formally absorbed by that company in 1872.

The Devon & Cornwall had completed the railway from Coleford Junction to Okehampton by October 1871 and by October 1874 an extension to Lydford had been completed. This was all part of a plan for the LSWR to gain access to Plymouth. The single track was doubled in 1879, a task that included building a second Meldon Viaduct across the valley of the West Okement, some 120ft above the ground. However, the powers obtained by the Central Cornwall Railway to build a line to the Bodmin & Wadebridge lapsed and it was to be many years before the LSWR felt able to proceed. The LSWR's subsidiary, the North Cornwall Railway, obtained the necessary Act of Parliament on

Above:
The North Cornwall Railway (NCR) from Halwill Junction to Padstow opened as far as Launceston in 1886, Wadebridge in 1895 and Padstow in 1899. For many years two goods trains per day traversed the line and during the 1950s most of the trains were in the capable hands of mixed traffic 'N' class locomotives; here No 31830 enters Launceston with a Wadebridge to Okehampton freight. The GWR station was adjacent, just to the right (north) of this photograph (see next chapter). *JV collection*

Right:
This is the remote Egloskerry station, some 4 miles from Launceston, looking towards Okehampton. The station boasted a passing loop, and a small goods yard, used for agricultural produce. It was located to the left, behind the signalbox.
JV collection

Lower right:
This view shows the brick-built Tresmeer station, looking in the up direction towards Okehampton. When the line opened, Tresmeer had a modest 182 inhabitants and throughout its life traffic was meagre. The station had a small goods yard and, until 1965, a passing loop.
JV collection

18 August 1882, by which time the line from Meldon Junction to Holsworthy had been built (and later on to Bude). The new line and the Bude branch used the same metals between Meldon Junction and Halwill Junction.

The proposed line was to be built across the bleak, thinly populated, rolling countryside of North Cornwall through Ashwater and Tower Hill, in Devon, to Launceston, Egloskerry, Tresmeer, Otterham, Camelford, Delabole, Port Isaac Road and St Kew Highway to Wadebridge, all in Cornwall. Launceston, a significant market town, 26¼ miles from Okehampton by rail, had a population of some 5,000 in 1890, while Egloskerry, for example, had only 406 inhabitants, Tresmeer 182 and Otterham 171. Camelford was larger than Launceston, but other stations served negligible populations, with Port Isaac Road being the most remote, located 'in the middle of nowhere' over 4 miles from the place on the coast that it purported to serve! When the word 'Road' or 'Highway' appeared in a station name the traveller needed to heed the translation, viz a long way away from the place name that preceded it!

Work on the line proceeded slowly because finance was in short supply. Also there were many costly and time-consuming embankments to be built and the weather offered no help to the construction gangs. After three years of effort the line from Halwill Junction to Launceston opened on 21 July 1886. From this date there was a coach connection to Camelford, Tintagel and Boscastle. It was to be a further six years before the next 7¾ miles to Tresmeer were opened, with Camelford being reached in 1893. The section to Delabole was opened on 18 October 1893 and Delabole through to Wadebridge on 1 June 1895. From 1886 the LSWR route from London via Okehampton to Launceston was much quicker than that offered by the GWR from Paddington via Plymouth. In 1890 the LSWR charged a return 1st Class fare of 62s 6d (£3.12) for the 440-mile round trip from Waterloo to Launceston. The entire line was single track but with passing loops and signalboxes at stations.

Just outside Launceston the railway from Halwill crossed the River Tamar, the Devon/Cornwall boundary, on a girder bridge, and shortly afterwards crossed the GWR's broad gauge branch from Lydford, Tavistock and Plymouth. The LSWR station was parallel to the GWR terminus and in fact from 1952 the 'rival' lines both used the LSWR station. A large goods yard and a single-track engine shed with turntable were provided at

Above:

This represents a typical NCR scene from September 1959. The graceful lines of 'T9' class 4-4-0 No 30715 from Exmouth Junction shed heading two Maunsell coaches, set No 28, an SR bogie utility van and a four-wheeled van working through from Padstow to Exeter are seen at Otterham. The station was a mile and a half from the village it purported to serve and was about a mile from the summit of the line, some 800ft above sea level.
Derek Cross

Launceston. From there the line climbed for 4 miles along the Kensey Valley to Egloskerry, which boasted a small goods yard used mainly for agricultural produce. From Egloskerry the line twisted and turned in a west-northwesterly direction to the remotely located, brick-built Tresmeer station, 34 miles from Okehampton, where a goods siding was provided. This was yet another example of the local station being over a mile from the village it served.

From Tresmeer the line continued to Otterham, some 5 miles distant. As with other stations on the line there was a siding for freight traffic. Otterham village was nearly a mile and a half from the station — just the job on a wet and windy Cornish winter's day! A mile or so beyond Otterham was the summit of the line, about 800ft above sea level. On summer Saturdays heavier trains than usual used to toil up the 1 in 73 to 1 in 78 on either side of the summit. The line then descended to Camelford, 43½ miles from Okehampton, which in later years had the distinction of providing a base for the only stationmaster on this section of the line. Without wanting to sound repetitive, the station was 1½ miles from the town!

Heading now in a southwesterly direction the line wound its way down to Delabole where a massive slate quarry was, and still is, located. The quarry, now owned by the Old Delabole Slate Co Ltd, dates back to the 16th century and is reputed to be the largest in the world. Following the installation of a stationary steam winding engine in 1834, the quarry had an operating narrow gauge tramroad by 1841. Prior to the coming of the railway the high-quality slate was 'shipped in considerable quantities from the little harbour at Port Isaac, 6 miles distant'. The slate traffic was once an important source of income for the railway with over 10,000 tons being shipped per annum. The railway was so welcome that the quarry/landowner gave the LSWR sufficient land for three-quarters of a mile of track with, of course, a company siding. Exceptionally Delabole station was located immediately adjacent to the village it served.

The line descended to Port Isaac Road station (50 miles), a misnomer if ever there was one! The original clock, which was once located in the station booking hall, showing the legend 'L&SWR — J F Fox late Jon. Gaydon — Barnstaple — 143', was until recently in the possession of the author. After passing through the only tunnel on the line, the 333yd Trelill Tunnel, St Kew Highway station was reached, approximately one and a quarter miles from the village, which had a population of 911 souls in 1901. None of the stations on the line had footbridges, only board crossings. South and west of Tresmeer the stations were all similar two-storey buildings of local stone. From there to Wadebridge the landscape was gentler and the bleak moorland feel disappeared. Just outside Wadebridge the line crossed the rivers Allen and Camel at almost sea level and joined the alignment of the Bodmin & Wadebridge Railway. The LSWR had owned the line for many years and there had been a station at Wadebridge for some 60 years, since 1834 (see Chapter 10).

The North Cornwall line was later continued through the established Wadebridge station to reach Padstow (62¼ miles) on 27 March 1899. The railway companies had had their eye on Padstow for many years and indeed it was once seen as a shorter route to Ireland. Although the Padstow goal had now been achieved, the envisaged line to Truro, for Falmouth and Penzance, was never built. Accordingly the North Cornwall line never achieved anything but branch status, even though Padstow enjoyed a direct service to London Waterloo as part of the famous 'Atlantic Coast Express'. The final stretch of line was almost level as it ran along 5½ miles of the sandy estuary of the River Camel. Padstow, with a population of nearly 2,000 at the time of the opening of the railway, had been a busy port for centuries. The SR built a new fish station there and some 1,000 wagonloads of fish could be

Right:
For many years the stationmaster at Camelford oversaw the other local stations between Wadebridge and Launceston (exclusive). Despite Camelford's large population the LSWR could not site its station nearer than 1½ miles from the market town centre, which made the railway vulnerable to road competition. Again a substantial station, goods yard and passing loop were all provided. Pausing with an up train with little evidence of business is 'N' class 2-6-0 No 31834. *David Lawrence*

Lower right:
Delabole station was opened in 1893. The area was notable for the vast Delabole slate quarry, reputedly the largest in the world, which once provided annually 10,000 tons of traffic for the railway. In this wonderful Edwardian scene a down freight has paused at Delabole and 10 people, including the LSWR train crew, pose for the photographer. *JV collection*

dispatched in a spring season. Long sidings served the harbour area and Padstow was provided with assorted goods sheds, turntable and rolling stock stabling roads. Coal was another important commodity.

The directors of the NCR stated that 'with the guarantee of the LSWR and having regard to the general conditions of the railway, they had no hesitation in submitting the undertaking as a safe and desirable investment'. They said that the proposed line would open up a new district for rail travel amounting to some 400 square miles and there would be a route of unbroken gauge from all parts of England. They also pointed out that only a 24-mile extension would need to be built from Wadebridge to Truro to make it a direct main line from London and the North to Falmouth and Penzance. Delabole was not forgotten and they estimated minimum annual traffic of 25,000 tons.

Despite early optimism there was little hope of the route making money, and after the line to Padstow opened little more was heard of the Truro extension. Local traffic was sparse and for most of the line's life four or five trains each way per day were deemed to be adequate for the traffic generated. On some summer Saturdays six or seven trains traversed the North Cornwall line and most passing loops were made use of. Most trains took well over 2 hours to travel the 62¼ miles from Okehampton to Padstow. The fastest time from London Waterloo to Padstow in 1935 was 6hr 37min. By 1954 the best time was 6hr 21min from

Waterloo off the 11.00am departure and, unbelievably, 6hr 21min from Paddington off the 3.30pm departure, changing at Bodmin Road! Except in the era of main up and down London trains, which did not normally stop at St Kew Highway, Tresmeer and Egloskerry (and Tower Hill and Ashwater in Devon), all trains stopped at all stations. There were one or two 'short' workings with morning up and down Launceston starters.

The North Cornwall line saw its share of goods traffic. Freight to and from Padstow, Wadebridge and Delabole ensured through traffic but there were also large quantities of livestock and processed meat shipped to and from Launceston. There was seasonal produce loaded at intermediate stations and incoming loads of coal, fertilizer, etc. In 1952 two goods trains per day traversed the North Cornwall line. In the down direction freight traffic off the 6.27am ex-Okehampton mixed train continued beyond Launceston to arrive at Wadebridge at 12.37pm, while the 10.44am from Okehampton arrived at Wadebridge at 7.13pm, after spending huge amounts of time at intermediate sidings. In the up direction freights left Wadebridge at 11.35am, arriving at Okehampton at 7.30pm, while the 4.30pm ex-Wadebridge ran to Salisbury, pausing at Okehampton from 9.45pm to 10.20pm.

Tender classes were generally favoured on the North Cornwall line, presumably because of the distances involved. The graceful 'T9' 4-4-0s were associated with the line from Edwardian times until finally displaced in 1961. The 'N' class 2-6-0 Moguls were

regular performers on both passenger and freight workings for 40 years and in the later years Bulleid light Pacific 4-6-2s made regular appearances, providing a strange spectacle heading lightly loaded two-coach trains across the Cornish countryside. On summer Saturdays they sometimes took six to 10 coaches up from Padstow, a demanding task but well within their capability. Standard and Ivatt 2-6-2T locomotives and the larger Standard 2-6-4Ts also worked the line from time to time. A wide variety of both GWR and SR motive power worked between Wadebridge and Padstow (see Chapter 10).

In common with so many other lines the North Cornwall lost money, and due to the sparse population the business case was even less robust than others. The additional summer traffic was insufficient to make a significant difference to receipts. There had been some mild rationalisation, such as the removal of the passing loops at Tresmeer and Otterham in 1965, but the line was a clear loss-maker. Freight gradually declined and all goods services were withdrawn from 7 September 1964. Diesel multiple-units were used on passenger services from the beginning of 1965 but they arrived too late to produce economies on such a scale that the line could be saved. The North Cornwall was of course included

in the Beeching list of lines for closure, by which time the former 'enemy', the Western Region, had assumed operational control of the line. Sure enough the closure notices were posted and the entire line closed on 3 October 1966, the same date as the Bude branch. Together they could certainly be classified as the LSWR's 'Withered Arm'. The Padstow extension was reprieved but only until 28 January 1967.

There is no doubt that the North Cornwall line had a unique atmosphere. Of course there were sunny days but the overall impression was of a remote railway infrequently serving small, scattered communities obscurely located in a rather barren landscape. The line faithfully served the North Cornwall area for over 70 years and little changed over that time. However, time could not stand still for ever, and sadly modern economics dictated the line's ultimate destiny.

Long after closure a group of enthusiasts descended upon Launceston with the objective of opening part of the closed Southern route towards Tresmeer. The 2ft gauge line became established as the Launceston Steam Railway and in the summer months regular services run over a distance of about 2 miles of the old North Cornwall trackbed.

Above:

This wonderful NCR scene from about 1950 shows Bulleid 'West Country' class 4-6-2 Pacific No 34004 *Yeovil*, in original form and resplendent in lined green livery, approaching St Kew Highway with a down evening stopping train. The sight of these express passenger locomotives on such lightweight loads on cross-country lines never ceased to fascinate. *B. A. Butt*

Below:

An all-Southern line-up at Wadebridge on 22 September 1959 finds, on the left, Class 0298 Beattie 2-4-0 well tank No 30587 toying with a brake-van while on the up main is 'West Country' class No 34033 *Chard* with a North Cornwall line train for Okehampton. On the right is Adams Class O2 0-4-4T No 30199 with a connection for Bodmin North. A Padstow-bound NCR train occupies the down road. With all this activity visible it is hard to believe that Wadebridge is now completely rail-less. *P. Q. Treloar*

Above:
This classic view of Padstow shows the location of the station in relation to the town and the River Camel. On a delightful summer's day in 1950 No 30712 and two carmine and cream coaches leave the terminus with, according to the photographer, a stopping train to Launceston. The turntable, which was long enough to turn a 'West Country' Pacific, is on the right. There are nine coaches on one of the centre holding roads and behind are freight sidings that once extended on to the quays. *B. A. Butt*

6. Launceston Branch (GWR)

With populations of 4-5,000 each, the towns of Tavistock and Launceston could not be omitted from the proposed network in the years of 'railway mania'. Surveys had been conducted as early as 1840 to bring a railway to Tavistock in order to serve a large agricultural and mining area. The Civil Engineer was James N. Rendel and he considered three schemes that, in the broadest sense, could be described as running to the north or south around the Dartmoor land mass or directly across it. One route was to run via Launceston and Okehampton, another via Teignmouth and Totnes and the other across Dartmoor with a 5½-mile branch to Tavistock. Even in those now far-off years the Plymouth area had a population of about 100,000, with strong naval connections, and a rail connection with Exeter and consequently London was considered highly desirable from both an economic and social viewpoint. The people of Plymouth and those likely to come up with the funds were consulted and by 1842 it became clear that a line to

the south of Dartmoor, which would serve centres of population, was the preferred route.

The history of railways between Exeter and Plymouth is not the remit of this book, so suffice to say that in 1843 the Exeter, Plymouth & Devonport Railway was formed to build the so-called South Hams route, which had been surveyed by Isambard Kingdom Brunel as early as 1836. That company joined forces financially with the Great Western, Bristol & Exeter and Bristol & Gloucester companies to substantially fund the venture. Capital of £1.1 million was to be raised, the aforesaid companies contributing a total of £400,000, with a prospectus being issued on 13 October 1843. The Exeter, Plymouth & Devonport changed its name in 1843 to the South Devon Railway and an Act was passed by Parliament in July 1844 to build the line. Rendel was again employed in 1844 to survey the best routes for a branch to Tavistock, but there followed a decade of wrangling with many diverse vested interests effectively blocking what many had hoped

Above:
As was the case with the Bude branch, only the terminus at Launceston (GWR station) on the Plymouth to Launceston (via Tavistock) branch was actually located in the county of Cornwall, all other stations being in Devon. Accordingly all the photographs feature the Launceston area. This view shows a small Prairie of the '4400' class, No 4408, at the station in GWR days, before departing for Plymouth. Some wag has opened a door on the offside of the leading carriage to secure notoriety. *P. Q. Treloar Collection*

would be a logical and immediate development, linked to the building of the Exeter to Plymouth line.

One landowner who was not as co-operative as others was Lord Morley. Whereas other noblemen had offered to provide every facility, Lord Morley was on the Board of the LSWR, which was threatening to 'invade' Plymouth with its Okehampton 'narrow' (standard) gauge line. A total of three different routes for a branch to Tavistock were proposed, including one along the valley of the River Plym, but there were various powerful objections to each of the routes. There was also the added complication caused by the South Devon Railway's decision to use the atmospheric means of propulsion on its entire system. However, there was a suggestion that the proposed steeply graded Tavistock branch would be

unsuitable for the atmospheric system and decisions were deferred. In 1847 the South Western Railway was again in Tavistock promoting its proposed line from the north.

There were lengthy disputes and delays between landowners, railway companies, engineers and Parliament, then in 1852 a company called the Plymouth & Tavistock Railway Company issued a prospectus to raise £150,000 to build a branch between the two locations. In the same year the rival South Devon & Tavistock Railway published its prospectus, which included a short branch to serve Lee Moor clay works. Still on the table was the subject of the Okehampton line. Out of a liaison of companies, the Plymouth, Tavistock, Okehampton & Exeter Railway Company was formed, but after many battles the South Devon &

Table 95   PLYMOUTH, YELVERTON, TAVISTOCK SOUTH and LAUNCESTON

WR Launceston branch timetable, summer 1958

Notes:
A 1 mile to Tavistock North Station
B 5 minutes later on Saturdays
D Second class only Mondays to Fridays. First and Second class on Saturdays
E Except Saturdays
K Arr 6 minutes *earlier*
L 8 minutes later on Saturdays
S Saturdays only
T Arr 9 22 pm
U Arr 4 minutes *earlier*
V Arr 9 20 pm
W Through Train from Saltash on Mondays to Fridays, Second class only (Table 94). First and Second class on Saturdays
Y Saturdays only. Through Train from Saltash (Table 94)
Z Arr 7 minutes *earlier*
② Second class only

Right:
The GWR reached Launceston in 1865, 21 years sooner than the LSWR's North Cornwall line. The stations were adjacent to each other and in 1952 GWR trains started to use the then Southern Region (SR) station as an economy measure, the GWR station area remaining in use as a goods depot until February 1966. This July 1939 photograph shows the layout looking towards the buffer stops and also the SR's signalbox on the left.
M. Dart collection

Below:
The GWR station at Launceston in 1880, before the arrival of the LSWR in 1886. The LSWR route is shown by the dotted line.
Crown Copyright

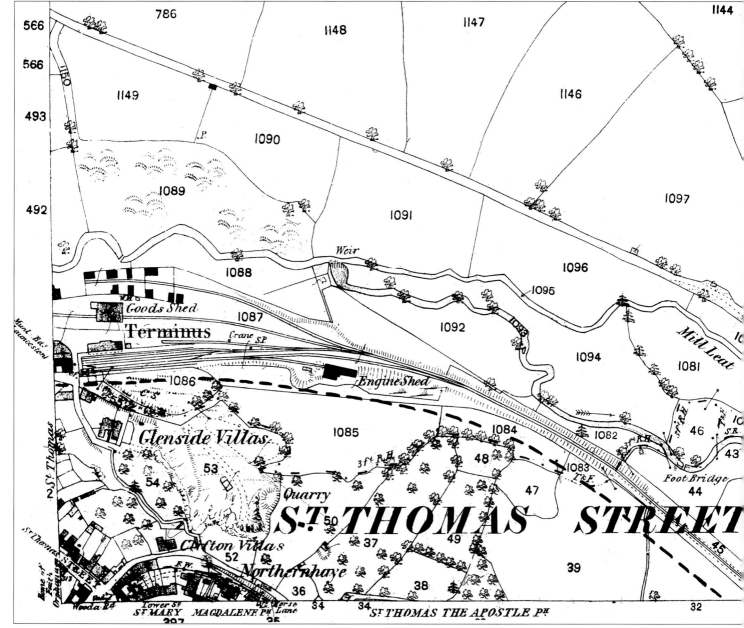

Above:
The Western Region train crew have time to share a story on the platform of Launceston South before departing for Plymouth on 23 June 1962. In 1958 there were only four round trips per day on the Launceston branch on Mondays to Fridays (with extras on Saturdays), and about five, plus freight, on the North Cornwall line, so line capacity at the 'Southern' station was never a problem. The last service on the GWR Launceston branch ran on 29 December 1962. *R. C. Riley, The Transport Treasury*

Tavistock company won the day, and a Bill was passed by Parliament in July 1854 approving the line.

The broad gauge line was to be 13 miles long and would leave the Devon & Exeter main line near Marsh Mills. To comply with the terms of the Bill all land had to be acquired by July 1857 and work had to be completed by July 1859. Work was heavy with three tunnels and six viaducts to construct, the longest viaduct being Walkham, 367yd long and 132ft high. Initially there were to be two intermediate stations, Bickleigh and Horrabridge. The line's engineer died in 1857, and his replacement was I. K. Brunel, who oversaw the rapid progress in construction. Finally, at the beginning of June 1859 Brunel rode the line and expressed himself satisfied. Accordingly, the line opened on 21 June, just days after the Royal Albert Bridge had opened, linking Devon and Cornwall by rail for the first time. There was much celebration in the market town of Tavistock, and in the early years the line was both busy and a financial success with good dividends for the investors.

To satisfy local demand a station at Marsh Mills, Devon, opened in 1861 but not at the junction with the South Devon line. When the South Western's line reached Okehampton in 1871 and Lydford in 1874, most Tavistock inhabitants wanting to travel to Exeter or beyond chose to travel by stagecoach to Okehampton. The South Devon Railway, which worked the Tavistock line, was amalgamated with the GWR in 1878, the South Devon & Tavistock having already been absorbed. Eventually stations were sited at Marsh Mills, Plym Bridge Platform (opened 1906),

Bickleigh and Shaugh Bridge Platform (opened 1907), and in the Meavy Valley were Clearbrook Halt (opened 1928), Yelverton (opened 1885), where a line to Princetown branched off (opened 1883), Horrabridge, Whitchurch Down Platform (opened 1906) and Tavistock South (the suffix used after nationalisation to differentiate it from the LSWR/SR Tavistock North station), 12 miles 71 chains from the junction with the South Devon main line. All of these stations were located in Devon and outside the scope of this book. There were also a number of goods sidings along the way, freight traffic at Tavistock commencing from 1 December 1860.

There had been all manner of schemes to provide Launceston with a railway, some dating back to 1836, and there is no doubt that from 1850 Launceston lost out from its isolated position and the population dwindled by some 1,000 folk between 1850 and 1860. The South Devon Railway had always wanted to extend its Tavistock branch to Launceston but preferred for others to plan and pay for it. Plans were prepared for a broad gauge line from Tavistock to Launceston via Mary Tavy, Lydford, Coryton and Lifton, and the line would be worked by the South Devon Railway for 50% of the takings north of Tavistock. The Bill became an Act of Parliament in June 1862. Fair progress was made and in 1865 Launceston was reached, 31 miles 67 chains from the junction with the main line at Marsh Mills, known as Tavistock Junction.

On 1 June 1865, a day of torrential rain, an inaugural double-headed 14-coach special train ran from Plymouth to Launceston, and despite the weather there were huge local celebrations in the

Right:
The classic GWR branch line motive power in Cornwall was the '4500' class 2-6-2 Prairie tank. With a steam leak in evidence No 4592 has just arrived at Launceston South (Southern) with a train from Plymouth. Two coaches was the normal load, with passenger loadings especially light beyond Tavistock. To the left of the LSWR signalbox can be seen the former GWR lines, which were used only for goods in later years. *W. A. Camwell/SLS*

Above:
This view incorporates both the Southern (right) and Western (left) locomotive sheds — the former looks as though it has been hit by a hurricane! It was common practice in later years for the branch locomotives to be turned on the ex-SR turntable but to be kept overnight in the more substantial ex-GWR shed. No 5541 performs a *tête-à-queue* on 2 May 1961. *R. C. Riley, The Transport Treasury*

Left:
Both Launceston stations have now been razed and part of the land is covered by a modern industrial estate. Fortunately the Launceston Steam Railway now runs narrow gauge steam trains over part of the old NCR line (see last chapter) during the summer months. The site of the SR station, seen here, is now the railway's car park and the LSR station is beyond the road overbridge, visible in the distance. *JV*

town. However, the railway inspectors required some minor unfinished works to be completed and the line was not opened to the public until 1 July, goods traffic being dealt with from 21 August. Between 1865 and 1873 traffic increased by 20% and some handsome returns were made. In 1874 the LSWR reached Lydford and it was proposed that a third 'narrow' (standard) gauge rail be provided from Lydford to Launceston along the existing branch. One can imagine the South Devon's response to that proposal! In July 1886 the 'narrow' gauge did finally reach Launceston when the LSWR built its North Cornwall cross-country line from Halwill to, eventually, Wadebridge and Padstow (see previous chapter). In 1876 the LSWR gained access to Tavistock (and beyond) from Lydford and from Tavistock to Plymouth via Bere Alston in June 1890. The GWR branch was converted to standard gauge in 1892.

Intermediate stations on the extended South Devon line were Mary Tavy (opened 1865 and renamed Mary Tavy & Blackdown in 1907), Lydford (until 1897 known as Lidford and opened in 1865), Liddaton Halt (opened 1938), Coryton (opened 1865) and Lifton (opened 1865), all in the county of Devon and not described in detail here. Having crossed the River Tamar and the boundary, the end of the line at Launceston, Cornwall, was reached. There were sidings at Pitt's Cleave Quarry siding, Leat siding and Cawdron siding, also all in Devon. On opening through to Launceston there were five trains from Plymouth and four in the reverse direction on Mondays to Saturdays and two round trips on Sundays. There was also a daily goods train to cater for freight movements. By 1906 there were 11 passenger trains per day to Tavistock, five of which continued to Launceston. In later years the service settled down to five trains per day each way on weekdays only, with at times an extra on Saturdays. The pace was hardly rapid and it took over 1½ hours to travel the 35½ miles to Plymouth Millbay.

In the early days a variety of GWR broad gauge locomotives worked the line, but the last broad gauge train working to Launceston was on 20 May 1892, when the line was converted to standard gauge, and from that time until World War 1 converted '3521' class 4-4-0s worked the route. However, once the '4500' class was introduced the Launceston end of the line became a tank engine preserve with GWR Prairies dominating. The class could haul 220 tons south of Yelverton and 240 tons beyond. Small 0-4-2T and 0-6-0PT locomotives worked auto-trains from Plymouth to Tavistock South, but larger classes were banned due to clearance and weight restrictions.

Launceston station comprised up and down platform lines, a centre road, engine shed, 45ft turntable, water column, goods shed and plenty of siding capacity for the large volumes of mineral, agricultural and livestock traffic. It had the suffix 'North' added to its name in June 1951 — a bit late — to distinguish it from the former SR station! In 1943, during World War 2, a spur between the GWR and SR lines was built for strategic purposes; the line was controlled by a ground frame and was SR property.

This connection was to sound the death-knell for the GWR station, because from 1 July 1952 all passenger trains from the branch used the Southern Region facility; with only four or five trains per day on the North Cornwall line there was plenty of spare capacity. The GWR station area continued to be used for goods traffic for a further 14 years.

Over the decades the branch continued to provide a regular passenger and freight service for the local community, although once the LSWR arrived most long-distance and London-bound travellers tended to use the Southern line. Both stations were located in the valley to the north of the town that is dominated by the partly ruined late Norman castle, where until the 19th century public executions were carried out. Although this book deals only with the branches and byways of Cornwall, the most picturesque parts of the branch were in Devon, where the hills and wooded valleys were a delight.

After World War 2 there was an increase in bus services working out of bomb-damaged Plymouth and an end to petrol rationing. A growth in private motoring and increased prosperity had a damaging effect on passenger numbers, and the reaction of the by then British Railways Board was to reduce train services so that by 1959 there were only three trains to Launceston, with Saturday extras, and no trains on Sundays. Receipts from the line had dwindled so much and so fast that the normally pro-railway Transport Users' Consultative Committee could not defend the continuation of train services and the Minister of Transport agreed with BR Western Region's proposals to close the line from 31 December 1962; this included complete abandonment of the track from Marsh Mills to Tavistock South and from Lifton to Launceston North. Thus the closure preceded the heyday of the 'Beeching' closures.

Fragments of line continued for freight, for example from Tavistock Junction to Marsh Mills for china clay traffic, Lydford to Lifton, and Lydford to Tavistock South, the last two being operated by the Southern Region, which also continued to serve Launceston North. Abandonment of even these freight services occurred during 1964 (Lydford to Tavistock South) and 1966 (Lydford to Lifton and Launceston). In May 1964 a steam locomotive hauled an inspection saloon between Launceston and Lydford even though the Launceston end of the branch was officially closed. There was drama on the line right at the end of passenger services when trains on the last day of service, 29 December 1962, were severely affected by heavy snowfalls and strong winds, with staff making herculean efforts to keep the branch trains moving. On 5 September 1965, after closure of the GWR branch but before closure of the North Cornwall line, a steam-hauled enthusiasts' special visited Launceston North for the very last time, to commemorate the centenary of the opening of the original broad gauge branch. After closure of the Southern line the market town of Launceston was deprived of all rail services, dashing the aspirations of the Victorian railway pioneers. Little evidence of the branch now remains west of the River Tamar.

7. Callington Branch

Whereas the areas around Bude and Launceston were largely agricultural, the land between Calstock and Callington and on the Devon side of the River Tamar was rich in mineral deposits. Kit Hill, to the west of Hingston Down, which at an altitude of just over 1,000ft dominates the area, was the centre of mining activity centuries ago, archaeologists having dated some of the workings back to Roman and Saxon times. The various mines produced copper ore, tin, lead, silver and arsenic, and the demands of the industrial revolution in the 19th century resulted in more mines being opened, facilitated by the advent of steam-driven pumping engines that kept deep mines free from water ingress.

The number of mines in operation was impressive. In no particular order, a far from exhaustive list includes Redmoor and Kelly Bray Mines, Kit Hill Great Consols, East and South Kit Hill Tin Mines, Hingston Down Consols including the Prince of Wales Mine, Holmbush Mine, New Consols Mine at Luckett, Drakewalls Mine, Greenhill Arsenic Works, Old Gunnislake Mine, Gunnislake Clitters, Wheal Edward, Wheal Arthur, Cotehele Consols (not far from the National Trust's Cotehele House) and Calstock Consols. Old Gunnislake Mine started life in the 17th century and many others were almost as old. Long before the arrival of the East Cornwall Mineral Railway a tramway had been built for conveying ores from the mines at Gunnislake down to wharves on the River Tamar. Some of these mines employed large numbers of workers; for example, in 1870 the Drakewall Mines employed some 340 men.

It does not take much imagination to envisage the huge volume of ore and minerals these mines produced. The only means of transporting their combined output and the large volumes of coal required for the pumping engines was by horse and ship using Calstock Quay on the River Tamar. In those days Calstock was a busy place with various quays, shipbuilding, market boats carrying passengers to Plymouth and local produce barges, each carrying about 50 tons of produce, sometimes formed into 'trains' and hauled by paddle tugs. Larger ships in the 150-300-ton category were used for the shipment of ores, granite and bricks towards Plymouth and coal and manure on the back-run. Liverpool and South Wales were the primary destinations for the ore traffic.

However, visitors to the area will be aware that much of the village of Calstock is at river level whereas the mines were on high land far above the river valley. It was expensive and hazardous to transport these materials by packhorses and horse and cart, and the mostly unmetalled local roads were primitive by today's standards. Hauling heavy loads up steep gradients in inclement weather was not a formula for the efficient transportation of minerals. Mining was at its zenith in the mid-19th century, and not before time, in 1862, a company called the Tamar, Kit Hill & Callington Railway Company was formed to connect Calstock Quay with Callington, a distance of 7 miles.

Right:
A much-needed railway line from Kelly Quay, Calstock, on the River Tamar, to the many mines located on much higher ground around the Kit Hill area was opened in 1872 under the auspices of the East Cornwall Mineral Railway (ECMR). At the end of the quay was a half-mile-long 1 in 6 incline that enabled wagons to gain over 350ft in elevation at the end of a 'wire rope' (cable). Shunting on the quay was performed by horses, as seen on the left. There was a passing loop halfway up the incline and the maximum load was two loaded or three empty wagons. Here two loaded coal wagons ascend the incline some 100 years ago.
Redruth Studies Library

The company 'jumped the gun' by cutting the first sod at Kelly Quay, Calstock, in November 1863 before an Act of Parliament had been obtained. A formal prospectus was issued in January 1864 and an Act was finally obtained in July 1864 authorising the proposed standard gauge line. While these formalities were taking place, work was progressing on an inclined plane up from Kelly Quay at Calstock and associated quayside buildings and infrastructure. In the meantime, in 1865, another Act was passed authorising the Saltash & Callington Railway, to construct a broad gauge branch of the Cornwall Railway, to link the towns in its name. The Tamar, Kit Hill & Callington had approval to link with the Saltash & Callington but a further Act was needed to enable the use of the broad gauge, although any connection would probably have resulted in mixed gauge operation. However, there was a general slump in 1866 and finance was not available to complete the Tamar, Kit Hill & Callington line, while the Saltash & Callington was not built at all.

A second railway to link Calstock and Callington was promoted in 1869 and an Act secured on 9 August of that year. The line was to be just over 7 miles 7 chains long, including the original incline and the track on the quayside at Calstock. The Act permitted the line to be constructed to a gauge of between 3ft and 4ft 8½ in; in the event, 3ft 6in was chosen. The line was not authorised to carry passengers. Having gained height via the incline, progress with construction of the permanent way across farmland to the north of Hingston Down and Kit Hill was rapid and the line was officially opened throughout on 8 May 1872. An Act in 1871 authorised a change of name to the East Cornwall Mineral Railway (ECMR). Two narrow gauge locomotives worked the line, while a stationary engine was used on the inclined plane and horses on the quay at Calstock. The line was an immediate financial success, the only limitation being the size of vessels that could navigate the Tamar as far as Calstock. Accordingly, the ECMR looked to connect with a railway that had access to the national system.

The ECMR line commenced 1 furlong east of the present Calstock Viaduct, which in 1863-64 had yet to be built. As modified by the ECMR there were over 450yd of rail-served moorings on the quay. Short of the western extent of the track layout on the quay there was a curved 1 in 6 incline to lift wagons 350ft above the quay. It was single track and just under half a mile long (35 chains) with a passing loop halfway up. Up and down wagons were counterbalanced, with the maximum load being two loaded wagons or three empties. Assistance was available from a 14hp stationary engine, wagons being attached to a 'wire rope'. Movements were controlled by electric bell codes and a midway semaphore signal. Located at the top of the incline were a winding house, engine shed and sidings for the wagons. Beyond the incline the line climbed to Drakewalls (Gunnislake) where there was a depot for public use, catering for coal and the needs of the agricultural community.

There were sidings aplenty in the area serving Drakewall's Tin Mine, Pearson's Quarry and Plymouth Works (via West of England siding) with an incline connection to Gunnislake Clitters Mine. Between Gunnislake and Callington were public depots at Cox's Park (Latchley), Monks Corner (Luckett) and various sidings serving mines and quarries, with the largest output being from Hingston Down and Kit Hill. The line speed limit was a curious 16mph and semaphore signals were provided at Cox's Park, Monks Corner and Kelly Bray. There were seven public road crossings, four of which had crossing keepers but were protected only by crossing gates. Trains could pass at two locations on the line, and on the steepest gradients trains were sometimes split.

The ECMR's motive power comprised two little 11¾-ton 0-4-0 saddle tanks built by Neilson & Co of Glasgow in 1871 (Works Nos 1660/1). They were reliable and lasted way beyond the time the line was taken over by the Plymouth, Devonport & South Western Junction Railway (PDSWJR) in 1891. In fact the second

of the two locomotives was regauged in the works at Callington and lasted until 1912. It was sold to the Selsey Tramway in Sussex, run by the famous Colonel H. F. Stephens, who in 1902 was appointed as Associate Engineer for the construction of the PDSWJR line. He obviously became familiar with the ECMR motive power and the sale may have had something to do with his previous connections with the line. After rebuilding again and being named *Hesperus* the locomotive was scrapped in 1927. The other narrow gauge locomotive, No 1, was in poor condition and was sold by the PDSWJR in 1911.

At this time the nearest railways were the Cornwall Railway main line from Plymouth to Truro and the Tavistock and Launceston branch of the South Devon Railway referred to in the previous chapter. A turn of the century guidebook shows that the nearest stations to Callington were Tavistock, 9 miles (GWR and LSWR), and Saltash, 9½ miles (GWR 'Motor'). By 1874 the LSWR had reached Lydford and, by mixed gauge line, Tavistock in 1876. In the same year the ECMR presented a Bill for a 7-mile extension from the top of the Calstock incline to Tavistock, where it would join the Tavistock & South Devon Railway. A branch of just over 1 mile to Morwellham Quay was also envisaged. The Act for the line was given Royal Assent on 15 August 1876, including a condition that required the ECMR to alter its existing line to standard gauge. The old speed limit was to be abolished and the carrying of passengers permitted. Unfortunately the finance was not forthcoming.

Other opposed schemes advocated by the Devon & Central Cornwall Railway included a direct railway from Lydford to Calstock, linking with the ECMR to Callington, which included a plan to extend the ECMR from Kelly Bray to Callington (until closure, Callington station was still at Kelly Bray, a mile from the town!). Opposition came from the GWR and the promoters of the Tavistock & Gunnislake Railway, but in May 1882 the House of Lords dismissed their objections and the D&CCR scheme was approved.

Unfortunately only 2% of the authorised share capital was forthcoming! The mining industry had begun to slow as world prices experienced another trough and the future of Cornwall's mines became less certain. Yet another scheme was submitted to Parliament, this time by the PDSWJR to construct a standard gauge railway from Lydford through Tavistock and Bere Alston to link up with the LSWR at Devonport, with a branch to join the ECMR at Calstock. The Bill received Royal Assent on 25 August 1883 and included powers to make agreements to acquire the D&CCR (and the ECMR). There were significant delays obtaining capital, but finally on 2 June 1890 the PDSWJR line through Devon was opened. The ECMR was taken over in 1891, although purchase was not completed until January 1894.

However, there was no money available to connect Bere Alston in Devon with Calstock in Cornwall and the powers to build lapsed. There was another flurry of activity regarding a Saltash to Callington branch but this came to nothing. The passing of the Light Railways Act in 1896 caused the PDSWJR to give consideration to a passenger-carrying narrow gauge connection from Bere Alston to Calstock to link up with the existing 3ft 6in gauge ECMR. The River Tamar would have to be crossed by a viaduct some 120ft above the water line, and the new line would be just over 4 miles in length. In 1900 the Bere Alston & Calstock Light Railway Order was made by the Board of Trade, but again little progress was made due to a shortage of funds. Deals were done with the LSWR whereby it would provide the capital, which was effectively secured on the entire undertakings of the PDSWJR. An amended order was made in 1905, changing the gauge from narrow to standard. As mentioned above, Colonel Stephens was appointed Engineer not only for construction but for converting the ECMR to standard gauge.

Authority was given to purchase second-hand locomotives and coaches from the LSWR or, if not available, to seek estimates for 'new build' locomotives. In 1906 the Colonel purchased goods

Right:
The Plymouth, Devonport & South Western Junction Railway (PDSWJR) took over the 3ft 6in gauge ECMR in 1894 and after much delay (see text), and in collaboration with the LSWR, authority to build a standard gauge line from Bere Alston to Callington was finally secured in 1905. This rare view, postally used from Tavistock in 1905, taken above Calstock and the River Tamar, shows the railway in the course of construction with the contractor's narrow gauge line running beneath this wooden pedestrian bridge. *JV collection*

Left:
This 1907 view of the quay shows that Calstock Viaduct has been completed but that the same cannot be said for the wagon lift. Although there seems to be plenty of business on the quay, with ships and wagons exchanging goods, the old ECMR incline was abandoned in 1908 when the standard gauge branch and the wagon lift were finally opened.
JV collection

Right:
This panorama shows Calstock Viaduct with the wagon lift in full operation. Even though there are 10 wagons on the quay with four more on the wagon lift siding at the end of the viaduct, traffic was so thin by 1912 that the full-time wagon lift operator was dispensed with. Gradually all freight traffic was taken out via the main branch and the wagon lift was finally abandoned in 1934.
JV collection

Above:
**This photograph shows the track layout at the Cornish (Calstock) end of Calstock Viaduct, with the sidings
serving the wagon lift in the right centre. The lift and its superstructure were demolished in October 1934.
Happily trains still run across the 290yd-long viaduct on their way from Plymouth to Gunnislake.**
JV collection

wagons and new locomotives to work the line; it was decided that two 0-6-2Ts for passenger workings and one 0-6-0T for freight would be sufficient, while one of the old regauged ECMR locomotives would be retained for pilot duties at Callington. The viaduct would have a wagon lift attached to it so that the old incline down to Calstock Quay could be abandoned; the difference in levels on the wagon lift was 113ft and the maximum load was one wagon weighing up to 20 tons. The full 9-mile 50-chain line opened on 2 March 1908, ECMR traffic having been suspended for only two days during the conversion of gauge to avoid disruption to the 200 tons of mineral traffic that was then dealt with daily. There were local celebrations but no formal opening ceremony. Stations were at Calstock, Gunnislake, Chilsworthy, Latchley, Stoke Climsland and Callington Road. Following complaints from within the parish, Stoke Climsland was renamed Luckett in 1909 and Callington Road became Callington for Stoke Climsland. The line was steeply graded and above Calstock there were long gradients of 1 in 38 on curves that caused adhesion problems from time to time. The steepest but short gradient was 1 in 33, on the approach to Callington station.

On leaving Bere Alston the line dropped away at 1 in 39 towards the Tamar Valley. Calstock station (1 mile 55 chains) was located on the Cornish side of the Tamar at the end of the impressive Calstock Viaduct. Although a crossing loop was provided, there was only one platform face. The original station was a corrugated iron structure similar in design to other Colonel Stephens lines. The line then climbed at a severe 1 in 38 on curves of 7 and 10 chains through leafy cuttings before turning through 180° and joining the old alignment of the ECMR on the way to Gunnislake. Before reaching Gunnislake there was a down-side siding serving a coal depot. The original Gunnislake station (4 miles 48 chains) comprised a single island platform with a multi-road goods yard and sidings.

On leaving Gunnislake there was Sand Hill Park Siding on the down side and old mines with sidings on the up side. The single platform face of Chilsworthy was at 5 miles 31 chains with down-

side brickworks and coal sidings immediately beyond. Whiterocks siding served a large quarry, and was followed by Hingston Down sidings, which included a loop. Latchley, at 6 miles 39 chains, was a small halt with a single siding and loading dock; the village it served was a mile away and was 500ft below the station site. Gradients were less severe over this part of the line. Near the 700ft summit of the line was the short-lived Seven Stones platform. Next was Luckett station (7 miles 58 chains), which had the benefit of a goods loop and loading dock. Three-quarters of a mile beyond Luckett was Kit Hill siding where a narrow gauge inclined tramway ran up to the granite quarries; it was later converted to standard gauge. Callington, at 9 miles 50 chains, had a single platform with a partial all-over roof, and a run-round loop outside the station. There was a two-road engine shed, goods shed, sidings and coal yard. The line had an overall speed limit of 25mph and there were no signalboxes, the few signals on the branch being controlled from small ground frames.

Despite the strong links with the LSWR, the PDSWJR operated the line from the opening in 1908 until the Grouping in 1923. Initially there were four round trip workings per day plus a 'short' from Bere Alston to Gunnislake; which was later extended to Callington on Saturdays. In the summer a late-night revellers' train was provided between Callington and Bere Alston, and return. In 1913 over 112,000 passengers were carried and business was booming, although the same could not be said for the freight business. The huge Devon Great Consols Mine had closed in 1899 and over the previous 20 years the same fate had already overtaken many mines in the Gunnislake and Kit Hill areas.

By 1909 goods traffic was 'practically at a standstill'. Kit Hill Granite Company restarted quarrying, causing a slight improvement, and Seven Stones Halt, between Latchley and Luckett, was opened in 1910, but closed in 1917. Colonel Stephens was effectively sacked when he failed to respond to a call for a meeting to discuss a full-time post. Nevertheless, in 1910 he purchased six coaches from the PDSWJR and in 1912 ECMR No 2 locomotive. In 1912 the wagon lift operator was

Above:
All 12 of Calstock viaduct's 60ft arches are featured in this fine study of a minimum-length 4.23pm Callington to Bere Alston branch train hauled by Class O2 0-4-4T No 30192 on 25 September 1954. The River Tamar is the boundary between Cornwall and Devon and the train has just left the Royal Duchy on its way to the junction with the LSWR's main line. *R. E. Vincent*

Below:
Other than for the very occasional engineering train the only locomotives to work over the Gunnislake branch in recent years have been on the annual weedkilling train. On 8 April 1990 the Chipman company's train, topped and tailed by Class 20 Bo-Bos Nos 20901 and 20904, eases across Calstock viaduct on its way to Gunnislake. *JV*

	BERE ALSTON and CALLINGTON.															
	Down.	**Week Days.**												**Sundays.**		
Miles		mrn	aft	aft	aft	mrn	mrn	turn	aft	aft	aft	mrn	aft	mrn	aft	aft
		T	8X	8O	8O	Y	T	T			8O	Y				
170	London (W.) dep.	0	1030	1030	..	8SO35	9L0	11 0	1 N0	3 0	3 0	..	..	110	1 04	0
—	Bere Alston ....dep.	819	11 3	11 15	1257	2 10	3 22	5 22	7 10	9	1 10	5	926	1222	515 7 21	10 0
1½	Calstock	825	11 9	11 21	1 3	2 16	3 28	5 28	7 16	9	9	1011	932	1228	523 7 27	10 6
4¼	Gunnislake	840	1124	11 36	1 16	2 30	3 42	5 42	7 30	926	1025	946	1242	537 7 41	1020
5¼	Chilsworthy	847	1131	11 43	1 24	..	3 47	5 47	7 35	934	1032	951	1247	541 7 46	1025
6¼	Latchley	852	1135	11 48	1 29	..	3 52	5 52	7 40	939	1037	956	1252	546 7 50	1030
7¼	Luckett	857	1140	11 53	1 34	..	3 57	5 57	7 45	944	1042	101	1257	551 7 55	1035
9¼	Callington G ..arr.	9 4	1147	12 0	1 41	..	4 4	6 4	7 52	951	1049	108	1 4	558 8 2	1042

	Up.	**Week Days.**										**Sundays.**			
Miles		mrn	mrn	aft	aft	aft	aft	aft	aft	mrn	mrn	aft	aft	aft
			T		Y	T	Y	8O						
	Callington G ...dep.	718	9 47	1257	T	423	620 9 5	1011	823	1130	6 30	8 15	9 10
1½	Luckett	724	9 53	1 3	..	429	626 9 11	..	829	1136	6 36	8 21	9 16
3	Latchley	729	9 58	1 8	..	434	631 9 16	..	834	1141	6 41	8 26	9 21
4	Chilsworthy	734	10 3	1 13	..	438	636 9 21	..	839	1145	6 45	8 31	9 26
5	Gunnislake	738	10 7	1 17	2 40	442	640 9 25	1026	843	1149	6 49	8 35	9 30
7½	Calstock	752	1021	1 31	2 52	456	653 9 40	1042	856	12 2	7 2	8 49	9 43
9½	Bere Alston 170 arr	8 1	1030	1 39	3 4	5 67	1 9 48	1050	9 5	1211	7 10	8 57	9 51
229½	173 London (W.) arr	2 24	A12 8	K37	10 8	355	..	..	..	350	7 44	..	..

O Except Sunday nights. Dep. 12 night on Weds.   G Sta. for Stoke Climsland (1 mile). Omnibus services, operated by the Western National Omnibus Company, run between Callington Station and Callington Village. also Callington Station and Stoke Climsland.   H Friday nights. Dep. 12 20 mrn on 30th July and 6th August only.   A Arr 4 33 aft on Sats.   K Arr. 7 35 aft. on Sats.   L Dep 8 45 mrn on Sats.   N Dep 2 0 aft on Sats.   8 O or SO Sats. only.   8 X Sats. excepted.   T Third class only.   Y Weds., Thurs., & Sats.

The Callington branch timetable in July 1938

Below:

An interesting working occurred on 3 July 1981 when experimental Class 140 diesel unit No 140001 worked a 14.45 special from Plymouth to Gunnislake. These four-wheelers and their Class 142 successors were unsuccessful on Cornish branches because of their rigid wheelbase and lack of sanding gear. The special is seen climbing above Calstock *en route* for Gunnislake. JV

dispensed with, such was the low level of activity at Calstock Quay now that the railway was linked with the main line. The old stationary engine on the Calstock Quay incline was sold in 1913. The PDSWJR continued to do a good job at marketing the line with various reasonably priced excursion tickets.

In 1913 the track layout at Callington was modified and in 1914 a siding was laid at Chilsworthy to accommodate the output of the local brickworks. In 1919 the platform and the cattle dock were extended at Callington. In 1921 the company acquired some bogie coaches from the LSWR to replace its old worn-out stock, which had originated on the North London Railway. Although mineral traffic had seriously declined, the market garden and agricultural business increased. By the time the Southern Railway absorbed the PDSWJR at the Grouping in 1923 there were five round trips per day between Bere Alston and Callington with one extra on Saturdays. The journey time for the 9½ miles was about 40 minutes.

Above:
Part of the PDSWJR motive power fleet was a pair of Hawthorn Leslie 0-6-2T locomotives and an 0-6-0T freight version. The locomotives were called *Earl of Mount Edgcumbe*, *Lord St Levan* and *A. S. Harris*. Here one of the '757' class 0-6-2Ts makes a vigorous departure from Gunnislake on its way to Callington. Its sister locomotive can be seen in the up road. The goods yard is on the right. *M. Dart collection*

Centre right:
From 6 November 1966 the Callington branch was truncated and Gunnislake became the terminus of the line. The original Colonel Stephens type of corrugated iron station building survived well into the 1970s. Seen here at Gunnislake on 20 June 1970 is a two-car DMU on working 2C40, waiting to return to Plymouth. The former LSWR main line through Bere Alston had closed in 1968 and from that date all branch trains worked through from Plymouth. *JV*

Lower right:
In the late 1990s the old Gunnislake station site was abandoned and the line shortened by a few hundred yards, enabling a low bridge over the A390 road to be demolished. The new station was marketed as an interchange point for buses, and a small car park for commuters was provided. In this July 1999 view a single-car Class 153 unit, No 153362, is working the branch. *John Frith*

Left:
This view of Chilsworthy, looking towards Gunnislake, shows the down brickworks and coal siding on the right. Note the single-faced platform and the siding points lever. *JV collection*

Right:
The PDSWJR Class 757s continued to work on the Callington branch until the mid-1950s, when Ivatt 2-6-2Ts arrived. On the heaviest trains they occasionally worked in tandem, and in this rare photograph, which dates back to 1949, No 758 *Lord St Levan* double-heads sister locomotive No 757 *Earl of Mount Edgcumbe* as the PDSWJR duo pound up the 1 in 36 climb above Calstock with a heavy Callington-bound down freight.
M. Dart collection

Left:
Latchley station was 1 mile (and 500ft in elevation) from the village it was supposed to serve. Basic passenger facilities were offered but, as can be seen in this shot looking up towards Gunnislake, a siding with loading dock was provided. The station closed in 1966. *JV collection*

Seven Stones Halt was located near to the 700ft summit of the line between Latchley and Luckett; opened in 1910, it was closed by 1917. Passing the crumbling remains of the platform with a down goods train is No 30757 *Earl of Mount Edgcumbe* in the early days of BR. *JV collection*

The line continued to operate successfully. A Sunday service appeared in 1924 comprising two trains each way, and in 1934 the wagon lift was finally abandoned. Traffic had remained mainly in the hands of PDSWJR motive power, the 1907 Hawthorn Leslie-built trio of 36-ton 0-6-0T No 3 *A. S. Harris* and 50-ton 0-6-2Ts Nos 4 *Earl of Mount Edgcumbe* and 5 *Lord St Levan*, until 1931 when the freight 0-6-0T was transferred to Eastleigh, Hampshire. However, in the early days of the Grouping the SR briefly but unsuccessfully tried other classes of motive power on the line. In 1929 the first LSWR Class O2 0-4-4T appeared on the branch, and these were to be regular performers until 1961. World War 2 came and went with only heavy loadings on some of the trains being of special note. The 0-6-2Ts could haul a maximum of six bogie coaches on the branch but this was sometimes exceeded, requiring double-headed workings. British Railways was formed in 1948 and between 1950 and 1958, and again in 1963, the line was deemed to be Western rather than Southern Region.

This change caused the remaining PDSWJR locomotives to be transferred away to Eastleigh where they ended their lives as Works shunters. From 1952 the Western Region had introduced ex-LMS Ivatt 2-6-2Ts on to the Callington branch, which in the mid-1950s rendered old Nos 4 and 5 redundant, a fate that befell the Class O2s in 1961. In the mid-1950s 400 vans and 50,000 packages of flowers and 300 vans and 66,000 packages of fruit were dispatched from Calstock and Gunnislake but by the 1960s there was closer scrutiny on the cost of operations. By this time there were six trains per day with an extra on Saturdays, and four Sunday trains, some being mixed.

The transfer back to the Western Region in 1963 seemed to be a turning point for the branch. During that year trials were conducted using diesel-hydraulic locomotives, but the Ivatt 2-6-2 tank engines survived to the end of steam in September 1964. From 7 September that year the service was in the hands of diesels, first locomotives then multiple-units. Yet again it was Dr Beeching who identified the line as loss-making and, in the eyes of some, the Western Region needed little encouragement to close a line of its former rival. Freight services were withdrawn in early

1966. The Callington branch was truncated from 6 November 1966, from which time the terminus became Gunnislake. BR had tried to close the entire branch but the terrain was so difficult that no viable public transport alternative could be provided. The LSWR main line from Okehampton to Bere Alston closed on 6 May 1968 when the line to Bere Alston and Gunnislake effectively became a branch line from Plymouth.

After the closure the track was rationalised and the LSWR's double track was lifted completely between Bere Alston and Meldon Quarry near Okehampton and singled between St Budeaux and Bere Alston, where branch trains reversed at the old Southern station with the train guard changing the points. The line from Bere Alston to Gunnislake is and always was single track, but was now without loops, sidings or points. In the late 1990s Gunnislake station was resited south of the main A390 road so that a low 12ft bridge over the road could be demolished. The new station has car parking and bus interchange facilities. Since 1968 there have been about eight return journeys on the branch on weekdays.

The journey from Plymouth to Bere Alston is outside of the scope of this book, but the ride from Bere Alston to Gunnislake is spectacular. The highlight is crossing Calstock Viaduct but there are many views of the River Tamar, the old village of Calstock, abandoned mines with ivy-covered chimneys, old stone cottages and pleasant pastures. The ride is highly recommended. The DMUs were popular because they afforded passengers excellent views of the line. There was an experiment in 1981 with a prototype four-wheeled railbus, and later Class 142 units were tried but they had door-opening problems and their rigid wheelbase and lack of sanding gear rendered them an almost inevitable failure on West Country branches. Services then continued in the hands of the old and faithful DMUs, until replaced by utility Class 150/2 and single-car Class 153 diesel-hydraulic units. In recent years there have been line promotions as part of a 'Dartmoor Explorer' ticket, with sponsored Sunday trains being introduced to the timetable during the summer. It is refreshing to write about an interesting branch line that in part remains open!

From the opening of the standard gauge branch in 1908 until 1909 Luckett station was called Stoke Climsland, but following protestations from the villagers, who suggested that the name was a misrepresentation, it was changed to Luckett. Callington Road then became Callington for Stoke Climsland. The station was 7 miles 58 chains from Bere Alston and it boasted a goods loop and loading dock, which can be seen in operation in this 1947 view. *JV collection*

Right:
Now in private ownership the Luckett station site can be clearly identified in this March 1992 view. The passenger platform, building foundations and loading dock can all be seen but the trackbed is now but a silent testimony to the flurry of action that took place here between 1872 and 1966. In ECMR days the siding near to this point was known as Monks Corner. *JV*

Left:
Three-quarters of a mile beyond Luckett was Kit Hill siding. There had been substantial mines and quarries in the Hingston Down/Kit Hill area years before the railway arrived, and the ornate chimney on top of Kit Hill is a landmark that can be seen from a great distance. This view shows Kit Hill siding with a loading crane and the start of the incline to the quarry on the right. *JV collection*

Right:
This wonderful study shows the three-rail Kit Hill rope incline in a state of disuse on 28 April 1951, although the quarry did not close until 1955. At the bottom of the incline, to the right, can just be seen the loading crane featured in the previous photograph. There was an 'escape track' at the foot of the incline to prevent any runaways reaching the main branch or the public road beyond. Wagons using the incline gained an altitude of some 300ft and the centre rail was used by both descending and ascending wagons (but not at the same time!). Note the winding rope, rollers and distant passing loop.
JV collection

Below:
LMS Ivatt 2-6-2Ts eventually replaced the ex-PDSWJR motive power and the LSWR Class O2s. On a bright 27 April 1962 Class 2MT No 41315 runs along the northern slopes of Hingston Down near Luckett with the 3.15pm Bere Alston to Callington train, formed of a typical SR branch consist. *J. C. Beckett*

61

Above:

With the chimney on the top of Kit Hill looking on, veteran Class O2 0-4-4T No 30236 enters Callington with a train from Bere Alston on 30 August 1954. Members of the class were regular performers on the branch between 1929 and 1961. Note the sidings left and right, the SR concrete sign and fences, and the engine shed behind the train. *R. C. Riley, The Transport Treasury*

Right:
In 1964 there was still freight traffic at Callington. Having completed its shunting operations, Ivatt 2MT 2-6-2T No 41316 prepares to leave for the junction at Bere Alston. The branch starting signal is upper quadrant whereas in the previous photograph it was of lower quadrant LSWR design. *M. Dart collection*

Above:
Although DMUs replaced steam locomotives, the immediate post-steam era saw Class 22 diesel-hydraulic locomotives used on the Callington branch. The first formal day of diesel operation was Monday 7 September 1964 and this view shows No D6323 posing under the all-over roof upon arrival with the 5.24pm from Bere Alston. There seems to be much cheer on this obviously very wet day. *Andrew Muckley*

8. Looe Branch and Liskeard & Caradon Railway

The Looe branch is, arguably, the best known of all Cornish branch lines. Whether this is because the line has such a fascinating history, or is the most scenic, or because the name of the seaside town it serves has other connotations would be pure speculation! The branch has certainly attracted the attention of railway historians, and at least four books and three comprehensive magazine articles have chronicled the history of the line. I would suggest that most authors have been intrigued by the menu of early mining history, transportation of minerals by canal and early tramways, rugged high country and meandering river valleys, ports, main line connections and viaducts, reversals in direction, steep climbs, branch line termini and semaphore signals, culminating in a thoroughly absorbing and Beeching-beating branch line that is still very much alive.

At over 1,200ft Caradon Hill forms a northern backdrop to the town of Liskeard, some 4 miles distant, while just over 7 miles to the south 'as the crow flies' (over 9½ miles by rail) is the coastal town of Looe. Both were to have an enormous influence on the transport scene in terms of canal and railway history. The acid soil in the area required manure, and whereas sea sand was used in north Cornwall, as mentioned in the Bude chapter, in the south use was made of both limestone, producing lime in limekilns, and sea sand (hence the origins of the hamlet Sandplace). Several of these limekilns were located between Looe and Liskeard in the East Looe valley; indeed, the remains of one installation can still be seen at Moorswater. This involved the transportation of lime by packhorse through narrow lanes for considerable distances; wagons did not come into common use until the 19th century. As long ago as 1774 consideration was being given to building a canal. A further survey in 1795 produced a plan for a canal linking the two towns, but the large number of locks required ruled out the proposals at that time.

In 1823 a Liskeard solicitor called a public meeting to discuss improvements in transportation, and by implication communication, between Liskeard and Looe by 'a Turnpike Road, a Rail Road or Canal' from Looe, via Sandplace to Looe Mills (below Liskeard). By the end of that year a plan for a canal had been produced. There was strong opposition from Lostwithiel and Fowey mainly on the grounds that the canal feeder would deplete the waters of the River Fowey. The plan provided for a towpath wide enough to accommodate 'Gentlemen's carriages' to appease an influential landowner. The Bill for the Liskeard & Looe Union Canal (L&LUC) received Royal Assent on 22 June 1825. Traffic would include lime, corn, timber, slate, coal and the products of the mines and quarries: tin, copper, lead and granite. The canal would run from Moors Water *(sic)* to Terras Pill, the tidal limit of the East Looe River.

Progress was rapid and within a month of the first sod being cut and a celebratory dinner in July 1825 construction commenced. The canal would carry boats with a 20-ton maximum capacity. Some locks were in operation in mid-1826, part of the canal was in use in 1827, and it was opened throughout in March 1828.

It was, however, not all 'plain sailing' as one or two landowners held out for higher compensation payments. Also some of the work was 'slovenly and unfinished', repairs were necessary in 1829 and not all associated works were completed until 1830. A handful of tramways connected individual limekilns to the canal, and the canal had an immediate beneficial effect on the price of coal, sand and lime. Although there was something of a depression in the world of agriculture in the mid-1830s and lime traffic suffered, all other traffic increased in volume. At about this time mining activity around Caradon Hill was about to increase significantly and there was a good chance that any shortfall in payload would be compensated for by mineral traffic. This was particularly fortuitous because the canal boats often worked back to Terras Pill empty.

The canal went from strength to strength as construction on connecting roads progressed. By 1849 annual traffic on the canal exceeded 21,000 tons and by 1859 the canal boats were carrying over 48,000 tons. There was even congestion on the canal at times. Part of the problem was the negotiation of 24 locks within 7 miles and a journey time of 8 hours! There were 13 canal boats and each carried an average payload of 16 tons, resulting in a theoretical annual capacity similar to the 1859 total.

By 1857 consideration was being given to a railway connecting Moorswater with Looe and a report with costings was prepared on 30 September 1857. As a result a Bill was prepared to put before Parliament and on 11 May 1858 the Liskeard & Looe Railway Act receive Royal Assent. However, before describing the building of the railway or the decline of the canal, further commentary is needed on the mines of Caradon Hill.

There had been evidence of tin mining and quarrying around Caradon Hill for centuries. This was shallow mining similar in some respects to Californian Gold Rush miners initially finding nuggets on the ground. Mining in Cornwall goes back to the days of the Romans and even the Phoenicians. These primitive workings were open cast, often using the 'streaming' technique — straining rock sediment in streambeds to find ore. Tin had been mined at nearby Herodsfoot and Menheniot from the 16th century until the early 19th century and there was plenty of evidence of numerous lodes in the area. It was a widely held belief that the discovery of significant mineral deposits would be exclusive to the geographical area west of Truro but in 1836, after some samples of copper ore were taken from Caradon Hill, that myth was exploded. There was no doubt that the samples were good quality but finance for further exploration and mining was hard to come by.

In 1837, 130 tons of ore were raised in an area that was to become South Caradon Mine, and this was sufficient to raise the interest of many who, until then, had stood on the sidelines. Other lodes were cut, shafts were sunk, and rich deposits were found in several, but not all, areas around Caradon Hill. Between 1837 and 1861 the population of nearby St Cleer increased by 400%, and the same phenomenon was seen at Crows Nest, Tremar, Darite

Right:
Its day's work having been completed DMU set No P571 leaves the Looe branch to join the main line at Liskeard station on 7 June 1980. The track configuration was later modified and access can now be obtained only from the up main line, seen here on the left. The short semaphore starting signal survives but a colour light has now replaced the advanced starter, seen in the distance at the end of Liskeard Viaduct. The down siding has also been removed. *JV*

Above:
There is a wonderful sleepy atmosphere to this September 1959 photograph at the Looe branch platform at Liskeard, which is set at right angles to the main line platforms. Having been detached from its coaches upon arrival from Looe, '4500' class No 4585 simmers in the sun before running round its stock. *Peter Gray*

Above:

The last day of steam operation on the Looe branch was 9 September 1961. Few realised that an era on our railways was about to end for ever and three coaches were more than sufficient to accommodate passengers. On that last day '4500' 2-6-2T No 5531 in lined green livery passes Liskeard Branch Signalbox with the 10.45am up from Looe. This box was subsequently closed and control was transferred to the main line signalbox.

M. L. Roach

and other nearby villages. But the miners worked in poor conditions for a small wage, and with an average income of only 50 shillings per month there was plenty of poverty. By 1863 there were 4,000 men, women and children working in 35 mines!

On Stows Hill one John Trethewey obtained permission from the Duchy of Cornwall to quarry granite at Cheesewring. Mines sprang up all over Caradon Hill, some of the better known being West Phoenix, Witheybrook, Phoenix United, Marke Valley, Wheal Jenkin, Gonamena and South Caradon. Some of these mines had several shafts, all with their own names, such as Holman's Shaft and Rule's Shaft at South Caradon. Many also had their own extensive tramway systems, above and below ground, such as South Caradon, which had a 3.4-mile tramway system! The output of all these mines and quarries was colossal. For example, Marke Valley produced 128,500 tons of copper ore between 1844 and 1890, Phoenix United produced 82,000 tons of copper and 16,000 tons of black tin between 1844 and 1898, and South Caradon, which once employed 650 persons, 217,820 tons between 1837 and 1885 (the date of closure). All of these minerals had to be transported to the head of the canal at Lamellion Bridge, Moorswater, at huge cost; for example, it cost 8 shillings per ton to convey the quarried granite.

In 1842 consideration had been given to building a railway from the Caradon Mines to the canal, including Cheesewring and Tokenbury branches, as the only practical means of coping with the growing output. In addition, the mines were consuming coal, iron and timber, so a back-load was guaranteed. The line was to be gravity worked on the downhill journey to the canal, with horses bringing back the empties and those with a back-load, even though Robert Coad, the engineer of the L&LUC, recommended horsepower throughout. No time was lost and Royal Assent was given to the Liskeard & Caradon Railway Act on 26 June 1843. The directors of the company had connections with either the mines or the canal.

MAY, 1890, and until further Notice.

LOOE RAILWAY.

DOWN TRAINS.	1 2 3	1 2 3 *	1 2 3	1 2 3 *
	A.M.	P.M	P.M.	P.M.
MOORSWATER......dep.	9·45	2·15	3·46	7·10
CAUSELAND ....arr.	9·58	2·28	3·59	7·23
SANDPLACE ....arr.	10·5	2·35	4·6	7·30
LOOE ....arr.	10.15	2·45	4·16	7·40

UP TRAINS.	1 2 3	1 2 3 *	1 2 3	1 2 3 *
	A.M.	P.M.	P.M.	P.M.
LOOE.. ....dep.	10·55	3·0	4·56	8.30
SANDPLACE ....arr.	11·5	3·10	5·6	8·40
CAUSELAND ....arr.	11·12	3·15	5·13	8·45
MOORSWATER .....arr.	11·25	3·30	5·26	9·0

* ON FRIDAYS ONLY.

FOR THE USE OF COMPANY'S SERVANTS ONLY.

MAY, 1890, and until further Notice.

Liskeard and Caradon Railway.

UP.	A.M.	P.M.
MOORSWATER.................dep.	7·0	12·15
POLWRATH ... .arr.	7·36	12·51

DOWN.	A.M.	P.M.
POLWRATH ...:...............dep.	8·45	2·45
MOORSWATER ....arr.	9·15	3·15

April 16th, 1890.

HERBERT G. T. HAWKEN,
Traffic Manager.

To Mr J. H. Smythurst

Below left:
This very rare survivor shows the timetable issued to Liskeard & Caradon Railway employees in April 1890. *JV collection*

Right:
The photographer's car just happened to stop on the new Liskeard bypass as Class 37 No 37019, left Liskeard for Moorswater at 10.50 on 11 April 1990 with a rake of empty CDA air-braked china clay hoppers. The branch platform can be seen in the background and the train will shortly turn through 180° to pass beneath Liskeard Viaduct on the left. *JV*

Left:
Snow in this part of Cornwall is relatively unusual but on 19 January 1985 there was sufficient to justify an overnight journey from Sussex to Cornwall! Here single-car Class 122 No 55025 is about to pass under the 150ft-high Liskeard Viaduct, which carries the Cornish main line over the valley, forming the 12.07 Liskeard to Looe service. *JV*

Right:
In order to travel to Looe from Liskeard all branch trains need to reverse at Coombe Junction. Until 1901 the Looe branch ran to Moorswater and there was no junction with the main line. However, in that year the GWR constructed a steeply graded connection, which DMU No L433 can be seen climbing on its way to Liskeard on 17 April 1981. Coombe Junction signalbox was closed a few weeks after this photograph was taken and these semaphore signals were felled. The line to Looe is on the right. *JV*

Left:
In recent years only a couple of trains per day were booked to call at Coombe Junction, and if the train crews saw nobody on the platform they would often 'give it a miss'. The author wanted to ensure that the Network SouthEast (NSE)-liveried DMU No L708 called at the platform, so he persuaded his late and greatly missed mother to take the single journey up to Liskeard. With the driver probably muttering and with the destination blind showing 'Shirley' (in Birmingham!) the DMU accelerates from the junction to make the pick-up. It was all well worth the £1 single fare! *JV*

The Looe branch timetable from the early days, November 1888, (*below*) before connection with the main line, and (*bottom*) the summer 1958 timetable.

LOOB RAILWAY.

Fares.			Down.	mrn	aft
1 cl	2 cl	3 cl			
0 9	0 6	0 3½	Moorswatr	9 45	3 50
1 0	0 7	0 5	Causeland..	9 58	4 3
1 6	0 9	0 7	Sandplace..	10 4	4 9
			Looe....arr	1012	4 17

Fares.			Up.	mrn	aft
1 cl	2 cl	3 cl			
0 6	0 4	0 2	Looe ..dep	1056	5 0
0 9	0 5	0 3½	Sandplace..	11 4	5 8
1 6	0 9	0 7	Causeland..	1110	5 14
			Moorswatr	1123	5 27

Table 96 — LISKEARD, CAUSELAND and LOOE

Miles									Week Days											Sundays					
		am S	am	am S	am E	am S	am E	am S	am E	pm	pm	pm E	pm S	pm E	pm S	pm	pm	am	am	pm	pm	pm	pm
—	Liskeard .. .. .. dep	550	7 15	8 45	8 55	9 52	10 5	1125	1155	1 23	2 52	4 35	4 40	5 50	555	7 45	9 13	9 0	1040	12 15	2 10	4 35	7 40
2	Coombe Junction Halt ..	...	7 23	8 55	9 3	10 5	1015	1133	12 5	1 33	3 4	45	4 47	5 49	22	9 8	1048	12 23	2 18	4 43	7 48
3¼	St. Keyne Halt	...	7 28	9 0	9 8	1010	1021	1138	1210	1 36	3 8	4 50	4 55	6 46	9 7	589	269	13	1053	12 28	2 23	4 48	7 53
5	Causeland Halt	...	7 32	9 5	9 12	1014	1026	1142	1214	1 40	3 12	4 54	4 59	6 8	6138	29	309	17	1057	12 32	2 27	4 52	7 57
6¼	Sandplace Halt	...	7 37	9 9	9 17	1019	1030	1146	1218	1 45	3 16	4 58	5 3	6 12	6178	7 9	359	22	11 2	12 37	2 31	4 57	8 2
8¼	Looe .. .. arr	620	7 44	9 17	9 24	1026	1037	1155	1228	1 53	3 23	5 5	5 10	6 20	625	8 14	9 42	9 30	1110	12 45	2 40	5 8	8 10

Miles									Week Days										Sundays					
		am S	am	am E	am S	am S	am E	pm	pm S	pm	pm E	pm S	pm	pm	pm	am	am	pm	pm	pm	pm
—	Looe .. .. dep	635	7 50	8 10	8 40	9 30	9 45	1045	1215	1240	2 0	345	5 10	5 15	6 45	8 30	9 50	7 45	11 20	1 25	2 50	6 30	8 20
2¼	Sandplace Halt	...	7 56	8 16	...	9 35	9 50	1050	1221	1246	2 6	351	5 16	5 21	6 50	8 36	9 55	9 51	11 26	1 30	2 56	6 36	8 26
3¼	Causeland Halt	...	8 0	8 20	...	9 39	9 54	1054	1225	1250	2 10	355	5 20	5 25	6 54	8 40	9 59	9 55	11 30	1 34	3 0	6 40	8 30
5	St. Keyne Halt	...	8 4	8 24	...	9 43	9 58	1058	1229	1254	2 14	4 0	5 24	5 29	6 58	8 44	10 3	9 59	11 34	1 38	3 4	6 44	8 34
6¼	Coombe Junction Halt ..	.	8 14	8 32	...	9 53	10 6	11 6	1236	1 1	2 21	4 10	5 33	5 38	7 6	3 51	1010	10 7	11 42	1 47	3 12	6 52	8 42
8¼	Liskeard .. .. arr	7 5	8 24	8 42	9 10	10 2	1017	1117	1246	1 11	2 33	420	5 44	5 50	7 16	9 1	1021	1016	11 52	1 58	3 22	7 1	8 51

E Except Saturdays   **S** Saturdays only

Right:
The four-wheeled coaches of the two-car Class 142 units, known as 'Skippers' in the West Country, were supposed to be the new generation of motive power on Cornish branch lines. However, the 'techies' did not allow for tight curves (no bogies), steep gradients (no sanding gear) and dodgy doors (they often failed to open). Hence their period of residence was rather short. On 22 April 1987 No 142027 is about to reverse at Coombe Junction with the 09.08 Liskeard to Looe service, while in the background Class 37 No 37175 waits for the road with ex-Moorswater china clay 'hoods' destined for Fowey. *JV*

Below:
The Liskeard & Looe Union Canal that preceded the railway was opened throughout from 1828, and ran from Moorswater, below Liskeard, to Terras Pill, the tidal limit of the East Looe River. It was connected to the various mines around Caradon by railway from 1846, and was so successful that by 1859 the annual payload being carried by boat was 48,000 tons. However, in 1860 Moorswater and Looe were connected by railway, which was the death-knell of the canal. The line of the old waterway can be seen in the foreground as No 37175 heads from Coombe Junction to the Moorswater works with china clay empties on 22 April 1987. *JV*

Construction of the standard gauge line started at the Cheesewring and good progress was made, although due to surveying errors some changes from the original plan had to be made. The railway encountered problems just north of Moorswater where the line passed through some Duchy of Cornwall land, and in terms of price the Duchy, as the Americans say, 'played hardball'. Thus the line was opened but only to Tremabe, south of St Cleer, on 28 November 1844. The opening celebration sounded fun, with the workmen being 'regaled with roast beef and strong beer'! The line was opened throughout in March 1846. The Cornwall Railway showed interest in purchasing the line but it seems that it too was short of funds. At this stage the Tokenbury branch had not been built and the traffic on the branch from South Caradon to the Cheesewring was rope-worked up the lower section of the Gonamena incline. Wagons descended to Moorswater individually, controlled by brakemen, returning in a coupled formation hauled by hired horses; over half of the 27 employees were brakemen. There were no passing loops.

The line was profitable from the start. In 1849, 10,000 tons were carried and this tonnage trebled within a decade. The mine owners of the Phoenix Mine built a small narrow gauge tramway from the mine to the Cheesewring branch, and in the summer of 1858 the Kilmar Railway was built to serve the nearby quarries; worked by the L&CR, in the first year of operation 10,000 tons of granite were carried.

By 1859 everything was booming, and although a handful of the mines had 'peaked' in production others were hugely increasing output. The canal was working to capacity and the Cornwall Railway had opened its main line from Plymouth to Truro, the Royal Albert Bridge having been completed that year. It was apparent that the subject of locomotive haulage on the L&CR would need to be revisited and further finance authorised. This was done by a further Act in 1860 that included the use of locomotives, the purchase of the Kilmar Railway and the building of the Tokenbury branch.

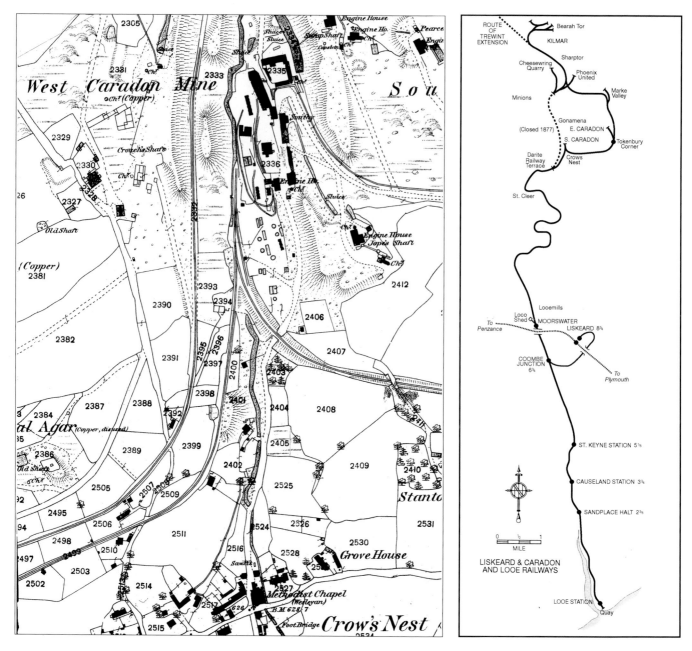

Above:

The main 1880 map *(Crown Copyright)* shows the remarkable track layout at South Caradon Mine with the Gonamena line to Minions on the left (abandoned 1877), while running parallel (to its right) is the low-level line from Moorswater. Trains reversed to reach Tokenbury Corner, Marke Valley, Cheesewring Quarry and Phoenix Mines. Note the extensive mine tramways, top right. The map above right shows the overall Liskeard & Caradon and Looe railways.

In the meantime, as mentioned earlier, the L&LR had been approved in 1858 with the objective of relieving, some might say replacing, the canal. The rail and granite blocks were ordered but later, during the construction process, longitudinal wooden sleepers were used. The standard gauge line was to run beyond the end of the canal at Terras Pill to Looe. There was a grand opening on 27 December 1860 using L&CR trucks and *Liskeard*, an L&LUC hired four-coupled tank engine. Passengers were carried in wagons that had been fitted with seats. At this time the canal company (L&LUC) still owned the Moorswater to Looe line (L&LR). The contrast was dramatic: 300 tons being conveyed in 1 hour by train versus 160 tons being transported in 1 day by canal. The building of the railway had damaged the canal in places and there followed some 40 years of deterioration with, eventually, only small boats carrying a ton or two of sand being

able to navigate the waterway. The canal became silted and overgrown and sinking bridges caused headroom problems. After 1909 there seems to have been little or no traffic and the Liskeard & Looe Union Canal ceased.

In the meantime the railway took delivery of a six-coupled tank, *Caradon*, in 1862, although on the L&CR there is evidence that horses were still being used at that time. Improvements had been made at Looe to accommodate the burgeoning traffic including, in 1849, a new replacement bridge connecting East and West Looe. It was reported that 'every inch of space on the quays at East Looe is filled'. Even in 1861 the two railway lines were not connected at Moorswater, and of course the Cornwall Railway running over the Moorswater 'scene' had no connection with either road. Further 0-6-0T locomotives were acquired from Messrs Gilkes, Wilson & Co: *Cheesewring* in 1864 and *Kilmar* in

Above:
In 1902 the St Neot Clay Company started work on a pipeline to convey china clay in slurry form from Parsons Park on Bodmin Moor down to Moorswater for drying, and the clay dries opened in 1904. Traffic lasted 92 years but at the end of 1996 operations ceased and the works closed. In happier days, on 13 March 1989, No 37675, the second Class 37 to carry the *William Cookworthy* nameplate, has just propelled some wagons into the works. *JV*

Right:
After a period of being mothballed the Moorswater branch sprang into life again when Blue Circle Cement started using the site for storing and distributing its products. The cement, in bagged and slurry form, is dispatched by rail from Earles Sidings in the Hope Valley of Derbyshire. These trains run twice weekly and in Cornwall are now handled by Class 66s, such as No 66226 seen here propelling wagons along the Moorswater byway on 6 September 2001. *JV*

1869. A station was built at Moorswater to accommodate dry goods and parcels, and Looe station was enlarged.

On the L&CR a tramway from Bearah Quarry to the Kilmar Railway was opened in 1868, adding to the tonnage carried by the railway. A standard gauge branch was built in 1869 to the Phoenix Mine, replacing the narrow gauge tramway. In 1871 another lower level line was laid to serve Cheesewring Quarry. A line around Caradon Hill through Marke Valley to Phoenix Mine, thus avoiding the Gonamena incline, was undertaken in 1872, but the work ceased, due, yet again, to a lack of funds. In terms of tonnage, conditions continued to be favourable but with the expenses-to-receipts ratio ever decreasing the storm clouds were gathering. In 1877 the line around Caradon Hill, called the Kilmar Junction Railway, and a branch to Marke Valley had at last been built and opened but some of the mines served were, by then, past their peak. From that time the Gonamena incline was closed. South Caradon had just incurred its first trading loss and some mine owners were seeking a reduction in carriage fees.

Back in 1868 the residents of Looe had petitioned for the railway to carry passengers but it was not until 1879 that the necessary works and provisions were made. The line opened to the public on 11 September 1879 and was to be run as a light railway, subject to a 20mph speed limit. There was one intermediate station at Causeland; this closed in 1881 when the relatively nearby Sandplace opened, but it reopened in 1888. There was no advertised passenger service north of Moorswater, but many years earlier the L&CR had allowed the public to travel free but with a charge being made for carrying their hat, umbrella or whatever! Also, as long ago as 1850 there had been a temperance passenger special on the line. Another example was when a locomotive-hauled 10-wagon special worked the line in 1877; apparently the 'eminent company were covered with fine ash'! All of these practices ended by 1896 when the line became unsafe for freight let alone passengers, but restarted in 1901 when standards were improved.

Initially there were two trains per day each way between Moorswater and Looe with an extra on Saturdays. At the beginning of the 1880s Cornwall was about to experience one of its regular recessions in the mining industry as the price of copper plummeted, and some of the Caradon mines were forced to close because of the economic conditions. To make matters worse both Cheesewring and Kilmar quarries ceased production. This had an immediate impact on the railway not only in terms of outbound minerals but also inbound supplies. There was talk of approaching the LSWR and the GWR at various times to buy or run the line but little interest was shown. There was also a proposal to extend the line to the North Cornwall line, in the direction of Altarnun with a variety of minor extensions from 400yd to 5½ miles. Another plan was to link with the LSWR at Launceston but this was opposed. One proposal was for a connection with the main GWR line, seen as essential to boost passenger traffic, 'especially tourists and excursionists'; this line would be 1,210yd long at a gradient of 1 in 33. Receipts for the year 1884 were the lowest ever, but Parliament nevertheless authorised a 9½-mile extension from Trewint to Launceston (see right map, page 72) and an agreement for the L&CR to lease the L&LR (L&LUC) for 30 years from 1888.

Work started on the Trewint extension in 1884 but the project would fail ultimately. The funds ran out, receipts were down, the company could not meet its liabilities and accordingly a Receiver was appointed on 13 October 1886. The decline of the L&CR had

Below:
For very many it will be the sight of a GWR Prairie 2-6-2T hauling a couple of coaches, rather than a 125-tonne Class 66, that will be the epitome of a West Country branch line. Based on this fine study by Peter Gray they could perhaps be excused. On 7 May 1960 No 4559 accelerates away from Coombe Junction with the 5.55pm Liskeard to Looe. *Peter Gray*

Right:
Workings by locomotives south of Coombe Junction are unusual and are normally confined to the annual weedkilling train and very occasional permanent way trains. Approaching the diminutive St Keyne station on 8 April 1990 are Class 20s Nos 20901 and 20904 'topping and tailing' the return up working of the Chipman's weedkiller. The halt opened in September 1902. On the right is the site of an old limekiln. *JV*

Below:
The Looe branch meanders down the delightful valley of the Looe River. Causeland was originally the only intermediate station between Moorswater and Looe, opening on 11 September 1879, the first day of regular passenger services on what was then the Liskeard & Looe Railway. Here one of the reliable little Class 121 'bubble car' DMUs, No 55000, approaches the halt with the 17.24 Looe to Liskeard service of 2 April 1990. *JV*

Left:
Some 84 years separate the next two photographs showing the single-faced platform of Sandplace. In 1902 the Liskeard & Looe Railway (L&LR) hired a 4-4-0 saddle tank from the GWR and No 13 stayed on the line for the next 20 years. Here in 1909 No 13 heads some GWR stock towards Liskeard, while during the pause some dignitaries seem to be posing on the platform. The L&LR stock had just been condemned by the GWR, describing it as 'obsolete with filthy gas fittings, split panels and roofs and bad under-frames'.
JV collection

Centre left:
In 1993 the small station building and the long exit gate on to the road were still features but the motive power in the shape of an incongruous NSE-liveried two-car DMU fails to stop at the request 'halt' with the 17.35 Looe to Liskeard service. In the winter months trains do not stop at the unlit intermediate halts after dark.
JV

Lower left:
This remarkable photograph shows one of the last public excursions to run down to Looe in 1901 using the original Liskeard & Caradon Railway (L&CR) stock. There being too many people for the old Metropolitan Railway Carriage & Wagon Co coaches, the little four-wheeled goods wagons were, as usual, pressed into service. The 1864 Hopkins, Gilkes & Co-built 0-6-0ST locomotive *Cheesewring* seems to have a good head of steam south of Sandplace. The original stock was all stored from the opening date of the new extension with the GWR main line later in the year. *P. Q. Treloar collection*

Right:
The 1827-8 Liskeard & Looe Union Canal to Moorswater started at Terras Pill, south of Sandplace. After the opening of the railway in 1860, use of the canal gradually declined resulting in abandonment in about 1909. Passing the just visible old lock gates and a small partially sunk boat at Terras Pill, is Class 153 No 153362 forming the 09.45 Liskeard to Looe service of 13 September 1995. The East Looe River can be seen behind the single-car diesel-hydraulic unit. *JV*

Above:
By the summer of 1993 the suburban DMU classes were well into the autumn of their lives and it was a pleasant surprise to find a unit painted in GWR chocolate and cream but with BR 'lion and wheel' emblems working the Looe and occasionally St Ives branches in Cornwall. Here three-car Class 117 unit No 305 forming the 16.50 Looe to Liskeard service crosses a minor road at Terras Pill. Note the raised wooden pavement to keep the feet of pedestrians dry during very high tides. *JV*

been rapid. Every possible economy was then made, costs were reduced, pay cuts imposed, rates reduced and new traffic found. However, despite a brief resurgence of activity in 1888, by the turn of the century mining on and around Caradon Hill had ceased completely. Cheesewring Quarry staggered on but traffic was minimal, and the infrastructure was in very poor shape. In 1892 another proposal for a connecting line between the L&LUC railway at Moorswater (Coombe Gate/Lamellion) and Liskeard (GWR) was made. The line would climb at 1 in 40/45 to gain the 150ft altitude difference between the lines, and would be known as the Liskeard & Looe Junction Railway. The name of the L&LUC would become the Liskeard & Looe Railway Company — a railway company at last!

An Act was passed in 1895 but funding was to prove difficult until a Captain Spicer bought into the company on such a scale that he gained control of the Liskeard & Looe Railway. The first sod was cut in June 1898, and new locomotives and carriages were purchased. After travelling up from Looe trains would change direction at Coombe Junction to reach Liskeard. During the course of construction the barely used canal had to be

diverted. The line climbed in a sort of horseshoe and ended in a branch line terminus at right angles but adjacent to the GWR main line station. At Liskeard there were goods sidings and a single line connection with the main line, used only for freight and stock movements. All workings until the official opening on 15 May 1901 used the old stock but from that date only the new acquisitions were used. Moorswater station closed on the opening of Coombe Junction, and the now demolished building was still in use as a bungalow after World War 2.

There were tremendous celebrations on opening day, especially at Looe. Passenger figures of 24,000 per annum before connection was made to the main line more than doubled to 55,000 in 1902, the first full year of operation, and later increased to 70,000. Mineral traffic was increasing slightly with Cheesewring still in operation on the L&CR line. In 1902 the St Neot Clay Company gave notice that clay would be piped down from Parsons Park works to a new installation at Moorswater for drying. A siding was laid in 1902 and in 1904 the first shipment of china clay was transported by rail to Looe. St Keyne station had opened in 1902.

In 1902 the new locomotive acquisition, 0-6-0ST *Looe*, was

sold to the London & India Docks Company, having been found unsuitable for the line. A 2-4-0T, *Lady Margaret*, was bought from Andrew Barclay and GWR 4-4-0ST No 13 was hired, the latter becoming a regular performer on the branch for nearly 20 years. The condition of the L&CR resulted in maintenance costs three times that of an average railway line. However, the line kept going and in fact there was a resurgence of interest in the Phoenix Mine and South Phoenix Mine in 1907. After the L&LR ran into financial difficulties, a situation not helped by the state of the L&CR, a disgruntled shareholder sought to have a Receiver appointed, but for political reasons the GWR came to the rescue.

A working agreement between the companies was made in August 1907 and from 1 January 1909 the line became part of the GWR. The GWR also took over the maintenance of the L&CR. However, by the start of World War 1 poor-quality tin and increasing costs resulted in the end of mining in the Caradon District; truly the end of an era. A modicum of granite continued to be produced, but this too fizzled out. The tracks were lifted in 1917 and sent to France to assist with the war effort. There was talk of reopening at a later date but it never happened, and final

legal abandonment took place in 1931. In 1906 there had been a serious accident on the L&LR when six empty carriages accidentally got a 'nudge' from a locomotive at Liskeard and ran away down the steep 1 in 40 bank to Coombe Junction. At an estimated 60-70mph they stayed on the rails at Coombe Junction and took to the Moorswater line, careering into a carriage shed and demolishing several coaches. Amazingly nobody was injured but 13 redundant coaches from the Mersey Railway had to be purchased as replacements at a cost of more than £1,000.

The GWR took over the serviceable L&LR locomotives, *Cheesewring*, *Kilmar* and *Lady Margaret*, and renumbered them 1311, 1312 and 1308 respectively. *Cheesewring* was transferred to Old Oak Common in London and was withdrawn in 1919, *Kilmar* remained on the line but was withdrawn in 1914, and *Lady Margaret* was transferred away, ending its days in 1948. The branch was mostly worked by GWR 0-6-0STs of the '1901' or '2021' classes. From the Grouping GWR Prairies of the '4400' and '4500' classes dominated the motive power scene with only occasional interlopers. The GWR also set about widening bridges to accommodate its own rolling stock. At the Grouping the L&LR

was completely absorbed by the GWR. The GWR had been taking thousands of trippers from Plymouth to Looe by its steamers, and later promoted the line as part of a round-trip sea-rail excursion. Looe began to prosper as a seaside resort and in 1928 the platform was extended, a situation experienced at Liskeard in both 1924 and 1937. In 1922 50,000 tickets were issued at Looe, a level that was maintained until 1929.

Although passenger traffic had been encouraging in the early 1930s, local traffic declined as did freight. Increasingly the china clay was 'tripped' up to the main line for dispatch from Fowey, rather than from the small harbour at Looe, leaving only coal traffic for Looe and a handful of box vans for local traffic, which once included fish. Traffic figures were also badly affected by World War 2 as holiday traffic was decimated. In 1935 the GWR proposed the building of a direct 7-mile branch to Looe from the main line near Trerulefoot; this would require heavy earthworks, but streamlined diesel railcars would make the journey from Plymouth to Looe in 35 minutes. Some earthworks were undertaken before World War 2 but the scheme was never revived and any acquired land was sold off in the 1950s. During the war there had been six round trip workings on the branch but this increased to seven, then eight trains once hostilities had finished. Journey times were static at just under the half-hour for the journey, including reversal at Coombe Junction.

After nationalisation the line operated under the auspices of the Western Region of BR and there was a slow postwar recovery. By the mid-1950s there were nine trains per day each way Monday to Thursday, 10 on Friday, 11 on Saturday and even six on Sunday. Holiday traffic continued to make a big contribution to receipts but was of course seasonal. Normally a pair of '4500s' would be sub-shedded at Moorswater to handle all branch traffic. Diesel traction was tried in 1960 and from 11 September 1961 the entire branch timetable was handled by a diesel multiple-unit, with considerable savings in operating costs and efficiency. Moorswater shed was closed and freight services withdrawn completely from 4 November 1963, except for the Moorswater clay traffic. Car ownership was on the increase and passenger volumes on the branch decreased, particularly off-season. In 1963 the line 'lost' over £1,000, although the costing algorithm was never disclosed! A closure notice was posted in 1966 but not executed. Railway employees were dispensed with at Looe station in 1968. In 1978 some 100,000 passengers were using the line but it was in receipt of a large public subsidy, in the region of £50,000 per annum. In 1981 the signalbox controlling Coombe Junction was closed and replaced by ground frames, to be operated by train crews, and the second line (part of the old run-round loop) was removed.

In the winter months a single 'bubble car' unit replaced the usual two- or three-car DMU, and the branch soldiered on through the 1980s and 1990s. A 'park and ride' scheme was introduced at Liskeard for those wanting to travel to Looe, and the car park extended. New motive power arrived in 1986 in the form of two-car Class 142 units. However, they had no sanding gear, were four-wheelers with no bogies, and had door problems, so their stay was a relatively short one and the DMUs were drafted back in. In the 1990s Class 150/2 two-car and Class 153 single-car diesel-hydraulic units were introduced, by which time the privatisation of the railways had occurred and the Wales & West company was running the services. A major blow to the line occurred in April 1997 when the English China Clay Company stopped shipping china clay from Moorswater works. However, since then use has been made of the line to Moorswater for twice weekly cement trains from Earles Sidings in the Peak District of Derbyshire. In the winter of 2001 there were still eight round trip passenger workings Monday to Friday and 10 on Saturday; a Sunday service operates for a few weeks in the summer peak period only.

Even today the ride from Liskeard to Looe is interesting and picturesque from start to finish. The old Liskeard branch station and awning are still used, even if some of the timetable connections with main line trains are appalling. On leaving Liskeard the single line descends at a ruling gradient of 1 in 40 twice passing beneath the Liskeard bypass, built in 1974, in a 180° sweep before running beneath the impressive 150ft-high Liskeard Viaduct, which carries the Plymouth to Penzance main line. Descending through cuttings below Bolitho the single line reaches the junction with the single line up from Looe at Coombe. The train guard contacts the Liskeard signalman by telephone and operates the points. Only two trains per day in each direction continue to call at the Coombe Junction platform (2 miles 5 chains) on the Moorswater alignment. The crew of trains using the goods line to Moorswater must operate another ground frame, housed in a wooden hut beyond the platform, before proceeding. Moorswater Viaduct dominates the valley to the north. The train reverses and continues past a sewage farm into the delightful valley of the East Looe River, running parallel with the old L&LU Canal, remains of which can be seen in abundance throughout.

St Keyne station is 3 miles 64 chains from Liskeard, and just down the road is Lametton Mill, where a famous organ museum is located. The line meanders south through the most delightful woodland with rustic views in every direction. Occasionally a small cottage is passed before another segment of old canal is spotted. Causeland station at 5 miles 9 chains is a splendid rural 'halt' that for many years boasted only a simple hut but in recent years, in common with other intermediate stations, has had a more permanent building constructed on its curved platform. The East Looe River is parallel to the line as it runs down towards the estuary and the sea. The next station is Sandplace (6 miles 39 chains), which once boasted a siding for loading sand and other produce, installed in 1879 and removed in 1956. The tide no longer reaches Sandplace but the now heavily overgrown canal basin was located here after the railway was built.

South of Sandplace the country opens out slightly and the old canal is crossed twice before Terras level crossing is reached; it is no longer gated or signalled and trains must stop briefly and sound their horn before proceeding. Just north of the crossing is Terras Lock, the entry point to the old canal. The old lock gates can still be seen on the east side of the line (see the accompanying photograph on page 77). The line then hugs the hillside on the east side of the valley, affording splendid views of the river before reaching Looe (8 miles 51 chains). Here there was once a small goods yard, engine shed, run-round loop and tracks and sidings down to the quay, but the line has now been truncated short of the station's original location. The quay lines were closed in 1954 and all freight had disappeared by 1963. A short walk takes passengers into the narrow streets of ancient Looe. The journey time is still just under half an hour, due to speed restrictions.

Once steam had ended, the china clay trains from Moorswater were worked by Class 22 diesel-hydraulics. Introduced in 1962, many of these unsuccessful locomotives had a life of a mere six years before they were withdrawn and scrapped. Some lasted until 1971 when Class 25 1,250hp diesel-electrics were drafted into Cornwall and they were regular visitors to the line until displaced by Co-Co Class 37s in 1980. The 1,750hp Class 37s were the 'kings' of the china clay scene until replaced by new Class 66s in 1999/2000. Class 20s appeared on weedkilling trains but other larger locomotives were barred from the line due to various restrictions. The only locomotives on the line south of Coombe Junction in recent years have been the annual visit by the weedkilling train and the occasional ballast train when trackwork is being undertaken. Very occasionally enthusiasts' specials have worked down to Moorswater but there are restrictions on 'C1' route main line coaches on the Looe section.

With more emphasis being placed on the environment and with implied political pressure to retain branch services, it seems likely that the Looe branch will continue to operate for many years to come. However, some loadings are light and if ever subsidies are withdrawn and a truly commercial regime is imposed that future could be less rosy. A case of use it or lose it, I fear.

Above:

They don't come much smaller than Looe Signalbox, seen here on the right! In fact, the signals seen here were removed shortly after this photograph was taken, on 29 July 1958. No 4585 has just arrived with the 2.52pm train from Liskeard comprising three non-corridor coaches. The tracks in the foreground that ran to sidings and down to the quayside have long since been removed. *Peter Gray*

Left:
This Victorian photograph at Moorswater station can be dated between 1881 and 1901 because the main line Moorswater viaduct was rebuilt about 1880 (the old piers can be seen) and Moorswater station closed in May 1901 when the new connection from Coombe Junction to the GWR main line was opened. With original L&CR coaching stock the railway's first new locomotive, *Caradon*, an 0-6-0ST built by Messrs Gilkes, Wilson & Co of Middlesbrough in 1862, faces north. The stone yard siding is on the right. *P. Q. Treloar collection*

Centre left:
This wonderful view shows *Caradon* hauling 10 wagons loaded with granite that have probably travelled around Caradon Hill from Cheesewring Quarry. The train has just arrived on the lower line and reversed at Crows Nest, near the South Caradon Mine complex, before heading towards Moorswater. The brake-van is ex-GWR. The line visible at the top of the photograph is the old Gonamena line to Minions. *JV collection*

Lower left:
A June 1934 view of the two-road locomotive shed at Moorswater, which remained open as a sub-shed of St Blazey until the end of steam. The line to Caradon and the Cheesewring is on the right. The old shed, which was also two-road, can be seen to the left of the water tower. Most of this interesting site was razed when the much-needed Liskeard bypass road was built. *JV collection*

Right:
Granite had been quarried for centuries in the area of the Cheesewring, and construction of the L&CR began there once Royal Assent was given in June 1843. In this view dating from the turn of the 20th century a boy stands on the main line of the tramway within the quarry while a spur line leads to other quarry sidings. Tens of thousands of tons of granite were taken from the quarry by horse-drawn rail wagons. *JV collection*

Centre right:
Most of the track of the L&CR was removed in 1917 to assist with the World War 1 effort. However, the granite block sleepers were left behind and grazing sheep have ensured that such remains can still be seen. In this September 2001 scene a couple of pieces of track (centre) and some granite blocks (left) have survived to testify that once railway wagons really did penetrate this now silent quarry. A visit is highly recommended. *JV*

Below:
There are 46 people and one dog visible in this remarkable study of a Sunday school outing at Railway Terrace, Darite, adjacent to the Polwrath depot. Such excursions were suspended in 1896 but recommenced in 1901 after the L&LR had made improvements to the track. Here 0-6-0ST *Caradon* heads three primitive three-plank goods wagons and a brake-van. *JV collection*

Left:
There were a vast number of shafts and engine houses within the Phoenix Mines complex and from about 1850 a significant narrow gauge tramway connected not only internal sites but made a junction with the standard gauge L&CR at Minions. A standard gauge branch to the Phoenix Mine replaced the external part of the tramway in 1869. As usual it was a question of 'ore out, coal in'. This view of the mine dates back to about 1904.
JV collection

Centre left:
Although there was a resurgence of interest in the Phoenix Mine in 1907, ore from the mine and granite from Cheesewring Quarry gradually fizzled out and the lines were closed and lifted in 1917. On an exceptional day in January 2001, nearly a century after the previous photograph, the gaunt remains of part of Phoenix Mine were photographed from the same spot, making a fascinating comparison. *JV*

Below:
This interesting June 1934 illustration was taken from the top of the hill featured in the centre photograph on page 82 but looking north along the 1844 to 1877 high-level line to Minions via the Gonamena incline. Half a dozen abandoned mines that were all once part of the South Caradon complex can be seen on the right. The low-level line, which reversed at Crows Nest and ran around Caradon Hill via Tokenbury Corner, is out of sight in the valley to the right. *JV collection*

9. Bodmin General Branch and Boscarne Junction

The history of the Cornwall Railway could fill a book in its own right but, to summarise, a Bill was prepared for a railway through Devon and Cornwall, from Exeter to Falmouth, as early as 1835. The Bill was rejected but the importance of linking the counties by rail would remain an issue of the day. Later, plans for a so-called 'coastal route' emerged. There were battles between the LSWR and the GWR in respect of which would be first to have its plans approved by Parliament, but at the end of the day it was a consortium of the GWR, the Bristol & Exeter Railway and the South Devon Railway — associated companies — that won the race. Isambard Kingdom Brunel had been instrumental in a new Bill, for a double-track railway from Plymouth to Falmouth with a number of branches, becoming an Act of Parliament in August 1846. However, these plans required capital of £1,600,000 to be raised. They envisaged a branch line to Bodmin, as due to the difficult terrain it had not been possible, on grounds of cost, to route the main line through what was then the county town, even though the population of over 5,000 persons would have made a welcome addition to traffic volumes. A first sod was cut near Truro in 1847 in respect of the main line.

At one time all work stopped on the main line as the dire financial climate of the period took hold. Work was later restarted, but in 1852 the plans for all branch lines, except that to Bodmin, had to be shelved. As it transpired, even the Bodmin branch was 'forgotten'. Much effort was exerted in order to reduce construction costs, such as the main line's track being single only. It was decided that the residents of Bodmin would have to change at Bodmin Road, the planned junction station, nearly 4 miles from the town, and use the turnpike road to reach Bodmin.

Even though Bodmin had been rail connected since the inauguration of the Bodmin & Wadebridge Railway in 1834, the line ran only to Wadebridge with no connections to the outside world. As the county town Bodmin was home to many important institutions and it was considered vital to have a rail connection to the main line, London, Plymouth and Truro. The broad gauge Cornwall Railway main line was ready for service on completion of the Royal Albert Bridge in 1859 but nothing more was done regarding a branch line to Bodmin. Another attempt to link Bodmin to the main line was made in 1873, but this also failed. The plan was to have two lines, one to the town of Bodmin and the other linking with the Bodmin & Wadebridge Railway, which until 1895 would remain isolated from its by-then LSWR parent. The reason this also came to nothing was the non-availability of the necessary funds. In 1876 the Cornwall Railway became part of the GWR, which feared that competition, in the shape of the LSWR encroaching into the area via its soon to be constructed North Cornwall line, would cream off lucrative traffic. After years of pressure an Act was finally passed in 1882 for a 3-mile 43-chain standard gauge branch from Bodmin Road to what later became known as Bodmin General (the suffixes 'General' in respect of the GWR and 'North' for the LSWR station were not added until September 1949, but I have used the names in the text in the interests of clarity).

Construction of the branch was not easy. The line had to climb some 300ft and this involved embankments, cuttings, bridges, a 1 in 37 gradient and many curves. The line was and still is very picturesque, although trees and foliage spoil some of the vistas. At

Right:
A rather quiet Bodmin Road station is seen in 1922. The footbridge and signalbox (now a café) survive, but the oil lamps, down goods yard, water tower, up goods yard platform and semaphore signals have all disappeared with the 'progress' of time. Even the name has changed to Bodmin Parkway, suggesting that you need a car to get to the station, which is over 3 miles from Bodmin. *JV collection*

Above:
The branch from Bodmin Road to Bodmin General opened on 27 May 1887. It was built to standard gauge, whereas until 1892 the GWR main line was broad gauge, resulting in the transfer of all goods and passengers at Bodmin Road. This magnificent 1890 view was taken from the branch and shows a wonderful assortment of headgear and facial hair! *Bristol City Museum, B&WR*

Left:
The West Country was one of the first areas of BR to be dieselised. As with the Liskeard to Looe branch, the 1961-2 period would see the end of steam traction, as far as everyday service was concerned. The death-knell for steam has been sounded as Class 22 diesel-hydraulic No D6317 waits at Bodmin Road's island platform to depart for General on 14 July 1961. *R. C. Riley, The Transport Treasury*

the junction there had to be a transfer shed between the standard and broad gauges, siding space, junction lines and run-round facilities, and the River Fowey had to be diverted somewhat. Enhanced buildings on the up-side platform were built and other work included the provision of a covered footbridge. At Bodmin General a stone terminus building was built with goods shed, small locomotive shed and sidings, provision being made for the extension down to Boscarne Junction where a link with the Bodmin & Wadebridge was planned. There were no intermediate stations, although on the Boscarne 'extension' from 1906 to 1917 there was a platform for St Lawrence Hospital. The line finally opened on 27 May 1887 (a few weeks after the Helston branch). By 1888 there were 10 trains in each direction, the journey times

being 10 minutes in the up direction and 13 on the uphill down journey. The 2-mile 56-chain connection to Boscarne opened on 3 September 1888, and was also a steeply graded line with stretches of 1 in 37.

In June 1886 there had been discussions between the LSWR and the GWR about the latter gaining access to Wadebridge. Agreement was reached but one wonders whether things would have been so amicable if the LSWR's North Cornwall line had at that time been opened to Wadebridge, which did not happen until 1895. The LSWR needed to reconstruct its 4-mile 64-chain line from Boscarne Junction to Wadebridge, provide a junction signalbox at Boscarne and a house for the signalman to live in. A new station terminus, signalbox and substantial goods shed were also built at Wadebridge in anticipation of the extra traffic. A deviation at the junction with the Ruthern Bridge line to ease a tight curve was also approved and constructed. In 1886 the LSWR suspended all passenger services in order to make these changes.

The line leading south to Ruthern Bridge left the main line at Grogley Junction, and its history is dealt with in the next chapter. There were also a number of schemes to link, for example, Ruthern Bridge with Roche on the Cornwall Minerals Railway's Newquay branch and also Ruthern Bridge with Truro. In the meantime, in 1888, the GWR commenced operations through to Wadebridge. While there were no first day opening celebrations it was soon realised that the service through to Bodmin Road was having a beneficial impact on the district, and it was reported that the line greatly added to the importance of Wadebridge as a centre for both trade and tourism. At this time an omnibus service connected Wadebridge and Padstow. Initially there was an excellent service from Bodmin Road to Wadebridge of 11 trains per day, but with no Sunday service. However, both before and after the opening of the North Cornwall Railway in 1895 a sense of rivalry existed between the LSWR and the GWR.

From March 1899 the line was extended the 5½ miles along the banks of the River Camel to Padstow (see Chapter 5). This tipped the GWR/LSWR balance in the area as passengers now had a direct train service to London Waterloo. There was also rivalry for Wadebridge and Bodmin traffic, and the LSWR station, Bodmin North, was nearer to Bodmin town centre than General. As mentioned above, due to the upgrading of the line and other modifications, services to Bodmin North had been suspended between November 1886 and November 1895, almost as if the LSWR was waiting for the North Cornwall Railway to arrive, and when it did a few of the NCR trains, or portions of them, ran through to Bodmin North. The LSWR opened new halts between Bodmin and Wadebridge at Dunmere, Nanstallon and Grogley in 1906 and steam railmotors were introduced. From that time services were greatly increased (see Chapter 10). The GWR did not call at these halts, a situation that continued well into the post-1948 nationalisation period.

Another development that followed the opening of the GWR lines, particularly after the change of main line gauge in 1892 that avoided the transhipment of materials at Bodmin Road and

Above:
In December 1989, long after the end of freight services at Bodmin Road and some six years after English China Clays stopped shipping clay by rail from Wenford via Bodmin General, the Fitzgerald Lighting Company, located on the Walker Lines Industrial Estate in Bodmin, used the old Fulford Trumps siding to convey some of its products by rail. This resulted in a weekly revenue-earning freight train traversing a privately preserved railway. After a period of uncertainty the English, Welsh & Scottish Railway (EWS) substantially increased its charges and in 2001 the contract was lost to road. The wagons were dropped into an exchange siding by the Bodmin & Wenford and collected by a BR/Transrail/EWS (depending on the year) locomotive. On 25 March 1992 No 37417 collects a couple of vans from the up yard at Parkway, with preservationists' stock on the right and the main line on the left. *JV*

Right:
On 9 May 1975 the scene at Bodmin Road was very different, with the up yard still used for freight wagon movement and storage. With the stove in the mandatory brake-van smoking and some 'clay hoods' waiting for the run to Wenford Bridge, the daily early morning goods from Wadebridge has just arrived behind Class 25 No 25223. The Class 25s replaced the Class 22s in about 1970 but they were in turn ousted in favour of the Class 37s just 10 years later. *JV*

Table 97 BODMIN ROAD, BODMIN GENERAL, WADEBRIDGE and PADSTOW

WEEK DAYS ONLY (¶¶)

Miles from Bodmin Road	Miles from Bodmin Nth		am S	am B	am	am T	am	am	am E	am E	am S	am S	am E	am M	am S	am	pm E	pm S	noon S	pm E	pm S	pm E	pm S
		Bodmin Road .. .. dep	6 55	.	..	7 50	..	..	.	857	915	..	..	10 10	1040	..	..	..	12 0	1220	1238	1 5	1 22
3¼		Bodmin Gen. A.. arr	7 10	...	...	7 58	...	...	...	9 5	923	...	...	10 18	1048	...	...	...	1210	1228	1248	1 13	1 30
		Bodmin Gen. A.. dep	..	.	..	8 10	..	..	9 0	.	.	..	..	10 35	..	..	..	..	..	1236	1251	..	..
—		Bodmin North. dep	...	...	7 22	...	8 43	...	...	...	...	...	...	...	...	11 20	...	...	...	...	...	...	...
—	1½	Dunmere Halt	..	.	7 26	..	8 47	..	.	.	.	..	..	..	..	11 24	..	..	..	..	..	..	..
6¼	2¼	Nanstallon Halt	..	...	7 29	8 18	8 50	...	...	...	...	...	...	...	...	11 27	...	...	...	1245	1258	...	...
8	3¼	Grogley Halt	..	.	7 33	..	8 54	..	.	.	.	..	..	..	..	11 31	..	..	..	..	..	..	..
11	6¼	Wadebridge.. arr	...	...	7 41	8 30	9 2	...	918	...	...	...	...	10 55	...	11 39	...	...	...	1257	1 10	...	...
		Wadebridge.. dep	..	712	7 44	8 43	..	9K12	.	.	.	1015	1030	11S15	..	11K43	12 3	1220	..	..	..	..	..
16½	12¼	Padstow .... arr	...	722	7 55	8 50	...	9K22	...	...	...	1024	1039	11S24	...	11K50	1214	1230	...	...	...	...	...

	pm S	pm E	pm D	pm	pm	pm S	pm S	pm E	pm	pm E	pm E	pm S	pm S	pm E	pm	pm	pm	pm	pm	pm S	pm T	pm	pm
Bodmin Road .. .. dep	..	..	..	..	2 30	3 30	..	..	..	4 25	..	4 55	..	..	..	6 15	..	..	7 26	8 0	9 2	9 42	1050
Bodmin Gen. A.. arr	...	...	...	...	2 39	3 45	...	...	...	4 33	...	5 5	...	...	...	6 25	...	...	7 35	8 8	9 15	9 50	1058
Bodmin Gen. A.. dep	..	..	..	..	2 48	..	..	..	..	4 50	.	5 18	..	..	..	6 30	..	..	7 43	..	9 18	..	..
Bodmin North. dep	...	...	...	2 0	...	...	4 5	4 23	...	...	...	...	5 36	5 48	...	...	6 45	...	...	...	...	...	...
Dunmere Halt	..	..	..	2 4	..	..	4 9	4 27	..	..	..	..	5 40	5 52	..	..	6 49	..	..	..	..	..	..
Nanstallon Halt	...	...	...	2 7	...	...	4 12	4 30	...	4 57	...	5 27	5 43	5 55	...	6 37	6 52	...	7 50	...	9 28	...	...
Grogley Halt	..	..	..	2 11	..	..	4 16	4 34	..	..	..	..	5 47	5 59	..	..	6 56	..	..	..	9 32	..	..
Wadebridge .. arr	...	...	...	2 19	3 6	...	4 24	4 42	...	5 9	...	5 39	5 55	6 7	...	6 49	7 4	...	8 2	...	9 40	...	...
Wadebridge .. dep	1 15	1 45	2 3	2 23	..	..	4 25	..	4 50	..	5 24	..	..	..	6 13	..	7 8	7 48	..	..	9 41	..	..
Padstow .... arr	1 29	1 59	2 14	2 34	...	...	4 35	...	5 0	...	5 33	...	...	...	6 22	...	7 19	7 58	...	...	9 51	...	...

Miles	Miles		am	am		am E	am	am S	am H	am	am E	am T	am E	am	am E	am E	am S	am S	am N	pm E	am E	pm S	pm E
		Padstow .. .. dep	..	..	..	..	..	..	8 10	8 30	..	9K 3	9 35	..	1055	..	11 0	..	1135	..	1155	1210	1258
5½	5½	Wadebridge.. arr	...	...	...	...	...	...	8 19	8 39	...	9K12	9 44	...	11 4	...	11 9	...	1144	...	12 4	1219	1 7
		Wadebridge.. dep	6 52	..	..	..	8 1	..	8 30	..	..	9 19	..	9 48	..	11 7	..	..	1153	..	1225	1226	..
8½	8½	Grogley Halt	7 0	...	...	...	8 9	...	8 40	...	...	...	...	9 56	...	...	...	...	...	...	1233	1236	...
10	10	Nanstallon Halt . ..	7 4	..	..	..	8 13	..	8 44	..	..	9 32	..	10 0	..	1119	..	..	..	..	1237	1240	..
—	10¾	Dunmere Halt	7 8	...	...	...	8 17	...	...	...	...	...	...	10 4	...	...	...	...	...	...	1241	1244	...
—	12¼	Bodmin North. arr	7 12	..	..	..	8 21	..	..	..	..	..	..	10 8	..	..	..	..	..	..	1245	1248	..
13	—	Bodmin Gen. A .. arr	...	...	...	...	...	...	8 55	...	...	9 42	...	...	...	1129	...	...	1215	...	...	...	...
		Bodmin Gen. A .. dep	..	7 25	..	8 15	..	8 30	8S58	..	9 18	9 45	..	..	..	1134	..	1134	1223	1245	..	..	..
16½	—	Bodmin Road .. .. arr	...	7 35	...	8 22	...	8 37	9S 5	...	9 25	9 54	...	...	...	1141	...	1141	1230	1252	...	...	...

	pm S	pm S	pm	pm	pm	pm	pm S	pm E	pm E	pm	pm S	pm	pm	pm	pm	pm S	pm T		pm	pm		pm	pm
Padstow .. .. dep	..	1 0	..	2 52	3 13	..	4 40	5 6	..	..	..	6 0	..	..	..	..	8 4	..	8 30	..	..	10 5	..
Wadebridge.. arr	...	1 9	...	3 1	3 22	...	4 49	5 15	...	...	...	6 9	...	...	...	...	8 13	...	8 39	...	...	1014	...
Wadebridge.. dep	..	..	1 23	3 7	..	3 24	5 11	..	5 18	5E34	5 56	..	6 18	..	7 5	..	8 15	..	..	8 42	..	..	..
Grogley Halt	...	...	...	3 17	...	...	5 19	...	5 26	...	...	...	6 26	...	...	...	8 25	...	...	...	...	...	...
Nanstallon Halt . ..	..	..	1 35	3 21	..	..	5 23	..	5 30	5E46	6 8	..	6 30	..	..	..	8 29	..	..	8 54	..	..	..
Dunmere Halt	...	...	...	3 25	...	...	5 27	...	5 34	...	...	...	6 34	...	...	...	...	...	...	...	...	...	...
Bodmin North. arr	..	..	..	3 29	..	..	5 31	..	5 38	..	..	..	6 38	..	..	..	..	..	..	..	..	..	..
Bodmin Gen. A .. arr	...	...	1 45	...	...	3 47	...	...	...	5E56	6 18	...	...	...	7 25	...	8 40	...	...	9 4	...	...	...
Bodmin Gen. A .. dep	1 0	..	1 50	..	..	3 53	..	..	..	6 0	..	..	..	6 43	..	7 38	8 44	..	..	9 15	..	..	1020
Bodmin Road .. .. arr	1 7	...	2 0	...	...	4 1	...	...	...	6 8	...	...	...	6 53	...	7 45	8 51	...	...	9 32	...	...	1027

A 1 mile to Bodmin North Station
B Saturdays only. Runs 12th July to 6th September inclusive
D Saturdays only. Runs 28th June to 23rd August inclusive
E or E Except Saturdays
H Through Train Padstow to Bodmin Road on Saturdays
K 5 minutes later on Saturdays
M Through Train Bodmin Road to Padstow on Saturdays
N Saturdays only. Through Train between Padstow and Bodmin Road
S or S Saturdays only
T Through Train between Bodmin Road and Padstow
¶¶ On Sundays passengers holding through rail tickets may travel by Southern National Omnibus between Bodmin Road and Wadebridge or vice versa—see Table 22

WADEBRIDGE and BODMIN ROAD.—Great Western.

Wadebridge .....dep	....	8 10	9 45	1130	....	3 10	....	....	6 15	8 30
Bodmin .... arr	....	8 30	10 5	1150	....	3 30	....	....	6 35	8 50
Bodmin .... dep	7 54	8 41	1011	12 8	1 0	3 [illegible]8	4 25	6 2	6 45	8 57
Bodmin Road 19, 18	8 1	8 48	1018	1210	1 7	3 45	4 32	6 9	6 52	9 4

Bodmin Road .dp	....	8 12	9 1	1038	1240	1 16	4 0	4 45	6 21	7 8	9 14
Bodmin.... arr	....	8 22	9 11	1045	1250	1 2[illegible]	4 10	4 58	6 31	7 18	9 24
Bodmin.... dep	7 40	....	9 16	1051	1256	....	4 18	....	....	7 24	....
Wadebridge ..arr	7 58	....	9 34	11 9	1 14	....	4 36	....	....	7 42	....

Above and left:
The frequency of weekday trains between Bodmin Road and Bodmin General varied little between November 1888 and the summer of 1958 (main timetable)

permitted through running of stock, wagons and locomotives, was the possibility of transporting freight, mainly in the form of china clay, from the Wenford Bridge line to the southern port of Fowey for shipment. Although wagons would have to reverse at Boscarne Junction, Bodmin General and Bodmin Road, the prospect of using Fowey compared with the very limited facilities, in terms of tides and size of vessel (and therefore destination), at Wadebridge and Padstow was attractive to the clay companies.

Business at Bodmin General was brisk and in 1903 over 38,000 tickets were issued, over 20,000 parcels and 600 tons of goods forwarded, and over 12,000 tons of coal, minerals and goods received. Even 200 wagons of cattle had been handled. Although in 1933 90 season tickets were sold at Bodmin, the number of other tickets issued had reduced by 30% compared with 1903, as had goods forwarded. Coal, minerals and goods received had halved, although curiously the amount of livestock handled

Above:
An idyllic pastoral scene of a rural, albeit demonstration, freight climbing away from the Glynn Valley at Bodmin Road (Parkway) and making for Bodmin General. Grazing cattle are undisturbed as green-liveried Class 20 No 20166 *River Fowey* hauls six wagons and two brake-vans past Charlie's Gate during the Diesel Gala on 23 September 1995. (Taken on a Nikon F301 camera with Nikkor 35mm f2 lens, using 1/500th sec at f8 on Ilford XP2 film.) *JV*

increased. The railway was feeling the impact of a recession and the appearance of omnibuses and motor lorries in greater numbers. None of the above statistics included the china clay traffic, which did not originate at Bodmin General.

The GWR branch continued to perform its almost classic task of serving a growing community with a frequent train service, running to a junction station that had connections to the national network. Train services varied from year to year with a daily average of about 10 round trips between Bodmin Road and General, most but not all of which ran through to Wadebridge. First thing in the morning and last thing at night trains started and finished at Bodmin General because the branch steam locomotives worked off Bodmin GWR shed. In motive power terms, once the GWR Prairie 2-6-2Ts were introduced they completely dominated the scene, and it is difficult to find a photograph when a '4500' class or slightly heavier '4575' series is not at the head of a train! They were the staple motive power for decades, although from time to time Southern Railway/Region locomotives, mainly in the shape of Class O2 0-4-4Ts and 'N' class 2-6-0 Moguls worked over Great Western/Western Region metals.

There was some blurring of the former 'battle lines' of the GWR/LSWR rivals when in 1950 control of the former Southern lines west of Exeter was transferred to the Western Region, then back to the Southern in 1958 and finally to the Western in 1963! As with the Looe branch, diesel traction in the form of DMUs and Class 22 diesel-hydraulic locomotives was tried in 1961 and they soon replaced steam. After April 1962 steam locomotives ceased to be shedded at Bodmin General, but locomotive haulage on the branch could still be experienced as Class 22s hauled the carriages from the age of steam. Except for the china clay trains, the passenger services were soon to be solely in the hands of DMUs. In 1964 there were changes at Boscarne Junction when economies were carried out. Instead of trains running from Wadebridge to both Bodmin General and Bodmin North an exchange platform was built at Boscarne, and passengers using Dunmere and Bodmin North were shuttled to and fro on a four-wheeled railbus to connect at Boscarne Junction with the Bodmin Road/General through trains to and from Wadebridge.

Once steam ended, the china clay trains were briefly in the hands of Class 22 Bo-Bo diesel locomotives, although a 204hp Drewry shunter worked the Wenford branch for a while. A Class 08 shunter normally worked the Wenford goods, then 'tripped' its load up to Bodmin General and on to Bodmin Road. However, 08s were restricted to eight loaded wagons from Boscarne, and after the Class 22s it was Class 25 diesel-electrics and later Class 37s that hauled the heavier trips from Boscarne to the main line.

By the mid-1960s there seemed to be doom and gloom on the branch line scene with the increasingly affluent motoring public spurning the railway. This, combined with the so-called 'Beeching era', created a bad climate for branch line viability. To the surprise of some, closure notices were posted and on 30 January 1967 all passenger services between Bodmin Road, Bodmin General and Padstow, including Bodmin North, were withdrawn, with the signalbox at General closing later in the year. The North Cornwall line from Okehampton through Launceston and Camelford to Wadebridge had closed the previous year, so after 133 years both Bodmin and Wadebridge were, once again, without a passenger service, the GWR branch having lasted for less than 80 years. The branch platform road was taken out of use at Bodmin Road where replacement bus services for Bodmin, Wadebridge and Padstow were provided.

Freight traffic from Bodmin Road to Wadebridge (and Wenford Bridge) continued until January 1979, one of the last commodities being slate dust from Delabole Quarry to Tonbridge in Kent. A siding had been provided in 1973 between Bodmin General and Road for Fulford Trumps, and this was later to become part of the Walker Lines Industrial Estate. The track from first Padstow then Wadebridge to Boscarne Junction was lifted, leaving Boscarne as merely a reversal point for china clay wagons to and from Wenford Bridge. The clay train ran with decreasing regularity and into the 1980s operated 'thrice weekly as required' — and on occasions it was not required! Finally in September 1983 even the clay traffic ceased and the signalbox at Bodmin Road (Parkway) closed; it was later to become a café on the down station platform. Was this the end of an era? Well, not quite.

After passenger services to Bodmin General ceased, the South West Group of the Great Western Society leased the disused engine shed, and located its '1361' class 0-6-0ST No 1363 and Hawksworth coach No 7372 at Bodmin General. Both were used on demonstration runs on a number of open days using the adjacent BR sidings. Much enjoyment was had riding 'Camel', a platelayers' trolley of 1875 vintage. The delightful Bodmin General station building was used as a furniture store, which saved it from demolition, a status not enjoyed by the old engine shed, or the large goods shed that was demolished in the summer of 1978. Just after the end of the Wenford goods traffic in 1983 Bodmin Road was renamed Bodmin Parkway to encourage the folk of Bodmin to leave their cars in the old down goods yard while they rode the train. 'Road' and 'Parkway' have the same meaning — they are both a long way from civilisation!

In 1984 the Bodmin Railway Preservation Society was formed with the objective of reopening the lines to Bodmin Road (Parkway) and Boscarne Junction, the track still being *in situ.*

Right
Although the end of the steam era is rapidly approaching there is still plenty of action at Bodmin General on 18 March 1961. '4500' class No 5539 has just climbed up from Boscarne with the 3.24pm train from Wadebridge while No 4565 takes a breather on shed between branch workings. The sight of a GWR Prairie arriving at Bodmin could soon be replicated when the B&WR's No 5552 has been restored. The engine shed in the photograph was demolished but the preservationists have completed a new two-road shed in the same position as the original. *Peter Gray*

Lower right:
On the same day as the previous photograph there is a quiet interlude as 2-6-2T No 4552 arrives on a freight and indulges in a little shunting, with both general goods and china clay traffic being switched. The 1961 infrastructure is remarkable with branch engine shed and water tower, signalbox, semaphore signals and goods shed all surviving. Although much has been swept away, the B&WR is gradually restoring the site.
Peter Gray

For a share issue the Bodmin & Wenford Railway plc was incorporated in 1985 and happily the issue was successful. In 1987 the Cornish Steam Locomotive Preservation Society moved its stock from Imperial Clay No 1 Dries, near Bugle, to Bodmin General, including the little ex-Par Harbour Bagnall 0-4-0ST *Alfred*, and an extensive workshop was built at General. The North Devon Shunter Group also moved its three small diesel shunters to the site in 1988. A Light Railway Order was granted in August 1989 and trips within the environs of Bodmin General commenced. On 17 June 1990 regular services began between General and Parkway, a great day for the preservationists as well as giving the public the opportunity of changing trains at the junction in order to reach Bodmin; however, British Rail discouraged car-bound passengers from starting their journeys from Bodmin Parkway. After much track and infrastructure work was undertaken on the line to Boscarne Junction it opened to passengers on 14 August 1996.

An interesting aside occurred in December 1989 when the Fitzgerald Lighting Company on the Walker Lines Estate used the old Fulford Trumps siding to convey some of its products by rail.

The train of three or four wagons ran once a week from Walker Lines hauled by one of the preservation society's diesels, normally a Class 08 or a 1,000hp Class 20 Bo-Bo. The wagons were deposited in an exchange siding at Bodmin Parkway where they were collected by a BR, later EWS (English, Welsh & Scottish Railway), locomotive. The traffic ceased between July 1991 and September 1996 when British Rail withdrew its 'Speedlink' freight services, but although it recommenced, following a significant increase in charges it ceased again in July 2001. It was refreshing indeed to see commercial, revenue-earning freight being hauled over a preserved line.

In the past few years the railway company has made significant progress in every department. Colesloggett Halt, an intermediate station between Bodmin General and Parkway, was built in 1992 and the newly constructed platform at Boscarne continued to be improved. Progress has been made in all departments including the construction of a replica signalbox and the installation of relevant semaphore signals. Attention has been given to detail, such as platform lamps, milk churns and luggage. Many items of stock have been refurbished and the railway has been wise enough to have an impressive collection of both steam and diesel locomotives; diesel multiple-units have also been acquired. In addition to ex-BR coaches, a fine assortment of goods wagons has also been preserved, including some of the famous china clay 'hoods'. Most of the stock is stored at Bodmin General and Walker Lines siding, with a handful of items at Bodmin Parkway.

Over the past 12 years or so numerous famous and well-liked locomotives have visited the line and attended steam galas, including GWR Prairie tanks that once worked the line in GWR/BR days. The modern railway companies have also supported the line by providing freight locomotives of the day to work the line for special events and diesel galas. In the year 2000 new EWS Class 66 and 67 locomotives appeared and HM The Queen travelled over the line. Despite a forecast recession there are even plans to extend the line towards Wadebridge. As with the railways of old, funds will have to be found, presuming that the cost can be justified in the first place. A visit to this standard gauge preserved line, its shop and buffet is highly recommended.

Left:
After the last china clay trains ran in 1983 the Bodmin Railway Preservation Society was formed with the objective of reopening the branch. The Bodmin & Wenford Railway plc was formed in 1985 and a successful share issue followed. A Light Railway Order was granted in 1989 and in June 1990 services between Bodmin General and Parkway commenced. During one of the many special days, in this instance the Diesel Gala of October 1991, visiting 'Hymek' Class 35 diesel-hydraulic No D7017 prepares to take over the next up working. *JV*

Right:
On 8 June 2000 0-6-0 saddle tank No 62 *Ugly*, built by Robert Stephenson Hawthorn in 1950, had the honour of hauling a Royal Train over the line during a visit to Cornwall by Her Majesty The Queen and HRH The Duke of Edinburgh. In July 1999 the locomotive, in smart lined green livery, waits to depart from Bodmin General. Progress is visible in the shape of the water tank and the signalbox. It is hoped that the operation will continue to go from strength to strength. *JV*

Left:
The 2-mile 56-chain line from Bodmin General down to Boscarne Junction, where a connection was made with the Bodmin & Wadebridge Railway (B&WR), opened on 3 September 1888, and GWR trains then worked through to Wadebridge and later Padstow. In common with the Bodmin Road line, this stretch of track was also steeply graded with a 1 in 37 section. In July 1951 '4500' class No 4559 exercises the check rail as it approaches Bodmin General with a couple of coaches. *B. A. Butt*

10. Bodmin & Wadebridge Railway

The Bodmin & Wadebridge Railway is one of the best known in Cornwall and has certainly captured the attention of the media more often than any other 'Southern' line in the county. It has several claims to fame. It was the first standard gauge railway line in Cornwall, the very first to use a locomotive for motive power — earlier railway lines, tramways and plateways in the mining areas had been of narrow gauge and had used horses and ropes to move wagons — and in BR days it was the last in the county to use steam as a means of propulsion. The B&WR was also the home of the Class 0298 2-4-0 Beattie well tanks that had their origins on the LSWR back in 1862. Three 1874-5 locomotives, built by Beyer Peacock of Gorton Works in Manchester, arrived on the railway in 1893 and except when away under repair they survived until 1962, a 'reign' of 69 years! Most railway photographers went 'on safari' to photograph these veterans during their lifetime. Finally, the route, particularly from Dunmere Wharf to Wenford Bridge, which meandered through magnificent countryside, small woods, across compact fields, through attractive cuttings and past minor industrial sidings, all within a few yards of the River Camel, was an unforgettable journey for those who had the privilege of riding the freight.

Below:
The B&WR is of great historical significance in that although there were earlier lines in Cornwall, it was the first standard gauge line in the county and the first to employ locomotives as motive power. The line opened in 1834 and two locomotives called *Elephant* and *Camel* worked the line, but in 1863 a Fletcher Jennings & Co of Whitehaven 0-4-0ST called *Bodmin* arrived and provided the staple motive power for 30 years. In this ancient 1888 view *Bodmin* is at the head of a B&WR formation at the sand drops at Bodmin (North). The photograph includes all four B&WR passenger-carrying coaches, and there are 14 directors and VIPs in the open coaches.
JV collection

Left:
The LSWR Adams Class O2s were synonymous with B&WR passenger operation between Bodmin North, Wadebridge and Padstow for many decades. For years the line was isolated from the rest of the railway system and although the GWR connected at Boscarne from 1888, it was not until 1895 that the B&WR, by then owned by the LSWR, was connected with its parent company when the North Cornwall line opened (see Chapter 5). With an interesting rake of rolling stock in tow, No 30203 approaches Wadebridge with a train from Bodmin North.
R. C. Riley, The Transport Treasury

Right:
After 87 years of service the three '0298' class 2-4-0 Beattie well tanks were displaced by three outside-cylinder pannier tanks of the '1366' class. However, their reign was short due to dieselisation in Cornwall, which was completed by 1965. Here No 1368 shunts wagons at the west end of Wadebridge station. The wharf fronting the River Camel is in the right background.
G. D. King

Left:
Following a period of great transition, when steam was replaced and regional boundaries were being changed, the WR services from Bodmin Road to Wadebridge and Padstow were in the hands of diesel units, such as the single power car seen here. About to depart from Wadebridge on 7 September 1964 is the 12.5pm from Bodmin Road to Padstow. Note the oil tail lamp on the bracket of the green machine.
Andrew Muckley

Right:
It is hard to believe that a place that was once as busy as Wadebridge is now rail-less. The only sign of the railway is the old goods shed and down station building and awning seen here. The rest of the area is incorporated in a housing estate, while the station building is now the 'John Betjeman Centre for the Retired', as seen in this August 1998 view. *P. G. Barnes*

Above:
This pleasing photograph should be compared with the previous one in 'before and after' terms. On 15 August 1959, 39 years earlier, Beattie well tank No 30586 has just added two box vans to a Bodmin North train. Often one of the three tanks was working the Wenford goods, one was on station pilot duties at Wadebridge and the other was spare. *D. Fereday-Glenn*

As explained in the Bude and Looe chapters there was a huge inland demand for manure for use in agriculture and this was normally supplied by either lime or limy sea sand. A scheme for a canal from Guinea Port, near Wadebridge, to Dunmere had been proposed in 1797 but was never built. In 1831 an influential local landowner, Sir William Molesworth from Pencarrow, commissioned a survey to explore the viability of a railway from Wadebridge along the valley of the River Camel to Wenford Bridge with branch lines to Ruthern Bridge and Bodmin. There were also a few mines and quarries in the area that might be able to use the railway, thus providing a back-load. The engineer, Roger Hopkins, presented his positive report in January 1832, stating that the line could be built for £26,000, a price that included buildings, a locomotive and rolling stock; he recommended standard gauge.

The Act of Incorporation of the Bodmin & Wadebridge Railway Company received Royal Assent on 23 May 1832, and Sir William Molesworth was appointed Chairman of the railway. Nine tenders to construct the line were received with the contract going to the Yniscedwyn Iron Works; a first turf was cut in a field near Drinnick Bridge. Full use was made of local granite with blocks being used as sleepers, and full-width granite blocks at rail joints. All other lines in Cornwall were using horses to haul wagons but the railway board decided to order a small locomotive from Neath Abbey Iron Works. This arrived in kit form and was assembled at Wadebridge under the supervision of the makers. By July 1834 the locomotive, called *Camel*, was working the line during construction. The first train of two wagons worked to Ruthern Bridge on 6 August 1834.

The grand opening of the 'main' line from Wadebridge via Dunmere to Wenford Bridge took place on 30 September 1834, with over 300 tickets being issued for the shareholders and invited guests. The train comprised 18 wagons and a coach, called the 'omnibus', and a special constable was allocated to each rail vehicle. The labourers were given a 'tenner' for their own, probably liquid, celebration! The train was highly decorated with flags and foliage, and a band in full uniform was amongst the passengers. It was reported in the press that 'the scene defied description, a more grand and imposing sight was never, perhaps, witnessed in this County'. The train left Wadebridge at noon and soon speeds of up to 10mph were reached. The locomotive stopped to take water at Dunmere, Tresarrett and at the Wenford Bridge terminus. On the return journey Bodmin was reached at 5pm 'amidst the cheers of the multitude assembled to witness the arrival'. The entire journey was without incident, much to the relief of the directors, no doubt.

Throughout the 149-year life of the Wenford section of the line there were never any scheduled passenger trains. In terms of rolling stock it is just as well because other than perhaps for early four-wheelers, route restrictions, curvature and clearances would have prevented most coaches from using the line. However, in the early years of the line passengers were unofficially carried in a 'tool wagon', which was effectively a match wagon between locomotive and train. On the Bodmin branch the single fare between Wadebridge and Bodmin was eightpence in an open coach and 1 shilling in covered accommodation. For a few months the locomotive *Camel* worked satisfactorily but it was prone to steam leaks and there were some breakages. When the locomotive was out of action the railway company hired horses at £2 10s 0d per week. The railway could barely cope with the demand for sand despite the daily train, and in the first nine months of the service receipts from this source of traffic exceeded £400, which must have been very encouraging for the directors. By contrast passenger receipts were a modest £23; however, bearing in mind that a single passenger train ran only on Wednesday and Saturday, it may not be surprising. There was an overall operating surplus. The railway employees must have been an officious bunch as fines for trespassing on the railway amounted to £3 11s 6d!

Expansion was soon needed and an Act in 1835 authorised capital for work on the wharves at Wadebridge and Bodmin and on the Ruthern Bridge branch, and, most important, the procurement of two locomotives and 40 wagons. Before any of this could be implemented *Camel* was up to her old tricks by suffering several further breakages, with horses coming to the rescue. On one occasion the locomotive and train fell between the rails! Throughout this period plans had been floated from time to time for extensions to the railway to link it with other lines. Extensions to Delabole, Launceston and Calstock were all mooted and the directors gave their support to the London, Salisbury, Exeter & Falmouth Railway, no doubt hoping that their line would feature in the LSE&FR plans. In 1845 a railway from Delabole (where there was an enormous slate quarry — see Chapter 5) to Rock, near Wadebridge, was proposed; after a meeting with the B&WR directors the line was changed to join the B&WR at Wenford Bridge. However, yet again nothing more was heard of the proposal.

The sand traffic was booming and in the six months to the end of September 1835 over 13,500 tons had been carried and 2,320 passengers, resulting in a net operating profit of over £600. The sand was recovered from the estuary and conveyed in 10 barges, which had a 12-ton capacity. A turning point for the railway came in 1836 when one of the new locomotives arrived at Wadebridge on the sailing vessel *Sophia*. The locomotive carried the name *Elephant* and was out on test in early June; in mid-June both *Camel* and *Elephant* were out on the same day working to Wenford Bridge with two excursions of 14 and 17 wagons (plus 'omnibus') respectively. *Elephant* was in trouble early on, on one occasion being 'worked home (to shed) by cattle'! Indeed, problems occurred with such regularity that they are too numerous to mention here. Problems also continued with *Camel*, but nevertheless the railway managed to get by.

In the late 1830s the volume of sand traffic stabilised and there was return mineral traffic comprising tin and iron from Ruthern Bridge, copper, iron, tin and lead from Nanstallon, and copper, iron and granite from Wenford Bridge. In 1840 a special train was organised for the population of Wadebridge to witness the public execution of the Lightfoot brothers at Bodmin. However, by the early 1840s there were signs that traffic was reducing, a fact that became only too apparent when losses of £400 per year were reported. To make matters worse the relatively small-scale mining operations in the area resulted in minimal downward traffic. Wage decreases were imposed and the locomotives were used only on passenger trains that ran on Saturdays and fair/market days, horses being used at other times. In 1844 an average of only 210 tons of sand per week was landed at Wadebridge. These were hard times for the B&WR and the directors were obliged to take radical action. It seemed that their only hope was to sell the railway to a larger company.

Both the broad gauge Cornwall Railway, which had connections with the South Devon Railway and Great Western Railway, and the standard gauge Cornwall & Devon Central Railway, supported by the London & South Western Railway, offered to purchase the B&WR. After due deliberation of all the issues the Board of the B&WR decided to accept the non-conditional offer from the C&DCR; presumably they were thinking that as a standard gauge organisation the C&DCR might incorporate the B&WR in its envisaged route from Exeter to Falmouth. Two Bills for the proposed takeover were submitted to Parliament in 1845 and 1846 but both were rejected. In the meantime the C&DCR failed, and the LSWR assumed the B&WR's responsibilities, without the usual Act of Parliament. The reason why the LSWR showed any interest was to keep the Cornwall Railway (later the GWR) out of North Cornwall and Wadebridge — at this time the nearest LSWR line was at Dorchester in Dorset!

From 1846 a daily passenger service from Wadebridge to Bodmin was introduced, and life on the railway continued as before, except in 1852 when the LSWR sent a replacement

Right:
The Ruthern Bridge branch opened on 30 September 1834 and left the B&WR in the vicinity of Grogley Halt. Tin and iron mines provided the main source of traffic in the early days but the mines gradually closed. In 1914 a new loop was constructed 6 chains nearer Grogley and in 1926 the line was slightly shortened, before being abandoned at the end of 1933. Here a pair of wagons await collection at Ruthern in 1926, viewed from the buffer stops. *JV collection*

Left:
An interesting mix of a typical SR-style concrete station sign and an equally typical GWR corrugated tin 'pagoda' hut grace the platform of Nanstallon Halt. Four-wheeled railbuses were used on a Bodmin North to Boscarne Junction shuttle from 15 June 1964 and here, in September 1964, one of the AC company's units was out of course as it headed for Wadebridge to have its steps repaired. The destination blind almost shows 'Cirencester Town'! *Andrew Muckley*

Right:
Even though the Bodmin & Wenford Railway now runs to Boscarne Junction it is doubtful that there will ever again be a crowd such as this at the location. After the Wenford Bridge line closed BR (Cornish Railways) showed enterprise in organising a nine-car DMU special to Bodmin General and Boscarne. After a lunchtime ramble, crowds prepare to rejoin the wreathed train on 20 November 1983. The line to Bodmin General is on the left, to Wenford (and formerly Bodmin North) on the right, and beyond to Wadebridge. *JV*

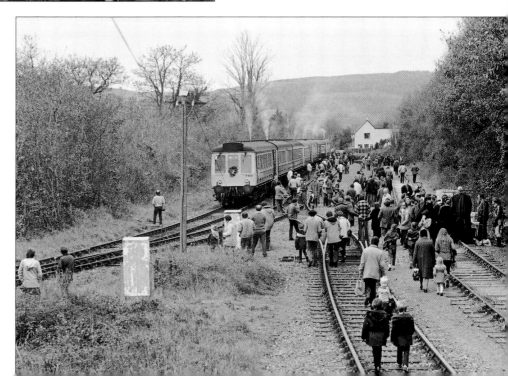

0-4-2T locomotive called *Atlas* to replace the worn-out B&WR motive power. *Atlas* was a little heavy for the poor track and *Pluto*, a lighter 0-4-2T, subsequently replaced the earlier locomotive in March 1855. The LSWR also supplied a couple of composite coaches. The track was in bad shape and in the early 1860s the B&WR again resorted to horses for power. By 1862 there was a significant development when china clay extraction in the area produced a further opportunity for the railway, but a proposal to extend the Ruthern Bridge line to a nearby iron mine was rejected as being too risky in financial terms. In 1864 Joseph Beattie declared that if a new 0-4-0 saddle tank, *Bodmin,* was to be used on the line much permanent way work would need to be carried out. Accordingly, in 1865, an Act was passed allowing the LSWR to raise £100,000 capital effectively to rebuild the line, including certain realignments at Dunmere and Grogley. The line was subsequently relaid but the realignments were not executed at that time.

In the meantime the Launceston, Bodmin & Wadebridge Railway had obtained an Act of Parliament in 1864 to build a line linking Launceston and Wenford Bridge, then southwards from Ruthern Bridge to Truro, with running powers over the B&WR. This proposal was not pursued. A later proposal from the Devon & Cornwall Railway saw a Meldon (near Okehampton) to Wenford via Holsworthy line as feasible. Other proposed lines in the Bodmin and Wadebridge area are dealt with in Chapter 9; suffice to say that they involved a broad gauge line from the Cornwall Railway's main line and the Cornwall Minerals Railway. Other approvals included the 1882 North Cornwall Railway's (later LSWR's) line from Launceston to Wadebridge and Padstow. Also, following the approval of the GWR's plans for a Bodmin Road-Bodmin (General)-Boscarne (Junction) standard gauge branch, an agreement was drawn up between the GWR and LSWR to control the former's access to Wadebridge and to impose on the latter the B&WR rebuilding (including a new station at Wadebridge and the aforementioned Dunmere and Grogley deviations). After decades of 'illegal' ownership of the B&WR (because of the absence of an authorising Act) the LSWR legalised the situation by another Act of 1 July 1886.

On the motive power scene there were plenty of changes over the years after the arrival of *Bodmin* and when it was being repaired. By the 1870s the passenger services had been reduced to Mondays, Wednesdays, Fridays and Saturdays; there were two round trips on Saturdays. The original B&WR locomotives, *Atlas* and *Pluto*, were all sold for scrap in 1865. In 1874 a 2-4-0WT *Scott* was in use, and in 1885 it was 0-6-0ST *Jumbo*. In May 1893 the first of three Beattie 2-4-0WTs arrived by sea from Southampton; these tanks were widely used on LSWR London suburban services but by this time trains were getting heavier and they were being replaced by later and more powerful designs. In 1895 Manning Wardle 0-6-0ST *Lady Portsmouth* arrived but was not fit for service. In 1898 all 'up-country' Beattie well tanks had been withdrawn and in 1900 first a Class O2 0-4-4T and later an 'Ilfracombe Goods' were tried as potential replacements. They failed to impress on the Wenford and Ruthern parts of the line and a decision was made to keep the Beatties. Numbers 0298, 0314 and 0329 were retained and the class became known as the '0298s'. The '0s' in their numbers were replaced by '3s' (eg 3298) in 1931 and under British Railways they became Nos 30587/5/6. In 1899 an Adams 'B4' 0-4-0T was used at Wadebridge for shunting duties but it was returned in 1901. In the early part of the 20th century a pair of Adams '415' class Radial 4-4-2Ts were used, which performed mixed traffic duties through the railmotor years until the 1920s. The Radials were then replaced on Bodmin North passenger trains by Adams Class O2 0-4-4Ts. Whenever the Beattie tanks were away being repaired or, as in 1921-2 and 1931-5, rebuilt (by Urie, then Maunsell), other classes of locomotive were tried on the B&WR lines. These included a 'P' class 0-6-0T and a PDSWJR 0-6-0T. We will return to the motive power scene later.

Passenger services on the B&WR were suspended from 1 November 1886 so that the above-mentioned extensive works could be completed. The GWR branch from Bodmin Road to Boscarne Junction was opened throughout on 3 September 1888, and after 54 years of splendid isolation the B&WR was at last connected with a main line and the outside world, but not via the tracks of its LSWR owners! An Act to reconstruct the Bodmin (North) branch was passed in 1891, the main work being a deviation to avoid a main road crossing on the Bodmin side of Dunmere Junction. It was not until 1 November 1895 that train services between Wadebridge and Bodmin (North, after 1949) recommenced, five months after the last section of the North Cornwall line from Delabole to Wadebridge opened (see Chapter 5).

From 1895 there were eight trains per day, one of which included through carriages from Waterloo. By contrast the GWR operated six or seven trains, so Wadebridge became a very busy place! In 1899 the 5½-mile line from Wadebridge to Padstow opened with plenty of implications for an extended Bodmin Road/North/General to Wadebridge service; both North Cornwall and some local trains served Padstow. In June 1906 32-ton steam railmotors were introduced but they had little trailing load capability, were difficult to drive and fire, had a maximum load of 40 passengers and were gas-lit; they lasted until the end of World War 1. Also in 1906 the LSWR opened halts at Grogley, Nanstallon and Dunmere, even though the surrounding population was sparse. From that date there were 10 round trips plus one mixed train in each direction, with minor changes to this pattern in seasonal and Saturday timetables. The GWR service comprised five round trips plus two mixed trains in each direction. A daily freight ran from Wadebridge to Bodmin, with another train working to Wenford Bridge picking up on the outward journey at Ruthern Bridge when there was any traffic. Only the LSWR trains stopped at the halts, a situation that continued until the 1960s.

The LSWR had a brief look at the possibility of running passenger trains on the Wenford branch but after an unsuccessful trial the proposition could not to be justified. The freight trains to Wenford and intermediate sidings continued, with china clay being the principal commodity in tonnage terms. Most of the china clay was shipped from Fowey rather than Wadebridge or Padstow in later decades. There followed a period of consolidation with few changes, except that sand traffic had finished just prior to the Grouping in 1923, when the LSWR became part of the Southern Railway. On 30 December 1933 the lightly used line to Ruthern Bridge was closed to all traffic, having not seen a train for some time. The mines had long closed and just a modicum of agricultural traffic was carried from Ruthern each year. There were mild festivities in 1934 to celebrate the centenary of the line, including a local exhibition and a special train from Wadebridge to Bodmin (North) and back.

During World War 2 the line between Wadebridge and Boscarne Junction was upgraded so that should the GWR or LSWR main lines out of Plymouth be blocked by bomb damage trains could be diverted via the North Cornwall, Bodmin & Wadebridge and Great Western lines. This involved four reversals but was used from time to time. During the war a number of armoured trains patrolled the area and a Great Eastern 2-4-2T worked at least one

Right:
This stirring photograph by Sid Nash shows that not all Bodmin North workings were in the hands of small tank locomotives. On 17 May 1962 'N' class 2-6-0 No 31860 moves briskly away from Dunmere Halt with the 12.25pm train from Wadebridge. These Moguls regularly worked into Bodmin North on freight but although they were regular performers on SR Cornish lines, none were allocated to Wadebridge shed.
S. C. Nash

Above:
A general view of the track layout at Bodmin North finds 'O2' class No 30236 arriving from Wadebridge on 4 October 1958. The word 'North' was added in 1949, to differentiate the station from Bodmin General on the then new 'British Railways' network. The grim-looking Bodmin Gaol can be seen between the train and the freight wagon in the siding. *L. King*

of these. In August 1946 new 'West Country' class 4-6-2 No 21C116 was worked through to Bodmin (North) to receive the name *Bodmin*; the locomotive has, happily, been preserved.

It is easy to dismiss decades of reliable branch line service in a few paragraphs, but for many years little changed. The LSWR services continued with a service of between seven and nine trains per day Monday to Saturday with a daily freight Monday to Friday on both the Bodmin North and Wenford Bridge lines. Most of the passenger trains to and from Bodmin North served Padstow, whereas only some of the trains from Bodmin Road/General worked through.

A postwar resurgence in passenger traffic peaked in the mid-1950s but, as stated in many chapters of this book, the public started its great love affair with the motor car, and rising prices on the railway, combined with an industrial dispute or two and a reduction in services, generated a vicious circle of fewer passengers and more economy measures. This was all complicated by frequent changes in the structure of British Railways two years after nationalisation in 1948. It is worth repeating here that in 1950 all the former SR lines west of Exeter were placed under the control of the Western Region of BR. They reverted to the Southern Region in 1958, only to return to the Western in 1963. By then there was a heavy government focus on costs and subsidies and Dr Beeching had concluded that all of the lines in this chapter (and many more) should be closed completely, in accordance with the grand 're-shaping' plan.

Returning to the motive power scene, the ubiquitous Prairies continued to work the GWR passenger and freight services (see Chapter 9). The Class O2s continued to work Southern passenger services until 1960 when Western 0-6-0 pannier tanks were drafted in to Wadebridge, with a single Class O2 available as

spare. The Beattie '0298' well tanks also continued to labour on the Wenford freights with occasional appearances on passenger trains when there was an availability problem. However, after 69 years of service in the area the old veterans were finally replaced in 1962 when a trio of 1934-built Collett '1366' class outside-cylinder 0-6-0PTs were allocated to Wadebridge. These Western engines lasted only two years before being replaced by Class 03 Drewry shunters in 1964. Some Bodmin North services and the daily freight were often in the hands of the capable Southern 'N' class 2-6-0 Moguls that worked off the North Cornwall line (see Chapter 5). Wadebridge also saw graceful Drummond 'T9' 4-4-0s and Bulleid light Pacifics that worked between Okehampton, Wadebridge and Padstow. In 1962 the '5700' class 0-6-0PTs were transferred away and ex-LMS Ivatt 2-6-2Ts were drafted in to work the Bodmin North services, lasting until dieselisation took place in 1964. Class 22 diesel-hydraulics headed some Western Region services in the early 1960s until DMUs were widely available. The '1366' 0-6-0PTs were the last British Railways steam locomotives operating in Cornwall.

As mentioned in the last chapter, one of the economies to be made on the B&WR occurred in 1964 when a small wooden transfer platform was built at Boscarne Junction with the idea that the Bodmin North services would be operated by a four-wheeled railbus 'shuttling' four or five times per day between the two points, making connections with the services from Bodmin General to Wadebridge. Only cynics would suggest that if the Southern Region had been in control it would have been the Bodmin Road/General services that would have been subjected to the railbus shuttle! By then most of the Western services were comprised of a single-car diesel unit, which was adequate for the number of passengers. In 1965 the number of railbus workings and

Below:
The railways of Bodmin, Wadebridge and Wenford

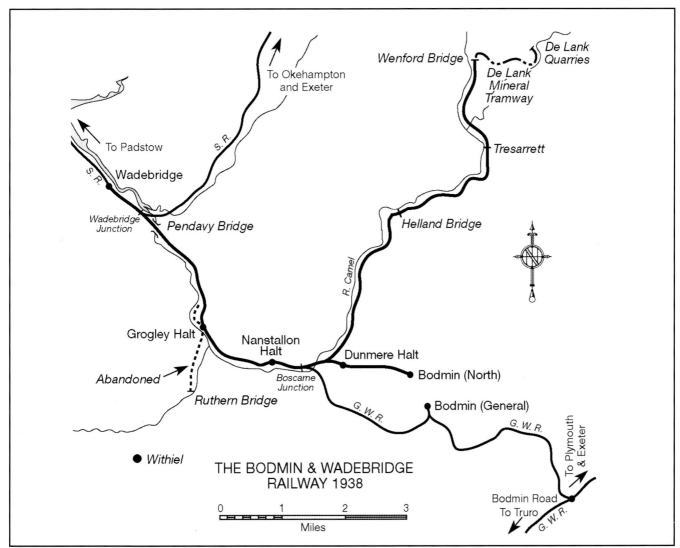

THE BODMIN & WADEBRIDGE
RAILWAY 1938

other branch trains increased and a couple of times a day the unit worked to Bodmin General to make a couple of round trips to Bodmin Road. However, by 1966 the writing was on the wall and from April there was a drastic curtailment of services to Bodmin North. The railbus had gone and just two trains per day worked to the Southern terminus; originating at Bodmin Road, they reversed at Boscarne Junction before continuing to Bodmin North, where they again reversed for the trip to Padstow. Later in the year all services were withdrawn on the North Cornwall line. Eventually the familiar closure notices were posted, and all passenger services ceased from January 1967 between Bodmin Road/General/North, Wadebridge and Padstow. The track from Wadebridge to Padstow was lifted with almost indecent haste.

Freight services between Bodmin Road and Wadebridge and from Boscarne Junction to Wenford Bridge continued. There were freight trains on most days but over the next decade the traffic was in terminal decline. Class 25 locomotives took over from the Class 22s on the Wadebridge trains and Class 08 0-6-0 shunters dominated the Wenford Bridge branch, the Drewry Class 03 shunters having been transferred away. By 1979 the Wadebridge traffic was so thin that proposals were published to withdraw freight services and in that year the last-ever train left

WADEBRIDGE and BODMIN.

Miles	Down.	Week Days only.						
		mrn	mrn	mrn	aft	aft	aft	aft
	Wadebridge .... dep.	7 5	8 26	10 0	1255	3 14	4 45	6 35
3	Grogley Halt	7 13	8 35	10 8	1 4	3 22	4 53	6 43
4¼	Nanstallon Halt	7 17	8 40	1012	1 9	3 26	4 57	6 47
5½	Dunmere Halt	7 21	8 44	1016	1 14	3 29	5 1	6 51
6¾	Bodmin D .... arr.	7 25	8 49	1020	1 19	3 34	5 5	6 55

Miles	Up.	Week Days only.						
		mrn	mrn	mrn	aft	aft	aft	aft
	Bodmin .... dep.	7 32	9 0	1128	1 55	4 20	5 15	9 12
1¼	Dunmere Halt	7 36	9 4	1132	2 0	4 24	5 19	9 16
2½	Nanstallon Halt	7 39	9 7	1135	2 4	4 27	5 22	9 19
3¾	Grogley Halt .... [above	7 43	9 11	1139	2 9	4 31	5 26	9 25
6¾	Wadebridge 179 and .... arr.	7 51	9 19	1147	2 18	4 39	5 34	9 33

NOTES.

D 1 mile to Great Western Station.

☞ **For other Trains** BETWEEN **Wadebridge and Bodmin** .. PAGE **46**

WENFORD BRANCH.

For Special Instructions as to the working of trains over this Line, see pages 61 and 62 of the Western Appendix to the Working Time Tables.

Distance. M.	Distance. C.	DOWN WEEK-DAYS.	SX C arr.	SX C dep.	SO arr.	SO dep.	SO arr.	SO dep.
			a.m.	a.m.	a.m.	a.m.	p.m.	p.m.
—	—	**Wadebridge**........	...	10C 0	...	*10 0*	...	*1 45*
4	32	Nanstallon Siding . .	10C12	10C20	.	.	.	
4	62	Boscarne Junction......	10C23	10 50	*10 15*	*(10 30)*	*2 0*	*(2 25)*
5	07	Dunmere Junction . .	10	54	.	.	.	.
5	25	Dunmere Siding........	10 55	11 15	...	...	..	...
8	12	Helland Siding . . .	11 44	11 49	Commences 20th September.			
10	28	Tresarrett Siding	12 2	12 12				
11	28	China Clay Co.'s Siding	12 17	12 37				
11	63	**Wenford**........	12 41	...				

Distance. M.	Distance. C.	UP WEEK-DAYS.	SO arr.	SO dep.	SX arr.	SX dep.	SO arr.	SO dep.
			a.m.	a.m.	p.m.	p.m.	p.m.	p.m.
—	—	**Wenford**........	...	...	...	1 20	.	.
0	35	China Clay Co.'s Siding	.	.	1 25	1 50	Commences 20th Sept.	
1	35	Tresarrett Siding	Commences 20th Sept.		1 55	2 0		
3	51	Helland Siding . . .			2 13	2 18		
6	38	Dunmere Siding........			2 41	2 43		
6	56	Dunmere Junction . .	.	.	2 44	3 4	.	.
7	01	Boscarne Junction......	*(10 15)*	*10 30*	3 9	3 45	*(2 0)*	*2 25*
11	63	**Wadebridge**	*10 45*	.	3 58	.	*2 40*	.

C—On Thursdays stop at Speed Restriction Board at 2¼ m.p. between Wadebridge and Nanstallon Siding and on Fridays stop at Nanstallon Down Distant Signal to change lamps, then run 6 minutes later to Boscarne Junction.

Above:
The LSWR timetable from Wadebridge to Bodmin (later Bodmin North) in January 1927 and (below) the Wenford goods working timetable from June 1952.

Left:
Many railway enthusiasts have for years held the Wenford Bridge branch in high regard, almost affection. The age of the line, its sinuous path, its unique motive power, its lifelong 'freight only' status and its against-the-odds survival for some 149 years made it rather special. On 7 September 1962 0-6-0PT No 1369 passes Dunmere Junction (the junction with the Bodmin North branch) with the 9.35am Wadebridge to Wenford Bridge freight.
S. C. Nash

Wadebridge. One of the last commodities handled was slate dust from Delabole. The service then comprised only a daily Class 08 working from St Blazey to Bodmin Road, General, and Boscarne to Wenford Dries, the line beyond to Wenford Bridge having been closed in 1967 and truncated in 1971. This service became less frequent and by 1980 was thrice weekly, as required.

The Class 25s were subsequently withdrawn or transferred away from Cornwall and from 1979-80 1,750hp Class 37s became the standard main line freight power in the county. These locomotives would 'trip' china clay wagons to and from Boscarne Junction when loadings exceeded that permitted for a Class 08 shunter. Sometimes a week or two would pass without a train. The end came in September 1983 when the 1834 line up the valley of the River Camel closed completely. Much of the old trackbed was converted to a footpath/cyclepath dubbed the 'Camel Trail'. For post-closure preservation developments see the previous chapter.

The B&WR was always based at Wadebridge. With trains arriving from and departing to Bodmin North, Bodmin Road, Padstow, Okehampton and beyond, plus freights on all of the above lines as well as Wenford Bridge, there were some 50 daily train movements at Wadebridge. Add running-round movements, going on and off shed and short trips to the wharf, and Wadebridge station became a surprisingly busy place. There were sidings on the Padstow side of the ancient bridge across the Camel to serve the quays in addition to a two-road engine shed, coaling and watering facilities, 50ft turntable (insufficient for the Bulleid Pacifics, which used Padstow), sidings, goods shed and a sand dock. A new stone platform was built in 1888 and in 1895 the island platform was added to cope with the North Cornwall and extra Bodmin North traffic.

On leaving Wadebridge the line ran along the south bank of the Camel estuary. In just under half a mile the North Cornwall line branched away to the north towards Camelford, and until July 1907 a signalbox controlled junction movements. At this location there was a siding to the nearby Guinea Port quay. The Bodmin line crossed the River Camel on Pendavey Bridge and at 1-mile 40-chain Rifle Range Platform was located on the down side, built in the 1880s to serve a nearby shooting range. Before reaching Grogley Halt at 2 miles 72 chains the old pre-1888 alignment to Ruthern Bridge diverged to the south. After 1888 trains for Ruthern Bridge would normally be up trains that would reverse at Grogley into a shunting neck, effectively part of the old line, before proceeding forward once more down the branch. Ruthern Bridge, at just over 4 miles from Wadebridge, comprised two simple sidings with a run-round loop. There was a small siding to an ochre pit but it was lifted before 1912. The last train ran in 1933 and the line was lifted in 1936.

Grogley Halt was a single wooden platform until 1957 when a standard concrete structure with a small shelter was constructed. The line continued up the valley and at 4 miles 25 chains Nanstallon wharf siding diverged on the down side. The siding closed in 1960 and was removed in the following year. Originally a halt with a wooden platform, Nanstallon Halt (4 miles 32 chains) was rebuilt with concrete facings and coping stones and blessed with a 'pagoda' hut for waiting accommodation. The small adjacent signalbox controlled signals and the crossing gates across a local lane. Just beyond Nanstallon was Boscarne Junction, access to which was controlled by Boscarne Junction signalbox (closed at the end of passenger services in December 1967). There were sidings at Boscarne (4 miles 62 chains) that were used mainly for china clay wagons to and from the Wenford Bridge line. At the east end of the sidings the Bodmin North/Wenford line divided from the GWR/BR(WR) Bodmin General line. Broadly in the 'V' of the junction two exchange platforms (one at rail level) were in use in 1964 to facilitate access to and from the Bodmin North line railbus.

Just 10 chains beyond Boscarne and across the River Camel was Dunmere Junction (5 miles 7 chains) where the Wenford

Bridge line took a left-hand fork, with the right-hand line going to Dunmere Halt and Bodmin North. Taking the Bodmin line, which was realigned in 1895 to ease curvature and gradient, the 1906 Dunmere Halt was a mere 13 chains from the junction. As with the rebuilt Nanstallon, the platform had a 'pagoda' hut to accommodate passengers. The average gradient from Dunmere Junction to Bodmin North was 1 in 47, although with light branch trains this was not a formidable obstacle. The line passed the famous Bodmin Gaol just before Bodmin North terminus, at 6 miles 31 chains. Sand drops were an important part of the original Bodmin site but after the rebuilding was completed in 1895 the area they occupied was covered by an enlarged goods yard and stone-built goods shed. The site had a gasworks siding, signalbox (closed on 30 January 1967, the day of the last train), turntable and run-round loop. There was a single platform face and a single-storey stone-built station building. A road, supermarket and car park now occupy the old 'North' site.

Returning to Dunmere Junction, the Wenford line was effectively a siding worked on a 'one engine in steam' principle. For many years it was protected by a gate and the train guard or shunter had to walk to Boscarne Junction to obtain the electric tablet from the signalman, without which the train could not proceed. Just 18 chains beyond Dunmere Junction was Dunmere Siding (once known as Borough Bounds Wharf) where the line crossed the main Bodmin to Wadebridge road. The guard stopped traffic by showing a red flag as the train crossed. The short siding that was used mostly for grain from the nearby Hawke's Mill closed in May 1969. The line meandered north along the valley of the River Camel and within a mile Penhargard siding, a loop used for timber traffic, was reached. A further 60 chains towards Wenford was one of the most photographed sites on the line, the water tank in Pencarrow Wood. The source of the water was a nearby stream, and due to their limited water capacity it was essential for the small tank engines that worked the line to stop for replenishment.

The next major feature on the line was the very picturesque Helland Crossing, where the line ran between two old Cornish cottages and crossed a minor ungated road. There was also a siding at Helland (Wharf), 8 miles 12 chains from Wadebridge, used mainly for feedstuffs. The small siding was taken out of use on 2 May 1960. The line continued through rural and thinly populated countryside to a point at 9 miles 71 chains where, between approximately 1911 and 1934, there was a siding that diverged from the main branch on the down side to serve a company that produced road stone (see the accompanying unique photograph). The stone travelled to the site by a narrow gauge tramway that crossed the River Camel on its way from the quarry to the loading point. A few yards further along the branch on the opposite side to the road stone siding was Parkyn's Clay Company's Stump Oak siding that was in operation from 1880 until the 1920s; it was removed by the beginning of World War 2. The remains of the loading wharf and the works on the hillside above are buried in undergrowth.

At 10 miles 28 chains was a minor road and Tresarrett siding. Adjacent to the crossing was a wharfinger's cottage, this being

the site of one of the original 1834 wharves. In fact there was a siding on the east side of the branch (removed in 1932) and a loop on the west side; the latter was closed in 1970 and lifted shortly afterwards. Another minor road was crossed before the 'China Clay Company's Sidings' were reached, 11 miles 28 chains from Wadebridge. There were extensive clay dries at this point, totalling six coal-fired kilns, some of which were later converted to use alternative fuel. These kilns once resulted in considerable inbound coal traffic. Originally there were three parallel lines here but one was removed before 1922. The china clay was piped down in slurry form from the vast site on Stannon Moor located in the hills some 4 miles away. For many years prior to the closure of the railway in September 1983, the china clay from this site was the only source of traffic on the branch. After 1967 the clay sidings effectively became the end of the line, but prior to that year they continued to Wenford Goods depot at 11 miles 63 chains. This location had the distinction of being the furthest point on the Southern Railway from London Waterloo station. The depot was used for general traffic but coal for domestic use was the main import and timber the primary output, although the farming community was also served. Until De Lank Quarry stopped shipping granite by rail in the very late 1940s, for every ton of traffic received at Wenford 3 tons were dispatched. Sidings, a 5-ton crane and a goods office were all features at Wenford.

Above:
One of the many rural delights on the Wenford line was Helland Crossing where the line ran between two Cornish cottages. On the outward journey of the Wenford goods on 13 July 1961 No 30585 attracts some local attention. A siding, known as Helland Wharf, was in use at this location until 2 May 1960, handling mainly feedstuffs for local farmers. *Peter Gray*

Above:

This previously published photographic gem was a prize-winner in a 1953 *Trains Illustrated* magazine competition. In perfect conditions Class 0298 No 30585 (old LSWR No 314) chuffs through Pencarrow Woods with 10 clanking four-wheelers in tow on 3 September 1953. At this time the freight left Wadebridge at 10am and allowing for shunting at intermediate sidings arrived at Wenford at 12.41pm — 2hr 41min for 11 miles 65 chains! The return trip left Wenford at 1.20pm arriving in Wadebridge at 3.58pm — 6 hours in all to travel 23½ miles! What a great day's work, if you could get it! *S. C. Nash*

Below:

One of the most interesting intermediate sidings on the Wenford line was located on the down side at the 9-mile 71-chain point between Helland and Tresarrett. The siding, known as Road Stone Company's siding, was open between 1911 and 1934. Standard gauge wagons were loaded via a 'Heath Robinson'-type hopper, which was fed by a narrow gauge tramway that crossed the River Camel between the quarry (visible in the background) and the siding. Taken by a Mr Whale of Blisland in the late 1920s, this is the only known photograph of the siding, with a superb collection of SR/LSWR/GWR wagons. *JV collection*

Left:
The china clay dried at Wenford clay dries is piped down from the Stannon Works high on the moor, over 4 miles from Wenford. In its heyday large numbers of china clay wagons would be taken to Boscarne and would then be 'tripped' to Bodmin Road and on to Lostwithiel. In the 1970s the once-daily train gradually dwindled to thrice weekly and by the early 1980s it ran as and when required. The last train ran on 26 September 1983. In this view there is little activity as the crew partake of lunch in one of the tin huts on the left. *JV*

Right:
Wenford goods depot was at the end of the branch and the site had been considerably enlarged in 1926 to cope with demand. For example, in 1928 there was 48,748 tons of goods and minerals shipped from Wenford Bridge and 15,374 tons received. Here on 22 September 1959 No 30585 has brought its clay loads up to the terminus from the dries to incorporate them in the return consist. The half a mile of line beyond the clay dries to Wenford Bridge closed to traffic in 1967.
P. Q. Treloar

Left:
Beyond Wenford Bridge a single standard gauge track crossed a minor road and continued up a three-rail 1 in 8 incline to De Lank Quarry. The incline was worked by cable on a counterbalance system, and the maximum single movement load was two wagons. The quarry is still open but shipment by rail ceased in the early 1940s. Horses were used for all non-incline wagon movement until 1925 when a small Simplex petrol-powered shunter was used. This view at the top of the incline dates back to June 1934.
JV collection

Above:
This incredible postcard, postally used from nearby St Breward in 1902, shows the upper section of De Lank Quarry. There is a standard gauge line and incline on the left, a single wagon at another level and two narrow gauge tramways, one of which enters the dressing sheds below. The quarry had an internal railway system until about 1950, and supplied much of the granite that was used in building bridges across the Thames in London.
JV collection

A most interesting feature of the Wenford branch was the connection with De Lank Quarry at St Breward. A single line extended across a minor road beyond Wenford Goods, past a couple of short quarry company sidings and up a standard gauge 1 in 8 incline towards the quarry. There were several spurs within the quarry and a further incline at the upper level. The line was opened in the 1890s to the site of the dressing sheds, where high-quality granite was prepared for customers, ranging from grave headstones to granite blocks for London's bridges. The incline used a cable-operated counterbalance system, and no more than two wagons could be worked up or down the incline at any one time. Horses were used to move wagons until the quarry became a subsidiary of Thos W. Ward Ltd in 1925. A Simplex four-wheeled petrol-powered shunter was imported from St Helens in Lancashire in 1926 for quarry shunting, and this small locomotive lasted until the internal quarry railway closed about 1950, when it was taken to Birmingham and later scrapped. The quarry is still open but the last shipment by rail was well over half a century ago.

It is hard to believe that the entire Bodmin & Wenford Railway 'network' has now closed and that everything described in this chapter is now history. The grand plans of those early pioneers served a purpose for nearly 150 years but now only photographs survive to show us scenes of everyday operation. After closure of this outstanding line and the start of the preservation movement described in the last chapter, there was some talk of reintroducing a freight service to serve the china clay industry at Wenford, with traffic travelling over the preserved line to reach Fowey. Indeed, much money was spent on looking at feasibility and the local authority was involved. Interested parties also spent large amounts of time on the necessary legalities and there were meetings aplenty. However, there were subsequently numerous changes in the china clay industry, including a takeover of English China Clays, volumes would not have been that great, lorries were handling the traffic successfully, and at best the huge capital expenditure would show marginal, if any, cost benefits. The case would then have had to depend on environmental issues, and in this respect there were some local objections to the proposed re-instatement of the railway and even conflict between the walkers and cyclists using the Camel Trail and those who wanted to get clay lorries off the road. However, in 2001 it seemed likely that clay production at Stannon would end and so would the clay drying at Wenford. In romantic terms it would be great to see trains trundling through Pencarrow Woods again, but in reality it is never likely to happen.

In the long term the preservationists may project their plans beyond Boscarne to Wadebridge and even Padstow, but the physical obstacles would be many. Consolidation has much to commend it because such grandiose plans would need a very large chequebook. Others would advocate a 'grow or die' policy. I will be content for readers to make their own judgements on the subject!

11. Fowey Branch

Lostwithiel was and still is a town of immense interest, with narrow streets, old buildings and an ancient bridge across the picturesque River Fowey. Not far away is the imposing Restormel Castle. Lostwithiel was once the ancient capital of Cornwall and a strategically important town that grew from river level on to the surrounding hills to become prosperous through local mining interests, a once active river trade, thriving markets, and its administrative role. However, the coming of the railway in the shape of the broad gauge Cornwall Railway in 1859, linking Truro with Plymouth and the outside world, was seen as a new opportunity to revive the slightly flagging fortunes of the town in the mid-19th century. This view was reinforced when the CR decided to locate its main workshops adjacent to Lostwithiel station. This installation included machine shops, a lifting shed, blacksmithy, machine shops, carpenters' shops, paint shop and associated administrative buildings, and the railway became a significant employer in the area.

In addition to the workshops and main line station Lostwithiel was eventually to have a substantial broad gauge goods shed, a milk depot/creamery, sidings, goods yards on the up and down sides, two signalboxes and crossing gates. As mentioned later, it would also become a junction when a branch line to Fowey was opened. The river trade was considerable in the Middle Ages but the inlet at the top end of the Fowey estuary was tidal and susceptible to silting up, so only relatively small vessels could use Lostwithiel as a port whereas just 5 miles down the river at Fowey there was a deepwater port capable of taking the largest vessels of the day. By the time the main line opened, mining activity was decreasing but volumes of china clay were on the increase and the railway entrepreneurs had their eye on Fowey as an ideal point for transhipment from rail to ship. There was, however, plenty of opposition. Clay was being shipped in volume from the increasingly busy but artificial and tidal harbour at Par, Looe was about to become a minor player, Charlestown, although not rail connected, was still a very busy centre, Pentewan was relatively 'small beer' by today's standards but was still thriving, and Newquay in the north also made a contribution. However, logic dictated that Fowey would be a port worthy of development and that meant a railway connection.

Accordingly, in 1862 the Lostwithiel & Fowey Railway published proposals to connect the CR main line at Lostwithiel with Carne Point, just half a mile north of the town of Fowey, by building a broad gauge branch line. The L&FR wanted to raise £60,000 to finance its plans, which included a line of quays from Upper to Lower Carne Point, various harbour works, including embankments and dredging, and the creation of a heavyweight Fowey Harbour Board that would levy rates, act as a local authority and oversee pilotage. The proposed Board would have 13 representatives, six members being nominated by the railway company. There were some local objections because building the railway to Fowey would sound the death-knell for river trade at Lostwithiel and deprive officials of their ancient rights, under

charter, concerning control of the river. The Corporation of Lostwithiel and other locals, perhaps parochially, saw the railway as a disadvantage to their fortunes. Locals also said that the huge cost of £60,000 to build the line and develop jetties at Carne Point would be a high-risk investment. They also suspected that the tolls and levies would be excessive and injure local trade.

However, once the dust settled and the various formalities were dispensed with construction began. The broad gauge line hugged the river on the west side passing Golant, the only intermediate village on the line, by a short causeway along the harbour front. The line stopped short of Fowey, although there were plans to extend it when circumstances permitted, and a total of only three jetties were built. Messrs Mead and Lang of Liskeard built the line, the Cornwall Railway was charged with operating it, and it opened on 1 October 1869 without ceremony. The line was essentially freight only but early records show that there was an excursion or two over the line using 'wagons with a passenger coach'. Initially traffic volumes looked promising, climbing to 29,000 tons by 1872, and this level was generally sustained for another two years until 1874, when storm clouds began to gather for the Lostwithiel & Fowey Railway.

In July 1873 the Cornwall Minerals Railway Act had been passed whereby lines of the Treffry Tramway, broadly from Newquay on the north Cornwall coast to St Blazey and Par on the south coast (plus branches) would be joined and upgraded for use by locomotives. Plans included certain deviations to the existing route to eliminate a tunnel and an incline. An integral part of the plans was a new direct route from Par/St Blazey to Fowey. Joseph Thomas Treffry had considerable land holdings at Fowey and, as with the L&FR, the company wanted to develop not only Par Harbour but also the deep waters and potential facilities at Fowey (see the next chapter). The CMR opened to traffic on 1 June 1874, and with its far better access to many of the clay works than the L&FR the impact on the latter was immediate. By 1875 traffic from Lostwithiel to Fowey was less than 9,000 tons, a mere third of the 1874 figure and equivalent to only 36 tons per working day. There was an increase to just over 11,000 tons in 1877, but by the end of the decade the annual tonnage was a modest 8,000, reflecting not only the impact of the opposition but a downturn in the china clay industry.

The competition between the railways included a price war with each company successively undercutting the tariffs of the other, but the Cornwall Railway and the L&FR could not compete with the CMR and lost the financial battle. There was no money available for infrastructure expenditure and one of the small bridges over an inlet on the L&FR became unsafe resulting in the complete closure of the Lostwithiel to Fowey line on 31 December 1879. The broad gauge line then went into slumber for over 15 years. However, many developments took place prior to the closure and just after the reopening of the line in 1895. Those having the greatest impact were the GWR finally taking over the CR in 1889 (having had a majority interest from 1876), the

	PAR and FOWEY.			
	Down.	**Week Days only.**		
Miles	Par ....dep.			
	St. Blazey			
4½	Fowey (below). arr.			

	Up.	**Week Days only.**		
Miles			aft	
	Fowey..............dep. 9 50			
4	St. Blazey			
4½	Par 22, 27, above. arr. 10 8			

		LOSTWITHIEL, GOLANT, and FOWEY.			
	Down.	**Week Days only.**			
Miles		W mn mrn mrn aft aft aft aft aft			
...	Lostwithiel ...dep. 7 6 9 10 10 25 11 25 12 40 2 50 4 20 6 40 8 5 9 32				
3¾	Golant............ 7 15 9 20 10 35 11 35 12 50 3 0 4 30 6 50 8 15 9 42				
5¼	Fowey (above). arr. 7 20 9 25 10 40 11 40 12 55 3 5 4 35 6 55 8 20 9 47				

	Up.	**Week Days only.**			
Miles		mn mrn mrn non aft aft aft aft			
...	Fowey..............dep. 8 0 9 55 10 50 12 0 2 0 3 35 5 30 7 25 8 55				
1½	Golant............ 8 7 10 2 10 57 12 7 2 7 3 42 5 37 7 32 9 2				
5¼	Lostwithiel 22, 27, arr. 8 15 10 10 11 5 12 15 2 15 3 50 5 45 7 40 9 10				

w Workmen's Train.

Left:
These timetables compare the
Fowey branch service of January
1927 (above) with the summer
of 1958.

Tables 98–99

Table 98	LOSTWITHIEL and FOWEY				
	WEEK DAYS ONLY—(Second class only)				

Miles		am	am	am	am E	am S		pm S	pm E	pm S		pm S	pm S	pm	pm S		pm S
...	Lostwithiel ... ... dep	7 5	8 20	...	9 5	10 15	...	10 20	12 10	12 25	1 5	... 2 25	3 15	... 4 5	5 5	... 6 10	7 0 ... 8 10
3¾	Golant Halt	7 14	8 29	...	9 14	10 24	...	10 29	12 19	12 34	1 14	... 2 34	3 24	... 4 14	5 14	... 6 19	7 9 ... 8 19
5¼	Fowey ... ... arr	7 20	8 35	...	9 20	10 30	...	10 35	12 25	12 40	1 20	... 2 40	3 30	... 4 20	5 20	... 6 25	7 15 ... 8 25

Miles		am S	am E	am	am E	am S		pm S	pm E		pm S	pm S	pm E	pm S	pm E	pm S		pm S	pm S
...	Fowey ... ... dep	7 25	7 30	8 40	...	9 30	9 45	...	11 35	11 55	...	12 35	1 35	1 45	3 35	4 20	4 35	... 5 35	6 30 ... 7 25 9 5
1½	Golant Halt	7 30	7 35	8 45	...	9 35	9 50	...	11 40	12 0	...	12 40	1 40	1 50	3 40	4 25	4 40	... 5 40	6 35 ... 7 30 9 10
5¼	Lostwithiel ... ... arr	7 40	7 45	8 55	...	9 45	10 0	...	11 50	12 10	...	12 50	1 50	2 0	3 50	4 35	4 50	... 5 50	6 45 ... 7 40 9 20

E Except Saturdays   S Saturdays only

Right:
Lostwithiel was a significant location for the Cornwall Railway (CR) when it opened from Plymouth to Truro in 1859, with both offices and workshops in the ancient town. In 1869 a broad gauge branch was built from Lostwithiel to Carne Point, Fowey, to take advantage of the deepwater port there. The freight-only line opened on 1 October 1869 but due to competition from the Cornwall Minerals Railway (CMR) and the lack of funds for maintenance it closed at the end of 1879. However, under the control of the GWR the route reopened as a standard gauge passenger and freight branch in 1895. In this vintage view of the transitional steam to diesel age North British large 'Warship' No D601 *Ark Royal* heads a down main line train into Lostwithiel in July 1959, while '1400' class 0-4-2T No 1419 waits in the bay platform with the Fowey branch train.
P. Q. Treloar

Lower right:
A 'Metro' 2-4-0T and clerestory coach on a Fowey branch train dates this photograph at Lostwithiel, which was taken on 23 May 1922. The down station buildings were demolished in 1976 and the up buildings in 1981. In 1923 over 59,000 tickets were sold at Fowey station; however, in the long run bus competition took its toll and in later years residents were more likely to want to travel to St Austell than Lostwithiel to shop. *JV collection*

Above:
With part of the old CR buildings in the background (at the southwest end of Lostwithiel station) Railfreight Class 37 No 37670 runs 'wrong line' into the station area, having just come off the Fowey branch with empty CDA wagons for Goonbarrow Junction on 16 June 1989. The down yard seems to be devoid of wagons, while at the end of the down platform can be seen the starting signals for the main line (right) and the Fowey branch (left). *JV*

change of the main line gauge from broad to standard in 1892, and the GWR taking over the entire Cornwall Minerals Railway, by a 999-year lease in 1877 and outright purchase in July 1896.

At Fowey the two lines from Lostwithiel and Par respectively had never been connected, but in 1895, after the GWR takeovers mentioned above, the entire Lostwithiel to Fowey line was rebuilt to standard gauge and extended to Fowey to connect with the CMR line, and a passenger service was introduced. The line reopened on 16 September 1895, affording Fowey two passenger routes. During the years of closure of the L&FR line the docks at Fowey had never been busier. As a result cargo-handling capacity had to be increased and this was done by linking the two lines and improving the jetties. In the late 1880s the average annual tonnage of china clay handled by Fowey was 110,000, followed by Par at 85,000 tons, Charlestown 55,000 tons, Pentewan 20,000 tons, Newquay 4,000 tons and lesser amounts from other Cornish ports.

By 1896 Fowey was handling 263,000 tons, with seven jetties available to shipping, and the intermediate station of Golant had been opened. Many other improvements to Fowey Docks were made by the GWR such as extending in length the three original L&FR jetties and equipping one former CMR jetty with an elevator and conveyor belt using electricity from a purpose-built generating station. Shipments peaked at nearly 600,000 tons before World War 1, but at the end of the war in 1918 volumes had fallen to 400,000 tons. Slowly business recovered and in 1923 the GWR built an eighth jetty. There had been two signalboxes at

Carne Point but in 1925 one was replaced by a more modern example located on the east (river) side of the sidings at the north (Lostwithiel) end. By 1937 tonnage had increased to 730,000 tons, but this figure was more than halved by the events surrounding World War 2. From 558,000 tons in 1956 business boomed and by the end of the century shipments from Fowey exceeded 800,000 tons.

Although mineral traffic was the primary purpose of the branch, with a population of about 2,300 persons the ancient town of Fowey was deserving of a passenger service. Between 1869 and 1879 the L&FR line was freight only and it was not until 1874, when the CMR arrived from the Par direction, that locals could 'ride the train', then from the date of reopening a passenger service was provided between Lostwithiel and Fowey. As mentioned above, there was only a single intermediate station between the towns, at the small village of Golant, 3¾ miles from Lostwithiel; this became Golant Halt in September 1955. The 5¼-mile branch had a reasonable service, which was gradually increased over the years. For example, there were three up and three down workings on opening in 1895, five return workings in 1910 and 10 in 1927, and by 1938 this had grown to 13; also in 1938 there was a summer Sunday service with no fewer than nine workings each way. The journey time was 15 minutes in each direction.

The timetable for October 1935 was slightly discouraging because the best overall timing between London Paddington and

Fowey was off the 10.30am departure that resulted in an arrival in Fowey at 4.2pm. However, beside the arrival time was a letter 't', and this was explained in the small print as being 'by road motor from Par, heavy luggage not conveyed'. The best time for a complete journey by rail, changing at Lostwithiel, was 6¼ hours, off the noon departure from Paddington. In the early days rakes of up to five or six small-capacity passenger coaches worked the branch hauled by a variety of tank locomotives. Increasingly from the 1930s the service ran in push-pull mode with a variety of auto-trailers but this was never exclusively the case and on some days, almost to the end of steam, locomotives would run round their one- or two-carriage trains.

In the early days 'Metro' and '3581' 2-4-0T classes worked the passenger trains. These were replaced in turn by '1400/5800' 0-4-2T and '4500' 2-6-2T Prairie types. Use of the Collett 0-4-2Ts was uncommon in Cornwall because most other branches were steeply graded, much longer than the Fowey line and several had long through trains in summer, while the relatively level track along the banks of the River Fowey ideally suited the '1400s'. In the early 1960s DMUs were used on the line, mostly single cars. Over 45,000 tickets were sold at Fowey station in 1903 and by 1923 this had swollen to over 59,000; some of these were for the ex-CMR St Blazey/Par route but traffic on that line was sparse and it substantially closed in 1925 (see the next chapter). By the end of the 1920s improved local road transport began to make inroads into the railway's receipts and by 1933 the number of tickets issued had shrunk to less than 34,000.

The line was closed for seven months during World War 1 and on three occasions during World War 2, the last time being five months in 1944. However, those periods of closure were insignificant compared with the events of the 1960s when, on 2 January 1965, the line closed to passengers completely, depriving Fowey of a passenger rail service. It would have been interesting to see the detailed accounting processes that resulted in closure. With the line well used for china clay trains the cost of running the passenger service should have been marginal. However, on the basis of the rules then extant it was a loss-maker, Fowey was well served by buses, especially to Par and St Austell, and after 70 years the service was withdrawn. On the last day of service a two-car DMU shuttled backwards and forwards.

The line has been regularly featured in the itineraries of railway enthusiasts' specials, which normally stop short of Fowey Docks and are usually 'topped and tailed' to avoid a run-round. There was an interesting development during 1994-5 when the Lostwithiel Chamber of Commerce sponsored the running of four round trip services along the scenic line on four summer Sundays. Two-car Class 150/2s were used and proved generally popular, but a change in BR's cost/profit centre structure in 1996 resulted in significant increases in costs, so the successful experiment was not subsequently repeated.

Other than for the substantial volumes of clay traffic Fowey was not a great centre for freight. Over the years general goods forwarded barely reached the 2,000-ton level compared with, for example, incoming general goods, coal and coke of nearly 2,000 tons in 1903, over 3,000 tons in 1923 and 2,500 tons in 1933. However, prior to World War 1 parcels traffic was impressive, with over 22,000 items being forwarded. By 1933 this had fallen to 19,000. After passenger services were withdrawn in 1965 all non-china clay freight traffic ceased.

On leaving Lostwithiel the Fowey branch once had its own dedicated line from the station's down bay platform whereby the branch trains could run up and down without affecting main line movements. However, the track layout was rationalised in November 1972 when the junction was moved 13 chains to the west. From that date one section of the bridge over the River Fowey became disused and clay trains for Fowey had briefly to join the down main line to either gain or leave the branch. China clay trains now leave for Carne Point, Fowey, either from the down sidings or from the loops on the up side of the station complex and via the main line. A happy reminder of yesteryear is the lower quadrant semaphore signalling that even in 2002 still controls movements around the station area and on to the branch.

After crossing the Fowey the single line branch heads south and takes a course that broadly follows the river. The main line runs parallel with the branch for about a mile but as it climbs towards Milltown and Treverrin this is not immediately apparent. Across the river can be seen the delightful hamlet and ancient church at St Winnow, then the small estuary to Lerryn. The line clings to the ledge at the foot of the gentle hills on the west side of the river for nearly 4 miles before the small harbour and village of Golant comes into view. As mentioned before, a small halt here was the only intermediate station. All trains slow for a minor road access to the river, used mainly by the yachting community, after which the line crosses another tidal inlet before reaching Carne Point.

Right:
Hugging the banks of the River Fowey, having just passed one of the public parks in Lostwithiel, Class 50 No 50043 *Eagle* makes for Carne Point, Fowey, with a long rake of empty 'clay hoods' on 23 April 1987. It was always an immense pleasure to see these 100mph express passenger locomotives working clay trains on branches, which normally occurred when they were being run-in after repair at Plymouth's Laira depot. The main line can just be seen above the wagons. *JV*

Right:
Except for the village of Golant the Fowey branch is fairly inaccessible by metalled road. The track crosses the tiny harbour on a purpose-built causeway and the views can be spectacular, such as this scene of grey Railfreight-liveried Class 37 No 37196 trundling down to the docks at Carne Point with a rake of 'clay hoods' on 3 April 1986. The River Fowey can be seen in the background but in the harbour the tide is out. *JV*

Above:
This is the junction at Lostwithiel with the main line climbing up to Treverrin Tunnel on the left and the broadly level branch down to Fowey in the foreground. Ambling south on 8 August 1959 is '4575' series '4500' class push-pull-fitted Prairie No 5572 (now preserved) with the 5.5pm train from Lostwithiel. In the early days of steam the line was worked by railmotors, and in later years auto-trains operating in push-pull mode were the norm. *Peter Gray*

Below:
One of the most delightful and tranquil spots in the whole of Cornwall is the hamlet of St Winnow. On a still sunny morning with a high tide the view of the Fowey branch across the river is superb. From the back of the ancient cemetery and with the aid of a medium focal length telephoto lens, refurbished Hunslet-Barclay Class 20/9 No 20901 is seen heading the annual Chipman's weedkilling train towards Lostwithiel on 8 April 1989. *JV*

Left:
The only intermediate station on the line was a small halt at Golant, which opened in 1896. There were three round trip workings per day between Lostwithiel and Fowey in 1895 and this had grown to 13 workings by 1938. However, by the end of the 1950s passenger loadings declined and like so many other branch lines it succumbed on 2 January 1965. Passing the site of the long demolished halt, at the south end of the little harbour, in June 1997 is No 37671 with down clay empties. The road is a boat ramp that drops down to river level. *JV*

The English China Clay Company leased the whole of the dock complex from BR in 1968, after passenger services ceased, and accordingly the area beyond the Carne Point stop board is now private property. Although now controlled by a ground frame, until 1954 the comprehensive sidings were controlled by a signalbox at the north end of the complex, which had, in turn, replaced an earlier one in 1925. The line then continued past a thriving dock area with, at various times, up to eight jetties in use, the eighth having been constructed in 1923. In 1950 jetties Nos 5 and 6 were closed and in 1962 jetty No 7 was reduced. In 1968, under the ownership of ECC, there was a complete modernisation of the docks area that resulted in a reduction to four well-equipped operational jetties, three for use by road and rail and one used for loading china clay in slurry form. A 22,000-ton bulk store was built and all jetties were equipped with modern loading equipment with a capacity of about 1,000 tons per hour. Further changes were made in 1987-8 to cater for new hopper wagons, the old wooden-bodied 'clay hoods' having finally been retired in February 1988.

The line continued through a 90° bend to reach Fowey station. Just before reaching the station on the land side of the line was a steeply graded track to the China Clay Company's generating station. The GWR greatly expanded the station site and the track layout, compared to the former CMR installation, with two through platforms, a 'centre road' and a bay platform at the west (St Blazey) end. There was a signalbox on the down platform at the Lostwithiel end of the station. An imposing footbridge of standard GWR pattern once connected the platforms but the third platform line became a siding in 1936 when buffer stops were erected at the west end, and the line was lifted altogether in 1951. The old up platform was removed and the footbridge demolished. There was originally a goods shed at the Lostwithiel end of the station but it was the general goods yard at the St Blazey end that latterly boasted an operational goods shed; this yard was lifted in July 1965. The entire Fowey station site was razed in 1968 when the line to St Blazey and Par closed and was converted to a private road for the exclusive use of ECC lorries carrying china clay to the docks.

After the steam engine disappeared from the scene, the withdrawal of passenger services and the closure of the St Blazey line, clay trains continued to use the old L&FR line. All classes of diesel locomotive associated with the Cornish freight scene have headed trains on the line including Classes 22, 25, 37, 42, 43 ('Warships'), 45, 46, 47, 50, 52 and 66. Class 08 and 10 shunters have been used for dock shunting at Carne Point and there were once plans to use a Class 09 to shuttle clay trains along the branch. Traffic volumes vary according to demand, which can include not only customer needs but also weather in the English Channel. Traffic once originated from scores of small clay driers but in today's rationalised world the china clay originates at various points on the Drinnick Mill branch, Rocks driers on the Newquay line, and Marsh Mills near Tavistock Junction in Devon. There are about four round trip workings per day to Carne Point. On occasions, locomotives taking wagons to Carne Point wait for unloading then work the empties back to the various clay works, but on other occasions they return 'light engine'. The best places to watch the trains are in the public park south of Lostwithiel, across the river from St Winnow or at Golant. At the latter location the garden of the Fisherman's Arms public house gives excellent views of the little harbour and the railway!

The branch is alive and well and even though there has been a recent slight downturn in the industry, over three-quarters of a million tons of china clay still rumble down the branch every year.

Left:
The Fisherman's Arms at Golant (once known as the New Inn) on the left has a beer garden where one can enjoy a pint and watch the occasional china clay train running to and from Carne Point. Although it has remained open for freight, the line closed to passengers in 1965, but during 1994-5 the Lostwithiel Chamber of Commerce sponsored passenger trains over the branch on a handful of summer Sundays. Sadly increasing costs nipped this enterprise in the bud, and on the last day of service, 24 September 1995, Class 150/2 unit No 150239 forms the very last working towards Carne Point. Passengers were not allowed to alight there. *JV*

Right:
Postcard fairs can be rewarding
at times and the author purchased
this local gem for the princely
sum of £3.50, which gives a
fascinating insight into turn of the
century operation just a few yards
north of Fowey station. In the left
foreground is jetty No 2 with twin
wagon turntables. Beyond, at jetty
No 1, sailing vessels are being
loaded with china clay. On the
right casks (barrels) of clay wait
to be loaded from four-wheeled
wagons. At this time clay arrived
from both the Lostwithiel and
St Blazey directions. *JV collection*

Left:
In the early days horses executed
all shunting at Fowey docks with
locomotives delivering wagons to
the jetties. However, in later years
there was a resident locomotive at
Carne Point and from 1968, when
English China Clays (ECC) took
over the entire dock area, the
company used Class 10 and
later Class 08 diesel shunters.
On 9 April 1990 a ship from
Lübeck, Germany, is being loaded
with china clay while Railfreight
Class 08 No 08954 has just
finished positioning some CDA
wagons over the discharge point.
JV

Right:
Although the impressive sounding
Class 37s and the clanking 'clay
hoods' have now gone, the
modern scene still has much to
commend it when viewed in
surroundings such as this.
Whispering away from Golant at
low tide with quiet roller-bearing
CDA wagons on Monday
3 September 2001 is General
Motors Class 66 No 66141. The
securely tethered boat in the
foreground is called *Free Spirit!*
JV

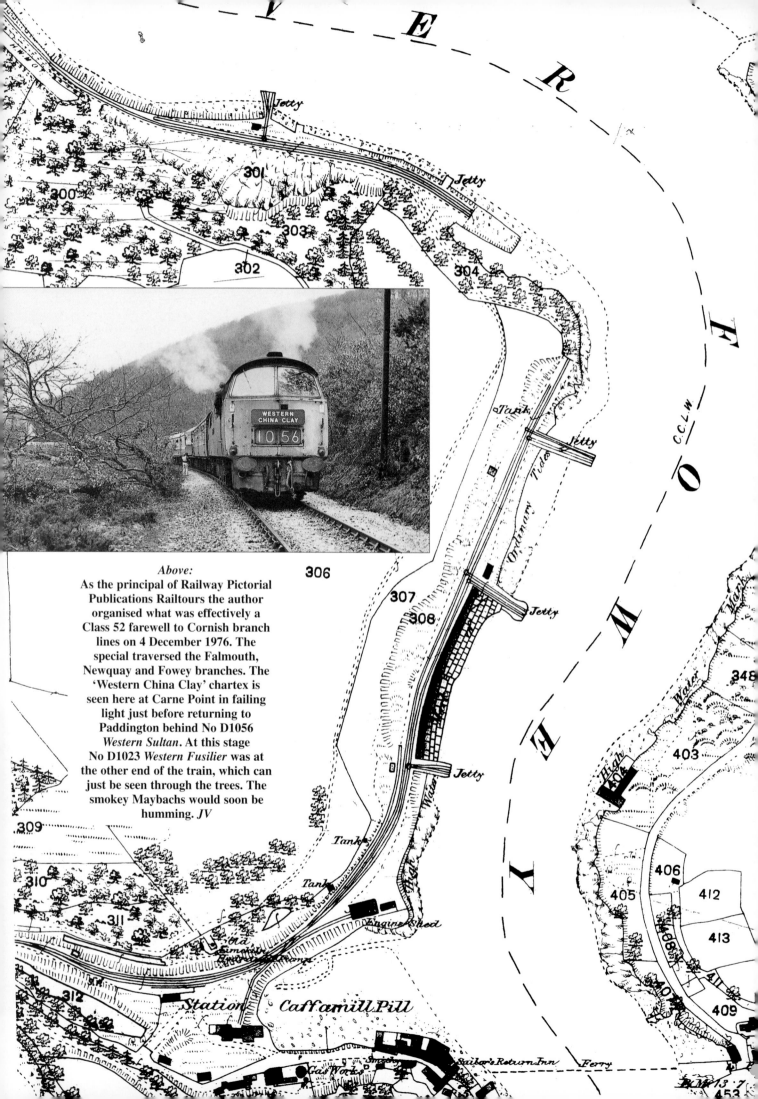

Above:
As the principal of Railway Pictorial Publications Railtours the author organised what was effectively a Class 52 farewell to Cornish branch lines on 4 December 1976. The special traversed the Falmouth, Newquay and Fowey branches. The 'Western China Clay' chartex is seen here at Carne Point in failing light just before returning to Paddington behind No D1056 *Western Sultan*. At this stage No D1023 *Western Fusilier* was at the other end of the train, which can just be seen through the trees. The smokey Maybachs would soon be humming. *JV*

Left:
This ancient Ordnance Survey first edition 1878 view of the deepwater port of Fowey shows the original 1869 broad gauge Lostwithiel & Fowey Railway (later GWR) line from Lostwithiel (top) unconnected to the Cornwall Minerals Railway (later GWR) 1874 line from St Blazey (bottom). The former line closed between 1879 and 1895, when the GWR reopened it as a standard gauge line and connected it with the St Blazey route. The docks were greatly enlarged by the GWR in 1923 and much modernised by the English China Clay Company in 1968. Passenger services from Lostwithiel were withdrawn in 1965 and in 1968 the St Blazey line closed and was converted to a road for the exclusive use of ECC lorries conveying china clay for loading. At its peak Fowey had eight loading jetties. *Crown Copyright*

Above right:
A typical GWR push-pull auto-trailer, No W130, with a 'Fowey' carriage board on the side and hauled by '1400' class 0-4-2T No 1419, leaves Fowey for Lostwithiel in May 1950. In the left background '4200' class 2-8-0T No 4298 is about to depart for St Blazey over the CMR route with empty wagons. On the right, across the River Fowey, is Bodinnick, which is served by a ferry from Fowey. *B. A. Butt*

Centre right:
A pleasant study of Fowey station on 14 June 1958 finds No 1419 quietly simmering after arrival from Lostwithiel with an auto-train. Note the decorative bargeboards and the down bay platform. The entire Fowey station site, including station, signalbox and all trackwork was razed in 1968 and all of this is now but a memory. *David Lawrence*

Lower right:
Early morning at Fowey in 1963 finds one of the large A1A-A1A 2,000hp 117-ton North British 'Warships', No D600 *Active*, relegated to china clay duties. The green machine with small yellow warning panel is coming off the line from St Blazey and making for Carne Point. The station once had two through platforms with a centre road, but even at this date rationalisation had taken place. *JV collection*

12. St Blazey to Par Harbour and Fowey

The ancient town of Fowey was a major naval base back in the 14th century, at which time naval history shows that over 700 sailors in 29 ships were dispatched from the port to take part in operations off Scotland and France. Over the centuries the town increased in importance as a port but it was somewhat restricted in transportation terms, being accessible only to packhorses and later wagons. One of the prominent landowners in the area was Joseph Thomas Treffry. He recognised the full potential of Fowey and in 1811 invested a considerable sum of money in building a new quay on the waterfront. However, the full potential could only be exploited if a railway was built, so in 1825 he planned one, but another powerful local family, the Rashleighs, who owned the rival port of Charlestown, would not allow him to build a railway across their land between Par and Fowey.

Treffry had many mining interests and he started building a tramway system between Ponts Mill, north of St Blazey, to the quarries near Luxulyan and the clay works and mines in the Bugle area. He was also active in the Newquay area with tramways from Newquay Harbour, which he purchased in 1838, to East Wheal Rose and to St Dennis and Hendra, thus serving both mines and clay works. The Treffry Tramways are described in more detail in the next chapter. The resourceful Treffry had also purchased 35 acres of land near Par in 1828 with the intention of building a large but entirely artificial harbour. After constructing a 1,200ft-long breakwater and associated wharves, Par Harbour received its first commercial vessel in 1833. Treffry also built a canal from Par Harbour to Ponts Mill, the terminus of his tramway, where all incoming and outgoing loads had to be transhipped from wagons to canal boats or vice versa. Treffry must have been very

frustrated in owning chunks of both Fowey and Par harbours but not having a rail connection between the two.

As will be explained in Chapter 13, following Treffry's death in 1850 the tramways lingered on until in 1872 an agreement was reached between the trustees of his estate and William Richardson Roebuck, an entrepreneur from London, to lease the lines, docks and harbours formerly owned by Treffry. The company headed by Roebuck was to become the Cornwall Minerals Railway and an Act of Parliament was duly passed on 21 July 1873. The Treffry Tramways were to be rebuilt with some realignment, 'missing' sections were to be joined up and a new line was to be constructed from the Par/St Blazey complex to the docks at Fowey. The objective was to join Fowey on the south Cornish coast with Newquay (and branches) on the north coast by a standard gauge railway line built to a standard that would support locomotive-hauled trains throughout. Work started immediately, although formidable earthworks would be necessary between St Blazey and Fowey (and in the Luxulyan Valley).

One of the obstacles to rapid progress on the line was the need for a 1,173yd tunnel at Pinnock, which was to become the longest tunnel in the county of Cornwall. To facilitate the arrival of the line from Par the CMR built three brand-new jetties at Fowey for the shipment of china clay and other minerals by sea. By February 1874 the western end of the line was all but finished, with track laid to the mouth of Pinnock Tunnel but with road bridge girders at Polmear, near Par Sands, awaited. The river and canal crossing at Par had been completed. On the eastern side of the tunnel blasting through the granite to complete it and its associated deep cuttings was well under way and progress was on target. The line

Left:
The CMR opened the line from St Blazey to Fowey in 1874 and passenger services started two years later, but loadings were never heavy and services were withdrawn in 1925. For many years the GWR heavy freight 2-8-0Ts and to a lesser extent 2-8-2Ts were regular performers on the line and on 10 August 1956 it is No 4247 that is starting its slog up to the 1,173yd Pinnock Tunnel with empties. *Les Elsey*

Above:
Steam trains running from St Blazey to Fowey always worked bunker first with the chimney behind the train crew, otherwise with a loaded train the locomotive's exhaust could cause footplate crew asphyxiation in the confines of Pinnock Tunnel. Having descended from Pinnock Tunnel and passing the campers on Par beach on 7 August 1956, 2-6-2T No 4526, is making for St Blazey yard. *Les Elsey*

was steeply graded, being 1 in 36/40 from Fowey to the tunnel and 1 in 49 from the tunnel down to Par Sands. A 'light' locomotive traversed the entire line on 27 April 1874, and in time for the grand opening on 11 June 1874 a stationmaster was appointed at Fowey and Par CMR (St Blazey), and certain other stations. From that date Fowey Docks was served by two unconnected railways, the L&FR from Lostwithiel and the CMR from Par/St Blazey.

Roebuck was extremely unlucky with the timing of his railway enterprise in that the storm clouds of recession were already looming, with big reductions in the prices the mine and pit owners could expect for their minerals, partly caused by significant over-production in the china clay industry between 1870 and 1873. By 1875 Roebuck and the CMR were struggling financially. His outlay had not only been for expensive railway construction but for 18 locomotives and eight steam cargo vessels. Sir Morton Peto, the contractor who had invested heavily in the CMR, was ruined financially. In an almost desperate attempt to increase income the CMR instigated a passenger service between Fowey and Newquay in 1876, for which it had purchased some bargain-basement, probably ex-Midland Railway, four-wheeled coaches, comprising three 3rd Class and three Composites. There were no intermediate stations between Fowey and Par CMR (St Blazey). The initial service was two trains per day between Fowey and Newquay; services left Newquay at 6.45am and 4.15pm, returning from Fowey at 8.20am and 7.15pm, the journey taking about 1½ hours for the 26 miles!

The passenger service made little impact on the CMR finances and in the areas served by the railway pits and mines were closing with alarming frequency (see the next chapter). The crunch had to come and in 1877 Roebuck approached the GWR in an attempt to rescue the ailing CMR. By an agreement dated 30 April 1877 the GWR undertook to work the whole CMR network for a term of 999 years. In January 1879 the CMR station at Par (effectively St Blazey) was officially renamed St Blazey and in July a standard gauge double-track connection between the main line station of Par and St Blazey was constructed. The main line was of course broad gauge at this time, so both passengers and freight had to change and be transferred at Par, and a large goods transfer shed was built for the purpose. From this time passengers travelling on the CMR could book through to any GWR station and vice versa.

After the 1875 crisis the fortunes of the line improved when, by 1885, china clay and china stone production had doubled, resulting in additional freight traffic for the hard-pressed line. Bradshaw's guide of 1888 shows that there were four down and five up trains between Fowey and St Blazey (and three through trains from Par/St Blazey to Newquay). By 1910 there were still five passenger trains in each direction over the 4 miles from Fowey to St Blazey and Par.

GWR rolling stock had begun to appear on the line in the 1880s and gradually the little CMR 0-6-0 tank engines were replaced (see the next chapter). In the meantime in 1895 the Lostwithiel & Fowey Railway had reopened to freight and a passenger service had been provided, giving the residents of Fowey the choice of two rail routes (see Chapter 11). Passenger traffic on the Fowey to St Blazey/Par line was never heavy and the introduction of frequent local omnibus services resulted in the GWR withdrawing passenger services on 8 July 1925. However, there was still a requirement for a single workman's train in each direction, which was provided until the end of 1934.

As mentioned before, the port of Par received its first commercial vessel over 40 years before the CMR connected Ponts Mill with St Blazey, the port of Par and Fowey. In the early days there was a variety of minerals shipped from the port but this considerably dwindled towards the end of the 19th century when many of the mines and quarries closed. The port of Par then became a significant centre for drying and shipping china clay, the volume of which had hugely increased after the opening of the Treffry Tramways; in 1855 some 15,000 tons of china clay left the port and within five years this figure had doubled. Business was booming — 44,000 tons of china clay left the port in 1865 and by 1870 the gross tonnage was 52,000. The over-production of china clay combined with a downturn in the business resulted in a considerable slowing in traffic volumes between 1875 and 1877, but by the late 1880s the crisis had passed and totals reached 85,000 tons per annum.

There could have been much commercial rivalry between Par and Fowey but they adopted different roles, the deep-water port at Fowey handling large ocean-going, long-haul ships while the tidal Par Harbour served small coasters on short-haul runs to other UK ports and cross-Channel destinations. Although most of the china clay arrived from the Hensbarrow Downs area, a series of

Left:
The line was steeply graded, being 1 in 36/40 from Fowey up to the tunnel and 1 in 49 down to level track at Par Sands. The gradient is very obvious in this photograph of Class 22 No D6342 on 9 May 1963 leaving Pinnock Tunnel with empties from Fowey. These locomotives had a short life: introduced in 1962, D6342 was withdrawn just six years later. In 1968 the entire line was converted from a railway to a roadway for the exclusive use of ECC lorries. *Carey Batchelor*

Centre left:
Towards the end of the line was the Par Harbour complex, a massive clay drying installation and distribution point with its own internal, standard gauge railway network. Over the years the clay company had a curious collection of motive power but there was nothing stranger than *Punch*, a primitive vertical-boilered locomotive that was converted in about 1936 by Sara & Burgess of Penryn from a more conventional 1879 Manning Wardle saddle tank. Photographed on 13 July 1938, *Punch* was scrapped in 1944. *Rev Wake, SLS*

Lower left:
Another locomotive owned by Treffry Estates Ltd, who owned Par Harbour, was an 0-4-0 Sentinel called *Toby*. This small locomotive was built in 1927 and had a vertical boiler and (geared) chain drive to the wheels, instead of the usual coupling rods. The locomotive seems to have been replaced by the arrival of two Bagnall 0-4-0 saddle tanks in 1937 and 1953. *JV collection*

Right:
Par Harbour received its first commercial vessel in 1833 and was fully operational in 1840. From 1835 it received minerals for export via a canal from Ponts Mill, where the output from Fowey Consols mine was loaded. The harbour has always been tidal. In this old Dalby-Smith local postcard at least 10 barques and schooners are berthed in the harbour. Wagons are on the quayside, one of which is being loaded from a horse and cart, and on the right there appears to be a 'clay hood', decades ahead of its time! *JV collection*

Par Harbour, Cornwall.
by S. Dalby-Smith, Mevagissey.

Left:
Alfred, one of the famous Bagnall 0-4-0 saddle tanks with cut-down cabs, was specially designed to allow a 7ft 6in overhead clearance so that it could pass beneath low bridges on the harbour railway system. In this scene at Par Harbour *Alfred* is scarcely higher than the clay wagons it is hauling. The main line is just above the cab roof and in the background clay is being dried on the Par Moor complex, now abandoned. *R. C. Riley, The Transport Treasury*

Right:
The harbour rail system has been hugely rationalised and now just a simple single track runs down from Par Bridge, near St Blazey, to the docks, where an adapted tractor does any shunting. In the early 1990s equipment for loading clay in slurry form was installed, and on 20 April 1993 Class 08 No 08955 propels three bogie tankers into the docks for loading. *JV*

clay dries were located just a few hundred yards from the harbour in the Par Moor complex, and most were served by rail from the sidings at Par Harbour. The spur ran under the main line via a very low bridge that required the resident shunting locomotives to have compact dimensions and cut-down cabs, resulting in locomotives no higher than the wagons they hauled, or in other words 'horse height'. This spur crossed the main coastal road to reach the series of dries.

Another aspect of china clay transportation that became increasingly important over the years, to the detriment of rail-borne volumes, was pipeline technology. This enabled the clay producers to pipe the clay in liquid slurry form from their primary works to remote drying plants, thus saving the need for a drying facility at every clay works. Clay could be piped several miles using a combination of pumps and gravity, a situation helped by the topography, with most of the works being on higher ground than the Par plant. Some of the clay was and still is piped from works over 11 miles away. The Par drying plant is still working 24 hours a day, seven days a week, and steam can be seen rising from its chimneys every hour of the day and night. In years gone by it is said that everything in the surrounding area was covered in a white dust. Par once had a large smelter and brickworks but they have now been consigned to the annals of history.

Volumes continued to increase at Par and while throughput could not be compared to Fowey, by 1933 shipments totalled over 100,000 tons. Much of the clay dried at Par was shipped from Fowey so shipping volumes are not the only indicators of total activity. By this time Par was handling 2,000-ton coasters and had come a long way from the days of the 50-ton wooden schooners. After World War 2 the English China Clay Company (ECC), which by then had absorbed hundreds of minor clay companies, took a 999-year lease on Par Harbour and over the subsequent years spent much money improving facilities. A total of 10 modern berths were built, the largest 280ft in length. All were constructed of concrete and modern loading equipment was provided. In 1964 ECC purchased the port outright and by 1965 1,500 vessels were loaded during the year.

There were two points of rail access into Par Harbour, one from St Blazey, which branched off the CMR Fowey line, and the other directly from the main line to the west end of the harbour area; the latter closed in 1965. There was a very comprehensive rail network within the harbour, with lines serving most quays and a number of large storage sheds, the largest of which was the 'Cambrian store'. This rail complex saw a number of interesting locomotives working its lines over the years. There was an old 1879 Manning Wardle 0-4-0ST called *Punch*, which was rebuilt with a vertical boiler in 1936, a 1927-built Sentinel called *Toby*, and, most famous of all, two Bagnall 0-4-0STs with cut-down cabs: No 2572 *Judy* of 1937 and No 3058 *Alfred* of 1953. This pair worked the lines for many years and happily both have been preserved. Other shunters worked in the harbour from time to time and most GWR/BR tank engine classes associated with the area delivered and collected wagons from the harbour sidings. However, once the domestic fleet was withdrawn in the early 1970s most of the internal complex was lifted and from that time a Class 08 shunter worked from St Blazey to some exchange sidings about once a day. Within the harbour a road-going tractor was and still is used to move a wagon or two into bagged china clay loading sheds.

At Fowey it was normally the locomotives that worked in from either Lostwithiel or St Blazey that were used for shunting along the jetties and in the many sidings, while horses were used on the actual jetties between the main branch and the loading point (see photographs). As mentioned earlier, the line from St Blazey was very steep and steam locomotives would normally work bunker-first so that the crews were in front of the chimney and avoided the potentially asphyxiating smoke and steam as they blasted up the climb to Pinnock Tunnel (which had only one ventilator shaft)

with a full load. For many years heavy GWR '4200' class 2-8-0T and '7200' class 2-8-2T types were used on the line because their superior tractive effort over the domestic panniers and Prairies could be put to good use. Smaller classes of steam locomotive were of course used on the line but with a correspondingly lower payload. After steam ended in 1964 and until 1968 Class 22, 41 and 42 diesels were used.

When returning from Fowey with empty wagons the locomotive would of course be chimney-first. The engine still had to work hard for the mile up to the diminutive Pinnock signalbox but once through the tunnel it was downhill all the way. The small 6-lever Pinnock signalbox, which opened in January 1908 and closed finally in 1958, is said to have finished up as a BR painters' shop at Par. Trains used to stop at the east entrance to the tunnel on the down run to have their brakes pinned down. There was a further stop board at the west end. The tunnel was bored through solid granite and, as already mentioned, was the longest in Cornwall. The single line then curved its way down to Polmear and Par Sands where in the summer holidaymakers and caravanners would wave to passing trains. At Par Sands trains again stopped to have their brakes picked up. The line then approached the Par Harbour branch and curved northwards to pass underneath the main line. The approach to Par Bridge crossing was controlled by the signals of Par Bridge signalbox, which closed with the line on 6 October 1968. The Fowey line and the Harbour branch converged just before the road crossing. Although the box has gone, the actual crossing survives for use by the daily, or so, train to Par Harbour. The crossing is still controlled by gates, operated manually by the train crew, a true anachronism in this day and age and one worth observing if you are lucky enough to find a train.

During the mid-1960s British Railways and ECC commenced discussions about the future developments at Par and Fowey. Significant capital was required to update the facilities at Fowey (as detailed earlier), which included a much-needed improvement to road access. Narrow Cornish lanes and 38-ton lorries carrying china clay were not an ideal mix but BR was desperate to secure long-term contracts with ECC for the conveyance of china clay by rail. As a result of these negotiations ECC made minimum annual tonnage guarantees to BR, and BR agreed to close the direct line from St Blazey to Fowey, which would be converted into a private road for the exclusive use of ECC lorries. This arrangement made sense because BR would still have access to Fowey Docks via Lostwithiel and to Par Harbour from St Blazey, and it would then not have the expense of maintaining the 3.2 miles of steeply graded track that ran from Par Bridge to Fowey. ECC would fund the conversion. Accordingly the old CMR line closed in October 1968 and work on the conversion started immediately. Five bridges and 13 overpasses needed attention, cuttings had to be widened to provide a two-lane road, a new bridge over the Fowey road at Polmear was needed and traffic lights had be provided for the single-road Pinnock Tunnel. In total 18,000 tons of hardcore and 15,000 tons of tarmacadam were used in the conversion, which was an unqualified success.

The St Blazey to Fowey line is a strange one to reflect on because passenger services ended so long ago that few anecdotes survive and despite extensive research not a single photograph of a pre-1925 passenger train on this stretch of line emerged. The nine years after closure to passengers are a bit of a mystery as one imagines the unadvertised early morning workman's train emerging from Pinnock Tunnel with old carriages and dim lighting in the winter's gloom — what an experience that must have been! For many years the only recollection for many will have been hard-working steam locomotives thrashing up to the tunnel with loads or clanking down with empties, ahead of a rake of squealing white wagons with their brakes pinned down. Whatever, the line served a useful purpose in the development of Fowey Docks and to that extent it is an important part of Cornwall's railway history.

Above:
The main railway entrance to Par Harbour was from a junction with the Fowey to St Blazey line just south of Par Bridge but there was also access from the west. Here the west end siding is in the foreground while on the main line 'Hall' class 4-6-0 No 7916 *Mobberley Hall* moves briskly away from Par with a down express.
R. C. Riley, The Transport Treasury

Sheet 1032

474 578

578

579

Stone

78

S.P.

482

Stone

480

481 Stone

St. Blazey Station
521 Stone

580

532

526

525

Signal Box

Goods Shed

race
522

523

Quarry
524

Old Shaft

Consols Mine
(in disused)

565

568

564

Old Shaft

567

566

617 Old Shaft

619

Foot Bridge

618

620 621

628

622

629 Chimney

625 Methodist Chapel

581

583

1569

GREAT WESTERN RAILWAY

LOOP LINE

589

S.P.

588

590

634

Sluice
Foot Bridge

634

632 631

633

630

630

592

594 595

593

Methodist Chapel
(Wesleyan)
598

Cornwall Minerals Railway.

PENZANCE AND PLYMOUTH TO NEWQUAY AND FOWEY.

		WEEK DAYS.						SUNDAYS.	
	1	2	3	4	5	6	1	2
	1 3	1 2 3		1 2			1 2 3	
	A.M.	A.M.		P.M.			A.M.	
PENZANCE ...de.		7 0		3 50	...	...	6 50	
Falmouth		7 25		4 35	...	...	7 30	
Truro		8 6		5 16	...	...	8 12	
PAR ......ar.		8 50		5 57	...	...	8 56	
				1 2 3				
PLYMOUTH ....d.		6 50		3 20	...	...		
PAR ....ar.		8 28		5 0	...	...		
	1 3	1 3		1 3			1 3	1 3
	A.M.	A.M.		P.M.			A.M.	P.M.
FOWEY ......de.	7 45	8 45	5 10	7 10	...	...	9 5	8 5
PAR ....ar.	8 0	9 0	5 25	7 25	...	...	9 20	8 15
PAR (Saint Blazey) ...d.		9 5		8 15	...	...	9 25	
Bridges		9 20		8 30	...	...	9 40	
Bugle		9 25		8 35	...	...	9 45	
Victoria		9 35		8 45	...	...	9 55	
Halloon (Saint Columb)		10 0		9 10	...	...	10 20	
NEWQUAY ...a.		10 20		9 30	...	...	10 40	

NEWQUAY AND FOWEY TO PENZANCE AND PLYMOUTH.

		WEEK DAYS.						SUNDAYS.	
	1	2	3	4	5	6	1	2
	1 3	1 3	1 3	1 3			1 3	1 3
	A.M.	A.M.	P.M.	P.M.			A.M.	P.M.
NEWQUAY ...de.	6 45		4 15		...	...		4 15
Halloon (Saint Columb)	7 6		4 36		...	...		4 36
Victoria	7 26		4 56		...	...		4 56
Bugle	7 36		5 6		...	...		5 6
Bridges	7 42		5 12		...	...		5 12
PAR (Saint Blazey) ...ar.	8 0		5 30		...	...		5 30
	A.M.	A.M.	P.M.	P.M.				P.M.
PAR ....de.	8 5	9 0	5 35	6 30	...	...	8 40	5 35
FOWEY ......ar.	8 20	9 15	5 50	6 45	...	...	8 55	5 50
	1 2 3		1 2					
	A.M.		P.M.					
PAR ....de.	8 28		7 50		...	...		
Truro ....ar.	9 27		8 37		...	...		
Falmouth	10 0		9 15		...	...		
PENZANCE ...ar.	10 45		10 4		...	...		
PAR ....de.	8 50	12 14	5 57		...	...		5 57
PLYMOUTH ...ar.	10 25	2 0	7 35		...	...		7 35

☞ AN OMNIBUS RUNS BETWEEN THE CORNWALL RAILWAY AND CORNWALL MINERALS RAILWAY STATIONS AT PAR.

Left and right:
The CMR timetable from November 1888 (left) shows three trains per day to and from Newquay. The very old timetable from March 1878 (right) shows the passenger timetable just two years after the opening of the line. Four of the intermediate stations are shown by their old names (see text). Note that an omnibus operated between the main line Cornwall Railway station at Par and the CMR station (St Blazey). This situation was remedied in 1879 when a double track spur connecting the sites (but not the lines due to a difference in track gauges) was opened. The map shows St Blazey in 1880 with the famous nine-road engine shed and turntable near the foot of the page. Eventually the parcels of land shown as 482, 526 and 568 were covered with sidings. The CMR signalbox shown here was replaced in 1908. *Crown Copyright*

CORNWALL MINERALS.—G. W.					[Sec., H. Gibbs.					
		gov	mrn	mrn	gov	**UP.**	gov	mrn	aft	gov	gov
Miles from Par	PaddingtonSta.			5 30	11½	Newquay.dp	7 20	11 2		5 30	
	4 LONDON .dep	9 0				St.Columb R.	7 36	1118		5 46	
	18 EXETER .. "	2 40	8 40	1158	4 10	Victoria (for	7 52	1134		6 2	
	18 PLYMOUTH "	6 50	11 0	2 40	6 55	Bugle [Roche)	7 59	1141		6 9	
	Par ....dep	8 40	1245	4 23	7 25	Bridges †	8 5	1147		6 15	
½	St. Blazey	8 45	1250	4 25	7 30						
—	St. Blazey .dp	8 46	1251	4 29	7 31	Fowey.dep	8 0	1142	3 50	6 10	8 20
4	Fowey ....arr	8 58	1 3	4 41	7 43	St.Blazey a	8 12	1154	4 2	6 22	8 32
4	Bridges, fr Luxu-	8 56	1 1		7 41	St. Blazey ..	8 20	12 2	4 7	6 30	8 40
6¾	Bugle .....[lyan	9 2	1 7		7 47	Par 19, 18ar	8 22	12 4	4 9	6 32	8 42
8¾	Victoria *	9 9	1 14		7 54	19 PLYMTH ar	1018	1 50	6 5	8 10	1026
14½	St. Columb Road	9 23	1 29		8 8	19 EXETER . "	1240	3 55	9 26	1020	
20¾	Newquay ...arr	9 35	1 42		8 21	3 LONDON . "	6 0	8 51½		4 0	
b 1&2 class. * Station for Roche; † for Luxulyan.											

Below:
A remarkable survivor and certainly a Cornish byway is the line from St Blazey to Par Harbour. The train normally runs daily and St Blazey's resident shunter usually provides the motive power. Passing under the Plymouth to Penzance main line with five 80-ton Polybulk wagons bound for St Blazey is No 08792 on 18 March 1994. The old line to Fowey diverged to the left at this point. *JV*

Left:
Forty years earlier the goods from St Blazey was also propelled, by another 0-6-0, but this time in the shape of pannier tank No 7709. Just through the arch of the main line bridge the Fowey to St Blazey line can be glimpsed. Also note the evidence of soot on the next arch, caused by hard-working steam locomotives with loads bound for Fowey. *R. C. Riley, The Transport Treasury*

Centre left:
One of the last sets of manually operated crossing gates in Cornwall is at Par Bridge on the harbour branch and it is one of the last workings that often incorporates a brake-van. In this 1994 view Class 08 No 08792 makes for St Blazey. The load includes a Cargowaggon containing bagged clay destined for mainland Europe. *JV*

Lower left:
Arriving at St Blazey on 8 September 1955 is one of the ex-GWR '4200' class 81-ton Churchward-designed 2-8-0 tanks, No 4206. St Blazey normally had two of the class included in its steam locomotive allocation. In trailing tonnage terms the 2-8-0s could haul 60% more than a '4500' class 2-6-2 Prairie tank. The left-hand semaphore signal controls the Fowey route, while that on the right relates to the Par Harbour line. Par Bridge signalbox closed in 1968. *Peter Gray*

13. Newquay Branch

Much of the early history of the Newquay branch, as we know it today, can be attributed to one man, Joseph Thomas Treffry (born as Joseph Treffry Austen in 1782 but who changed his name upon inheriting his grandfather's Treffry estates when his uncle died). The family home was at Place, near Fowey, where they owned vast tracts of land. They also owned a large number of mines and other mineral works within a radius of about 15 miles of Fowey, including the vast Fowey Consols at Tywardreath, which contributed large sums of money to the family coffers in the early and mid-19th century. Treffry seems to have been an astute businessman and he realised at an early age that the deep-water facilities at Fowey had enormous potential and, properly developed, could rival and indeed surpass the harbour at Charlestown, which at that time was at the top of the league of tonnage shipped.

As a first step Treffry built a new quay at Fowey between 1811 and 1813. However, he recognised that it would be difficult to grow business there with the transport infrastructure then existing. All materials to and from the docks had to be carried by packhorse and, in later years, by horse-drawn wagon. The maximum single journey payload was 3 tons and, particularly in winter, roads became deeply rutted and at times were barely passable. His mind therefore turned to canals, railways and docks. There had already been some tramways laid in the Redruth/Camborne mining area and Treffry knew that there would be a significant return on investment if he could secure the necessary land, rights and finance. The profitability of many of the mines and pits was marginal and even a small saving in transport costs could mean the difference between prosperity and total closure.

Above:
The station of 'Par, change for Newquay' in May 1922. A train comprised of clerestory coaches from Newquay has just arrived at the island platform and several passengers can be seen waiting for an up main line service. The single coach in the down platform looks as though it has been detached from a down working. The main line at Par was not connected with the CMR until 1879 and before 1892 a change of gauge required all goods and passengers to be transferred. *JV collection*

Above:
In terms of motive power this is an extremely rare shot. Large '5101' class 2-6-2 Prairie tank No 4167 double-heads a down Newquay-bound through train with heavy freight 2-8-0 Class 4200 tank No 4247. The powerful pair makes a vigorous start from Par on 2 September 1954. The signalbox and the main line are on the right.
R. C. Riley, The Transport Treasury

Below:
This 1986 impression shows a similar scene but was taken from the up end of the island platform; the station awning is the common reference point. Class 50 No 50039 *Implacable*, heading the 17.10 Newquay to Wolverhampton train, is skilfully brought into Par by St Blazey driver Percy Wherry. The train comprises Mk 2 air-conditioned InterCity coaches. The old transfer goods shed seen in the photograph on the previous page has long gone. *JV*

Right:
Deep snow at Par station early in the morning of 19 January 1985 finds a pair of Class 37s easing around the bend from St Blazey on their way to Newton Abbot. The author, who had been watching the previous day's weather forecast and had travelled down to see the anticipated snow, had just stepped off the overnight sleeper (as a 'waker') from Paddington. A fill-in flash illuminates the signalbox, semaphore signal gantry and Nos 37207 *William Cookworthy* and 37230. *JV*

Left:
The original CMR Par station was renamed St Blazey on 1 January 1879, when a connecting double-track spur to Par main line was opened. The station finally closed in 1925 (1934 for workmen's trains) but the building survived into the 1970s, while the platforms, the signalbox and the semaphore signals have survived. In the background is St Blazey depot and the lines to the left go to Par. This view dates back to 20 February 1982. *JV*

Right:
The roundhouse at St Blazey became one of the most architecturally interesting railway structures in the West Country and it is now a listed building. Access to the nine roads, each capable of holding two of the original CMR 2-4-0 tank locomotives (the entire fleet of 18), was via a single turntable. The shed continued to be used by the GWR and BR until 24 April 1987, and each 'bay' is now used as an industrial unit. On 3 April 1986 it is Class 47 No 47240 whose nose peeps out into the daylight. *JV*

The influential Rashleigh family thwarted Treffry's early plans. They owned the harbour at Charlestown and some of the land between Par and Fowey that Treffry would need in order to drive a railway through. Seeing him as competition, they refused to sell. So Treffry purchased 35 acres of land at what was to become Par Harbour and by 1828 he had drawn up plans for the construction and development of a tidal harbour. This would take 10 years to construct and the major piece of engineering would be a 1,200ft breakwater. Much of the stone used in construction came from Treffry's Clift Quarry, near Pentewan, via Pentewan Harbour. In 1829 the original horse-worked narrow gauge Pentewan Railway had been opened to the outskirts of St Austell, but Treffry was sufficiently astute to have secured guarantees from major china clay producers John Lovering and Robert Martin to use Par in preference to other ports. Although work had not been completed, Par received its first commercial vessel in 1833.

The copper ore from Fowey Consols was brought down the hill to Ponts Mill at the foot of the Luxulyan Valley via a half-mile double track 1 in 9 inclined plane. It was therefore logical for Ponts Mill to be linked by canal with the newly opened harbour at Par, and a 12ft-wide canal was duly built and opened in 1835. There were also other inclined planes in the area all contributing to the success of the canal. Once the canal hurdle had been crossed Treffry made public his intentions to link Newquay on the north Cornish coast with Par on the south coast, beginning with a section from Par to Molinnis, near Bugle. He had also been on the acquisition trail, adding to his collection Par Consols, shipping interests, granite quarries in the Luxulyan area, and various china clay works in the Hensbarrow Downs area, as well as the land needed to build his proposed tramway. Another important purchase occurred in 1838 when Treffry bought from Richard Lomax the whole of the Newquay Harbour complex. This fitted Treffry's plans perfectly.

After one abortive attempt to get the new tramway started the management was handed over to William Pease, who was to become Treffry's 'right hand man'. In 1837 the surveying and quantity surveying had been completed. The tramway would rise 300ft from Ponts Mill by a 2,840ft-long incline at a gradient of 1 in 9, powered by a waterwheel fed from a number of leats; it would be on the east side of the Luxulyan Valley and would become known as the Carmears Incline. The port of Par became fully operational in 1840 and the first stage of the tramway, to Colcerrow Quarry, was opened in 1841. From the top of the incline the line ran on broadly level ground, but in order to reach the Molinnis/Bugle area it would have to cross the imposing Luxulyan Valley. A massive viaduct was built, 648ft long and 98ft above the ground, constructed of local granite, each block weighing some 5-6 tons. The viaduct took three years to build at a cost of £6,708. It also performed the role of an aqueduct and although the rails have long been removed, water still flows underneath the granite slabs comprising the 'floor' of the structure.

The line then continued past Luxulyan village and across open farmland at Bowling Green to reach Molinnis, effectively Bugle. The terminus was accessible from a number of china clay works but also from local tin mines. The standard gauge horse-worked line was nearing completion in August 1843 and opened in 1844. The main outgoing traffic was copper ore, china clay and china stone, lead ore and granite, while incoming loads included coal, timber and lime, the latter for agricultural use. Treffry again let it be known that his intention to link the tramway at Molinnis with Newquay, with a branch down to St Dennis and Hendra, was very much alive. Indeed, work commenced in earnest in 1844 on the north Cornish coast, from Newquay to East Wheal Rose and also to St Dennis and Hendra. The line up from Newquay Harbour also started on a steep cable-hauled incline through a tunnel and made its way through the streets of the town to what was to become the site of Newquay station. The tramway then had to cross the

substantial Trenance Valley by a spindly wooden viaduct, known as 'the spider'. After crossing farmland past the sites of what were to become Quintrel Downs and St Columb Road stations the tramway entered the 530yd Toldish Tunnel, near Ruthvoes, before reaching St Dennis Junction (then Bodmin Road Junction).

In 1846 Treffry was taken ill and was confined to his home at Place, relying on the trusted William Pease to administer the estate. Nevertheless he continued to purchase various mines and pits. In 1849 the Treffry Tramway from Newquay to St Dennis and Hendra, as well as the branch to East Wheal Rose, was in operation. Sadly, the following year Treffry died and with Pease having defected to the Fortescue family it was left to a distant relation, Dr Edward Wilcox, to progress Treffry's unrealised plans. Wilcox changed his name by deed poll to Treffry. An incline up to the Hendra works was built in 1852 and, more importantly, in 1855 the tramway was extended from Ponts Mill to Par Harbour, thereby rendering the canal redundant. However, Molinnis and St Dennis (Junction) were still not linked by the tramway. In the late 1850s a major downturn in the mining industry occurred as world prices crashed. Fowey Consols, for example, mined over 15,000 tons in 1836 but by 1860 this had plummeted to less than 4,000 tons. It closed completely in 1867 following another downturn in the industry.

Meanwhile in the Luxulyan Valley the original line from the top of the Carmears Incline to Colcerrow Quarry and Carbeans Quarry was extended in 1855 by a branch line via Gatty's Bridge to Cairns Quarry, to the northeast of Luxulyan village. Horse-drawn loads of granite swelled the traffic travelling down the Carmears Incline but by 1880 the 'new' branch had closed. There were also developments along the floor of the Luxulyan Valley when between 1868 and 1870 the South Cornwall Granite Company built a tramway from Ponts Mill to Rock Mill Quarry with a branch to Orchard Quarry. This tramway was used during the construction of the 1874 CMR deviation from the old Carmears Incline route. At about the turn of the century the quarries were taken over by John Freeman of Penryn, and although in the early part of the 20th century the demand for granite declined, the quarries struggled on until World War 1, when this track and the rails on the Carmears Incline were both lifted to help with the war effort. During the early 1920s a clay kiln known as Trevanny Kiln was built on the valley floor and track was relaid not only to the clay driers but also to the quarries, possibly to facilitate the transportation of granite blocks used in the construction of the clay kiln. The entire line was lifted again in 1938, although subsequently relaid to Trevanny Kiln only. The siding from Ponts Mill finally closed on 31 December 1967. Small 'Simplex' four-wheeled petrol locomotives were used to move wagons from the BR siding at Ponts Mill.

The Cornwall Railway (GWR) broad gauge main line through Cornwall was opened in 1859 and a group of clay producers approached Dr Wilcox/Treffry with a view to closing the gap between Molinnis and St Dennis and extending the line from Hendra through 'clay country' to join the main line at Burngullow. As a result, the Newquay & Cornwall Junction Railway was formed (see Chapter 19 for more detail). A report in 1860 was prepared to determine the suitability of the tramway for locomotive usage, and found that the track at 42lb per linear yard was too light and that viaducts and tunnels were unsatisfactory. By 1870 the tramway had become something of an anachronism, being one of only two horse-drawn lines in the county (excluding shunting operations). The saviour of the situation arrived in 1870 in the shape of W. R. Roebuck, an entrepreneur from London who was looking to invest his cash in Cornwall. Meaningful discussions took place in 1872 and as a result the idea for a Cornwall Minerals Railway emerged, with Roebuck leasing existing lines from Treffry Estates. Part of the deal included building the 'missing link' and converting and upgrading the whole line for use by locomotives.

Above:
An excellent, if somewhat hackneyed, location for railway photography is near the end of the single-track Newquay branch, on the approach to Middleway Crossing, where the railway, the River Par and the old canal to Ponts Mill all run parallel. In striking 'large logo' blue livery Class 37 No 37175 runs down to St Blazey with mixed clay wagons from Goonbarrow Junction on 23 April 1987. *JV*

Right:
Far removed from the tramway and steam eras with horses and old wheezing 2-4-0T steam locomotives as motive power are the impressive 'high-tech' North American-built GM Class 66s. These 125-tonne whispering giants are the latest generation of freight locomotive ordered by the post-privatisation English, Welsh & Scottish Railway. Their first revenue-earning run on a Cornish china clay train occurred on 9 January 1999. No 66123 was photographed near St Blazey Gate heading for the ECC (now Imerys) Rocks Works at Goonbarrow Junction in July of that year. *JV*

Left:
Ponts Mill was an important transportation centre in times gone by. Minerals were transported down from the mines and pits by ropeways and tramways, and there were grinding mills, clay dries and a canal where barges carried the output down to Par Harbour. It seemed that transport activity would end when the last clay train left the works on 21 April 1992, but when photographed in June 1997 this siding off the Newquay branch was being cleared and was subsequently kept manicured for the occasional overnight stabling of the Royal Train, normally when the Prince of Wales visits his Duchy of Cornwall estates. More recently the site was used for clay wagon refurbishment. *JV*

Right:
In happier times on 4 May 1989 the 'as and when required', but normally daily, Ponts Mill freight headed by shunter No 08955 removes two PRA wagons from the now demolished works. The brake-van is standing on the alignment of the original 1841 Treffry Tramway. The wagons will travel all the way to Fort William in Scotland where the china clay will be used in paper production. The focal point for comparison between the views is the telegraph post. *JV*

Left:
In addition to the original 1841 tramway that ran up the Carmears Incline and the CMR line on the course of the existing branch, a further tramway was built along the floor of the Luxulyan Valley between 1868 and 1870 serving Orchard and Rock Mill quarries. The last stone to leave the quarry by rail was in about 1928 and the track was lifted in 1938 (see text). In this rare 1922 view the Newquay branch crosses the tramway on Rock Mill Viaduct, while below Orchard Quarry is to the left and Rock Mill Quarry to the right. *JV collection*

Right:
The 1874 alignment up the Luxulyan Valley has always been a test for locomotives as they overcome the 1 in 37 climb in the 'down' direction. In the days of steam the heaviest trains were double-headed and sometimes a banker was also employed. However, on 19 July 1958 the 10.45am Par to Newquay local is double-headed by 'Grange' class 4-6-0 No 6858 *Woolston Grange* and one of the GWR's attractive Churchward Mogul 2-6-0s, No 6397. The photograph was taken from Treffry Viaduct, which spans the valley at this point. *Peter Gray*

Right:
Dwarfed by the magnificent surroundings of the Luxulyan Valley single-car Class 153 unit No 153373 descends from Luxulyan station towards St Blazey with the 10.15 Newquay to Par service of 22 September 1994. During the winter of 2001-02 there were just four round trip workings on the Newquay branch with no movement before 09.30 or after 20.50, with very poor connections at Par and hence few passengers. *JV*

Left:
A walk up the old Carmears Incline is still rewarding, in terms of industrial archaeology. At the top of the 1 in 9 climb from Ponts Mill are the remains of a checker's cabin. There is also a smithy, a coil of cable rope and the remains of the water wheel that supplied the power for hauling the wagons up the incline. This view shows the cabin on 3 September 2001, with granite setts, or sleepers, visible on the left. *JV*

Below:
The Newquay branch timetable for the summer of 1958

Table 99

PAR, BUGLE and NEWQUAY

MONDAYS TO FRIDAYS

Miles		am	am	am	am	am	pm	pm	pm	pm	pm	pm	pm D
	Par dep	6 10	6 45	7 20	9 30	1034	1220	2 40	3 20	4 25	6 25	7 45	9 20
4¼	Luxulyan	..	6 59	7 34	9 44	1049	1233	2 56	3 34	4 39	6 42	7 59	9 34
6¼	Bugle	6 29	7 4	7 40	9 50	1055	1247	3 3	3 40	4 45	6 48	8 5	9 39
8¾	Roche	6 35	7 10	7 46	9 57	11 1	1254	3 10	3 46	4 50	6 54	8 11	9 43
14¼	St. Columb Road	6 50	7 24	8 0	1012	1116	1 8	3 25	4 2	5 6	7 10	8 26	9 58
18½	Quintrel Downs	..	7 33	8 9	1022	1125	1 16	3 35	4 12	5 15	7 19	..	..
20¾	**Newquay** arr	7 5	7 41	8 16	1030	1131	1 25	3 45	4 20	5 25	7 30	8 40	1012

SATURDAYS

	am	am	am	am	am	am H	am	am	am	pm	pm	pm	pm	pm A	pm	pm	pm	pm	pm	pm	pm
Par dep	4 50	5 10	6 10	6 50	7 45	8 10	9 20	10 5	1045	1225	1 35	2 5	2 40	3 10	3 25	5 30	6 12	6 50	7 30	8 15	9 20
Luxulyan	..	..	..	7 6	8 0	..	9 34	..	11 0	1239	1 53	..	2 56	..	..	5 45	6 27	..	7 44	8 31	9 34
Bugle	..	..	6 29	7 13	8 6	..	9 42	..	11 6	1246	2 0	..	3 3	..	..	5 52	6 35	..	7 50	8 38	9 39
Roche	..	..	6 35	7 19	8 13	..	9 50	..	1110	1253	2 6	..	3 10	..	..	5 58	6 42	..	7 56	8 44	9 43
St. Columb Road	5 30	5 50	6 50	7 33	8 32	9 10	1010	1042	1130	1 12	2 23	2 44	3 25	3 50	..	6 18	6 58	7 35	8 16	8 59	9 58
Quintrel Downs	..	..	..	7 42	8 42	..	1020	..	..	1 21	2 33	..	3 35	..	..	..	7 7	..	..	..	..
Newquay arr	5 50	6 15	7 5	7 50	8 50	9 25	1031	11 0	1146	1 30	2 40	3 0	3 45	4 5	4 30	6 35	7 15	7 50	8 32	9 13	1012

MONDAYS TO FRIDAYS

Miles		am	am	am	am	pm	pm	pm	pm	pm B	pm	pm	pm B	pm	pm G
	Newquay dep	8 12	9 45	1045	1130	1250	1 45	4 45	6 0	7d20	8 5	9 8	9d45	1015	10d50
2¼	Quintrel Downs	8 20	..	1051	..	1257	..	4 52	6 7	..	8 11	9 16	..	1022	..
6½	St. Columb Road	8 30	10 0	11 2	1145	1 8	2 1	5 4	6 18	..	8 24	9 27	..	1033	..
12	Roche	8 44	K	1116	1159	1 21	2 16	5 18	6 31	..	8 38	9 42	..	1047	..
14½	Bugle	8 50	1020	1123	12 5	1 27	2 22	5 24	6 37	..	8 43	9 50	..	1052	..
16½	Luxulyan	8 55	..	1129	1211	1 33	2 28	5 30	6 42	..	8 49	9 56	..	1058	..
20¾	**Par** arr	9 9	1040	1143	1228	1 46	2 42	5 43	6 56	8 12	9 3	10 9	1042	1111	11 40

SATURDAYS

	am	am	am	am Z	am	am	am	pm	pm	pm	pm	pm	pm	pm	pm
Newquay dep	7d50	8d 5	8d50	10 0	11d0	11d15	1152	1230	12d40	1 45	5 0	6 0	8 0	9 8	1015
Quintrel Downs	..	..	8d59	..	..	..	1159	..	12d48	..	5 7	6 7	8 7	9 16	1022
St Columb Road	..	8d20	9d10	10 15	..	11d28	1210	..	1d 0	2 1	5 19	6 18	8 18	9 27	1033
Roche	..	8d35	9d24	..	..	11d42	1224	..	1d14	2 16	5 34	6 31	8 31	9 42	1047
Bugle	..	8d42	9d30	..	..	11d48	1230	..	1d20	2 22	5 40	6 37	8 37	9 50	1052
Luxulyan	..	8d48	9d38	..	..	11d54	1235	..	1d26	2 28	5 46	6 42	8 42	9 56	1058
Par arr	8 42	9 5	9 55	..	1147	12 9	1252	1 15	1 42	2 42	6 0	6 56	8 55	10 9	1111

SUNDAYS

	am	am	am	am	pm	pm
Par dep	8 35	9 30	1040	1115	5 8	7 5
Luxulyan	8 48	9 44	..	1129	5 22	7 19
Bugle	8 55	9 50	..	1134	5 28	7 25
Roche	9 1	9 56	..	1140	5 34	7 31
St. Columb Road	9 16	1012	1122	1157	5 48	7 46
Quintrel Downs	..	1021	..	..	5 58	..
Newquay arr	9 30	1030	1140	1210	6 8	8 0

SUNDAYS

	am	am	pm	pm	pm	pm	pm
Newquay dep	9 55	1110	1 50	5 17	7 5	7 20	9 5
Quintrel Downs	..	..	..	5 24	..	..	9 13
St. Columb Road	1010	1125	2 4	5 35	..	7 35	9 23
Roche	N	1140	2 19	5 49	..	7 49	9 36
Bugle	1029	1146	2 25	5 55	..	7 55	9 42
Luxulyan	..	1153	2 31	6 1	..	8 1	9 48
Par arr	1050	1210	2 44	6 15	7 53	8 15	10 4

A Will not run after 30th August
B Runs Fridays 1st, 8th, 15th and 22nd August only.
D Fridays only; also runs on Monday 4th August
d Passengers travelling by this train to certain stations beyond Par are required to hold Regulation Tickets (see page 30)
G Runs Fridays, 1st, 8th, 15th, 22nd and 29th August only.
H Runs [illegible]8th June to 23rd August inclusive
K Calls at 10 12 am to pick up passengers for London only on notice being given at the Station by 9 30 am
N Calls at 10 20 am to pick up passengers for London only on notice being given at the Station by 9 30 am
Q Calls to pick up passengers only
Z Restaurant Car Train to London (Paddington) arr 4 55 pm (Table 81)

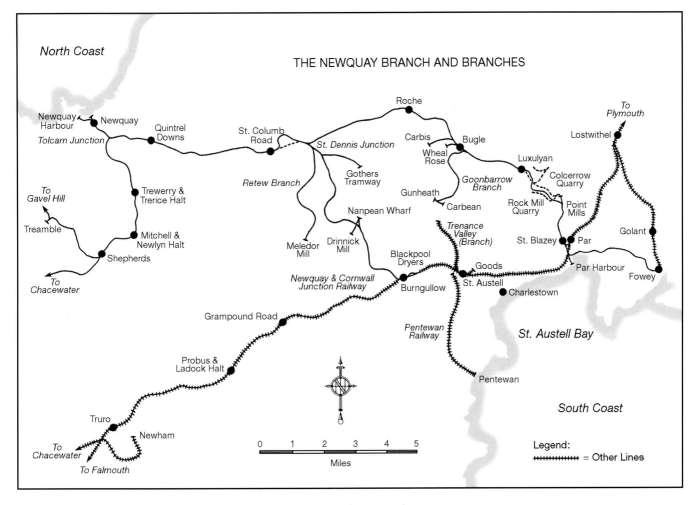

THE NEWQUAY BRANCH AND BRANCHES

North Coast

To Plymouth

Roche

Newquay Harbour — Newquay — Quintrel Downs — St. Columb Road — *St. Dennis Junction* — Carbis — Bugle — Lostwithel

Tolcarn Junction

Wheal Rose

Luxulyan

Colcerrow Quarry

Gothers Tramway

Retew Branch

Goonbarrow Branch

To Gavel Hill

Trewerry & Trerice Halt

Gunheath

Rock Mill Quarry

Point Mills

Nanpean Wharf

Carbean

Golant

Treamble

To Chacewater

Mitchell & Newlyn Halt

Shepherds

Meledor Mill

Drinnick Mill

Trenance Valley (Branch)

St. Blazey — Par

Blackpool Dryers

Goods

Par Harbour

Fowey

Grampound Road

Newquay & Cornwall Junction Railway

Burngullow

St. Austell

Charlestown

St. Austell Bay

Pentewan Railway

Probus & Ladock Halt

N

Pentewan

South Coast

Truro — Newham

To Chacewater

To Falmouth

0 1 2 3 4 5
Miles

Legend:
++++++++ = Other Lines

Below:
Back in 1950 when railway embankments and rights of way were maintained and permanent way workers had huts, a grubby Prairie 2-6-2T pounds up the valley towards Luxulyan with a Par to Newquay local. Standing 98ft high in the background is Treffry Viaduct, completed in 1844, which carried a leat and the original tramway from Ponts Mills to Molinnis (Bugle) across the valley. *B. A. Butt*

Above:

There is plenty of scope for nostalgia in this shot of railway infrastructure at Luxulyan on 13 July 1961.
So much has now gone, including the water tower, the 'pagoda' hut, the signalbox and signals, the passing loop,
the water column, the sidings, the main station building, the pick-up goods and of course steam traction. Even
the chimney of Treskilling clay works (top right) has gone! Pannier tank No 1664 departs with a Goonbarrow
Junction to St Blazey mixed freight. *Peter Gray*

William Richardson Roebuck lost no time in making himself known to a number of prominent land and mine owning Cornish families. He made a number of acquisitions and even became the principal stakeholder in the Cornish Consolidated Iron Mines Corporation, incorporated in 1872 to extract, process and ship iron ore from the Perran Lode, mentioned in Chapter 21. Under the plans lodged for the Cornwall Minerals Railway (CMR) there would be, in addition to the items mentioned in the last paragraph, a new railway line between Par/St Blazey and Fowey. Major earthworks would be needed to construct a new line up the Luxulyan Valley to avoid the obstacle of the Carmears Incline, the low tunnel at Toldish would also need to be bypassed and a new viaduct over the Trenance Valley required. Branches to Carbis Wharf, near Bugle, to Melangoose Mill (the Retew branch) and from East Wheal Rose to Treamble were included in the Act, as was amalgamation with the Newquay & Cornwall Junction Railway. The CMR was incorporated by order of an Act of Parliament on 21 July 1873.

Roebuck employed considerable manpower on the various works, which were divided into three major groups. The granite tunnels at Pinnock on the Fowey line and at Luxulyan posed major problems and impeded progress, but nevertheless by the end of 1873 the works were on target. There was much building work at St Blazey to produce a nine-road roundhouse, turntable and an office block. Jetties had to be built at Fowey and roads had to be crossed on many stretches of line, the bridge on Goss Moor over the main (A30) highway requiring the greatest earthworks. Both local labour and Irish navvies were employed in the construction and the CMR was criticised by the Methodist Church for allowing work on Sundays. An engine shed was built at Newquay and 12 of the 18 Sharp, Stewart & Company 0-6-0 tank locomotives ordered to work the line were delivered. The first few dozen of the 400 wagons ordered by the CMR also started to arrive. A light locomotive traversed the entire line on 27 April 1874 but a May inspection by the Board of Trade called for further works to be undertaken. The CMR finally opened on 1 June 1874, just 11 months after the passing of the Act!

J. C. Richardson, the General Manager of the CMR, flagged away the first train. Some of the workings in the early days were not orthodox, especially on the branches, in that the locomotive was often in the middle of the train due to a lack of sidings and run-round facilities. The freight-only lines were operationally successful but luck was not on Roebuck's side because by the time the railway became established there was a downturn in the mining industry, especially in the iron ore business. The branch to Treamble and on to Gravel Hill was badly affected as the Perran Lode gradually declined, and with it some of Roebuck's fortune,

as the CMR was planned to be heavily dependent on iron ore traffic. He had just spent out over £43,000 on 18 locomotives and purchased eight steam cargo vessels, in addition to a proportion of costs associated with the construction of the CMR. To make matters worse there had been over-production in the china clay industry in the 1870 to 1873 period and this affected its production in 1875-6. By 1875 Sir Moreton Peto, the contractor for the CMR, who had invested heavily in the company, was ruined financially.

The CMR made an almost desperate attempt to augment its income by introducing a passenger train service between Fowey and Newquay. Six ex-Midland Railway four-wheeled coaches were purchased 'for a song' and stations were located at Fowey, Par (from 1878 St Blazey), Bridges (from 1905 Luxulyan), Bugle, Holywell (later Victoria and finally, in 1904, Roche), Halloon (from 1878 St Columb Road) and Newquay. Quintrel Downs Platform was opened by the GWR in 1911. While mentioning names, Bodmin Road Junction became St Dennis Junction, and Newquay Junction became Treloggan Junction then finally Tolcarn Junction! The first day of passenger service was 20 June 1876. The train was highly decorated with flowers and greenery, there were festivities at all intermediate stations with two bands in attendance, and a civic dinner and speeches by local dignitaries at Newquay. The initial passenger service saw two trains per day between Newquay and Fowey. A horse-drawn coach service connected Par (CMR) with Par (GWR) and St Columb Road and Wadebridge. During the next two years there were still but two trains a day each way and by 1878 the Sunday service, comprising a single round trip, was axed. In 1877 and 1878 mines and pits continued to close.

By April 1877 Roebuck could stand the financial strain no more and approached the GWR in an attempt to launch a rescue package. The GWR was sympathetic and also, no doubt, saw a future investment opportunity in controlling a greater chunk of Cornwall's railways. By an agreement dated 30 April 1877 and sanctioned by Parliament the GWR undertook to work the line for a 999-year term from 1 July 1877; in fact the takeover did not take place until 1 October. A total of 45 miles and 47 chains of railway were relinquished to the GWR; there were also financial guarantees from the GWR, while the CMR was to hand over more than 53% of the gross receipts. Gradually the mining and china clay industries improved but the iron ore traffic never recovered and after a period of disuse the Gravel Hill extension was lifted in 1888. In 1879 a double-track standard gauge spur between Par and St Blazey was constructed, resulting in a junction station on the main line but one at which all passengers and freight had to be transferred from one gauge of train to another.

Left:
The east end of the loop at Goonbarrow is not often photographed but the semaphore signals there are a joy. On a damp 25 July 1986 No 37135 approaches Goonbarrow Junction with a long haul of empty 'clay hoods' from Fowey. The old-fashioned speed restriction notice instructs drivers not to exceed 15mph until clear of the points. *JV*

Right:
The changing of tokens between train driver and signalman for the single-line sections still takes place at Goonbarrow Junction, where the WR semaphore signalling system has survived into the new millennium. Signalman Peter Hamley of Wadebridge makes the change with the driver of the 10.14 Newquay to Par service of 12 June 1986. The unit, Class 142 No 142025, was one of a small batch of 'Skippers' allocated to West Country branches, but the experiment was unsuccessful and after a relatively short stay they were transferred away. *JV*

Left:
A smiling fireman shares a gesture with a shunter at Goonbarrow Junction as a train from Newquay enters the loop behind one of the ubiquitous GWR 0-6-0 pannier tanks and three coaches. Passenger trains from Fowey and St Blazey to Newquay commenced in 1876 but in those days Goonbarrow was known as Rosevear Siding. It became Goonbarrow Junction when the Goonbarrow branch to Carthew opened in 1893.
Hugh Davies

Above:
Another rash one-day trip to the Royal Duchy was on 23 November 1991 when a Manchester to Newquay enthusiasts' special, organised by Pathfinder Tours, was diagrammed for haulage by three Class 50s over the Newquay branch. The special was well over an hour late but the wait at the top of a lighting gantry was worth it when a pair of gleaming 'Hoovers' passed the shortened stack of Wheal Henry at Goonbarrow. Train 1Z37 was powered by No 50008 *Thunderer* in shining blue livery and 50015 *Valiant* in immaculate engineers 'Dutch' grey and yellow livery. Both locomotives had white wheel rims and yellow axlebox covers. No 50033 *Glorious* was at the other end of the rake of InterCity-liveried Mk 1 coaches. *JV*

Below:
Goonbarrow Junction is a fairly sleepy place with four branch trips per day in each direction plus, perhaps, an equal number of china clay trains to ECC (Imerys) Rocks Works. However, a highlight on summer Saturdays was when a pair of 125mph IC125 units actually used the passing loop at Goonbarrow to cross, giving the impression of hyper-activity. On 22 August 1992 the 14.40 Newquay to Leeds train (left) passes the famous 'Atlantic Coast Express', the 11.05 Paddington to Newquay. The trains are seen between withdrawn slurry tanks on the left and 'Tigers' on the right. *JV*

There was a steady recovery in traffic and at one point in 1885 volumes increased by 9% in a six-month period. Bradshaw's timetable for 1888 shows four down and five up passenger trains between Fowey and St Blazey (see the previous chapter) and three trains in each direction between Par/St Blazey and Newquay. After cessation of the broad gauge in 1892 the service to Newquay increased to five return trips per day. The revised gauge also affected the workings of the CMR's Newquay & Cornwall Junction line to Drinnick Mill (see Chapter 19). Money started to roll in and the CMR undertook two further ventures: a 3½-mile line into the very heart of china clay country from Roskear Sidings (now Goonbarrow Junction), near Bugle, to Carbean, and a short half-mile branch from Bugle to Martin's Goonbarrow and Great Beam clay kilns. The lines were known as the Goonbarrow branch and the Wheal Rose branch (not to be confused with the early CMR line to East Wheal Rose) and both were opened in 1893. From 1 July 1896 the GWR purchased the CMR outright and absorbed the network into its system; the CMR was then dissolved. The last act of the CMR had been to control the 1895 link-up with the GWR's Lostwithiel & Fowey Railway line at Fowey.

The CMR originally ordered 18 0-6-0 30-ton tank locomotives from Sharp, Stewart & Company, designed to work in pairs 'back to back', and the nine roads of the tailor-made roundhouse at St Blazey were designed to take a pair of locomotives. There were no coal bunkers and coal was inconveniently carried on top of the side water tanks. Four of the locomotives were named, but embarrassingly No 1 was delivered with the nameplates misspelt *Treffrey* rather than *Treffry*. All of the locomotives had Allan straight link motion, common on LNWR machinery. With the aforementioned downturn in traffic during the mid/late 1870s 18 locomotives were never required, and after the GWR takeover in 1877 half of them had never been steamed and were returned to the makers for resale. Apparently this settled a debt, only part of the original consignment ever having been paid for. Nos 1 to 9 were taken into GWR stock as Nos 1392 to 1400 and were all rebuilt as saddle tanks in 1883-4. Water capacity was increased, bunkers were fitted, 2 tons of weight was added and the driving cabs were extended. One locomotive was sold but the others had new boilers fitted by Swindon Works in 1895. They would eventually all be reallocated, many finding years of employment as Works shunters at Swindon. The final examples were scrapped in 1936.

There is no doubt that the GWR had rescued the CMR. There were a number of changes under the auspices of the GWR, including the introduction of more modern rolling stock during the 1880s. The GWR reopened its Lostwithiel to Fowey line in 1895 and in 1905 completed its Chacewater to Newquay line (see Chapter 21). Of particular importance was the introduction of through coaches from London Paddington to Newquay in May 1906, further opening up Newquay's potential as a major seaside resort for holidaymakers and trippers. The journey from London took 5 minutes under 8 hours. This was the precursor of through holiday trains from many parts of the country to Newquay, which during the 1930s and again in the 1950s made the resort one of Cornwall's most popular destinations. This heavy summer traffic resulted in the doubling of sections of track on the branch, from St Dennis to Tregoss Moor in 1921, from Goonbarrow Junction to Bugle in 1930, and at the Newquay end of the branch in the 1940s.

The GWR modified the track layout at many stations, expanded facilities and extended passing loops, and many of these changes are dealt with later. The uneconomic passenger service between Par/St Blazey and Fowey was withdrawn in 1925, although a single workman's train in each direction continued until 1934. The company closed the Newquay Harbour branch in 1926, the developments at Par and Fowey having rendered the small harbour redundant. After World War 2 the Treamble line (see Chapter 21) was closed and lifted. Other changes included infrastructure items such as notices, signs, lighting, permanent

way and above all signalling; between 1877 and 1916 the GWR closed and replaced every one of the original CMR signalboxes. In terms of motive power, as mentioned earlier, the CMR locomotives were eventually dispensed with and replaced by GWR classes of the era, mostly from the Dean stable but later by Churchward, Collett and Hawksworth types.

Even after the Grouping the GWR locomotives 'ruled' and the following classes could be found at St Blazey (83E): '1400' 0-4-2T (the replacement for the earlier '3500' 'Metro' 2-4-0Ts), '1366' 0-6-0T, '2021' 0-6-0PT, '2181' 0-6-0PT, '5700' 0-6-0PT, '4500' 2-6-2T, '5100' 2-6-2T, '6300' 2-6-0, 'Manor', 'Grange', 'Hall', 'County' and 'Castle' 4-6-0, '4200' 2-8-0T and '7200' 2-8-2T. In later years BR Standard 4-6-0s sometimes worked to Newquay. In the mid-1950s St Blazey had an allocation of about 35 steam locomotives, plus visiting engines. Prairie and pannier tanks normally worked local train services.

Except for the line from St Blazey to Par Harbour the Newquay branch now starts at Par on the Plymouth to Penzance main line. Branch passenger trains leave the outer face of the island platform, although there is an up goods loop for freight and postal trains. Par was opened in 1859 and once had a large transfer goods shed, loading dock and all the infrastructure items of the steam age, such as water columns. The down-side stone station building remains, and there is still a (roofless) footbridge and a signalbox. At the time of writing, lower quadrant semaphore signals survive and a visit to Par to witness their operation is worth while in itself. The up-side waiting shelter is modern. For many years the branch line services to Fowey and Newquay were shown in separate timetables. Over the years some Par to Newquay branch trains have started or ended at Plymouth. Newquay is now the only Cornish branch line that still has through trains to and from Scotland, the North, the Midlands and London on summer Saturdays. Since the removal of run-round facilities at Newquay the through trains are of necessity InterCity 125 units with a power car at each end.

The station platforms at Par were lengthened in 1913 and 1924. There was further track rationalisation in 1973, and from the early 1980s, when St Austell and Burngullow signalboxes were closed, Par signalbox had interface with Truro on the down main, Lostwithiel on the up main and St Blazey on the branch. The line around to St Blazey is double track and just before the site of the old St Blazey station (which closed in 1925, but where the platforms are still in evidence) is St Blazey yard. The site is the administrative and operational hub of railways in Cornwall, which includes all trains serving the china clay industry. St Blazey was designed by the great Victorian railway engineer Sir Moreton Peto and built in 1873 on 600sq yd of land adjacent to the old Treffry Tramway. The buildings were unusual in being built of red brick imported from the Plymouth area, as opposed to locally produced granite. Buildings included offices, a locomotive works, erecting and repair shops, a boiler house, smithy, fitting shop, wagon shop, goods shed and the nine-road roundhouse to accommodate the entire CMR locomotive fleet. There was a short, steeply graded siding to the coaling stage at the south end of the complex.

Over the years numerous changes have taken place and many of the buildings have been demolished. After the end of steam in 1964 the coaling stage was removed and as the diesels arrived, diesel oil refuelling equipment was installed. Although modern air-braked wagons are still maintained at St Blazey, the wagon shop stopped repairing the little vacuum-braked four-wheeled 'clay hood' wagons in 1988. A modern single-storey office building replaced the old high-ceilinged brick-built offices in the 1980s. The track layout has changed regularly over the years but the most significant change took place in 1987 when, after 113 years of use, the old ('Grade 2' listed) roundhouse was closed and leased as non-rail-connected industrial units.

There is still plenty of action at St Blazey with wagons to and from various loading points being marshalled into trainloads and postal trains being serviced. In recent times the only St Blazey locomotive allocation has been a couple of Class 08 shunters, but in the past it has either been the home of or serviced Classes 22, 25, 37, 41, 42, 43, 45, 46, 47, 50, 52 and 60 diesels, and most have worked the Newquay branch. The only classes now likely to be seen are 08, 60, 66 and 67, the 66s now hauling the clay trains. After years of operation by DMUs, local services are now in the hands of Class 150/2 or 153 units.

Beyond the old St Blazey station and the still operational signalbox, Middleway Bridge Crossing is passed; the diminutive signalbox that controlled the road crossing was taken out of use in January 1981. The line runs parallel with the old Par Canal and the River Par towards the Luxulyan Valley passing St Blazey Bridge Crossing. The next landmark is Ponts Mill siding, on the alignment of the old Treffry Tramway route to the foot of Carmears incline. Ponts Mill is steeped in railway history and industrial archaeology. In addition to the Treffry and valley tramways already described there was also a clay drying plant and narrow gauge tramway, which served the nearby Prideaux Wood china clay dry. Until 1912 there was also a siding from the Newquay branch to Prideaux Wood. There were once some ancient tin mines above the clay works, dating back to the Phoenicians. At Ponts Mill there was also a china stone works that closed in the mid-1960s. In its last years the Ponts Mill line saw a daily train, which was propelled from St Blazey by the resident shunter, and it was also used to berth the Royal Train on more than one occasion. Clay drying at Ponts Mill stopped in 1992 and the last train ran on 21 April. In 1997 the overgrown track was cleared for use as a stabling point for the Royal Train, and in 2001 the works area was being used for shotblasting and refurbishing CDA clay wagons, but this work has now ceased and concrete blocks have been placed on the track preventing further usage.

The Newquay branch crosses the 52yd Prideaux Viaduct, the 92yd Ponts Mill Viaduct and the 52yd Rock Mill Viaduct while making its way up the valley, and then passes under the Treffry Viaduct. Trains then enter a sheer granite cutting before entering the unlined, 52yd Luxulyan Tunnel. After passing the old connection with the original Treffry Tramway line Luxulyan station is reached. Here, in 1910, an island platform replaced a more conventional configuration and provided a passing loop between St Blazey and Goonbarrow Junction. A year later a GWR signalbox replaced the CMR original. There was a goods yard on the north side of the line and a connection to Treskilling Clay

Below:
Molinnis, which is immediately adjacent to Bugle station, was the terminus of the original Treffry Tramway. The line pre-dated the Ordnance Survey and the precise location is not known but the old down loading wharf at Bugle would seem logical. Bugle signalbox was located at Molinnis Crossing, and passing the now ungated road on 23 October 1996 with the 10.10 Newquay to Par service is Regional Railways Class 153 No 153305. The sign would seem to indicate that a steam train is following! *JV*

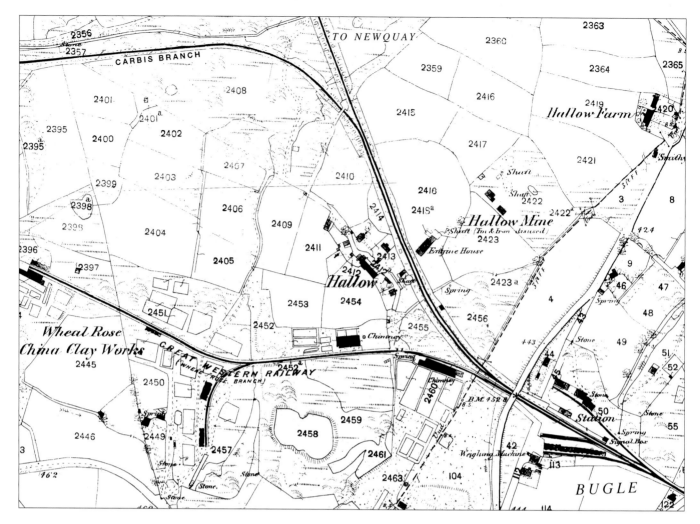

Above:

The Bugle area in about 1895. The down loading dock with its two sidings and the up goods yard with just a single track (which was later enlarged) can be seen bottom right. Bugle then boasted just a single-faced platform, which was converted to an island platform in about 1930. On the Wheal Rose branch the first works on the down side beyond the junction was Wheal Hope (also known as Treleavens Kiln) and on the up side East Goonbarrow Kiln. The branch then divided with the lines serving Wheal Virgin, Martin's Goonbarrow, Wheal Rose and Great Beam Nos 1 and 2. The track layout shown here was subsequently enlarged and a run-round loop was provided. The Carbis branch at the top of the map served West Goonbarrow, Rosemellyn and Great Wheal Prosper clay kilns. *Crown Copyright*

Works, which was served by a short narrow gauge tramway. A camping coach once graced a siding. Nearly all the railway infrastructure was closed and removed in 1964, leaving just a single line serving a basic unstaffed halt. The single line continues through Bowling Green to Goonbarrow Junction, adjacent to the huge Imerys Rocks Works.

Goonbarrow Junction is now the only passing place between St Blazey and Newquay. It was once the junction for the closed Goonbarrow branch and is now the geographical extremity of china clay operations along the branch. Goonbarrow Junction signalbox survives, as do lower quadrant semaphore signals and a number of sidings. The line continues for half a mile to Molinnis road crossing and Bugle station; this section was double track between 1930 and 1964. The Bugle area was the terminus of the original Treffry Tramway until 1874, when the line was extended to St Dennis Junction. Bugle is the only original station on the branch that has not changed its name, and had down loading wharves and an up-side goods yard. A GWR signalbox replaced a CMR installation in 1916, and at the end of the 1920s an island platform was constructed in readiness for the 1930 track doubling to Goonbarrow, replacing the original single-face platform.

Just beyond Bugle on the down side was the gated entrance to the Wheal Rose branch, opened in 1893, effectively a half-mile-long siding that served Wheal Hope, East Goonbarrow, Martin's Goonbarrow and Great Beam Nos 1 and 2 kilns, while a spur from the branch served Wheal Virgin air dry and Boss Allen's Timber Wharf. The branch closed in 1964. As at Luxulyan there has been considerable rationalisation at Bugle, with the removal of goods yard, signals and sidings, although the signalbox continued in use as a ground frame for some years. The second line from Goonbarrow Junction was latterly used as a long siding to Carbis Wharf.

On leaving Bugle the former junction with the Carbis Wharf branch is on the down side, then the line climbs steeply towards Roche passing the highest point on the line before the station. Roche is named after Roche Rock, a nearby landmark. A single original platform gave way to two platforms in later years providing a further opportunity for trains to pass on the branch. There was also an up-side goods yard, all controlled from a signalbox. Goods facilities were discontinued in 1964 and the signalbox closed shortly afterwards. As with Luxulyan, now just a single platform face and a single track survive. After curving

Right:
A very special day for connoisseurs of motive power on the Newquay branch occurred on 22 March 1992, when, straying far away from their Southern Region base, a pair of Construction Sector Class 33s appeared with an enthusiasts' special, the 07.15 Basingstoke to Newquay via Falmouth Docks! Nos 33050 and 33063 cross the road at Molinnis Crossing and approach a derelict-looking Bugle, shortly after the Carbis Wharf branch had been lifted. Class 37 No 37675 was at the back of the Network SouthEast Mk 2B/C rolling stock. The 'Cornish Construction Crompton' special had passed the branch DMU at Goonbarrow, which can be seen in the distance. *JV*

Left:
The CMR wooden signalbox at Bugle, seen here, was replaced in 1916, so this early photograph of the station is probably Edwardian. In 1929-30 Bugle was rebuilt with an island platform. On the left are casks of china clay waiting to be loaded, while the china clay business seems to be brisk at the main down-side loading wharf. The station is behind the wagons on the left. In 2001 houses were being built where the foreground clay wagons are standing. *ECC, JV collection*

Right:
This 1950s view shows the island platform layout at Bugle. There are plenty of china clay wagons in the up yard as the Par-bound branch train pauses for custom. In the distance the GWR signalbox stands next to Molinnis Crossing; this was closed in 1973. Until the Carbis Wharf branch closed in August 1989 the line in the right foreground was effectively a dedicated single track from Goonbarrow, used exclusively by Carbis Wharf trains. *W. A. Camwell, SLS*

Left:
This picture is a personal favourite because not only does it feature Bugle but it also shows a newsworthy event on a perfect day. On 4 October 1991 single-car Class 121 No 55006 failed at Newquay and had to be rescued. Passengers were conveyed by a hastily arranged replacement bus service but the photographer was more interested in securing a picture of Railfreight Class 37 No 37673 hauling the failure back to St Blazey for repair. The ensemble passes Bugle's up fixed distant signal. The abandoned Carbis branch on the left would soon be lifted. *JV*

Right:
The Wheal Rose branch (in fact a long siding) opened in October 1893 and was one of the last projects undertaken by the CMR. The line served Wheal Hope, Wheal Virgin, East Goonbarrow, Martin's Goonbarrow, Great Beam Nos 1 and 2 and Wheal Rose. The half-mile-long line closed completely from 29 November 1964, and this view, taken a quarter of a century later, shows the track set in concrete at the end of the Wheal Rose line. *JV*

Left:
West of Bugle the next station is at Roche, which is remarkable in that the station was known as Holywell from 1876 until 1879, Victoria from 1879 to 1904 and Roche from 1904 until the present day. Roche village is about three-quarters of a mile south of the station, and its name is derived from the French for 'rock', Roche Rock being a nearby landmark. The goods yard at the up end of the station closed in 1964, and the passing loop was removed and the signalbox closed in 1965. The up platform and buildings on the left were demolished years ago.
JV collection

Above:

The Newquay branch traverses the wilds of Goss Moor and in the process crosses over the main A30 trunk road on a low bridge with a 14ft 3in headroom, under which lorries driven by inattentive drivers regularly get stuck. The bridge can be seen on the far left in this 1958 shot. Probably taken on a summer Saturday, the view features double-headed 4-6-0s in the shape of 'Manor' class No 7816 and 'Grange' class No 6832, hauling a massive 14-coach 12.30pm Newquay to London Paddington service. Now that's what you call a train! *Peter Gray*

underneath the main A30 the branch then crosses over the same road before a straight run across the bleak Goss Moor. There is a road crossing at Tregoss Moor, and although it is now single track, a small signalbox once controlled the eastern end of a double-track section to St Dennis Junction.

St Dennis Junction was the point where the Newquay & Cornwall Junction line from Burngullow joined the Newquay branch and where the Retew branch headed south into clay country. Until December 1986 the junction was also an important passing loop. In later years there was a spoil tip at St Dennis and in 1990-1 some new-generation CDA china clay wagons were 'de-coated' in the sidings. Now all sidings, loops, the second track to Tregoss, signalbox and all branch connections have been removed. Continuing towards Newquay, the branch deviates from the old original tramway alignment, which went through the 1874-abandoned 530yd Toldish Tunnel, to reach St Columb Road station. This once had two platforms and passing loop, goods yard and a substantial loading dock, but again the mid-1960s proved to be a disaster for railway infrastructure and from January 1965 all of the above were removed, leaving only a single track and a single-face platform.

The line continues across Halloon Crossing and Coswarth Crossing before entering the 31yd Coswarth Tunnel. The 1911 Quintrel Downs Platform is the next stopping place. Prior to opening there had been a passing loop and sidings here, controlled by a signalbox, but after the single-platform halt was opened the track layout comprised the single-line branch and two sidings, controlled from a ground frame in a gatehouse. The sidings were closed in 1965 and the gates and ground frame were removed in 1981. The line continues across farmland and passes Chapel and Trencreek Crossings to the site of Tolcarn Junction where the line to East Wheal Rose and Chacewater branched off. There was a triangular connection at this point and from 1931 a new single signalbox controlled all movements; the triangle was sometimes used for turning tender locomotives. There was no need for the junction once the line to Chacewater closed in 1963 and

Trevemper siding just south of the junction closed in 1964. The signalbox operated for the last time on 23 November 1964.

Beyond Tolcarn the line runs on to Trenance Viaduct; the original was known as 'the spider', being a flimsy timber structure incapable of supporting locomotives. It was replaced by the CMR in 1873-4 but by the 1930s the single-track structure had become inadequate for the volumes of traffic at Newquay, especially in the summer months. The third viaduct was ready before World War 2 but the trackwork had not been completed. The first train to cross it did so on 27 March 1939 but it would be a further seven years before the second track was in use. Once across the viaduct the trackwork once fanned out into platform roads on the north side and carriage sidings and goods yard to the south. The replacement for the 1904 GWR signalbox, built in 1946, was located in the middle of the trackwork, just off the end of Newquay's longest platform.

The location of Newquay station can be traced to the 1849 Treffry Tramway. Although not immediately obvious to visitors, the station is located on a narrow strip of land between the Trenance Valley (not to be confused with the Trenance Valley branch) and the cliffs above Newquay Bay, and well positioned for the town that grew up around it. The station was opened by the CMR in 1876, two years after the line from Fowey and St Blazey had been opened for freight and mineral traffic. The original station was an unpretentious single-platform affair with a stone station building, and prior to 1904 there was a CMR signalbox, goods shed and engine shed. However, when traffic increased and the line from Chacewater was about to open in 1904-5 the whole area was redeveloped. A replacement signalbox, new locomotive depot, enlarged goods shed and goods yard and a much larger three-platform station layout were all built. The platforms were lengthened again in 1928 and 1934. The engine shed closed in the 1930s when it became no longer necessary to stable locomotives at Newquay overnight.

Holiday traffic at Newquay was really impressive and on a summer Saturday in the 1950s up to 20,000 passengers would

Above:

The site of St Dennis Junction featured here first saw tramway tracks in June 1849 when Treffry's Tramway was opened between Newquay Harbour and St Dennis and Hendra Crazey, with horses providing the motive power. In due course this became part of the Drinnick Mill branch (centre right). In 1874 the CMR line from St Blazey made a junction here (left) and at the same time the Retew branch down to Melangoose Mill opened (far right). The other line seen here, above the last carriage, is a siding used for tipping old ballast. On 8 July 1955 '5700' class 0-6-PT No 9673 negotiates the junction with the 6.35pm Par to Newquay train. Note the white spoil tips around Gothers Clay Works in the background. *R. C. Riley, The Transport Treasury*

arrive at the seaside resort. However, from about 1960 it was the usual story of rapid decline. The Chacewater line closed in 1963, goods facilities were being run down to end in 1964, sidings were removed, and platforms were reduced in length, one becoming unsafe. Eventually the run-round crossover was removed and in 1987 the signalbox was closed and the signals removed, leaving just a single-line stub using a single platform face. This meant the end of locomotive-hauled trains, unless they were 'topped and tailed'. As if this was not enough, in 1992 a true act of vandalism took place when BR demolished the original 1874 station building. With so much appalling 1960s-type modern architecture in the Newquay station area it is hard to believe that the railway and the local council could allow this rare piece of history to be destroyed. A primitive 'vandal-proof' shelter was constructed, which was promptly vandalised. Newquay station now has nothing to commend it!

Journey times over the years changed dramatically and from a 1906 time of 7hr 55min from London Paddington, the IC125 'Atlantic Coast Express' in 1989 took 4hr 43min. From 1987 only a single holiday train could use Newquay at any one time and up and down trains on summer Saturdays had to pass at Goonbarrow Junction signalbox or at St Blazey. On the positive side, Newquay is now the only Cornish branch line to have through workings from London, Scotland and the North on summer Saturdays. However, at other times, and especially in winter, traffic is very thin and the line must be loss-making. Traffic volumes are not

helped by the unbelievably inept train timers who, in the summer of 2001, had First Great Western's 'Cornish Riviera' express arriving at Par at 13.52 with the penultimate Wales & West Railway's Newquay train of the day leaving Par at 13.40! With only four trains per day and connections like that there would appear to be either a hidden agenda for closure or a lack of business acumen.

The Newquay line has had a remarkable history and the variety of scenery between Par and Newquay is hard to rival. The branch train is often a single-car unit and even in the 21st century there are three locations with operational semaphore signals and signalboxes. Whenever there is an availability problem, an accident on one of the ungated crossings or a lorry jammed under the low bridge on the A30 road across Goss Moor, bus substitutes are quickly provided. In 1987 there were plans to reroute the Newquay branch via the freight-only Drinnick Mill branch to connect with the existing alignment at the site of St Dennis Junction but at current passenger income levels the cost would be very hard to justify. In any event, the line from St Blazey to Goonbarrow would still have to be maintained for china clay trains. Much depends on whether the county council continues with plans to widen Cornwall's main trunk road across Goss Moor, current thinking being that a new route to the north is the preferred option. We must be grateful that the Newquay branch line is still open, but the hope for the future must be that somebody finds some scope to develop traffic to ensure its survival.

Right:
The sight of IC125 units on the Newquay branch always seems an anachronism. When photographed on 25 September 1993 the St Columb Road passing loop, goods yard and all other paraphernalia had long gone and only a scene of dereliction greeted the down 06.05 Leeds to Newquay service. At least the holidaymakers on board would be greeted by sunshine at Newquay. *JV*

Left:
In a scene from more civilised times, when St Columb Road station was staffed and a resident signalman controlled train movements, '4500' Prairie tank No 5519 pauses with a down Newquay-bound local in the 1950s. Prior to November 1878 the station was called Halloon. The goods yard here was very busy and was enlarged in 1910, while the passing loop was extended in 1931 and 1933. Strange, with that background, that it should become a single-track unstaffed halt from January 1965. *W. A. Camwell, SLS*

Right:
There was a siding and a signalbox at the site of Quintrel Downs long before the small station was opened in October 1911, and on that date the signalbox closed in favour of a gatehouse containing signal levers. Messrs Martyn & Lewarnes owned the private siding on the right. Just departing from Quintrel Downs with a Par to Newquay train in the early 1950s is No 4559. The crossing gates and the last of the signals were removed in 1981.
Donald Kelk

Above:
It is now exceedingly difficult to secure photographs of locomotives on the Newquay branch west of Goonbarrow Junction as all passenger trains are in the hands of diesel units and there are no run-round facilities at Newquay. However, Sunday 20 March 1994 was an exception in that engineers had occupation of the line resulting in a locomotive-hauled ballast train. Having re-ballasted a section of track near Coswarth Tunnel and visited Newquay, gleaming Class 37 No 37412, with No 37413 at the rear, hauls empty 'Dogfish' wagons back to St Blazey in perfect climatic conditions. The buildings of Newquay are on the horizon. *JV*

Above:
This 'little and large' motive power combination east of the short 44yd Coswarth Tunnel on 9 July 1960 comprises work-stained 'Grange' class 4-6-0 No 6875 *Hindford Grange* and '5700' class 0-6-0PT No 8702 powering the 12.40pm Newquay to Cardiff train towards Quintrel Downs. Diesels would soon relegate scenes such as this to the history book. *Peter Gray*

Below:
A very poignant day on the Newquay branch occurred on 4 October 1987, the last day of locomotive-hauled trains on the branch and the last day of operation of Newquay signalbox, and consequently the end of semaphore signals at the Cornish terminus. To commemorate the event a double-headed Class 50 excursion was run from Paddington to Newquay. Enthusiasts mill around the platform before the 17.40 departure behind Nos 50035 *Ark Royal* and 50034 *Furious*. All but one of the tracks, the signalbox, signals and main station buildings have since been removed. Subsequently the only locomotive-hauled passenger trains have been 'topped and tailed' Royal Trains (see also the photograph on page 137). Here (inset) HRH The Prince of Wales uses Newquay platform on his way to visit the Duchy of Cornwall estates on 26 March 1991. *JV*

Left:
This old postcard view of Newquay station in 1906 features a small 2-4-0T at the head of a short train; the awning on the right can be identified in the photograph on the previous page. Newquay station opened in 1876 and initially there were but two trains a day to and from Fowey. Gradually more trains worked to Newquay as holiday traffic grew and, in 1905, the Chacewater line opened. The posters are advertising beer and tobacco — some things never change! *JV collection*

Below:
At some locations photographs of the early diesel era are more difficult to come by than the age of steam, probably because the dyed-in-the-wool steam fan never bothered photographing diesels. On 31 July 1965, during the diesel-hydraulic era, Class 43 North British 'Warship' No D850 *Swift* heads the 11.45 train to York while the 10.05 to Paddington is triple-headed by Class 22s Nos 6325, 6322 and 6349. The nearest platform at Newquay became unsafe in later years and was fenced off. *T. Mahoney*

Left:
In my book *The Newquay Branch and its Branches* book I stated that 'what must surely be the ultimate in rationalisation and a depressing scene to boot is the Newquay of the 1990s..... for now only the old station buildings remain'. Well, it turned out not to be the 'ultimate' and things did get worse. The 'vandal-proof' shelter was vandalised and removed, and official vandals flattened the original 1876 station building to make way for a car park. This is now the desolate scene at Newquay and while the tiny new shelter is attractive, Newquay station is a miserable place. Winter and off-peak loadings are so light that the only surprise is that the town continues to have a railway service of any description. *JV*

14. Goonbarrow Branch

One of the last acts of the CMR, even though under the operational control of the GWR, was to open the Goonbarrow and Wheal Rose branches, near Bugle. The proposed 3½-mile Goonbarrow branch would penetrate the heart of china clay country and be riddled with sidings serving over 10 china clay and industrial installations. With a capital of £24,000, work started in 1890 but due to the number of embankments, overbridges, sidings and even a tunnel it was not until 2 October 1893 that the line opened. The branch was always a restricted route regarding locomotives passed to work the line. The CMR built a locomotive shed at Stenalees and to work the branch they acquired a 27-ton 0-6-0 saddle tank from Messrs Peckett & Sons of Bristol. The locomotive was appropriately named *Goonbarrow* and, absorbed by the GWR in 1896 and given the number 1388, was sold in 1911 to a South Wales colliery (other motive power is mentioned later).

As the splendid Ordnance Survey map of about 1880 reproduced overleaf shows, there was at that time a junction to some sidings on the site of the present Goonbarrow Junction, controlled by Rosevear Sidings signalbox. A single-line siding from Rosevear ran down to Wheal Fortune china clay works and continued to a head-shunt with a reverse siding making its way

Above:
The 3½-mile Goonbarrow branch was opened in 1893, during the last days of the CMR, and was constructed to penetrate deep into the heart of china clay country where a large number of clay pits and associated dries were located. The line left the Newquay branch at a point known as Rosevear, which was to become Goonbarrow Junction. In the 19th century there were clay works known as Hallivet, Rosevear and Wheal Anna in the area but now only the large Rocks works survives. At the beginning of the branch was Wheal Henry, seen on the right. Running round its train after arrival at Goonbarrow on 23 April 1987 is No 37175. *JV*

Above:

Part of the Goonbarrow branch closed in 1965 but it closed completely on 3 December 1978. Now only a section two or three train lengths long survives as a long head-shunt for Goonbarrow traffic. After a bit of 'bramble bashing' this location on the old branch can be reached, but it is a gamble whether an incoming train will travel this far up the line. On 18 March 1994 No 37412 arrives at Goonbarrow from Fowey with a train of a suitable length to necessitate a trip up the Goonbarrow branch stub. *JV*

Below:

The left-hand map *(Crown Copyright)* shows a fascinating illustration of Rosevear Junction in 1880 (which became Goonbarrow Junction in 1893) and the position of the CMR signalbox, replaced in 1893. When the Goonbarrow branch was opened in 1893 there were significant changes made at this location and now it is the site of many sidings and the substantial clay drying plant rejoicing in the name of Rocks. On the right is a not-to-scale map of the Goonbarrow branch that opened in 1893 and closed in stages between 1965 and 1978.

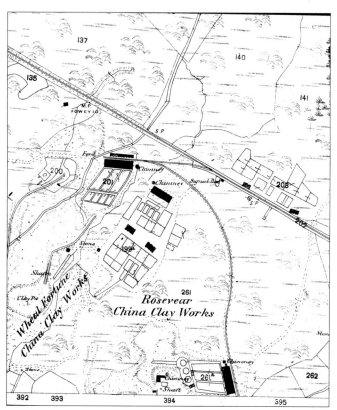

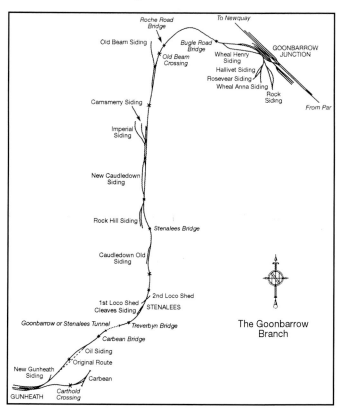

down to Rosevear works. Sidings called Hallivet, Wheal Anna and Rocks were later added to the track layout in the area. In 1890-3 the complex was hugely changed with the arrival of the Goonbarrow branch, and a new GWR signalbox replaced the old CMR example (replaced again by the present box in about 1909). The line left the junction and almost immediately on the down side was Wheal Henry, a coal-fired pan dry that closed decades ago. The line then climbed at 1 in 39 away from the Goonbarrow complex and part circled the village of Bugle by crossing both the Bodmin to St Austell and Bugle to Roche roads before reaching Old Beam Crossing. This was followed at the 288-mile 35-chain point by a reverse siding of the same name on the up side, which served the North Goonbarrow Clay Company, later ECC; this siding was taken out of use on 20 March 1969. The points giving access to the various works sidings were controlled by separate ground frames.

After passing over Carnsmerry Crossing there was a positive rash of sidings including Carnsmerry, Imperial, New Caudledown and Rock Hill. Within 25 chains (550yd) there were no fewer than five ground frames. All of these clay works sidings were on the up side and some of the sidings formed loops, which facilitated shunting operations. Just before New Caudledown Siding another rough road crossed the line at Netley Crossing. These clay sidings all closed between 1946 and about 1977. In February 1977 the Cornish Steam Locomotive Preservation Society set up camp at Imperial Clay Dries and moved both locomotives and rolling stock to that atmospheric location. However, track lifting on the branch took place in March 1979, which prevented the group from running trains over any significant part of the branch, although they regularly held 'open days' for the public, giving rides over a short stretch of line from their wooden 'Imperial Halt'. Following

notice of a huge increase in site rental by ECC in 1987 they moved to the Bodmin & Wenford Railway at Bodmin General.

Continuing to climb, the line crossed the Bugle to Stenalees road where, on the up side at 289 miles 18 chains, was Caudledown Old Siding. This wharf served not only the clay industry for outgoing traffic but also for incoming coal to fire the various pan dries. On the approach to Stenalees there was a water tower and it was at this site that the replacement locomotive shed was located. Cleaves Siding at 289 miles 40 chains followed on the up side and this was reputedly the site of the original engine shed; the siding closed back in 1933. After entering an ever-deepening cutting the line plunged into the 345yd Goonbarrow Tunnel at Stenalees. On leaving the tunnel the line climbed steeply to cross the Stenalees to St Austell road on a girder bridge. This was also the summit of the steeply graded branch, which then fell at 1 in 39 towards Gunheath. Trains were obliged to stop and 'pin down the brakes' in either direction.

Oil Siding, on the down side, was on the course of the original Goonbarrow branch alignment (see the accompanying photograph); the course was changed following the extension of Carbean clay pit in about 1910. Oil Siding opened in 1926 to serve Carbean electric sub-station. Another 31 chains down the branch a siding to H. D. Pochin & Co's New Gunheath works, No 4 kiln, was laid in 1921. This was another company that was to be absorbed by ECLP/ECC. The line then continued to reach Gunheath, where there were sidings and loading wharves. Trains for Carbean reversed at Gunheath and descended the single-line branch at 1 in 40 and 1 in 35. After passing the gated Carbean Crossing the line reached Carbean, 290 miles 75 chains. The layout at the tiny terminus was cramped and comprised a loading wharf, a short run-round loop and a head-shunt. Beyond the head-

Below:
The cooper's wagon has arrived with 80 empty casks for use in the transportation of china clay, while loaded casks can be seen in the wagons. This local Bugle photographer's view of about 1904 vintage shows one of the clay dries at the northern, Goonbarrow, end of the branch. When loaded these casks weighed a quarter of a ton each and approximately 40, or 10 tons, could be accommodated in an early five-plank four-wheeled wagon.
JV collection

Left:
When photographed in the mid-1950s there was a little traffic at Old Beam Siding on the Goonbarrow branch as '1600' class No 1626 picked up a few box vans, probably filled with bagged clay. The point giving access to the siding was removed on 20 March 1969, although there had been little traffic in the years immediately before. The trackwork is typical of many of the minor sidings. The Ford Consul car and the Thames Trader lorry help to date the picture. *Hugh Davies*

Right:
This picture shows New Caudledown Siding with a single box van standing adjacent to the linhay of the clay works. This siding effectively made a long loop with the branch, having access to the branch via points controlled by ground frames at both the northern and southern ends. In the 1980s the Cornish Steam Locomotive Preservation Society was located at the nearby Imperial dries. *JV*

Left:
This view shows the southern portal of the 341yd tunnel at Stenalees after abandonment of the branch. The gradient through the tunnel continued at 1 in 39 to the summit of the line, but within a few hundred yards of this point the line would descend at a similar gradient. This cutting has now been filled in, obscuring the portal. *JV*

Right:
The returning Goonbarrow branch goods, the 1pm from Carbean, is double-headed by a pair of '1600' class 0-6-0PTs on 13 August 1956. The train is approaching the water tower at Stenalees, once the site of a small branch engine shed. The massive clay tip in the background is that of Imperial works. This entire area was dominated by the china clay industry and further clay works stacks can be seen above the locomotives. *Hugh Davies*

Centre right:
Below Stenalees there was a deviation to the original route constructed in about 1910 to enable Carbean china clay pits to be extended. A short section of the remains of the old route, on the left, known as Oil Siding, was used to serve an electricity sub-station. The main branch, on the right, descended towards Gunheath, as seen in this June 1965 view. The stacks in the centre belong to the Carbean and Gunheath works respectively. *Maurice Dart*

Lower right:
On a dull summer's day in June 1956 an 0-6-0PT, probably No 1626, propels 13 empty wagons into New Gunheath Siding, while the shunter walks through the drizzle to uncouple the wagons. Gates, such as the one seen here (bottom right), protected many such sidings. In order to reach Carbean, the end of the branch, trains had to reverse at Gunheath and descend at 1 in 35 for about half a mile. The Carbean section can just be glimpsed at a lower level, centre left. *Hugh Davies*

Left:
The loading wharf at Carbean backed on to the main A391 Bodmin to St Austell road, and the track layout was very cramped, which generally resulted in a complex shunting process. The little terminus was 291 miles from Paddington via the original GWR route. Maurice Dart states that the tips in the background belong to Higher Ninestones, Penhale, Single Rose, Great Teverbyn and Lower Ninestones china clay pits. This section of line closed in 1965 but there had been no traffic since 1963.
Norman Simmons

shunt was a 291 milepost, the distance from Paddington via Bristol! At Carbean the Goonbarrow branch was less than a mile from the 1920-built Lansalson or Trenance Valley branch to the south, but due to the hilly terrain, connecting the two was never in prospect.

Other than the 0-6-0ST locomotive *Goonbarrow* one other small locomotive was used in the construction of the line, an 1872-built 0-6-0ST called *John Owen* built by Messrs Fox Walker for the Whitland & Taff Vale Railway. It became GWR No 1385 until sold in 1911. Also in the early days Manning Wardle 0-6-0ST *Ringing Rock* worked the line and it too was absorbed by the GWR and allocated the number 1380, until sold in 1912. This locomotive ended up on the Kent & East Sussex Railway but its name was transferred to another Manning Wardle tank locomotive on the Selsey Tramway in Sussex, another of Col Holman F. Stephens's lines. These locomotives were joined by the converted CMR tank engines described in the previous chapter. Two other classes worthy of mention were the '2021'/'2181' classes of GWR 0-6-0PT and their '1600' class 0-6-0PT successors, which all worked the line regularly. Diesel locomotives did put in appearances between the end of steam and the closure of the line, and they comprised Classes 08, 22 and 25. Other classes of steam locomotive worked the line from time to time but special permission had to be granted and they could work over only part of the branch.

One train per day normally traversed the branch and regularly two locomotives were employed because of the complexities of shunting the many sidings. Locomotives often 'topped and tailed' trains but they could sometimes be observed double-heading. Sometimes wagons were propelled and when only one locomotive was used a complex plan was devised so that certain sidings were visited only in the up or down direction. At times two locomotives would return with separate trains, one from the New Caudledown area and the other from Carbean/Gunheath. Trains up from Carbean were propelled. An overall speed limit of 10mph was imposed. In the 1950s the daily train left St Blazey at 8.10am and returned from Carbean at 1.00pm. There were never any signalboxes on the branch, the train staff being provided by the Goonbarrow Junction signalman.

Technology in the china clay industry was instrumental in the gradual demise of traffic on the branch. As mentioned, Cleaves

Siding closed in 1933 and as more clay was piped in slurry form to central drying locations, and as old coal-fired pan kilns were closed, particularly in the 1950s, traffic volumes diminished. The line beyond New Caudledown south ground frame to Gunheath and Carbean closed on 29 April 1965, having seen no use for two years. The rest of the line from New Caudledown to a point near Wheal Henry, south of Goonbarrow Junction, closed on 3 December 1978. The last working was a Class 25 diesel delivering CSLPS stock on 1 December 1978. The track was removed in 1979, except for a section beyond Wheal Henry that is still used as a long head-shunt for clay trains visiting Rocks Works at Goonbarrow.

Today little of the branch remains. Sections of it can be traced but many installations have been demolished and, as with most china clay pits, over time the entire landscape moves as spoil is deposited and various works take place. In Bugle the area around Imperial and New Caudledown still has evidence of the railway, with track set in concrete, and at Carbean a 'hole in the hedge' gives access to the old Carbean wharf. It was a fascinating line in that its full length lasted only seven decades but in its heyday it was the epitome of the china clay rail scene in Cornwall. The line never had a passenger service and was little known, so it is fortuitous that a few railway photographers recorded the scene.

There is still plenty of action at Goonbarrow Junction. Every weekday a number of trains leave Rocks for the docks at Fowey. ECC (now Imerys) Rocks has always been an important installation producing large quantities of china clay, so much so that the clay company normally employs a works shunter. In recent times this has been Rolls-Royce/Sentinel 0-4-0 No P403D called *Denise*, but this was later replaced by ECC-owned Class 08 No P402D *Annabel*. On occasions wagons are loaded for long-distance services to Stoke-on-Trent, Glasgow and even mainland Europe. The old signalbox is still operational and semaphore signals abound. As mentioned in the previous chapter, the only passing loop on the Newquay branch is located at Goonbarrow. The box contains single-line tokens for the section to St Blazey and behind it there is a shunter's office. The track layout has been changed many times at Goonbarrow and Rocks to reflect the changing needs of the railway and the industry. Perhaps the most encouraging aspect of the Goonbarrow branch is that there is still a tiny piece in operation.

15. Carbis Branch

The Carbis (Wharf) branch, or 'Carbis Siding' (originally Carbus) as it was known, was one of my favourites. There was nothing extraordinary about the branch; it simply presented a challenge to photograph a train on the line. The 1-mile-long siding started life as part of the original 1874 Cornwall Minerals Railway (CMR) network. Incorporated in the 1873 Act, its primary purpose was to serve the needs of the china clay industry, a matter of clay out, coal in! The line started at Bugle on the Newquay branch, a location that was effectively the terminus of the 1843-4 Treffry Tramway from Ponts Mill. Great Wheal Prosper and Rosemellyn clay works became particularly important in the 19th century, not only for volume but also for the quality of the clay that they produced, and the owners of the pits were the same people who owned the land for the envisaged trackbed, so the CMR had no problems in acquiring the land to build the railway.

Below:
For my *Illustrated History of China Clay Trains* book, now in its second edition, a photograph of a train on the Carbis branch was required. This was an approximately monthly event and good fortune was needed to be in the vicinity when the event occurred. A compassionate St Blazey management came to the rescue by making sure that whatever the circumstances, a photograph of such a train would be included in that book. On the above occasion, a wet day in October 1985, No 37207 *William Cookworthy*, proudly wearing its Cornish Railways insignia and crest, approaches Bugle with three 'clay hoods' in tow. The Newquay branch is on the right and the Wheal Rose branch once ran between the metal posts and across the road on the left. *JV*

The CMR left construction until very late in the day. In February 1874 work had still not commenced, yet by 1 June the line had been completed. The reason for the company's apparent complacency was that, being a very straight line with little in the way of gradients, construction was straightforward. William West's foundry at St Blazey provided the ironwork for a road overbridge support at Carbis Bridge, just as it had supplied similar materials to the CMR for building other parts of the railway, including the girders for the new Trenance Valley Viaduct at Newquay.

Although the branch left the Newquay line just west of Bugle station, from 1910 the branch was accessed via a separate line that served Bugle's down-side wharves and the Wheal Rose branch. The line curved to the southwest then straightened up until about half a mile down the track, at the 288-mile 56-chain point, where a single-track siding to Rosemellyn Works branched off on the down side. The line gently curved across Rosemellyn Crossing and under the Bugle to Roche road before branching into two short sidings. One siding was Carbis Wharf, where general merchandise and china clay from other pits was loaded into wagons, and the other reached Great Wheal Prosper, serving the china clay works of the same name. This was acquired by the Goonvean & Rostowrack China Clay Company, owned by Lord Falmouth, in 1937.

In 1901 the length of the two sidings at the end of the branch was doubled at a cost to the GWR and the Great Wheal Prosper China Stone & Clay Company of £331 16s 7d. At about the turn of the century the single-track Rosemellyn siding branched into two roads near the loading wharf. Originally a catch point was situated on the Carbis Wharf side of Carbis Bridge but this was later relocated to a point between Carbis Bridge and Rosemellyn Crossing. In 1912 another siding was laid, just on the Bugle side of Rosemellyn siding but on the up side, to serve the large pan dry at West Goonbarrow clay works. Rosemellyn Works was taken over by English Clays Lovering & Pochin (ECLP) in 1936 and was the first of the three installations on the branch to close its rail connection in 1948. West Goonbarrow, after many years of production, closed from 31 December 1967 and the track was removed in 1969. The second line at the Carbis Wharf terminus was also closed and removed, but the line soldiered on serving only the Goonvean company's old coal-fired clay dries, the last to operate in Cornwall.

Traffic on the branch had been heavy in the 1950s and sometimes the daily train was double-headed. Trains were always propelled to Carbis and hauled back because throughout the line's history there was never a run-round loop at the terminus. Just

beyond Carbis Wharf was Carbis brickworks where bricks were produced for building use throughout Cornwall. Gradually traffic dwindled, yet although lines and works were closing all around the area the Carbis branch survived. Following the complete rationalisation of the Bugle station area in 1973 and closure of the Wheal Rose branch, the former double track from Goonbarrow Junction became a very long siding that ran parallel to the Newquay branch but which served only Carbis Wharf. Towards the end of its life just a single Goonvean & Rostowrack Company customer received china clay from Carbis, the bathroom furniture and ceramic manufacturer Armitage Shanks near Glasgow in Scotland.

In the final years a single wagon would be propelled from Goonbarrow Junction every three to four weeks. Sometimes the locomotive would wait at Carbis for the wagon to be loaded but at other times the wagon would be dropped for between half a day and a couple of days pending pick-up. When the small 13-ton wooden-bodied wagons were withdrawn from long hauls in 1982 it was normally an 80-tonne (gross) 'Tiger' wagon on lease from Tiger Railcar Leasing's ECC International fleet that was used, and a new concrete loading 'base' was installed at Carbis to support the newcomer. The favourite was No TRL 11600, the same wagon being used in order to prevent cross-contamination of clays, although on rare occasions a smaller 32-tonne PGA wagon was used. If left at Carbis, wooden chocks would be placed under the wagon to prevent a runaway down the short 1 in 44 gradient towards Rosemellyn. Either a front-loading tractor or a small portable conveyor belt unit was used to load the wagon. Goonvean lorries were also loaded at Carbis.

The operation of the branch was inconvenient to British Rail, with workings infrequent and the payload small. After Bugle and later St Dennis Junction signalboxes closed, it was difficult to find a path for the Carbis freight because it was not possible to have two trains west of Goonbarrow Junction at the same time, even though effectively the Carbis branch was separate from the parallel Newquay branch; apparently this was due to the mechanism at the ungated Molinnis Crossing. Accordingly the freight had to run in any short gaps in the passenger service timetable, the favourite paths being early morning before the first branch passenger train or, if slick, during the late lunch period when the branch train was on its way to Par. The run was time-consuming because of a slow speed restriction, poor-quality track, crossing gates that were operated by the train crew and wagon coupling. The round trip would normally take about half an hour, without waiting for loading. As if to show its disinterest, BR had not dispatched the weedkilling train down the branch for at least

Above:
This nostalgic scene shows the Carbis byway to good effect. Pannier tank No 1626 pauses by a splendid wooden fixed distant signal during shunting operations in the summer of 1960. The shunter is throwing the point for West Goonbarrow siding, where a few wagons will be collected. The works closed in 1965 leaving only Great Wheal Prosper at the end of the line as a revenue-earner for the railway. *Hugh Davies*

a couple of years resulting in a slimy, weed-covered trackbed. This in turn had health and safety implications for train crews and resulted in even 107-tonne Class 37 diesels slipping badly on the track.

From the clay company's point of view it was not worth paying BR to keep the line open, as the cost of track replacement would have been prohibitive. Also the Goonvean company had another rail siding at Trelavour, near ECC Parkandillack, and with new pipelines about to be commissioned between Great Wheal Prosper and Trelavour any clay could be loaded there. Finally the old coal-fired pan dry was nearing the end of its life expectancy and closure was inevitable. In all the circumstances it was therefore decided to close the old CMR line and the very last wagon was loaded and hauled out from Carbis Wharf on 25 August 1989. There was a three-month trial, pending completion of the Goonvean pipeline, whereby china clay was conveyed by road from Great Wheal Prosper to Trelavour for loading on to railway wagons. The trial was successful and hence after 115 years of service the Carbis branch was finally closed to all traffic.

In the days of steam a small tank locomotive, or sometimes a pair, would work the line and in later years it was the '1600' 0-6-0 pannier tanks that dominated. The branch had its own dedicated brake-van, suitably stencilled 'For use between Goonbarrow and Carbis'. In later years it was Class 22, 25 and 37 diesels that worked the line, although only photographs of Class 37s have been forthcoming. A few years prior to closure a railway enthusiasts' DMU charter worked the line but otherwise it was always freight-only. The line was lifted in 1992. The passing of this old weed-covered line was the end of an era. Great Wheal Prosper was the last pan dry served by rail; it was one of the works not owned by English China Clay, workings were erratic, the line passed through the now sad site of Bugle, it was part of the original CMR, and above all it simply oozed atmosphere. To photograph a train was something of a safari and 'insider information' via St Blazey or the Goonbarrow signalman was essential. Without such help I might never have photographed action on the line and I am able here to thank publicly all concerned for ensuring a train ran at the appropriate time!

Right:
On 5 May 1989 Railfreight Class 37 No 37669 works the Carbis branch in the early morning. At 06.50 the locomotive is approaching Rosemellyn gates, which will be opened by the shunter who can be seen hanging on to the side of the locomotive. Even though closure is just three months away, the occasionally used gates have just been replaced following an 'incident'. *JV*

Left:
It was 'up with the lark' again on 2 September 1988 to record the Carbis freight on film. Most unusually an 80-tonne 'Tiger' wagon was not available and a much smaller 32-tonne PGA vehicle was used, with tarpaulin sheeting in place to protect the china clay. Having just passed the slip point at Carbis, No 37674 is backlit by the early morning sun as it makes for Goonbarrow Junction at 07.40. The stack belongs to West Goonbarrow. *JV*

Above:
In years gone by the loading dock on the right was for the use of both china clay and general freight at Carbis Wharf, while the track on the left was used solely by the wonderfully named Great Wheal Prosper Clay Kiln. Trains were always propelled to Carbis because run-round facilities were never provided. Slumbering at Carbis in July 1960 is 0-6-0PT No 1664 with a pair of GWR-style brake-vans. The chimney on the right belongs to Carbis brickworks. *Hugh Davies*

Right:
Carbis was a wonderful backwater and a great favourite of the author. Photography was always a challenge. No 37669 has just propelled a single 'Tiger' wagon, No TRL 11600, out from Goonbarrow Junction, the shunter has uncoupled the wagon and he is screwing down the manual brake. Wooden chocks were also placed under the wheels to prevent runaways down the 1 in 44 to Rosemellyn Crossing. Great Wheal Prosper Clay Kiln was the very last coal-fired pan kiln in Cornwall and the coal can be seen on the extreme left. The Goonvean & Rostowrack Clay Company owned the now derelict works, the last train running on 25 August 1989. *JV*

16. Retew Branch

The Retew branch was another line built to serve a growing china clay and china stone industry. The line is shown in the 1873 Cornwall Minerals Railway Act as railway 'No 3', with Retew spelt 'Ratew'. Although extended in later years, the branch was to be 2 miles and 1 furlong in length commencing 'in the Parish of St Columb Major by a junction with the New Quay (*sic*) Railway at a point about 260yd southeastward of the turnpike road from Truro to Bodmin passing through the Parish of St Denis (*sic*) and terminating in the Parish of St Enoder at or near the Melangoose clay works'. The line ran close to the course of the infant River Fal. Construction seems to have been fairly straightforward and the line opened, with the rest of the CMR, on 1 June 1874. Prior to the opening of the CMR there had been

missing sections of line between St Dennis Junction (then Bodmin Road Junction) and Bugle, and between Hendra, south of St Dennis Junction, and Drinnick Mill on the Newquay & Cornwall Junction Railway. Accordingly from the opening day any china clay transported by rail from dries on the Retew branch was able to reach Par and Fowey.

The traffic returns from the line were very encouraging and the GWR could see the potential as pits to the south of Melangoose grew in size, in terms of output and area. Accordingly in 1912 the GWR extended the line about 1½ miles southward from Melangoose to serve works at Virginia, West Treviscoe, Burgotha, Tolbenny, Melbur and Meledor. A further short extension to New Meledor Mill, later Collins Rotary Drier, was ready for service on

Below:
Another view of St Dennis Junction appears on page 146, but this 1947 view shows a line of wagons to the right of the signalbox on the alignment of the Retew branch. The line was opened with most of the CMR network in 1874 but was extended from its original terminus of Melangoose to Meledor Mill in 1912. The line was normally traversed by one train per day until decline set in during the 1950s and 1960s. *JV collection*

Right:
The first crossing on the Retew
branch south of St Dennis
Junction was Gaverigan, across
the Indian Queens to St Dennis
road. The branch was only 4 miles
2 chains long, yet there were a
huge number of sidings and
works with rail connections.
Returning to St Dennis Junction
in this 1950 shot is '4500' class
Prairie No 4526. *P. Q. Treloar
collection*

Left:
One by one the clay works closed
as pipeline technology improved,
small works were absorbed by
larger ones, small-capacity pan
kilns became uneconomic and
English China Clays absorbed
many small private companies.
Only 10 sidings were in operation
by 1950 and this rapidly reduced
thereafter. In the 1970s traffic
was very sparse and the last
recorded revenue-earning train
was taken out of Collins dries in
September 1980. The track was
lifted in 1983 and in this 1986
record of Melangoose siding and
clay works nature is reclaiming
the land. The 'main' branch is on
the right. *JV*

Right:
This rare view taken in the early
part of the 20th century shows
china stone being loaded into
wagons by wheelbarrow at
Virginia clay works. The siding
seen here extended a quarter of a
mile from the Retew branch, and
Virginia had its own internal
narrow gauge tramway. The
siding closed in 1965 and the
hugely enlarged works now covers
any evidence of the once busy
siding. *JV collection*

11 October 1921. At its peak the line was busy, serving over a dozen clay works and public wharves, and in addition to the standard gauge branch, many of the clay works had their own internal narrow gauge tramway systems. In researching the history of the Retew branch it became clear that the names given to the various sidings serving particular works were not always the same as the local names given to those works, while in other cases the names of the works had changed, for example McLarens (or Wheal Remfrey) Siding, New Trerice (or Trewella) Siding and Dry Kiln (or South Fraddon) Siding!

The junction at St Dennis is on the edge of Goss Moor and the single track Retew branch headed in a southerly direction and descended towards the first road crossing at Gaverigan, on the St Dennis village to Indian Queens road. The line fell at just over 1 in 200 to reach Trerice Crossing. Just beyond the crossing at 1 mile 35 chains on the up side was Trerice Siding, formerly serving Wheal Remfrey brickworks; this siding closed in 1966. Just 16 chains further down the branch was McLarens (or Wheal Remfrey) Siding, which formed a 180yd loop between the north and south ground frames. The siding came into use in 1924 and closed in 1966. On a falling 1 in 149 gradient New Trerice (or Trewella) Siding branched off on the down side at 2 miles 4 chains. A few yards further along the branch but on the up side was Fal Valley (or Retew) Siding, open between 1882 and 1972. Just beyond the ground frame was a third road level crossing, known as Retew.

At 2 miles 18 chains along the branch on the down side was a comparative newcomer, Dry Kiln (or South Fraddon) Siding, which has also been referred to as Great Halwyn. The siding opened in 1939 and was removed in 1973. At 2 miles 25 chains there was an interesting track configuration where on the up side there was a 9-chain loop called New Halwyn Siding, while on the down side between 2 miles 27 chains and 2 miles 36 chains there was another 9-chain loop, the Retew Loop. Although the lines were not parallel, a map of the line gives the impression of a triple track branch! Within a few yards of the Retew Loop south ground frame was Anchor Siding north ground frame, which controlled Wheal Benallick Siding. Beyond the Wheal Benallick Works the siding continued to Melangoose clay works. Anchor Siding south ground frame on the up side gave access to Melangoose Mill public siding. At 2 miles 43 chains Grove Siding diverged on the

up side, where there were deep wooden chutes angled down into the railway wagons for loading. This area was the terminus of the original 1874 Retew branch, although curiously the mileage was approximately 3 furlongs longer than that specified in the Act.

At right angles to the above sidings was the large Anchor china clay works, which was served by a reverse siding branching off at the 2-mile 52-chain mark on the up side. The siding was opened in 1906 and removed in 1972. Two sidings on the up side of the branch were added to this complex of trackwork in 1925, their main use being to accommodate shunting movements and for wagon storage. At this point the line turned sharply to the southeast through almost 90° and continued to fall at 1 in 40 towards Meledor. At 2 miles 62 chains, also on the up side, was Virginia Siding ground frame, which controlled the siding down through the picturesque Treviscoe Wood to the substantial Virginia clay works. The siding was virtually a short branch, extending over a quarter of a mile from the Retew branch. It opened in 1912 (the same date as the GWR extension to the branch) and was closed in 1965. After crossing the River Fal twice another siding with a 1912 to 1965 lifespan, West Treviscoe Siding, was reached, branching off on the down side at 3 miles 3 chains to form a loop with the main branch. At this point the Retew branch was, 'as the crow flies', only about half a mile west of Treviscoe on the Drinnick Mill branch.

The line continued to fall at 1 in 40 through pleasant woodland and crossed the River Fal twice before Tolbenny (sometimes known as Virginia) Crossing was reached. Opened in 1931 and closed in 1972, Tolbenny Siding branched off on the down side at 3 miles 44 chains. Just beyond was the start of Meledor Loop Siding and beyond that Meledor Loop. Branching away from the 1 in 95 loop on the up side was Burgotha Siding, serving Lower Burgotha. South of Meledor Loop south ground frame was another complex that on the up side included Melbur Siding and Meledor Mill public siding. Another loop for run-round and shunting purposes was adjacent to these sidings. From 1912 the branch ended at the 4-mile 2-chain marker, just short of Meledor road crossing. However, in 1921 the branch was extended across the road to reach New Meledor Siding, later Collins Rotary Drier. Manually operated crossing gates protected the road.

There were no signalboxes on the branch, and latterly all crossing gates were controlled by train crews. Nearly all the

Above:
No 3635 is shunting at Meledor Mill on 11 July 1955 with empties on the right having just been hauled down from St Dennis Junction. Loaded wagons are out of sight at the platform on the right. This was a public siding but the Retew branch never had a passenger service. In the right background is the stack of Tolbenny clay kiln, which also had its own dedicated siding and lasted until 1972. *R. C. Riley, The Transport Treasury*

Right:
This was the sad scene at the end of the Meledor Mill trackwork on 23 July 1986. The track to the right is just yards in length, witness the buffer stops, but the line ahead through the crossing gates was known as New Meledor Siding and came into use in 1921. This line accessed New Meledor (originally owned by the New Cornish Meledor China Clay Co), which later became known as Collins Rotary Drier, named after the captain of the works. A further visit was made in 2001 and this site is now completely buried in trees and undergrowth. *JV*

sidings were controlled and protected by single lever ground frames, although Tolbenny and Virginia sidings had multiple lever ground frames. As there were no passenger trains, facing point locks were not provided. The overall speed limit was 15mph and there were restrictions on the class of locomotive passed to work the branch. However, the usual small pannier and Prairie tanks working out of St Blazey presented no route availability problems. On occasions two locomotives worked a single train on to the branch but in this event they had to be at either end of the train. Locomotives were not permitted to run over some sidings, so wagons could only be left or collected if there was a rake of other wagons between the engine and those to be delivered/collected. At some steeply graded sidings 'stop bars' were bolted to the track to prevent runaways. With so many sidings to serve it was not surprising that even in the busiest years only two trains per day were booked to work the branch.

There is no doubt that, judging by photographs taken in the 1950s, some of the sidings on the Retew branch had been little used for years. Also the date of official closure bears no relation to the date that the last trainload left, and it is probable that some sidings had not been used for years before the closure date. Nevertheless the story of the decline of the Retew branch is curious in that it was a slow death, a case of closure by stealth. On the other hand, although the majority of official siding closure dates were in the 1960s and 1970s, the years 1966 and 1972-3 stand out, which would appear to reflect a change in policy regarding the transportation of china clay by the clay companies and/or the railway.

There is no doubt that in the later years 'big was beautiful' in respect of clay works, and some of the smaller pan kiln installations were probably uneconomic. New generations of drying equipment that eliminated the use of coal were introduced. Then there was expansion, where large works simply 'gobbled up' the land occupied by the 'tiddlers'. Technology, which has been discussed elsewhere, was another factor whereby clay in liquid slurry form could efficiently be transported many miles by pipeline for drying at a large centralised location where economies of scale could be exercised. This efficiency would show the almost cumbersome activities of the slow-moving freight trains, complicated shunting moves and wagon orders, combined with a decaying infrastructure, in a very unfavourable light. Then of course there was the agreement of the mid-1960s

between BR and ECC, which guaranteed a minimum annual tonnage of china clay by rail in return for the handing over of the Fowey to Par line and the Fowey Docks investment. It is not known whether this agreement worked against the Retew branch or not.

Whatever the reason for the decline in traffic by the end of the 1970s the line was finished. The last recorded passenger train was a railway enthusiasts' DMU in 1977. In the final years trains had become infrequent and traffic patterns erratic. The last recorded traffic from Collins Driers, at the end of the branch, was in September 1980. The annual weedkilling train traversed the line in the summer of 1981, and in mid-March 1982 a locomotive and van worked to the end of the branch and back, the last known movement before most of the branch was lifted in 1983. At some of the clay works the line was set in concrete and although some remnants can still be seen, much of the line is inaccessible, many of the old pan dry kilns have been demolished and tons of spoil and mica have been moved about, obliterating some of the trackbed. With ECC permission I managed to 'drive the trackbed' in 1989 with some difficulty. It would now be impossible.

In the past there were plans to extend the branch by several miles, following the course of the River Fal to St Just Pool in Carrick Roads, virtually across the river from Falmouth, but as with most such grandiose schemes this came to nothing. Once the clay wagons had come off the Retew branch at St Dennis Junction trains had to reverse in order to reach St Blazey, Par or Fowey. The journey was not easy in that a path had to be found between passenger workings to and from Newquay, brakes had to be pinned down over certain sections and the single track did not provide much in the way of operating flexibility. Some of the trains were double-headed from St Dennis Junction to St Blazey and occasionally one of the heavy but powerful '4200' class 2-8-0Ts or '7200' class 2-8-2Ts would deliver and/or collect wagons from St Dennis. They were not, however, permitted to run on the Retew branch.

The branch was not one of the better-known lines but it served a useful purpose for over 100 years. Having studied the trackwork I can only marvel at how the train crews knew how to marshal their trains and how to implement logically the various wagon orders. Nature has now reclaimed much of its land and yet again we must rely on the intrepid photographers of the day who pointed their cameras in the direction of this pleasant backwater.

17. Newquay Harbour

Back in the 16th century Newquay was known as 'Newe Kaye'. At that time it was a tiny hamlet with just a few fishermen's cottages. Although the harbour at Newquay had always been naturally sheltered by Towan Head, in the 16th century a refuge had been built to afford small ships greater protection from the angry seas. The main business of the harbour was landing pilchards, while the nearby Penpoll Creek at Crantock and Trevemper, the highest point reached by tidal influence on the River Gannel, had both been used to ship relatively small volumes of tin, copper and fleeces from sheep, commodities that were transported by packhorse. The first sign of any significant change took place in 1770 when Richard Lomax, Lord of the Manor of Towan Blistra, purchased the harbour and much of the surrounding area. By 1811 lead had been discovered at East Wheal Rose near Newlyn East and mines at Perranzabuloe were in production. Furthermore the china clay industry was growing and the transportation and shipping of the output was high on the agenda. Consideration had been given to building a canal from china clay country to the coast but the financial backing was not forthcoming. In 1825 a pier was built at St Columb Porth capable of taking schooners with an 80-ton payload potential.

In the meantime, under the influence of Lomax, Newquay Harbour was getting busier, and fish, corn, iron ore, china clay, sand, manure, limestone and salt were all being handled. Small ships tried to balance incoming and outgoing traffic but there was

Above:
Newquay Harbour has a fascinating railway history that surprisingly dates back to 1843, when the Act of Parliament authorising the plans of Joseph Thomas Treffry was passed. Landowner Richard Lomax had spent £10,000 enlarging the port in 1832-3 but he died in 1838 and Treffry bought the Harbour for a 'snip' at £7,000. Treffry planned to build a tramway from Par to Newquay, linking ports on both the north and south Cornish coasts, with an important mineral district in between. The line would end in a 1 in 4½ (mean) incline through a tunnel to the harbour. Work started in 1845 and the first wagons were horse-drawn through the streets of Newquay in 1849. This is the only photograph discovered in past research of a horse-drawn 'train' in the town of Newquay, which probably dates back to the 1880s. Two horses are hauling five or six empty wagons.
Woolf/Greenham collection

463

462

469

462ᵃ

463ᵃ

469ᵃ

Tithy Cove

Fish Cellars

Flagstaff

North Pier

B.M. 88·6

Red Lion Hotel   *Slip Cove*

Flagstaff

73ᵃ

South Pier

Jetty

94

Limekiln

491ᵃ

Sun Dial

490ᵃ

The Fort

Christian Chapel

Flagstaff

489ᵃ

High

488ᵃ

Water

487ᵃ

495

Mark

492

Lifeboat House

Flagstaff

The Island   50

Jago's Island

Fish Cellars   *Tides*

of   *Ordinary*

Engine House

493

Coastguard Station

Eothan

Fish Cellars

Fish Cellars

NEWQUA

50

530

Flagstaff

501

496

Baptist Chapel

500

499

496ᵃ

B.M. 91·1

Methodist Chapel
(Wesleyan)

497

86

B.M. 110·5

Conn Hotel

Methodist Chapel
(Congregational)

New Inn

522   525

530ᵃ   B.M. 105·3

St. Michael's Chur

Schools
(Boys & Girls)

TRAMWAY

Left:
This first edition *circa* 1880 Ordnance Survey map shows the alignment of the Newquay Harbour tramway. The standard gauge line opened in 1849 as part of the Treffry Tramway network and was formally closed to all traffic by the GWR in 1926. The incline that ran through a tunnel to gain access to the harbour and the sidings by the engine house for the whims that hauled the wagons up from quayside can be seen centre left. *Crown Copyright*

Inset left:
It seems hard to believe that a Town Council that could take the trouble to commemorate the tramway to Newquay Harbour could be the same organisation that approved the demolition of Newquay's original 1876 station building. However, the plaque near the start of the tramway contains several inaccuracies, for example the 'coming of the steam railway to Newquay in 1884', which should read 1874, and 'contracted to haul the trams or trucks singly by horse', where in fact the previous plate shows several wagons on the move. The 26 October 1849 date for the opening of the tramway is also debatable! *JV*

Above:
I have over 20 old postcards of Newquay Harbour and it is interesting to see how many wagons are on the quays in each photograph. This Edwardian view is interesting in that it shows two shunting horses standing to the right of two empty china clay wagons. Two loaded coal wagons are about to be cable-hauled up the incline, while a fifth wagon is on the end of the quay. The stone jetty within the harbour area was built by the CMR in 1873/4 to increase handling capacity. *JV collection*

Below:
Judging by the buildings around the harbour this photograph is much earlier than the last one. The large building on the hill is the Atlantic Hotel, built in 1892, and it would thus be reasonable to assume that this picture dates back to about 1900. There are two clay wagons on the central jetty, two in the middle foreground and at least one, barely visible, on the quay. A single coal wagon is at the dockside. This was still the age of sail with a schooner by the central jetty and a barque to the left.
Woolf/Greenham collection

little room for manoeuvre at Newquay. Accordingly, in 1832 Lomax embarked on a £10,000 harbour expansion scheme that would cover an area of 4 acres; a new south quay was built and the north quay extended. A total of 250 men were employed on the rebuilding, which was completed in 1833, at the same time that Treffry's Par Harbour received its first commercial vessel. In 1835 Treffry made his comments about wanting to connect the north coast of Cornwall with the south coast by building a tramway from Par to Newquay. It was therefore hardly a surprise that when Lomax died in 1838 Treffry almost rushed in to buy Newquay Harbour and some surrounding land for £7,000.

Treffry planned a tramway from the harbour, which would rise through a tunnel by an incline of 1 in 4½ and run through the streets of the town to the site of what, in 1876, was to become Newquay station. An Act of Parliament authorising the work was passed in November 1843 and work commenced on the harbour section the following year. This was about the same time that the Ponts Mill to Molinnis (Bugle) Treffry Tramway opened (see Chapter 13). The lines in the harbour would run along the quays to facilitate loading, and all wagons on the quays, through the town and on to the mines would be horse-drawn, the horses being owned and operated by the Hoytes family. By a series of points the harbour sidings converged into a single line that entered the 96yd tunnel. Initially wagons were hauled up the incline by a rope cable connected to a horse-powered whim, but later this was replaced by stationary steam engine whims operating a steel cable. The engine house was located just behind Fore Street, and the engines had very tall chimneys to increase the draught for the fires. There was a passing loop just beyond the top of the incline, behind the engine house, and horses were attached/detached at this point.

The tramway then curved past the bottom of Marcus Hill via Crantock Street, Manor Road, and Cliff Road and on to Island Crescent behind the Victoria Hotel to the site of the present Newquay station. The tramway was standard gauge throughout, in common with all Treffry Tramway lines, and the first wagonload was conveyed in January 1849. The line was just less than 1 mile in length and the harbour was 301 miles 41 chains from London Paddington via Bristol. In 1873 the CMR built a 100ft-long by 20ft-wide stone jetty within the harbour to increase handling capacity. At this time Newquay ship owners possessed 160 small, wooden vessels, while four small shipyards built schooners, ketches, etc. A new 150ft-long wooden trestle connected the jetty to the 'mainland' and carried a single track, which quickly switched into two roads, one serving each side of the new jetty. However, the completion of the CMR was not good news for Newquay Harbour because some of the china clay from

the St Dennis area started to be shipped from Par and Fowey in the south. Loads to Newquay Harbour were surcharged at 2d per ton.

A further major problem for Newquay Harbour occurred in the late 1870s when the iron mines on the Perran Lode failed, and this was compounded in 1885 when East Wheal Rose mine closed. Also, towards the end of the 19th century the days of the small 50-ton schooner were coming to an end, much larger ships were able to use Par and Fowey, and Newquay could not compete with the economics of the southern ports. While the railway to Newquay became well established, the infrastructure hugely extended, especially after the line from Chacewater opened in 1905, and business was booming, this could not be said of the tramway, where traffic dwindled to just a few wagons per week rumbling through the town.

It is uncertain when the last wagons were hauled down the tramway to the harbour but research shows that the last outbound cargo was in 1921, while the last incoming load in 1922 was agricultural fertilizer landed from the schooner *Hobah*. The line slumbered for four years before the GWR formally closed it in 1926. The wooden trestle to the stone jetty was removed in the early 1950s. Long after closure an aquarium was opened at the harbour tunnel mouth and in the 1980s the tunnel mouth at the top of the incline was unearthed during excavations for a new supermarket, which now occupies the site of the old winding engines. Just opposite the present Newquay station the alignment of the old tramway can still be traced and the local authority has thoughtfully erected a plaque outlining the history of the tramway, albeit with a few factual errors.

It is interesting to reflect that in 1858 horses took an impressive 2,788 tons of china clay down to the harbour at Newquay. Another interesting aside is that in 1879 the tramway was contracted to carry the Royal Mail between the Post Office in Bank Street and the railway station. Postcard views of the harbour were very popular and 20 early postcards in the author's collection contain a total of 49 wagons, an average of between two and three wagons at any one time, with a range of zero to five. There are still a handful of boats using the harbour but it is hard to imagine wagons running through this crowded tourist resort (in summer months). Section 60(1) of the GWR Act 1929 vested the harbour and tunnel to the Newquay Urban District Council, while the tramway track from Cliff Road to Crantock Street was conveyed from the GWR to the council on 3 June 1931, and the council purchased the whim engine house area from the British Transport Commission on 26 May 1953. The tramway was unique and it was undoubtedly one of Cornwall's more interesting byways.

Above:

In 1858 horses took 2,788 tons of china clay down to the harbour at Newquay, but once the CMR line opened through to Par and Fowey in 1874 most china clay headed towards the south coast ports. Loads to Newquay were surcharged at 2d per ton and the productive East Wheal Rose mine closed in 1885, all contributing to Newquay Harbour's decline. Also the age of the small schooner was coming to an end and larger iron steamships that needed deeper water and more manoeuvring space could not use Newquay. Traffic simply petered out, with the last outgoing load being taken down to the harbour in 1921 and the last incoming cargo in 1922. The line was formally closed by the GWR in 1926. Note the track layout in the area of the tunnel. *Woolf/Greenham collection*

Right:

A wander through the streets of Newquay from the railway station to the harbour following the course of the old railway is well worth while, but be prepared to encounter a supermarket where the old winding engines once stood. The central jetty has been without its wooden trestle since 1950 but the old tunnel mouth, once an aquarium and now used for storage, can be found amongst the lobster pots, as seen in this 1997 view. One wonders what percentage of the population or the visitors know that the harbour they are walking around was once a busy port with its own tramway. *JV*

18. Trenance Valley Branch

For many decades during the mid-19th century there had been various plans to build railways up the Gover and Trenance valleys to the northwest of St Austell. There were a number of clay pits in the area and historically their output had to be hauled out of the valleys and through St Austell to reach the harbour at Charlestown, although after 1829 the railhead of the Pentewan Railway south of St Austell was another option. However, none of the many schemes came to fruition in the 19th century mainly due to the inability to raise finance, despite the issue of an optimistic prospectus. In fact, although there were many branches that penetrated clay country, such as the Goonbarrow, Carbis, Retew and Drinnick Mill lines, plus a handful of tramways, the Gover Valley was never served by rail. Some abortive plans were made for extensions to existing lines, particularly the Pentewan, whose terminus was very near to the southern end of, particularly, the Trenance Valley, but the pits were on much higher ground and one plan called for a line that would require a gradient of 1 in 20 over part of its route.

In 1830 Francis Swaine Price, the manager of the Pentewan Railway, built a new 1¼-mile road up the Trenance Valley at a cost of £230 in an attempt to persuade the Charlestown-using clay producers to use Pentewan, but this had little impact. Also the Pentewan's owner, Sir Christopher Hawkins, showed little interest at that time in embarking on grander schemes. The final Bill put

Above:
The Trenance Valley line was the last of the Cornish branches to open and was always one of the more obscure. A line up the valley to serve the numerous clay works had been on the cards for decades but for a variety of reasons it never came to fruition until the GWR decided to build it. Work started in 1913 but due to World War 1 work was suspended and the line was not opened until 1920. In this rural scene with grass-covered tracks '4500' class 2-6-2T No 4552 stands in Lower Ruddle Yard in June 1958. The Trenance Valley branch can be seen just in front of the locomotive while the wagons on the left are stored in Boskell china clay works siding. The locomotive is facing Lansalson. *Norman Simmons*

Above:

Here is a wonderful 'men at work' scene on the 9.15am St Austell to Lansalson goods at Bojea Yard; in fact, the line was known by local railwaymen as the 'Bojea Branch'. The locomotive, a '5700' class 0-6-0PT, is on the main branch and the other four sidings are part of the yard. There was a loading dock at the far end. In 1920 John Lovering & Co built two new clay dries at Bojea and they added considerably to traffic volumes. The foreground wagon is on Carlyon Farm Siding, which opened in 1929-30 and closed in July 1964. Many of the clay kilns further up the valley can be seen above the 'Toad' brake-van. *Hugh Davies*

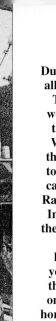

before Parliament with Pentewan links was in 1910, when Sir James Szlumper & Son conducted a survey of the proposed routes to Ruddlemoor in the Trenance Valley, up the Gover Valley and down to Mevagissey. They envisaged a huge deep-water lock, south of Pentewan Harbour, passenger trains and conversion to standard gauge, the cost being estimated at a colossal £211,000! The Bill failed at the Standing Orders Committee stage, one of the reasons possibly being that by then the GWR was planning its own branch up the Trenance Valley.

The GWR Bill to build the 1-mile 53-chain Trenance Valley branch was passed and construction work started in 1913. The timing was bad because after waiting so many years for a railway the clay companies and the GWR were thwarted by the onset of World War 1 in 1914, which brought an abrupt end to construction. Notwithstanding a significant downturn in china clay production during the war, work recommenced after the hostilities ended with the section to Bojea opening on 1 May 1920 and to the end of the line at Lansalson on 24 May 1920. Messrs John Lovering & Co owned the vast Higher and Lower Ninestones clay works and in 1920 they built two new clay dries at Bojea in the St Austell River valley, connected to the works by a private tramway. There were 13 other clay dries in the valley serving clay works, including Trethowal, South Ninestones, Ruddle, Wheal Martyn and Lower Lansalson, together producing some 100,000 tons of china clay per annum, which for the most part had to be transported to the branch in horse-drawn carts. Other clay works to the north used Carbean Wharf on the Goonbarrow branch (see Chapter 14).

On the main line a signalbox was opened in 1916 for the construction of the branch. The main line from St Austell to Burngullow had been doubled on 26 March 1899, and the Trenance Valley branch left it at the 286-mile 55-chain point. Initially the junction was double track, but on 13 November 1949 it was singled with access to the branch via the up main line only, rendering the signalbox redundant; it closed from that date and the points were then controlled by a ground frame under the auspices of St Austell signalbox. On the branch the short section of double track soon changed to single.

At 36 chains from the junction was Carlyon Farm south ground frame, a siding and loop that were added in 1929-30. Bojea south ground frame was located at 44 chains and this opened out into the four sidings that comprised Bojea Yard, which was in fact a mini marshalling yard with an island-shaped loading dock at the north end. At the end of the small complex at 66 chains was Bojea north ground frame. At 1 mile 19 chains was Lower Ruddle ground frame with a reverse siding on the up side to Lower Ruddle Yard,

where there was another two-road island dock for the loading of china clay. A little further on, at 1 mile 24 chains on the down side, was another reverse siding to Boskell china clay works, a single siding that branched into three. Just 15 chains on was Lansalson Siding ground frame, which controlled a single line that made a reverse connection with the branch. Beyond the ground frame was Lansalson Yard, the end of the line, where again a loading dock was part of the railway infrastructure. The distance to the final buffer stop was 1 mile 53 chains.

The china clay industry recovered after the war and for many years the Trenance Valley line made a welcome contribution to the coffers of the GWR. Volumes were no doubt helped by the closure of the Pentewan Railway in 1918. The gradual decline of traffic on the branch was similar in some respects to the Retew branch, whereby old-fashioned coal-fired pan dries became uneconomic, some of the smaller clay pits were worked out and pipeline technology improved. This enabled china clay in slurry form to be transported to centralised drying plants more efficiently and at less cost than the railways. Also company amalgamations and takeovers resulted, especially after 1935, in English China Clays dominating the scene, and that company would have ensured that a corporate strategy was in place, to the possible detriment of some of the older privately owned pits and works.

After World War 2 there was a further downturn in traffic resulting in the changes in track configuration at the junction. Closure by stealth followed, with the line beyond the Boskell Works (1 mile 35 chains), including Lansalson Yard, closing on 27 July 1964; the track was removed within a month. Carlyon Farm Siding and two of the roads and the loading dock in Bojea Yard were also taken out of use in that month. Finally, on 30 September 1968, Boskell china clay works and Lower Ruddle Yard gave up the ghost and the entire line was closed after a modest 48 years of service. The branch was the only dedicated china clay branch built by the GWR; it is now heavily overgrown and, although a cliché, it really has gone 'back to nature'.

The normal range of small tank engines that were allocated to St Blazey over the years worked the line, and both 0-6-0 pannier tanks and 2-6-2 Prairie tanks were regular visitors. After steam ended, the line was worked by a Class 08 shunter. There was never a passenger service but an enthusiasts' special with a 2-6-2T at each end worked the branch on 28 April 1962, virtually a farewell tour! The line was infrequently photographed and it has rarely been featured in articles in the railway press. The junction was just to the east of St Austell Viaduct, which spans the Trenance Valley, but it is now difficult to see any evidence that the branch ever existed.

Right:
Pulling a long line of wagons out of the three-road Boskell Sidings in June 1958 is Prairie tank No 4552. The entire branch was just 1 mile 53-chain long and there were 14 clay dries in the valley, producing at their peak about 100,000 tons of china clay per annum. *Norman Simmons*

Above:
On 28 April 1962 the Plymouth Railway Circle ran a brake-van charter over a number of china clay branches. This Cornwall Minerals special traversed the Trenance Valley branch and is seen here being propelled towards Lansalson by a pair of Prairie tanks in the shape of Nos 5531 and 4564. The well-patronised 11 brake-vans are passing through typical clay country and it is hard to believe that the participants are now all 40 years older! *Peter Gray*

Right:
The demise of the branch was very similar to that of the Retew branch, with old coal-fired pan kilns becoming uneconomic, pipeline technology improving and consolidation within the industry all contributing to a traffic downturn. The line beyond Boskell, including the Lansalson Yard terminus seen here in 1989, was closed in July 1964 and the entire branch closed on 30 September 1968. Note the two tracks set in the cobbles and the remains of the loading dock on the right. *JV*

19. Drinnick Mill Branch

As mentioned in other chapters, one of the emerging problems for the growing number of producers of china clay in the early part of the 19th century was transporting their product from the clay pits and dries to the coast for shipment to customers who, in those days, were mostly in the Potteries of Staffordshire. The nation as a whole was about to explode into the Railway Age and certain mining and industrial sites had already benefitted from the building of tramways to facilitate the transportation of materials. By 1829 the Poldice Tramway, the Redruth & Chasewater Railway and the Pentewan Railway had already become established in Cornwall (see Chapters 1 to 3), as well as a number of minor tramways in certain mines. However, the china clay industry was in its infancy and every few years it grew manyfold. As explained in previous chapters it was the Treffry Tramways that actually penetrated clay country (rather than the Pentewan, which ended a few miles from the clay works)

Above:

The Drinnick Mill branch was born as the Newquay & Cornwall Junction Railway (N&CJR) in 1869. The owners of china clay works and various mines had for years had to contend with a chronic transportation system where the output had to be conveyed for many miles by horse and cart with a maximum 3-ton payload over roads that were poor and in winter sometimes impassable. They were well aware of the potential of a railway into the heart of clay country and several proposals for a line had been made over the years. The N&CJR planned a 5-mile 13-chain single line from Burngullow on the Cornwall Railway main line to meet the CMR line at Hendra south of St Dennis Junction. The Drinnick Mill branch can be seen curving to the right at Burngullow station in this 1922 photograph. The station was closed on 14 September 1931. Note the old former broad gauge engine shed. *JV collection*

Above:

By 1976 just the signalbox and one of the up station buildings remained at Burngullow. Shunting a very long line of 'clay hoods' out of Blackpool dries on 19 May 1976 is 2,700hp 'Western' Class 52 diesel-hydraulic No D1023 *Western Fusilier*. The branch was built to broad gauge but the line had only reached Drinnick Mill when funds ran out. It was converted to standard gauge at the same time as the main line in 1892. *JV*

Below:

Rationalisation was almost complete when prematurely repainted 'Transrail' Class 37 No 37695 came off the Drinnick Mill branch on 24 August 1994 with a rake of CDA wagons — officially 'Transrail' was not launched until 9 September, to be succeeded by English, Welsh & Scottish Railways on 21 October 1996. The disused Burngullow signalbox, just visible, was later set on fire by vandals and subsequently demolished. By this time the main line had been singled from Burngullow to Probus. *JV*

Above:
Crugwallins clay dries, on the right, is a pleasant backwater that is still occasionally used by English China Clays' successor, Imerys. With the protecting gate locked on this day, Class 37 No 37135 descends from Lanjeth to the junction at Burngullow with mixed vacuum-and air-braked wagons on 22 February 1982. *JV*

and made a big impact from about 1844, but it was the Cornwall Minerals Railway and its many branches that truly satisfied the needs of the industry.

In broad-brush terms the CMR served the north side of the Hensbarrow Downs area where many of the china clay works were located. The lines from St Dennis Junction to Hendra, from Bugle to Carbis and, especially, the 1893 Goonbarrow branch to Carbean took the railway nearer to a number of large producers, but the south side of the Downs was still dependent on primitive roads and horse-drawn wagons. In 1843 the need for a railway was recognised and in November of that year plans were prepared for a line from St Austell to St Stephen. No fewer than 257 parcels of land would need to be acquired, and the line would run from the Pentewan Railway to Gover Mill, Trewoon, north of Methroes, High Street, Carpella, Foxhole, Drinnick and Nanpean, ending at Little Treviscoe. In 5¼ miles the line would have climbed over 400ft with a ruling gradient of 1 in 60, and a short inclined plane at 1 in 12. However, nothing came of the plan or similar proposals in 1858 and 1862.

In 1864 there was a scheme to build a 5-mile 13-chain single line from Burngullow on the Cornwall Railway's Plymouth to Truro main line to link up with the Treffry Tramway line from St Dennis Junction to Hendra. This line would serve a large number of clay pits and be known as the Newquay & Cornwall Junction Railway (N&CJR). On some early maps it is shown as the St Dennis branch but since the Grouping it has been known as the Drinnick Mill branch. In common with the main line the branch would be broad gauge throughout, and was authorised on 14 July 1864 with a capital of £27,000.

The prospectus for the line makes interesting reading and paints a very rosy picture of the future: 'The proposed line of railway is intended to be constructed from Burngullow station on the Cornwall Railway through the heart of the important china clay and china stone district of St Stephen and St Dennis to a junction with the St Dennis branch of the Par and Newquay Railway near the village of Hendra' (the Treffry Tramway and later CMR line). It continues: 'It is also intended to apply for powers to improve the Par and Newquay Railway so as to adapt it for locomotives as far as Ruthvoes within a little more than two miles of St Columb (to which it is intended to continue the railway if sufficient funds shall be subscribed for the purpose). The line to Hendra will be about five miles in length affording direct communication with Newquay, Par, Fowey and Falmouth.' More detail is provided: '...the curves and gradients will be easy and there will be no tunnels, viaducts or other heavy works. It is estimated that 80,000 tons of merchandise would annually pass over the line besides passengers. Needless to say, this would afford a very handsome return of the limited capital required.'

The prospectus was well received and the first sod was cut in a field near Burngullow on 15 November 1864. The contractor was to be William West & Son of St Blazey. By 1867 the money raised had run out but prominent landowner George Fortescue, who had been upset by the company choosing broad gauge for its line, nevertheless loaned it £1,000 and waived his dues for land purchase, enabling construction to continue. A further Act was obtained after it was found that a 1-mile 2-chain deviation from the original plan would be needed at an extra cost of £3,000. After a further two years of activity the line finally reached Drinnick

Right:
Just around the corner from the junction with the main line and once accessed by a reverse junction with the Drinnick Mill branch was Burngullow West Siding, opened by Trehidy Minerals Ltd in June 1898 and lasting until September 1974. Again the track was set in concrete adjacent to the linhay. With the old stack still extant, the works was photographed in June 1989. *JV*

Left:
The little Crugwallins dries, featured opposite, has its own resident shunter for gradually moving clay wagons past the loading facilities. On 21 April 1993 ECC-owned Sentinel No P403D *Denise* is in action. The clay company also has resident shunters at its Blackpool, Fowey, Treviscoe and Rocks installations. Some closed clay dries such as Moorswater also had domestic motive power, while at other locations, such as Par Harbour, road-going tractors have been adapted to perform the task. *JV*

Right:
The branch climbs away from the junction at a gradient of 1 in 38/50 towards High Street, Carpella and Foxhole. Descending from Lanjeth Crossing with a 500-ton load on 13 July 1961, with no doubt the brake-van performing its function, are a pair of purposeful pannier tanks, '5700' class No 9755 and '1600' class No 1624. These clay lines were always worked by small tank locomotives due to weight restrictions and route availability limits. *Peter Gray*

Mill and the railway was opened to that point on 1 July 1869. The contractor of the line had used two broad gauge locomotives during construction and in the early days it was these locomotives that worked the branch. One was a Manning Wardle 0-4-2T of 1866, purchased in 1869 and called *Newquay*, and the other was a Brotherhood (of Gloucester) six-wheeled, four-coupled locomotive of 1863 named *Phoenix*.

The first 2 miles of the branch had cost a staggering £22,000 and the cutting through granite to Nanpean had proved to be expensive. The railway was underperforming and it was not until the Cornwall Minerals Railway Act of 1873 that the situation was addressed. The powers for the construction of the line beyond Drinnick Mill, to Hendra, had expired and none of the required land had been taken up. The N&CJR was also in debt, a fact also mentioned in the Act. The upshot of all this was that the CMR was authorised to build a standard gauge railway 2 miles 4 furlongs and 5 chains long to connect Drinnick Mill and Hendra, effectively the 'missing link'. The line was efficiently progressed so that it was ready for service on the same day as the rest of the CMR system, 1 June 1874 (see Chapter 13). The work was undertaken with the complete co-operation of the clay companies and many sidings were laid into particular works. There was a break of gauge at Drinnick Mill, a situation that persisted until 1892 when the CR/GWR main line was converted.

In fact, the 1873 Act stipulated that the CMR should add a third rail from Drinnick Mill to Burngullow, thus providing mixed gauge working, but it never complied. The Cornwall Railway took the CMR to court over the matter and the CMR eventually laid some track but in such a way that it was unusable! Despite the original intentions no passenger service was ever provided on the line, which to this day remains freight-only. In 1907 there was disruption on the branch when the Carpella United Clay Company gave notice of its right to extract clay from the ground beneath the railway line. The GWR was the owner of the branch by then and it took the clay company to court claiming that the activity was not tantamount to the extractions of minerals under its preserved rights when the N&CJR was built. The case went to the House of Lords, which ruled in favour of the clay company. Accordingly from 1909 the line was severed between 290 miles 20 chains and 290 miles 40 chains, and through running was then no longer possible over what had become known as the 'Carpella gap'. It was not until 18 April 1922 that the GWR opened a deviation line to avoid the break, thus re-establishing through working between Burngullow and St Dennis. Presumably the delay in building the deviation had been due to a cooling-off, 'wait and see' period, as well as the advent of World War 1. It is

assumed that between 1909 and 1922 all clay was taken out of the area via St Dennis Junction.

The CR opened Burngullow station on the main line in 1863. The station was resited a little further to the west in 1901 and a new signalbox was opened at the west end of the down platform. However, there was never any significant population in the area and the station closed on 14 September 1931. Although the Drinnick Mill branch diverged from the main line at Burngullow, there was never a branch platform because there was never a branch passenger service! However, there was a broad gauge locomotive shed just north of the station. Some years after closure in 1986, after serving as a refuge for permanent way staff, arsonists destroyed the semi-derelict 1901 GWR box. Just to the east of Burngullow station there was, and still is, a large complex of lines serving only ECC (now Imerys) Blackpool dries, but in the past various sidings served Methrose, Wheal Louisa, Parkyn & Peters and Cornish Kaolin. The east signalbox overlooking the complex closed in 1935. In 1988-9 ECC spent £2 million modernising Burngullow, especially for loading large volumes of china clay slurry for a new Scottish papermaking customer.

The surviving Drinnick Mill branch curves away from the main line on a steeply graded curve at the 288-mile 50-chain point. Within a few yards the first of many clay company sidings is encountered, to Burngullow West on the up side, although only the shell of the clay dry, which closed in 1974, now remains. (In this text 'up' and 'down' are used in the conventional 'up to London' way, although in N&CJR days the 'up' direction was to St Dennis Junction.) The line continues to climb to the northwest at 1 in 38 easing to 1 in 50, and at 288 miles 67 chains is Crugwallins ground frame, leading to Crugwallins Siding, also on the up side. This drying installation is still open for infrequent traffic and employs its own shunter (see the accompanying photograph). The branch then continues to the ungated Lanjeth Crossing at 289 miles 27 chains, where the train crew operated the crossing gates until they were removed on 14 November 1966. At 289 miles 71 chains on the up side was the 1928 Beacon Siding, serving the clay company of the same name; the old wharf that closed in 1963 can still be seen. Immediately beyond Beacon was High Street Siding, also on the up side, where a narrow gauge tramway network once carried china clay from the linhay to the loading dock before abandonment in 1967.

The original route between High Street Siding ground frame at 289 miles 71 chains and Old Carpella Sidings ground frame at 290 miles 61 chains was abandoned in 1909 due to the Carpella break, but short lengths at the ends of each line were used as sidings, until taken out of use in 1917 and 1949 respectively. At

Right:
Another long-abandoned section of railway, just visible, is the siding to New Carpella (comedians might say that if this is the new one, what does the old one look like?). The siding came into use on 19 September 1921 to serve the Carpella United Clay Company works. The raised loading wharf can be seen on the right, while in the background the old engine house is being restored. Photographed on 9 April 1991, this area of private land is now heavily overgrown. *JV*

Left:
No 4508 with an 83E shedplate eases over the top of the climb from Burngullow and makes for Nanpean Wharf, near Drinnick Mill, with china clay empties on 30 July 1954. This was to be the locomotive's last run but it was later reinstated, eking out its days at Truro shed until 1959.
M. Dart collection

Right:
Drinnick Mill goods office was not only the administrative centre for wagon movements and associated paperwork but also the train crews' rest room where a cup of tea and a sandwich could be enjoyed. The resident shunter also 'resided' here and his waterproofs could be found hanging in the outer room. From time to time there may also have been an opportunity for a game of cards! On 11 June 1981 No 37207 is also enjoying a break as it stands idling on the line down to Nanpean Wharf. The building was demolished in October 1993. *JV*

Left:
Gradually the lines at the lower level, where there were several kilns, a clay mill and a bag store, fell into disuse as the older traditional clay dries were abandoned, and the last outgoing traffic was from Drinnick No 7 kiln on 14 May 1992. However, in the 1980s the lower line to the now demolished coal-fired power station saw some traffic as Drinnick was used commercially as a coal distribution point for Cornwall. In this view from the main branch on 22 July 1986 No 37696 in Railfreight livery is shunting HEA coal wagons; it has delivered seven loaded wagons and will remove two empties. *JV*

Below:
Nanpean Wharf was not only the reversal point to gain access to Drinnick lower but was also an important loading point in its own right in years past, when large volumes of clay were brought down from the pits by horse and cart for loading. In recent years the only product to be loaded here was pelletised calcified seaweed for agricultural purposes, otherwise it was used for storing crippled wagons. In June 1958 pannier tank No 9755 is performing shunting operations. The village of Nanpean can be seen in the background.
Norman Simmons

Above

This rare scene shows Drinnick No 8, North Carloggas kiln many years ago. The siding in the foreground is 'sunken' to facilitate loading, and four sheeted wagons await removal. What is particularly interesting is the narrow gauge clay works tramway that can be seen each side of the sunken siding, from where clay was obviously tipped directly into the standard gauge wagons. *Eric Lillicrap Snr, M. Dart collection*

Right

The Drinnick Mill complex is seen here in about 1880, when the line was still broad gauge. The line from Burngullow enters the map bottom right, and the two sidings top right serve Dubbers No 2 and No 1 kilns. The line beyond drops down to Nanpean Wharf where reversal was necessary to gain access to Drinnick and Carloggas, bottom left. At the top left the line heads west to Parkandillack and St Dennis Junction, while a siding curves away to the West of England clay works. Other sidings and run-round loops were added in later years but all except the 'main' branch have now closed. The track was converted to standard gauge in 1892. *Crown Copyright*

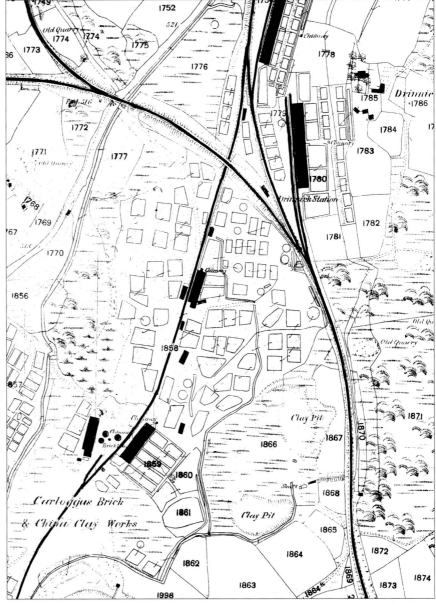

183

Left:
The diminutive Drinnick Mill signalbox can be seen to the right of this pannier tank, which was working the 10.50am Drinnick Mill to Burngullow goods of 20 June 1956. The box opened in 1921 and was closed in May 1966. Part of the West of England clay works can be seen in the background. The trace of stonework below the brake-van is the bridge over the low-level line.
Hugh Davies

Above:
This is a broadly similar view to the previous photograph, showing clay train operations in the diesel era. With a massive tiered spoil tip in the background 1,750hp Class 37 No 37674 drops down the 1 in 40 from Slip Bridge with five 'Tiger' wagons weighing 400 tonnes in tow, on 6 June 1997. The above-mentioned bridge over the low-level line is in the foreground. In many ways this is the heart of clay country, where there were once sidings serving the clay industry in abundance on both sides of the line. *JV*

Above:
InterCity on the Drinnick Mill branch, which has always been freight-only, is something of a rarity but on
20 February 1993 Hertfordshire Railtours visited the Duchy of Cornwall with their 'Par Snip' (ouch!) Railtour!
Led by Railfreight No 37673 the train was tailed by No 37670 over the Drinnick Mill branch, to the end of the
line at Parkandillack, and is seen passing the Drinnick Mill complex at a mandatory 10mph. In the early 1990s
there were plans to divert the Newquay branch over this route but they never came to fruition. *JV*

Below:
The odds of photographing a train on the old Rostowrack siding were only a little better than winning the National
Lottery! Fortunately on 19 February 1982 I was in the excellent company of resident shunter Ivor Trudgeon who,
of course, knew what was 'goin' orn'. On this day the rarely used siding saw one empty wagon delivered and one
wagon of china stone removed. The Goonvean & Rostowrack China Clay Co Ltd owned the siding but with such
little traffic it predictably closed during 1984. The main branch is in the centre of the photograph and the
foreground trackbed was known as Varcoes Siding, which was taken out of use in June 1965. *JV*

the beginning of the new deviation line New Carpella Siding on the down side was opened in 1921 at 290 miles 5 chains, even though the full deviation was not brought into use until the following year. Carpella Siding, beyond Old Carpella and on the down side at 290 miles 64 chains, was opened in 1898 and closed in 1968. Carpella was served by the Mid Cornwall Tramway, which delivered the clay to the loading wharf. Drinnick Mill south ground frame was at 291 miles 17 chains, until 1966 forming a 10-chain loop on the down side. Following removal of the south ground frame in 1966 only a reverse dead-end siding from Drinnick Mill north ground frame remains. Just beyond this on the up side was one of the old original 1869 sidings to some clay dries, Dubbers No 2 Siding; both Dubbers sidings closed about 1970.

At 291 miles 38 chains was a major divergence, with the main branch turning westward past Drinnick Mill signalbox (1921-66) towards Parkandillack, while the right-hand spur descended to Nanpean Wharf past the original 1869 siding to Dubbers No 1 Siding on the up side. The distance to the buffer stops at the Nanpean 'terminus' was 291 miles 60 chains. Just 14 chains from Nanpean Wharf there was a reverse connection on the down side that dropped away to pass under the 'main' branch to some coal drops by Drinnick Power Station, various Drinnick Mill clay dries and Carloggas Siding. At the far end of the complex were Barne and Rottery sidings. During the 1980s clay traffic ceased on the lower lines and their only use between 1985 and 1987 was for coal, Drinnick having briefly become a general coal distribution centre. The last train ran on 14 May 1992 when Class 37 No 37673 collected a Polybulk wagon from Drinnick No 7 kiln.

Nanpean Wharf with its loading docks dates back to the original days of the line but in recent years its only use, other than as a reversal point, was for loading calcified seaweed (later transferred to Truro) and for storing withdrawn wagons. In the early days 3-ton wagons each hauled by a trio of horses called at the wharf to transfer their china clay and china stone payload into railway wagons.

Back at the upper junction there was a goods office, with outside 'facilities', where all the local paperwork and dispatching activities were handled; this was demolished in 1993. From here the branch climbed away from Drinnick to the West of England New Siding ground frame at 291 miles 47 chains, which served the clay company of the same name until taken out of use in November 1973 after nearly 100 years of service. The Hendra Tramway served this once important siding. Beyond, Cathedral Quarry and Snell's Stone Wharf were served on the up side.

The steep gradient then continued with the 1873 Lukes Old Siding diverging on the down side at 291 miles 63 chains; this was removed in 1960. Just 14 chains further west Lukes New Siding diverged, also on the down side, which lasted three years longer than Lukes Old. This area is in the very heart of china clay country and all about there are artefacts that come into the industrial archaeology category. The summit of the branch is between Lukes and Slip, then it is downhill all the way to Parkandillack. Just beyond Slip Bridge were the two short Slip Sidings, controlled by a ground frame at 292 miles 11 chains and owned by the Goonvean & Rostowrack China Clay Company, where wagons were loaded with china stone until 1960. Rostowrack siding left the branch by a trailing connection on the up side just 7 chains further along the branch. China stone was infrequently loaded at the wharf from 1923 until 1984. Goonvean ground frame was at 292 miles 21 chains and controlled a siding that divided into Varcoes Siding, parallel to the main branch, and Goonvean Siding, which curved in a southerly direction for several hundred yards. This siding was opened in 1882 and taken out of use in 1976.

Between 292 miles 30 chains and 292 miles 38 chains was Little Treviscoe loop, on the up side of the line. Leading off the loop was Little Treviscoe Siding (and, many years ago, Gear's Siding), which was served by a narrow gauge tramway from the adjacent clay pit. Opened in 1907, the siding closed in 1969. An early closure in 1948 was Trethosa Siding, which trailed in on the down side at 292 miles 42 chains. Under the St Stephen road bridge on the up side is Kernick dries and beyond that Central Treviscoe dries, both still open to traffic, but the 1913 Kernick signalbox, which was opposite the works, closed in 1950. Opposite the complex on the down side was Great Treviscoe Siding, controlled by a ground frame from 1950 until 1967. The last of the sidings from Central Treviscoe rejoined the single line branch at the 292-mile 79-chain point. The Kernick/Treviscoe area has seen many changes in track layout over the years and much of the track is set in concrete. In one of Kernick's sheds lives *Elaine*, an interesting road/rail Trackmobile, used for shunting in the area.

One of the most important works on the line is ECC (now Imerys) Parkandillack, a major works that dispatches large volumes of china clay every day. There was a signalbox opposite the main works from 1911 until 1922. The various sidings serving Calciner and Buell drying plants include a run-round loop, and at the far end of the Parkandillack Sidings is Trelavour, the only rail connection used by the Goonvean & Rostowrack China Clay Company. At the time of writing the siding is still connected but unused (see Chapter 15). At the far end of the branch are stop blocks, 293 miles 60 chains from Paddington via Bristol. Beyond Parkandillack the line once continued to St Dennis Junction and much of the trackbed can still be traced. In 1987 there was a plan to resuscitate the line, which would then have become the Newquay branch, enabling the line from Goonbarrow Junction to St Dennis Junction to be closed. The county council could then have converted the A30 road across Goss Moor to dual carriageway and eliminated a low railway bridge, but nothing came of the plan.

Continuing towards St Dennis the old 1852 Hendra incline can still be seen at the 294-mile mark, and old spoil tips on the hills above the site are testimony to once extensive mine workings. Whitegates Crossing was to the east of St Dennis village and there was once a siding there as well as a small wharf for local produce and inward coal deliveries. Passing the siding ground frame on the down side at 294 miles 12 chains the line continued to Gothers or Pochins Siding at Domellick, where the 3ft 1in gauge Gothers Tramway from Gothers china clay works branched off. The line was about 2 miles in length, opened in 1879 and served Higher and Lower Gothers and Wheal Frederick china clay works. Clay had to be transhipped at Domellick into standard gauge wagons. Although the tramway closed in about 1930, the substantial stone wharf is still in evidence. The siding at Domellick formed a loop with the branch at 295 miles 5 chains. The line then continued to St Dennis Junction, where the Drinnick Mill branch, the Retew branch and the Par to Newquay lines all converged.

Between 1950 and 1966 the whole N&CJR was divided into two block sections: Burngullow to Drinnick Mill and Drinnick Mill to St Dennis Junction. Originally the CMR used the train staff and ticket system but the GWR introduced electric train staff working, an Annetts key on the train staff operating the many ground frames controlling the sidings. Some sidings had small cast nameplates attached to one of the levers and some of the frames were housed in small huts, while locking bars were used at some to prevent runaways. The line was busy from its opening, and as early as 1875 over 92,000 tons of china clay were shipped from Drinnick Mill. For many years there were two trains per day between Burngullow and Drinnick Mill and two from St Dennis Junction to Drinnick Mill, one of which worked through to Burngullow. By the end of steam, only one train per day worked south from St Dennis Junction and the line from there to Parkandillack closed in 1966. In more recent times there was a morning and an afternoon train on the surviving branch, with local 'clay hood' and later CDA workings as required to any of the surviving dries on the branch. The line is still an important feeder for the china clay industry.

Right:
No 9655, a '5700' class pannier tank, is standing to the east of Kernick dries, just beyond the point for Trethosa Siding. It is coupled to LMS-style brake-van No M730063 and is waiting to continue its return trip towards Drinnick Mill in July 1960. To the left was Little Treviscoe Siding, while in the distance on the right was Goonvean Siding.
Hugh Davies

Lower right:
Unsung workhorses of the Cornish motive power scene were the 16-wheeled 1Co-Co1 137-ton Class 46, or 'Peak', diesels. For many years Plymouth Laira had an allocation, but Gateshead members of the class regularly arrived on long-distance freights, particularly those from Mossend and Stoke-on-Trent. They also worked passenger trains in Cornwall, although somewhat restricted by their steam heating or 'no boiler' status. Here at Kernick dries on 16 May 1984 a tired-looking No 46027, which was just a few months away from the end of its working life, shows off its almost 68ft length while shunting a TGV Ferrywaggon on its way back to Burngullow and St Blazey. *JV*

There have always been motive power restrictions on the Drinnick Mill branch. With 18-chain radius curves, lightly laid sidings and weight-restricted overbridges only small 0-6-0 pannier and 2-6-2 Prairie tank locomotives worked the branch in steam days, and research failed to produce a single photograph of a tender locomotive on the line. In diesel days most classes common to Cornwall were used, but by far the heaviest were the 135/6-ton 1Co-Co1 Class 45/46 locomotives, although their eight axles resulted in an axle loading that was less than the 117-ton Class 47/50 six-axle locomotives. From about 1980 to 2000 the most common diesel class was the 105-ton Class 37 Co-Co. From January 1991 Class 47s and 50s were banned beyond Drinnick Mill due to weight restrictions on a road overbridge. However, after the new General Motors North American-built 126-ton 3,000hp Class 66s appeared in January 1999, structures were strengthened, permitting the use of the new locomotives through to Parkandillack.

The Drinnick Mill branch truly penetrates the fascinating terrain of china clay country. There are several vantage points to observe china clay trains, provided one knows that a train is on the move! The best approach is to survey the area with an Ordnance Survey map, then wait on the road bridge over the main line at Burngullow for a branch train to depart. With speed restrictions and a crossing, a chasing car can overtake the train without breaking speed limits! Shunting can be observed at the Kernick/Treviscoe complex from a road bridge and there is another road bridge at Slip. A farm path crosses the line on a bridge at Parkandillack but the clay company owns most of the land in this entire area and trespassing is prohibited. Also there can be heavy vehicles on the move and some of the ground is very unstable. To get the full atmosphere of not only the china clay industry at work but of the old clay works with their crumbling chimneys, a visit to this 'moonscape' served by a fully operational railway line is highly recommended.

Above:
Having just passed the long-abandoned Lukes Old and Lukes New sidings, No 37673 pokes its nose through a narrow bridge on the approach to Slip Bridge on its way to Parkandillack. Note that the tight curvature has necessitated metal rod 'ties' to be located between the tracks to strengthen the permanent way and maintain the gauge. The old pillars once supported a conveyor system from clay works on higher ground, all part of the fascination of railroading in clay country. *JV*

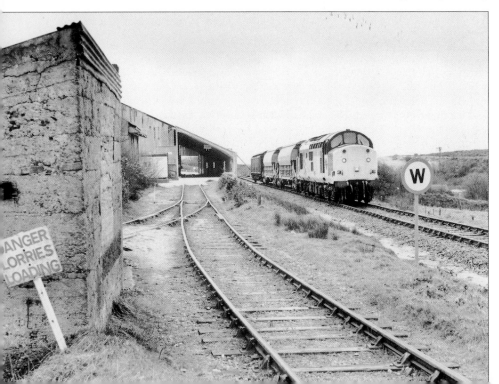

Left:
Immediately beyond Kernick dries is Central Treviscoe Siding. In this less familiar photographic vantage point at the north, or Parkandillack, end of the siding, No 37521 heads for Parkandillack on 18 March 1994 with three air-braked wagons for loading. The siding here was originally opened by the Central Treviscoe & General China Clay & China Stone Co Ltd in 1896 but it was closed between 1934 and 1964. *JV*

Above:
Parkandillack and behind it Trelavour are now at the end of the Drinnick Mill branch, but beyond the buffer stops on the left the line once continued to St Dennis Junction, where it connected with the Newquay branch. The section of line between St Dennis and Drinnick Mill was always standard gauge, and closed completely from 6 February 1966. Although Parkandillack is one of the busiest spots on the line, it looks semi-derelict in this 24 August 1994 photograph as 'Transrail' locomotive No 37695 runs round its train. On the right is Parkandillack Calciner and New Buell Siding. *JV*

Right:
The last week of operation of the 'clay hoods' occurred at the beginning of February 1988. These vacuum-braked 13-ton vehicles had been part of the Cornish railway scene since their introduction between 1954 and 1959, and were all built at Swindon Works. Having a rest from Class 1 passenger duties, 100mph Class 50 No 50045 *Achilles* has just arrived at Parkandillack on 4 February 1988. Today all traffic on the branch is in the hands of Class 66 locomotives. *JV*

20. Falmouth Branch and Newham Goods

Although in the mid-19th century the populations of Redruth and Penzance were greater than the City of Truro (with a population of about 12,000), the present county town was arguably Cornwall's most important business and cultural centre. Its position, not only in topographical terms but also as a port and business centre, was unrivalled. Architecturally Truro Cathedral dominated the city and this ecclesiastical centre of power had enormous influence over not only the surrounding parishes but also the county as a whole. To the south was the ancient port of Falmouth with a population of over 10,000, and thus it was entirely logical that both Truro and Falmouth should feature prominently in the plans of the early railway builders. The first proposal for an Exeter to Falmouth railway was back in 1835 but the House of Lords rejected it. However, on 3 August 1846 a Bill for the building of a railway from Plymouth to Truro and Falmouth became an Act of Parliament. Capital of £1.6 million was authorised for the Cornwall Railway's (CR) double-track main line between Plymouth and Falmouth plus several branches, and a consortium of the Great Western Railway, Bristol & Exeter Railway and South Devon Railway was to contribute £337,000. The West Cornwall Railway's scheme to connect Penzance with Truro was also approved. The former line would be broad gauge and the line to the West standard gauge.

The CR's first sod was cut 'in a spiritless manner' in a field near Truro in August 1847. Problems immediately ensued and progress was slow until a financial crisis brought proceedings virtually to a halt. Brunel tried to intervene but little came of his efforts. A cut-price scheme followed for a single-track main line and no branches (Bodmin to Bodmin Road had been excluded from the cuts but it was not built at this stage). When the contractor for the Truro to Falmouth section failed it was decided to leave the work part finished and to concentrate on the Plymouth to Truro section. This volume cannot detail the entire history of the CR, but suffice to say that after considerable difficulty the broad gauge line from Plymouth to Truro opened throughout on 4 May 1859, the 25-mile 11-chain standard gauge West Cornwall Railway (WCR) from Penzance to Truro having opened on 25 August 1852. The WCR's terminus for the three daily trains in each direction was at Truro Road, Highertown, west of the present tunnel.

On 16 April 1855 the WCR closed its terminus at Truro Road following the construction of the 2½-mile extension to Newham on the banks of the Truro River, a sort of 'South Truro' station. The line looped through some 90° from Penwithers Junction to a delightful little terminus with an overall roof over a pair of tracks, a goods shed and quay sidings fronting the river. Although the Newham site was to serve as a goods depot for over 100 years, its life as a passenger terminus was short-lived. From May 1859, when the CR opened its station (at the present site), most WCR trains were transferred there and Newham was closed to passengers on 16 September 1863. From that date the line served as a goods branch and thrived until the 1950s when, like so many other lines, traffic began to decline. At the 1-mile point on the branch there was once a short intermediate siding to Calenick Smelting Works, while a useful source of revenue in later years

Left:
The first railway from Exeter to Falmouth was proposed in 1835 but as described in the text it was 4 May 1859 before the Cornwall Railway (CR) opened to Truro, although the city had first been reached in 1852 by the West Cornwall Railway (WCR) from the Penzance direction to Truro Road station, Highertown. An Act of 1861 renewed powers to construct a line to Falmouth, and although not an easy task, the branch opened on 24 August 1863 to broad gauge standards. In this early 20th century view of Truro, with horse-drawn cabs waiting for custom in front of the station, the Falmouth branch bay platform is on the right. *JV collection*

Above:
The Truro scene during the transition from steam to diesel is featured here. On 22 July 1960 a pair of shiny new Class 22 locomotives is halted at the down main line platform with a van train while priority is given to the Falmouth branch working; 2-6-2T No 5537 departs from the bay platform for Perranwell, Penryn, Penmere Platform and Falmouth. *R. C. Riley, The Transport Treasury*

Right:
The little Class 121 and 122 single-car diesel units were regular performers on the Falmouth branch for many years. No 55009 has worked 'wrong line' from Penwithers Junction and is seen entering the down bay platform at Truro having worked the 11.53 Falmouth to Truro service of 24 March 1992. In the background is the weekly Mondays-only Truro to Ince UKF Shellstar fertilizer empties, now discontinued, worked by Railfreight Class 47 No 47350. For the time being the semaphore signals survive. *JV*

was coal for Truro Gasworks siding, brought into use in 1955 and lasting until December 1970. The loss of this traffic was 'the last straw' and the little 2-mile 31-chain branch, with its daily train (as required), closed on 6 November 1971.

The CR Truro station was an impressive structure with 1st, 2nd and 3rd Class entrances and waiting rooms! There were long arrival and departure platforms, with the standard gauge WCR trains using the outer face of the latter. There was a grand overall roof comprising two spans, each of over 40ft, together with a goods shed and a long two-road engine shed. To the west of the station it was necessary to bore a 70yd tunnel through the hillside to connect the WCR and the CR, and this was to become Highertown Tunnel.

In accordance with the WCR's Act the CR could call upon the other company at the appropriate time to make provision for broad gauge track from Truro to Penzance and this they were ordered to do in 1864. This resulted in dual gauge running, with the first broad gauge goods train working to Penzance over the dual gauge track in 1866 and the first passenger train on 1 March 1867.

An Act of 1861 renewed powers for the Falmouth extension, to be run by a new Joint Committee consisting of 12 members of the interested railway companies. Construction recommenced but the route was not an easy one, requiring a number of large embankments, eight of Brunel's timber-topped viaducts and a couple of tunnels. The single-track broad gauge line finally opened on 24 August 1863 with two intermediate stations at Perran (which later became Perranwell) and Penryn. In the early days there were five round trip passenger workings per day. One of the reasons for the interest in the line to Falmouth, other than to serve the sizeable population, was the prospect of the development of the docks, mentioned later, and this had an effect on the siting of the passenger terminus. The connection to the docks was opened in January 1864.

A full list of the wooden viaducts with masonry piers on the original Falmouth branch is as follows:

Penwithers Viaduct Length 813ft, height 90ft. Replaced in 1926 by a massive embankment.
Ringwell Viaduct Length 366ft, height 70ft. Replaced by an embankment with culvert in 1933.
Carnon Viaduct Length 756ft, height 96ft. Crossed the Redruth & Chasewater Railway. Replaced by a nine-arch all-masonry viaduct in 1933.
Perran Viaduct Length 339ft, height 56ft. Sometimes called Trewedna Viaduct. Replaced by a masonry viaduct in 1927.
Ponsanooth Viaduct Length 645ft, height 139ft. The highest viaduct on the branch. Replaced by a new masonry viaduct on a new alignment in 1930.
Pascoe Viaduct Length 390ft, height 70ft. Replaced by a culverted embankment on a new alignment in 1923.
Penryn Viaduct Length 342ft, height 83ft. Replaced by an embankment on a slightly different alignment in 1923.
Collegewood Viaduct Length 954ft, height 100ft. Built on a sweeping left-hand curve and the longest viaduct on the branch. It was the last survivor of the original viaducts, lasting 71 years, until replaced by a new masonry viaduct in 1934.

Within the 11-mile 29-chain distance of the original line between Penwithers Junction and Falmouth Docks station, the lengths of viaducts totalled almost a mile and tunnels nearly half a mile! The viaducts cost some £10,000 per annum to maintain and it is reputed that 55 full-time employees were needed to maintain them. The GWR formally took over the branch from the CR in 1889 and the track was converted from broad to standard gauge in 1892, in common with the rest of the CR (GWR).

On leaving Truro (CR) station the line enters Highertown Tunnel then runs straight to Penwithers Junction, where the former WCR line veers towards the northwest on its way to

Penzance. The junction configuration at Penwithers has changed many times over the years. Originally the WCR line to Newham crossed the Falmouth branch almost at right angles but in later years the Newham branch was a trailing connection from the down line to Falmouth, just before it went from double to single track. Penwithers Junction signalbox was closed in 1971, after closure of the Newham line, and the track was further rationalised, bringing the Falmouth branch under the control of Truro. The following description of the line includes the original viaducts detailed above.

Following Penwithers Junction was Penwithers Viaduct on track rising for a mile at 1 in 66. The line passes through the 924ft Penwithers cutting before entering the lined 491yd Sparnick Tunnel, the line then falling at 1 in 88/64 to the site of Ringwell Viaduct. About half a mile before Perranwell station the line crosses the impressive Carnon Viaduct. There was sand to a depth of 21ft in the riverbed at this location, mostly spoil from the mines, and the engineers had problems securing foundations for the 12 piers. The replacement masonry viaduct has nine arches. At 304 miles 78 chains is Perranwell station, where there was once a passing loop, goods yard and shed, loading bank and an elevated signalbox set at right angles to the line and straddling one of the sidings. A fine stone station building once existed but although the goods shed has survived, passengers now have to huddle in a glorified bus shelter. Goods services were withdrawn on 4 January 1965, the signalbox closed in 1966 and the passing loop was later lifted.

Perran Viaduct followed about 1 mile from Perranwell with the track rising at 1 in 66, easing to 1 in 100 on the entrance to the lined 374yd Perran Tunnel. After a climb of about 1 in 60 for a mile the line crosses Ponsanooth Viaduct, the fourth highest in Cornwall. The site of Pascoe Viaduct is followed by a deep cutting at Roskrow Hill. The line then tumbles at 1 in 60 towards Penryn station, 309 miles 12 chains, which is south of the site of the former Penryn Viaduct. A slight realignment resulted in the post-1923 station being built slightly to the west of the original structure, this time on a straight section of track. A large number of other changes were made in 1923, including the closure and replacement of the 1894 signalbox, extension of the sidings around the goods shed and the addition of sidings at the up end of the down platform. In its heyday Penryn goods yard was extremely busy. Not only did the 3,000 population and the many local businesses produce traffic, but Penryn was also a railhead for many outlying districts not otherwise served by rail. The passing loop survived until 1971 when the 1923 signalbox was closed and the signals and passing loop removed. Nowadays there is just a miserable, basic bus shelter perched on a single featureless platform, although to be positive at least Penryn still has a train service. Mileages south of Penryn are now 1 chain shorter than at the time of opening due to the various realignments.

From Penryn the line falls at a maximum of 1 in 51 through a cutting and on to the splendid 318yd-long, 100ft-high Collegewood Viaduct, which replaced the last of the old Brunel wooden-topped examples in 1934. The viaduct is the longest on the branch and overlooks the whole of the inlet and harbour area of Penryn. The line does a southerly sweep of the town of Falmouth and the alignment is attributable to the decision to end the line at the docks, rather than using the town site of Greenbank, as specified in the 1846 Act. At the 311-mile 13-chain point is Penmere Platform, a halt opened by the GWR on 1 June 1925 to serve a growing community to the southwest of Falmouth. From 1940 until 1967 there were four sidings to the south of the line, which also formed a freight loop, serving a Ministry of Defence oil depot. A tasteful new brick waiting shelter with conventional awning was added to the platform in 1999. The station is now tended by the 'Friends of Penmere' and their work has been commended in a Railtrack 'station of the year competition'. We must hope their efforts survive the local vandals.

Right:
The track layout at Penwithers Junction has changed many times over the years. Curving to the right is the main line to Penzance, while the Falmouth line (which changes to single track within a few yards) goes straight on. On the left of the Falmouth lines the Newham branch, part of the old WCR route to Truro, can just be detected. Passing Penwithers on 13 July 1957 is No 6808 *Beenham Grange* with an up lightweight freight.
R. E. Vincent

Centre right:
The compact WCR wooden station at Newham, for Truro, had a single platform and an all-over roof, as seen here on 14 August 1956. It had a short life as a passenger station, opening in 1855 and closing in 1863 when the present main line Truro station was made available to the WCR. However, after closure to passengers the Newham site operated as a freight depot for well over 100 years. *Hugh Davies*

Below:
The Newham Goods site south of Truro was not too far from the city, as can be seen from the position of the cathedral. In addition to general goods, another important commodity was the coal supply for Truro Gasworks. However, when the works closed in 1970 the line was doomed and formal closure took place on 6 November 1971. On 20 July 1960 about-to-be-withdrawn Prairie No 5552 runs beside the Truro River during shunting operations.
R. C. Riley, The Transport Treasury

Left:
When first built, the Falmouth branch had no fewer than eight major viaducts within the 11 miles 29 chains that separated Penwithers Junction and Falmouth Docks. However, at a later date embankments replaced four of the structures. A survivor is the 756ft-long, 96ft-high Carnon Viaduct seen here. DMUs dominate normal services but on 22 March 1992 no fewer than three locomotives were employed on a 'Chartex' for railway enthusiasts. Returning from Falmouth Docks is No 37675 *William Cookworthy* hauling nine Mk 2B/C Network SouthEast coaches (a set from the Waterloo-Exeter pool) and a pair of Class 33s, Nos 33050 and 33063, across Carnon Viaduct. *JV*

Table 101 — TRURO and FALMOUTH

Week Days

Miles		S am	E am	S am	E am	S am	E am	S am	E am	S am	am	S am	EH pm	E pm	S pm	S pm	S pm	S pm	S pm	EK pm	E pm
	Truro .. dep	5 35	6 45	6 50	7 28	7 47	8 8	8 25	8 50	9 10	1015	1112	1137	1210	1246	1 20	1 40	2 17	2 55	3 20	4 8	3 49	4 35
4½	Perranwell	5 45	6 56	7 2	7 38	7 58	8 20	8 36	9 0	9 20	1025	1122	1149	1220	1256	1 30	1 51	2 27	3 8	3 30	3 58	4 04	4 45
8½	Penryn	5 55	7 8	7 13	7 47	8 9	8 29	8 47	9 10	9 30	1035	1132	1159	1230	1 6	1 40	2 0	2 37	3 20	3 40	4 7	4 14	4 55
10½	Penmere Platform	6 0	7 14	7 18	7 53	8 15	8 35	8 52	9 15	9 35	1040	1137	12 4	1235	1 11	1 45	2 5	2 42	3 25	3 45	4 12	4 15	5 0
11½	Falmouth .. arr	6 5	7 20	7 24	7 58	8 20	8 40	9 0	9 20	7 40	1046	1145	1210	1242	1 18	1 50	2 11	2 50	3 30	3 50	4 20	4 20	5 5

Week Days—continued / **Sundays**

		SN pm	E pm	S pm	E pm	S pm	E pm	B pm	S pm	E pm	S pm	am	am	am	noon H	pm	pm	pm	pm	V pm	H pm	H pm
Truro .. dep		4 55	5 15	6 10	6 15	6 35	7 0	7 35	8 10	8 20	9 8	9 55	10 8	30	9 51	1120	12 0	2 0	4 0	5 14	5 50	7 45	9 15	..
Perranwell		5 8	5 25	6 20	6 25	6 46	7 10	7 45	8 21	8 30	9 17	10 4	7	22	8 41	10 4	1130	1210	2 10	4 10	5 24	6 0	7 55	9 26	....
Penryn		5 20	5 35	6 35	6 35	6 57	7 20	7 56	8 30	8 40	9 27	1012	7	33	8 50	1015	1139	1220	2 19	4 20	5 34	6 12	8 4	9 35	....
Penmere Platform		5 25	5 40	6 40	6 40	7 2	7 25	8 1	8 35	8 45	9 33	1017	7	38	8 55	1020	1144	1225	2 25	4 25	5 40	6 18	8 10	9 40	..
Falmouth .. arr		5 31	5 46	6 47	6 47	7 7	7 30	8 6	8 40	8 50	9 38	1025	7	45	9 0	1025	1150	1230	2 30	4 30	5 45	6 25	8 15	9 45	...

Week Days

Miles		S am	E am	S am	E am	ED am	S am	am	H am	S am	am	S pm	E pm	pm	pm	pm	pm	pm
	Falmouth dep	6 27	8 0	8 35	9 0	..	9 30	10 0	10 25	..	11 0	1125	..	1210	1220	1235	..	1 30	2 25	..	3 10	4 25
1½	Penmere Platform	6 32	8 5	8 40	9 5	..	9 35	10 5	10 30	..	11 5	1130	..	1215	1225	1240	..	1 35	2 30	..	3 15	4 30
3½	Penryn	6 37	8 10	8 47	9 10	..	9 42	1013	10 36	..	11 10	1136	..	1220	1230	1247	..	1 41	2 36	..	3 20	4 36
7½	Perranwell	6 47	8 19	8 56	9 20	..	9 52	1025	10 45	..	11 23	1150	..	1230	1239	1257	..	1 51	2 45	..	3 31	4 47
11½	Truro .. arr	6 57	8 30	9 7	9 30	..	10 5	1036	10 58	..	11 35	12 0	..	1241	1250	1 8	..	2 2	2 56	..	3 40	4 58

Week Days—continued / **Sundays**

		S pm	E pm	pm	H pm	pm	pm	am	am W	am H	pm	pm	pm	H pm	H pm	pm	pm
Falmouth dep		5 10	5 24	..	6 25	7 10	..	7 45	8 55	..	10 0	..	9 5	9 40	1045	..	1240	1 30	2 45	5	6 45	..	8 50	10 0
Penmere Platform		5 15	5 29	..	6 30	7 15	..	7 50	9 0	..	10 5	..	9 10	9 45	1050	..	1245	1 35	2 50	5 10	6 50	..	8 55	10 5
Penryn		5 21	5 35	..	6 35	7 20	..	7 55	9 5	..	1012	..	9 15	9 52	1055	..	1251	1 40	2 55	5 15	6 55	..	9 0	1010
Perranwell		5 30	5 45	..	6 47	7 29	..	8 5	9 17	..	1021	..	9 25	10 2	11 5	..	1 3	1 50	3 5	5 25	7 5	..	9 10	1020
Truro .. arr		5 42	5 56	..	7 0	7 40	..	8 17	9 28	..	1033	..	9 35	1015	1118	..	1 15	2 0	3 15	5 35	7 17	..	9 20	1030

B On Saturdays Through Carriages from Bristol dep 1 45 pm (Table 81)
D Through Carriages to London (Pad.) arr 4 20 pm (Table 81)
E Except Saturdays

H Through Train from or to Newquay (Table 100)
K Through Carriages from London (Pad.) dep 9 30 am (Table 81)
L Through Train to London (Pad.) arr 4 3 pm (Table 81)

N Through Carriages from London (Pad.) dep 10 35 am (Table 81)
S Saturdays only
V Through Carriages from London (Pad.) dep 10 40 am (Table 81)
W Through Carriages to London (Pad.) arr 5 10 pm (Table 81)

Above:
The Falmouth branch timetable for the summer of 1958. Note the number of through trains and carriage workings.

Above:
Originally most of the viaducts followed the Brunel timber-topped Class 'A' pattern, although those on the Falmouth branch were built by Brereton after Brunel's death. This well-known 1912 photograph shows Carnon Viaduct before its replacement by a masonry viaduct in 1933. Crossing is a Falmouth to Truro train headed by a '3521' class locomotive. In the foreground is the Redruth & Chasewater Railway from Devoran to Redruth (see Chapter 2), which closed in 1915. *Redruth Studies Library*

Below:
Looking down the valley towards Devoran on 5 April 1990 finds a two-car DMU scuttling towards Truro forming the 16.35 service from Falmouth Docks. The original piers from the 1863 viaduct that spanned the upper reaches of Restronguet Creek can be seen between the arches. The new viaduct cost £40,000 in 1933, but with some 70 years of service already under its belt it was a good investment. *JV*

Beyond Penmere the single line descends at 1 in 80 to a single-platform concrete halt that, from the date of construction in December 1970, was known as The Dell. At this time Falmouth Docks station was temporarily, as it turned out, abandoned for passengers, and this new station was much nearer to the town centre than the Docks. However, the latter station was reopened in 1975 and The Dell was renamed Falmouth Town, a much more sensible arrangement. Half a mile beyond the 1970 station is Falmouth Docks, the terminus of the branch, 312 miles 49 chains from London Paddington via Bristol. The original infrastructure here was impressive with a station building 200ft long and 90ft wide with a splendid 70ft-span all-over roof. There was a goods shed, goods yard with cranes and a two-road locomotive shed with turntable. In the early years there was also a turntable for turning rolling stock. The track layout at the terminus changed many times over the years but the greatest changes occurred in 1894 and 1903, a new signalbox being erected in 1894. A new turntable was provided for locomotives behind the engine shed in 1897 but removed when the shed closed in 1927.

When one considers Falmouth's illustrious past with full-length express trains to London, plus local trains to Truro and plenty of freight traffic, today's scene is bleak. The delightful long down platform and awning has survived but everything else has been razed. The total railway buildings comprise one Portakabin and the crumbling remains of a loading dock. However, Falmouth is still not quite a single-line stub because just outside the station on the down side is the rusting connection with Falmouth Docks, which was opened on Thursday 14 January 1864 and gave the Falmouth Docks Company direct access to the CR and the rest of the UK. Great hopes were pinned on the docks becoming a huge centre for commerce, with imports and exports keeping the many jetties busy, the railways active and the merchants rich! Furthermore Falmouth had designs upon the tourist industry and special efforts were made to develop this potential. By 1876 the town was included in the prestigious Thomas Cook holiday guide.

The docks blossomed and an extremely comprehensive railway network was developed extending to all parts of the harbour and on to the east, west and north piers. All jetties were served by rail as well as a large iron foundry. The detailed developments at the harbour, such as the opening of a new large dry dock in 1920, are too numerous to mention here, but the lines were so busy that a domestic fleet of dock company locomotives was necessary to handle both the internal and external traffic to the CR/GWR/BR interface. Although Falmouth Docks were very busy in the early days and at the beginning of the 20th century, because of their remote location from the major cities of the UK the complex never really lived up to the hopes of the early speculators. Falmouth did, however, develop as a major ship repair centre and to this day large vessels can be seen in the dry docks under repair. In the early days the docks fleet comprised small 0-4-0 vertical-boilered locomotives, or 'coffee-pots', but especially in the 1926-7 period 0-4-0 saddle tanks replaced them. Even in the mid-1970s three small tanks from the Hawthorne Leslie, Hudswell Clarke and Peckett stables were retained as docks shunters, but by 1980 the occasional movements by rail within the docks were in the hands of a 0-4-0 Sentinel diesel shunter. Although there is currently no goods traffic to or from the docks there were experiments with firstly fish traffic, secondly calcified seaweed and later with Freightliner containers and new-generation freight wagons, but no regular traffic resulted. The connection to the docks is extant but unused and weed-covered.

The Falmouth branch timetable has varied greatly over the years. The initial service saw five round trip workings, and at its peak 21 trains were run in each direction. In 1927 there were 16 trains each way, in 1958 it was 15, in 1984 it had reduced to 11, and in 2001 it was 12. There were always minor variations on Saturdays and until recent years there were always trains on the sabbath. Through trains and through coaches to London Paddington featured for many years but these finally came to an end on 29 September 1979, by which time just one train per week on summer Saturdays, the 09.10 departure, left for the capital. Details of the broad and standard gauge motive power used on the line in the last 140 years could fill a book in their own right, but unlike many other Cornish branches and byways the line was passed for large tender locomotives, including the 4-6-0 'Castle' class. In later years most branch line services were in the hands of '4500' class 2-6-2 Prairie tanks but their use was by no means exclusive. Rivalling the GWR workhorses for longevity has been the use of DMUs on the line between about 1963 and 1994. All diesel locomotive classes commensurate with other parts of the county of Cornwall have traversed the branch from time to time and the line has been the target for enthusiasts' specials bringing, for example, Southern Region Class 33 diesels to Falmouth. One of the problems has been 'pathing' and sometimes specials have run as locals because no other path has been available.

Except for the rusting connection to the docks the branch is now, beyond Penwithers Junction, an unsignalled single-line stub normally worked by a shuttling Class 150/2 diesel unit. Other than the train crew and permanent way contractors there are no staff employed on the branch, and it has its own dedicated bay platform at the west end of Truro station, where surprisingly the station movements are still controlled by manually operated lower quadrant semaphore signals, a welcome leftover from GWR/WR days. Trains arriving from Falmouth travel up the down main line between Penwithers Junction and Truro, a mildly unnerving experience! The line has always had a 50mph speed limit, with lower speed restrictions at some points. It is interesting to note that the down sleeping car service connection from Truro to Falmouth in 1888 (the 6.40am departure), stopping only at Penryn, took 22 minutes for the journey, exactly the same as the 2001 service stopping at all stations! For a while in steam days 37 minutes was allowed for the 11¾-mile journey. Today the service seems to be safe but it is anybody's guess whether the docks will ever see revenue-earning freight traffic again. The line is worth exploring.

Right:
Perranwell station, the first stop out of Truro, was noted for its unusual signalbox, which straddled one of the goods sidings at the end of the down platform. Today a single line runs through the station but once there was a passing loop, goods yard, goods shed and an elevated loading bank. Goods were withdrawn in January 1965 and the signalbox closed in 1966. In the mid-1950s the customary 2-6-2T, No 4549, pauses at Perranwell with a down train. *W. A. Camwell, SLS*

Lower right:
Penryn was the railhead for many outlying districts as well as its own population of 3,000, and became the most important intermediate location on the branch. This elegant Edwardian view shows a mid-morning up train approaching, while on the platform, which has the benefit of an awning, a handful of well-dressed passengers probably intend to travel 1st Class! The station lighting is also very stylish. Many changes were made in 1923 when a new station, built slightly to the west, was opened and additional sidings were made available at both the up and down ends of the down platform.
JV collection

Left:
By comparison with the photograph on page 197, what a miserable station Penryn is nowadays with no creature comforts whatsoever, except for the crudest of shelters. The passing loop survived until 1971 when the 1923-built signalbox was closed and the signals and redundant track were all removed. On 6 April 1991 Class 101 diesel unit No 874, comprising coaches Nos 53315 and 53330, forming the 11.20 ex-Truro service, pauses at Penryn to collect perhaps half a dozen passengers. *JV*

Right:
This photograph from well over 100 years ago shows that even the GWR did not always get it right. On 31 October 1898 the 5.20pm mixed 'Mail' train headed by locomotive No 3542 was derailed on the embankment south of Collegewood Viaduct, near Penryn, tearing up a length of track. The locomotive crashed down the slope but only the leading mail coach turned completely on its side. The driver, Mr Cotterill, died of scalding but none of the passengers was seriously injured.
M. Dart collection

Left:
This wonderful view, reputedly recorded in the 1890s, shows Collegewood Viaduct in its original state. It was the last of the Cornish timber viaducts to be replaced, in July 1934. The local two-coach train, comprised of two Brake 3rds of 1881 vintage, is hauled by one of the ubiquitous 'Metro' class 2-4-0 tanks and is steaming towards Falmouth, approaching the scene of the 1898 accident. *P. Q. Treloar collection*

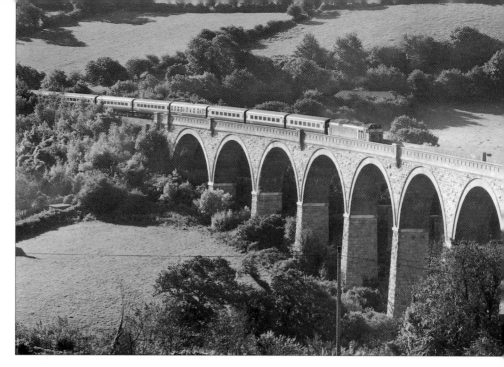

Right:
The branch was passed to take the larger classes of steam locomotive, such as the GWR 'Castle' class 4-6-0s, and for many years there were both through trains and through coaches from Falmouth to London Paddington. The tradition continued into the diesel era, but by 1979 there was just a single through train, which ran only on summer Saturdays. To secure this shot I asked a lady in a house that overlooked the viaduct whether I could use her back bedroom! Making a wonderful sight on 22 September 1979 is Class 50 No 50044 *Exeter* hauling the penultimate through train to Paddington across Collegewood Viaduct. *JV*

Above:
On 23 September 1994 there was a signalmen's strike in Cornwall and little was moving on the main line. However, the Falmouth branch train was performing its scheduled services and a day on the branch was rewarded by not only afternoon sunshine but also the rostering of a two-car Class 115 NSE DMU. With the harbour and town of Penryn as a backdrop, unit No L723 forms the 14.40 Falmouth to Truro service. Note the old piers of the original 1863 viaduct in the foreground. *JV*

Above:
The stark stone industrial building, the boats in the inner harbour and a generally misty atmosphere give this picture a distinctly Cornish flavour. Also on 23 September 1994, DMU unit No L723 crosses Collegewood Viaduct in the far distance as the 11.55 Falmouth to Truro service. At this time the branch service provided 13 round trip workings between Cornwall's only city and the south coast. *JV*

Left:
As the population of Falmouth grew, the GWR wanted to exploit the traffic potential of the southwest of the town, and Penmere Platform was opened on 1 June 1925. The line here was always single but there was a freight loop and sidings serving a Ministry of Defence oil depot between 1940 and 1967. In this 1950s view at least four passengers wait for a train.
JV collection

Above:
When deserved, it is a pleasure to be positive about our railways and in 1999 some extremely tasteful shelters, built with traditional materials in the traditional style, were constructed on some branch stations. Such a shelter, built of brick with a proper awning, now graces the platform of Penmere, the word 'platform' having disappeared from the timetable after 1961. The 'Friends of Penmere' now care for the station. Approaching the platform with a working from Falmouth is one of the current generation of multiple-units, Class 150/2 No 150261. *JV*

Below:
From Penmere the line continues via Falmouth Town, which between 1970 and 1975 was known as The Dell and was the terminus for passenger services, to Falmouth Docks. One can almost hear the bark of 2-6-2T No 5500 as it leaves Falmouth Docks and passes Falmouth signalbox on Sunday 17 May 1959 with the 6.45pm to Truro. The locomotive's side tanks sport the large BR 'lion and wheel' emblem. *Michael Mensing*

Above:
The down-side awning is a remarkable survivor from the days of steam. Unlike other termini no attempt has been made to shorten the corrugated-tin-roofed structure, despite gradual decay. This is especially surprising in view of the fact that only two-coach trains tend to use the station these days. Nestling amongst the weeds at the sad and neglected terminus in 1994 is a Class 115 DMU. The bird on the roof must not be deprived of its perch in the future! *JV*

Left:
On 1 July 1981 the docks' Sentinel diesel shunter No 129 is peeping out of its shed but there is otherwise little activity. Half a dozen box vans can be seen in the siding between the sheds and another can be glimpsed on the left. Some of the trackwork has been lifted and clearly the docks system is in decline. Even though it is still a major ship repair centre, Falmouth never really fulfilled the aspirations of its owners, its distance from the industrial centres of the UK having always been a disadvantage. *JV*

Below:
In the early days primitive vertical-boiler locomotives worked the docks area but in 1926-7 they were replaced by a number of 0-4-0 saddle tanks. In the 1970s there were still three steam engines left in service from the Hudswell Clarke, Hawthorne Leslie and Peckett stables. This shot shows *Falmouth Docks & Engineering Company No 1*, a product of the Hawthorne Leslie company. The docks have seen fish traffic, calcified seaweed, experimental Freightliner workings and tests with new-generation wagons, but unfortunately there is still no regular freight traffic. *JV collection*

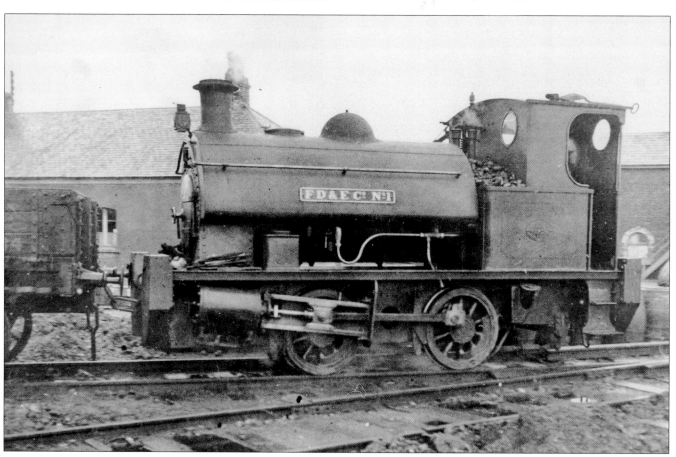

21. Chacewater to Newquay Branch including Treamble and Gravel Hill

In today's world of the motor car nobody in their right mind would have built a railway for profit between Chacewater and Newquay. The countryside between the two places was pleasant enough but the only towns with a significant population were St Agnes, with just over 4,000, and Perranporth, which was to become a popular summer holiday destination. A railway would certainly make the journey from Newquay to Truro easy and there would be the opportunity of picking up a little freight along the way, but the reasons for building the line were strategic.

For many years there had been a real threat that the rival LSWR would invade GWR territory by building a line from Wadebridge to Truro, possibly via Newquay; indeed, the LSWR ran a connecting bus service from Wadebridge to Newquay for many years. The LSWR was also making its way through North Cornwall, and by 1895 had finally reached Wadebridge, and in 1899 Padstow. There was also an earlier LSWR proposal to link Ruthern Bridge, off the Bodmin & Wadebridge line, which it owned, to Roche, on what was then the Cornwall Minerals Railway. Although the CMR was wholly taken over by the GWR in 1896, the LSWR remained a threat.

In 1894, in anticipation of the LSWR's incursions, the GWR proposed a direct line from Truro to Newquay but the plans were rejected by Parliament. The companies agreed not to fight over this corner of Cornwall, but nevertheless a further GWR plan for

Above:
Opened in part in 1903 and throughout in 1905, the branch line from Chacewater to Newquay was a comparative latecomer. Although the holiday trade along the North Cornwall coast was growing, the rural population was sparse and freight traffic potential was never heavy. Nevertheless the GWR built the line for the strategic reason of heading off the LSWR, which had reached Padstow by 1899. Some branch trains started and terminated at Chacewater, while others ran to and from Truro. In this mid-1950s shot No 4559 calls at the island platform at Chacewater with a Truro to Newquay working. *W. A. Camwell, SLS*

a line between Truro and Newquay, over a totally different route, submitted before the turn of the century, was approved. Although Truro is almost due south of Newquay and about 11 miles away 'as the crow flies', the revised route was far from direct in that the branch left the ex-WCR main line at Chacewater, 5 miles west of Truro, and travelled to the North Cornwall coast by a circuitous route via St Agnes, Perranporth and Shepherds, a total overall mileage of 23¾.

Another factor no doubt taken into consideration by the GWR was that for over 5 miles at the northern end of the proposed branch there was already a standard gauge railway line *in situ*, part of the route having been opened as long ago as 1849 as the Treffry Tramway to East Wheal Rose mine. In 1873-4 the CMR extended the line to Treamble and Gravel Hill via Shepherds to exploit iron mines in the Perran Lode. Unfortunately for the GWR, large-scale mining in the St Agnes area and at East Wheal Rose, as well as iron ore traffic from Gravel Hill, had ceased long before the new line opened in the 1903-5 period. None the less, although upgrading would be necessary, construction of the new route over the CMR line would be that much easier. Large-scale changes took place at Newquay in 1904 in anticipation of the arrival of trains from Chacewater (see Chapter 13).

Chacewater station on the WCR's Penzance to Truro route was opened in August 1852, and was about half a mile north of the small town it purported to serve. As a junction station for the new line it was ill-equipped, but it would be 1912 before extensive rebuilding took place, when an island platform was provided for branch train use. The main buildings at Chacewater and the signalbox were on the down side, and a pair of sidings was provided at the down end of the down platform, forming a small goods yard. From 1924 a line separate from but running parallel to the main line was provided for branch trains as far as the actual junction at Blackwater.

The GWR did not do things by halves and at Blackwater Junction, at the time of opening, there was not only a double-track connection from the main line to the single-line branch, which headed north, but also a double-track connection from the Redruth direction, forming a double-track triangle. The west-to-north spur was very much a secondary link, being used only for infrequent passenger trains and occasional freights; it survived until 1916 for passenger traffic and 1919 for freight, although it was not until November 1924 that the tracks were finally lifted. The original triangle was expensive to signal with three signalboxes in use — Blackwater East, North and West, and after 1924, as mentioned above, the branch junction comprised just a single track from the direction of Newquay that extended all the way to Chacewater station; the three signalboxes were closed in that year and the branch was then under the control of Chacewater signalbox. To provide the additional running line the cutting had to be extended on the north side.

Although it could never be said that the Chacewater to Newquay line had conveniently located stations for all the villages and hamlets it served, the meandering alignment attempted to have regard to these local communities while

Right:
Steam in action at the diminutive Mount Hawke Halt finds Prairie No 5562 heading towards Truro with the daily up branch freight. This halt was opened in 1905 but the small village it purported to serve was over a mile away and traffic was very light. The platform, in common with other similar halts on the line, was graced with a corrugated metal 'pagoda'-style waiting hut. The farmer (top right) is making hay while the sun shines! *G. Clarke*

Left:
In population terms St Agnes and Perranporth were the principal towns on the line, but St Agnes station was some distance from the town. This 1922 photograph shows the original configuration, but in 1937 considerable rebuilding took place when an island platform was built and St Agnes became one of three passing places on the branch. The nearest sign reads 'Parcels Office and Cloak Room'. *JV collection*

Right:
One corridor coach, one compartment coach and a four-wheeled van comprise this 1950s Newquay to Truro branch train, slowing for a pause at the delightfully named Goonbell Halt. No 5500 with large 'lion and wheel' emblem on its side tanks has steam to spare as the vacuum brakes are applied. There were around 10 trains per day each way, with half as many on summer Sundays. *G. Clarke*

working within the constraints of the topography. A few months after the railway was opened throughout on 2 January 1905, the GWR opened half a dozen modest single-platform halts, each with a couple of lamps, a sign and a basic 'pagoda' hut, to serve the minor hamlets along the line; they were ready for service from 14 August.

The rural branch left Blackwater Junction on an embankment, which can still be seen today, then climbed for 1 mile 9 chains to Mount Hawke Halt serving a hamlet over a mile away; as in the case of the other halts there were no sidings. The brick-faced platform now sits below an infilled cutting. The line then continued on an embankment, which is visible from the B3277 St Agnes road. It must have been disappointing for the inhabitants of St Agnes when they realised that the much-heralded new railway would be three-quarters of a mile from the village centre. The red-brick station initially had a single platform but was considered important enough to have a stationmaster. In 1937, some 34 years after opening, a long 300ft island platform, providing a passing

TRURO, CHACEWATER, and NEWQUAY—(One class only).

Miles	Down.	mrn	mrn	mrn	mrn	D	aft	aft	aft	D	aft	aft	aft	Sundays mrn	D	non	aft	aft
—	Truro.......dep.	..	7 26	9B33	1028	10B53	1B30	3B15	4A35	5K35	6 3	7B0	8B30	9 15	..	12 0	2 55	6 5
5¼	Chacewater ¶	6 30	7 37	9 46	1039	11 10	1 45	3 30	4 46	5 55	6 15	7 20	8 50	9 26	1130	1212	3 7	6 17
8¾	St. Agnes	6 40	7 47	9 56	1049	11 18	1 55	3 40	4 55	6 3	6 25	7 30	9 0	9 36	1140	1222	3 17	6 27
13¼	Perranporth	6 55	8 4	1011	11 4	11 32	2 10	3 55	5 13	6 15	6 42	7 45	9 15	9 52	1157	1238	3 33	6 43
17¾	Shepherds	7 10	8 19	1029	1118	11 48	2 25	4 10	5 28	6 30	6 57	..	9 30	10 7	1212	1253	3 48	6 58
23¾	Newquay ¶ (below) .. arr.	7 25	8 34	1044	1135	12 0	2 40	4 25	5 43	6 45	7 13	..	9 45	1022	1230	1 10	4 3	7 13

Miles	Up.	mrn	S	mrn	mrn	aft	D	aft	D	aft	aft	aft	aft	Sundays mrn	aft	aft	aft	D
—	Newquay ¶.......dep.	7 34	..	8 43	1130	1225	10 15	2 5	4 44	6 12	7 35	..	8 45	1030	1 45	4 40	7 20	7 45
6	Shepherds	7 52	D	9 2	1147	1243	10 27	2 25	5 2	6 30	7 53	..	9 3	1048	2 3	4 58	7 38	8 0
10½	Perranporth	8 2	9 0	9 15	1158	1254	10 36	2 36	5 14	6 41	8 4	8 40	9 15	11 0	2 15	5 10	7 50	8 10
15¼	St. Agnes	8 19	9 10	9 32	1215	1 11	10 50	2 53	5 31	6 58	8 21	9 0	9 30	1117	2 32	5 27	8 7	8 25
18½	Chacewater ¶ 26	8 28	..	9 41	1225	1 20	11 0	3 2	5 40	7 7	8 30	9 10	9 43	1126	2 41	5 36	8 16	8 35
23¾	Truro 26, 31, 63...arr.	8B43	9 30	9B55	1234	1B37	11J12	3B15	6B0	7B20	8B45	9 20	9 52	1138	2 51	5 46	8 25	..

¶ "Halts" at Mount Hawke, between Chacewater and St. Agnes; at Goonbell, at Mithian, and at Perranporth Beach, between St. Agnes and Perranporth; at Goonhavern, between Perranporth and Shepherds; at Mitchell and Newlyn and at Trewerry and Trerice, between Shepherds and Newquay.

B Change at Chacewater D 1st and 3rd Class. J Change at Chacewater. Arr. 11 17 mrn. on Sats.
K Change at Chacewater. On Sats. dep. 5 15 aft. S Saturdays only.
OTHER TRAINS between Truro & Chacewater, page 26

Table 100 TRURO, CHACEWATER, PERRANPORTH and NEWQUAY
(Second class only except where otherwise shewn)

Miles		Week Days am	am S	am E	am	am E	am S	am T	pm	pm	pm P	pm	pm E	pm S	pm T	pm S	Sundays am	am	am T	am	pm	pm	pm	pm T	pm T
	Truro .. .. dep	6 5	7 10	717	8H45	10 8	1010	1140	1H15	2J48	3 45	4L15	5H43	6 15	7 42	910	845	9 25	1125	1155	151	.	440	542	725
5	Chacewater	616	7 25	729	9 15	1020	1023	1154	1 35	2 58	3 55	4 39	5 58	6 25	8 0	922	...	9 37	1140	12 6	2 2	...	451	553	736
6¾	Mount Hawke Halt	621	7 30	734	9 20	..	..	1159	1 40	3 3	..	4 44	6 3	6 30	8 5	927	.	9 42	1145	1211	2 8	.	456	558	741
8½	St. Agnes	626	7 35	739	9 25	1028	1030	12 4	1 45	3 8	4 5	4 49	6 8	6 40	8 10	932	...	9 47	1150	1216	214	...	5 1	6 4	746
9	Goonbell Halt	629	7 38	742	9 28	..	..	12 7	1 48	3 11	..	4 52	6 11	6 44	8 13	935	.	9 50	1153	1219	217	.	5 4	6 7	749
10¾	Mithian Halt	634	7 43	747	9 33	....	....	1212	1 53	3 16	....	4 57	6 16	6 49	8 18	940	...	9 55	1158	1224	222	...	5 9	612	754
13	Perranporth Beach Halt ..	639	7 48	752	9 38	1038	1040	1218	1 59	3 21	..	5 2	6 21	6 55	8 22	945	.	10 0	12 3	1229	227	.	513	617	759
13¼	**Perranporth**	641	8F 2	8B29	9 41	1040	1044	1221	2 4	3 23	4 20	5 5	6 24	6 57	8 24	948	912	10 2	12 5	1230	230	435	515	620	8 1
15¾	Goonhavern Halt	649	8 10	810	9 49	..	..	1230	2 12	3 31	..	5 14	6 33	7 5	8 32	.	.	1010	1212	..	237	442	523	628	8 9
17¾	Shepherds	656	8 17	817	9 56	1052	....	1236	2 19	3 39	....	5 20	6 40	7 11	8 39	...	...	1018	1218	....	244	449	530	637	816
19	Mitchell and Newlyn Halt.	659	8 20	820	10 0	..	..	1240	2 22	3 43	..	5 24	6 43	7 15	8 43	.	.	1022	1222	..	248	453	534	641	821
21	Trewerry and Trerice Halt.	7 4	8 25	825	10 5	....	....	1245	2 27	3 48	....	5 29	6 48	7 20	8 48	...	...	1027	1227	....	253	458	539	646	826
23¾	**Newquay** .. .. .. arr	712	8 32	832	1015	11 6	..	1255	2 35	3 55	..	5 36	6 56	7 29	8 55	.	940	1035	1235	..	3 0	5 5	547	655	835

Miles		Week Days am S	am E	am K	am	am S	am ET	am	pm	pm S	pm E	pm	pm	pm	pm	Sundays am	am T	pm	pm	pm	pm T	pm T	pm
	Newquay .. .. .. dep	7 20	7 24	..	9 12	..	11 0	1150	1 35	2 55	3 20	4 35	5 52	7 55	9 15	10 0	1050	..	1 30	4 0	620	8 0	8 50
2¼	Trewerry and Trerice Halt.	7 27	7 31	....	9 19	....	....	1157	1 42	3 2	3 27	4 43	5 59	8 2	9 21	10 6	....	....	1 37	4 6	626	8 6	8 56
4¾	Mitchell and Newlyn Halt.	7 33	7 37	..	9 24	..	..	12 3	1 48	3 8	3 33	4 49	6 5	8 7	9 27	10 12	..	..	1 43	412	633	812	9 2
6	Shepherds	7 37	7 41	....	9 28	....	1114	12 7	1 53	3 12	3 38	4 53	6 9	8 11	9 32	10 17	11 3	....	1 47	417	637	817	9 7
8	Goonhavern Halt	7 43	7 47	..	9 33	..	1120	1212	1 58	3 17	3 43	4 59	6 14	8 16	9 37	10 22	..	..	1 52	422	642	822	9 12
10½	**Perranporth**	7 50	7 54	8 15	9 39	11 0	1125	1220	2 4	3 24	3 49	5 5	6 23	8 25	9 43	10 28	1116	1 10	1 58	428	649	828	9 18
10¾	Perranporth Beach Halt ..	7 51	7 55	..	9 41	11 2	1127	1222	2 5	3 25	3 51	5 7	6 25	8 26	9 47	10 30	..	1 11	2 0	.	651	830	9 20
13	Mithian Halt	7 58	8 2	....	9 48	....	....	1229	2 12	3 32	3 58	5 14	6 32	8 33	....	10 37	....	1 18	2 7	...	658	837	9 27
14¾	Goonbell Halt	8 4	8 8	..	9 54	..	..	1235	2 18	3 38	4 4	5 20	6 38	8 39	..	10 43	..	1 24	2 13	.	7 4	843	9 33
15¼	St. Agnes	8 7	8 11	8 28	9 57	1114	1139	1238	2 21	3 42	4 7	5 23	6 42	8 42	9 58	10 46	1130	1 27	2 16	...	7 7	846	9 36
17	Mount Hawke Halt	8 11	8 15	..	10 1	..	..	1242	2 25	3 46	4 11	5 27	6 46	8 46	..	10 50	..	1 31	2 20	.	711	850	9 40
18¾	**Chacewater** ...... arr	8 17	8 21	....	10 7	1121	1148	1248	2 31	3 52	4 17	5 33	6 52	8 53	10 9	10 56	1139	1 37	2 26	...	717	856	9 46
23¾	Truro .. .. "	8H35	8H34	8 48	10 20	1133	12 2	1H13	2Z41	4 5	4H50	5D55	7 2	9 3	1020	11 6	1150	1 48	2 36	.	730	9 6	10 0

B Arr 7 55 am
D Change at Chacewater. On Saturdays arr 5 45 pm without changing
E Except Saturdays
F Arr 7 50 am
H Change at Chacewater
J Change at Chacewater on Saturdays
K Saturdays only. First and Second class. Through Train to London (Pad.) arr 3 55 pm (Table 81)
L Change at Chacewater, dep 4 25 pm on Saturdays without changing
P Saturdays only and not after 30th Aug. First and Second class. Through Carriages from London (Pad.) dep 8 25 am (Table 81)
S Saturdays only
T Through Train from or to Falmouth (Table 101)
Z Change at Chacewater on Saturdays and arr Truro 3 5 pm

For OTHER TRAINS between Truro and Chacewater, see Table 81

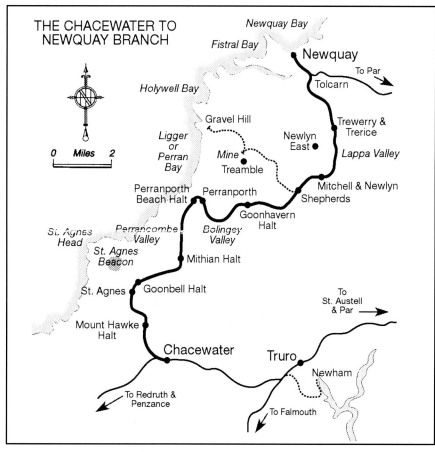

THE CHACEWATER TO NEWQUAY BRANCH

Left:
The July 1938 Chacewater to Newquay branch timetable (top). Note that Bradshaw cares to refer to the halts only in the narrative on the right. Below is the summer 1958 timetable, showing all stations and halts. The line still had a through working to and from London Paddington on summer Saturdays but only to and from Perranporth.

Above:
Prairie tanks did not have the complete monopoly of the branch and on occasions one of Truro's 0-6-0 pannier tanks ably handled services. Beyond Goonbell, and 5 miles 7 chains from Blackwater Junction, near Chacewater, was Mithian Halt. Passing the running-in board is No 7715 with the 11am Newquay to Truro train of 11 July 1961. *Peter Gray*

Right:
This map of the Chacewater to Newquay branch shows the circuitous route adopted to travel from Truro to Newquay.

Above:
Even back in the 1930s the branch workings were '4500' class-hauled. With a remarkable selection of rolling stock in tow, including GWR auto-coach No 82, No 5504 passes the water tank and enters Perranporth station with a train from Truro. *Dr I. C. Allen, M. Dart collection*

Below:
Just on the Truro side of Perranporth was Perranporth Beach Halt, built in 1931 to take trippers nearer to the sands. Unlike the halt the main station had every facility, including the large goods shed seen on the right. The lower quadrant semaphore signal is 'off' for this typical branch train of the mid-1950s, which is waiting to leave for Chasewater. *W. A. Camwell, SLS*

Above:
Perranporth signalbox was sited at the Newquay end of the island platform, whose buildings had deep awnings and commodious waiting rooms. Having filled the tanks with water, the engine driver on the left is looking at his mount, No 5500, while waiting time with a Chacewater to Newquay working. In 1958 a through train on summer Saturdays left Perranporth at 08.15am and arrived in London Paddington at 3.55pm, a journey of 7hr 40min. *W. A. Camwell, SLS*

Above:
This view of Goonhavern Halt, opened on 14 August 1905, dates back to 5 June 1922. Down trains had a 2-mile slog up from Perranporth along the Bolingey Valley to reach here, and there were heavy earthworks in this area including cuttings and three road overbridges. Signs of the local hamlet and the village chapel can be seen on the right. *JV collection*

loop, and a signalbox were constructed; the platform was connected to the original station building by a footbridge. The station had a goods yard and goods shed on the down side, and was 2 miles 57 chains from the junction.

Leaving St Agnes the line veered sharply eastward and a mere 45 chains down the line was Goonbell Halt serving a few nearby buildings collectively known as Goonbell. The line then continued across the five-arch 140yd Goonbell Viaduct, and at the 5-mile 7-chain point was Mithian Halt, conveniently located to serve a small community. The line then descended the Perrancombe Valley at gradients of up to 1 in 45 to within a short distance of Cornwall's north coast at Perranporth. In 1931, at 7 miles 16 chains, just before the line swept around the valley at 90°, a halt was constructed for the 'bucket and spade brigade'. Called

Perranporth Beach Halt, it opened on 20 July 1931, just in time for the peak summer invasion of holidaymakers.

From the date of opening Perranporth had a substantial island platform, goods shed, cattle dock, signalbox and other railway infrastructure items. The station had very deep awnings and between 6 July 1903, when the first part of the line opened, and 2 January 1905 it was the terminus. Although Perranporth suffered from the lack of a central focal point, its beach was splendid and by the 1950s its popularity was at its zenith. This was recognised by the railway and on summer Saturdays in the 1950s there were through workings between Perranporth and London Paddington, with an overall journey time of approximately 7hr 45min. After leaving Perranporth at 7 miles 47 chains the railway ran along the Bolingey Valley in a broadly easterly direction before crossing the

Right:
The East Wheal Rose mine dates back to 1814 and by 1818 it was one of Cornwall's top producers of lead. It was 1849 before Treffry connected the mine to Newquay Harbour by tramway but by then the mine was in decline, closing completely in August 1885. Some years after closure of the Chacewater to Newquay branch, part of the trackbed was used as a narrow gauge tourist line, called the Lappa Valley Railway. The route happily incorporates some of the land around the remains of the East Wheal Rose engine house, seen here as 15in-gauge *Muffin* departs with the 11.50 train from Benny Halt on 11 August 1998. *P. G. Barnes*

89yd Cox Viaduct at 8 miles 51 chains to reach Goonhavern Halt at 9 miles 76 chains, serving a sprinkling of houses in the vicinity near the Newquay to Redruth road.

The line then curved to the northeast and through a cutting before descending to Shepherds at 11 miles 71 chains, the junction for the freight-only line to Treamble. Shepherds was built on conventional lines with up and down platforms, allowing trains to pass. There was no goods yard, just a short refuge siding and a signalbox on the up side. Other than in the companion OPC book *The Newquay Branch and its Branches*, little has been written about the Treamble branch, which is hardly surprising because the line never sprang to prominence and received little publicity, having originally been built to serve the iron ore industry. In the 18th and 19th centuries iron ore had been extracted from the Perran Lode that ran from Holywell to the downs around Newlyn East, but it had to be hauled some 9 miles for shipment and that added to the unit costs in a competitive marketplace. Although there had been an application to Parliament in 1865 to construct a railway from the iron lode to Newquay, it was the CMR in its 1873 Act that extended the Treffry Tramway line (which the CMR subsumed) from East Wheal Rose to Treamble.

The main mines in the area were at Gravel Hill, Duchy Peru and Deer Park. The CMR described the line as '4 miles and 7 furlongs in length, commencing in the Parish of Newlyn by a junction with the existing tramway from New Quay *(sic)* to East Wheal Rose about eight hundred yards or thereabouts from the termination thereof, and terminating in a field in the Parish of Perranzabuloe at a point one hundred and sixty yards or thereabouts to the southward of a mill known as Treamble Mill'. The company

Centre right:
Resembling a Class 52 diesel is *Duke of Cornwall*, which once ran on a now abandoned narrow gauge railway along the sands at Carlyon Bay to a naturists' beach! It now resides on the Lappa Valley Railway, and with some interesting track in the foreground it heads some semi-open stock at East Wheal Rose. The main line extends to just over a mile and it is now the only working reminder of the old branch. *P. G. Barnes*

Lower right:
Beyond Shepherds the next station was Mitchell & Newlyn, the '&' giving away the fact that the tiny halt did not adequately serve either community. The halt was built amongst the spoil from East Wheal Rose mine adjacent to a minor road and was nearer to Newlyn East than Mitchell. The halt is one of the few surviving sites on the branch where platform and 'building' survive. By 1998 nature had almost finished its reclamation process and it is now hard to imagine that a train ever passed this place. *P. G. Barnes*

Left:
The last halt on the line before reaching Newquay was Trewerry & Trerice Halt. As with Mitchell & Newlyn the halts were originally built with wooden platforms, such as that seen here, but were later rebuilt with concrete platforms. The crossing gates were operated manually and three oil lamps comprised the entire illumination for passengers and train crews! The crossing box rejoiced in the name of 'Trewerry Crossing Ground Frame'. *IAL*

mentioned that the success of the line would depend on the output levels from the mines. In addition to the Treamble line, a 1-mile 4-chain extension from a trailing point near the terminus was built to Gravel Hill, at the eastern end of Perran Beach. Construction of the extension took just 10 days, the company having the landowner's permission but not Parliamentary authority.

The entire line was opened, in common with the rest of the CMR, on 1 June 1874, but despite early optimism the mines were not efficiently worked, production slumped and there was a downturn in the industry. As a consequence prices fell, and the Cornish Consolidated Iron Mines Corporation was dissolved in 1884. On the Treamble line there had been an intermediate siding at Deer Park, which was served by a tramway from the iron mine of the same name, but this was exhausted by 1886. The extension to Gravel Hill closed in 1888 and the track was lifted during the following year. Traffic volumes to and from Treamble were never high and the line was not worth retaining. Duchy Peru mine (and Great Retallack mine) was also served by a tramway that ran down to Treamble but production also ceased there. This was the last straw and the whole branch closed under the auspices of the GWR at the end of 1916, the track being removed in 1917. By then the government was looking for surplus rail for the war effort and the track went the same way as that on the Treffry Tramway lines around Carmears and also the Pentewan Railway.

These events should have been the end of the story but, to the surprise of many, the GWR announced that 'as and from Tuesday 16 February 1926 the Treamble branch, which forms a connection with the Perranporth branch at Shepherds, had been reinstated and was opening for goods traffic'. The 3-mile 60-chain branch would provide accommodation for 14 trucks at the private siding terminus and would be controlled by Shepherds signalbox on the 'train staff, one engine in steam or two coupled' principle. Trains would run thrice weekly, on Tuesdays, Thursdays and Saturdays.

From Shepherds the first mile of the line descended at 1 in 60/88/41, followed by the second mile falling at 1 in 40/100/60. At the 2-mile mark the line fell even more steeply, at 1 in 50/40 for over a mile, then undulated after the 3-mile marker. The 1926 trackwork was single throughout from Shepherds to the loop just outside the Treamble terminus. The locomotive would always run round its train in the loop then propel the wagons into the private siding. There was a gate across the track just beyond the GWR boundary. Beside the loading wharf at Treamble there was also a 2ft-gauge tramway worked by a pair of small Kerr Stuart 0-4-2T steam locomotives serving the C. M. Powder Co Ltd, which manufactured gunpowder. The little tramway closed in 1942.

Traffic volume at Treamble continued to be small and the 14-wagon loop was never filled to capacity. The overall speed restriction on the branch was 10mph and the freight was allowed a leisurely 1hr 35min for the round trip, including shunting. Due to the gradients stop boards were fixed at 47 chains and at 2 miles 59 chains and brakes were picked up at 2 miles 41 chains and at Treamble loop. Whistle boards were situated on either side of a crossing near Rejerrah, and propelling was banned in either direction. After a handful of wartime troop trains and some 'as and when required' freight workings, traffic finally petered out in the summer of 1949. Closure was formally posted in January 1952 and the track was removed in the spring of 1956. The line can be traced in a couple of locations but it is otherwise heavily overgrown.

Back on the Newquay line, from Shepherds station, where in times gone by a camping coach with a clerestory roof was located, the line passed Fiddlers Green before crossing Penhallow Moor. The next halt at Mitchell & Newlyn, 13 miles 14 chains, was the most remote on the line and was accessible only by a footpath. Needless to say, it was convenient for neither Mitchell nor Newlyn (East)! After the construction of the 1873-4 CMR extension to Treamble the East Wheal Rose mine effectively had its own siding; facing Newquay on the up side at 13 miles 46 chains, it closed in the last years of the 19th century. East Wheal Rose, a major producer of lead, opened in 1814 but closed in 1831 due to a slump in price. However, it reopened in 1834 and by 1846 employed no fewer than 1,200 men, women and children! The mine was wet and in 1842 steam pumping engines were removing 734 gallons of water per minute! In 1846 there was a terrible disaster when the mine flooded killing 39 miners. By the time Treffry built his tramway in 1849 the mine was already in decline again but it soldiered on until August 1885.

Part of the alignment of the Chacewater to Newquay branch has been used for the Lappa Valley 15in-gauge tourist railway that opened in 1973, running from Benny Halt terminus to East Wheal Rose. The area around the mine has been developed to attract tourists and the many features include a boating lake and a miniature railway. Both steam and diesel locomotives are used on the line, which is open in the season and well worth a visit (see the accompanying photographs).

The final halt on the line was at Trewerry & Trerice at 15 miles 6 chains. The halt, in common with Mitchell & Newlyn, had its original wooden platform replaced by concrete slabs. There was a coal siding at Trewerry but this was closed in September 1948. Between Trewerry and Trevemper Siding the CMR line deviated from the original Treffry Tramway alignment. At 16 miles 76 chains there was a reverse siding on the down side to some

coal drops, and in fact Trevemper Siding itself survived (from the Newquay end) for eight months after the main branch line closed, being less than half a mile south of Tolcarn Junction, where the Chacewater line joined the Par to Newquay branch. Tolcarn was a triangular junction, although the south-to-east curve, closed from 1888 until 1931, was used more for turning locomotives and stock than for any form of through running.

From six trains in each direction on weekdays in 1910 services increased to eight in 1927, 12 in 1938, falling to 11 in 1958. In later years there was a Sunday service. The trains varied from single railmotor (and trailer) in the early days to steam-hauled branch trains of between two and four coaches in later years. Motor-fitted 2-4-0Ts worked trains in the early days followed in later years by 2-6-2T and 0-6-0PT tank locomotives, based on Truro shed. During the last year or two firstly diesel locomotives then DMUs put in appearances. Light tender locomotives, such as GWR 2-6-0 Moguls, appeared on the branch at times and in summer pairs of tanks were sometimes rostered. The last train on the branch was a four-car DMU formation. There was a 40mph speed limit on the line and the full 23¾-mile Truro to Newquay journey time was 1 hour, for one of the few semi-fast trains, to 1hr 15min for the normal stopping service. If a change at Chacewater was necessary journey times were about 15 minutes longer.

There were always many more trains to Newquay on the Chacewater line compared with the Par line but in the summer months all through holiday trains to Newquay used the older line. The Chacewater line reputedly had some 600 passengers per day, or about 30 per train, as well as a daily freight, but by the criteria used in the 1960s the line was losing money. Total receipts from the line covered only 65% of the full operational costs of running it, and it was a duplicate line simply in terms of travelling to Newquay by train. Closure notices were therefore posted and after all formalities were executed the line closed completely on 4 February 1963. Only the short section to Trevemper Siding remained open but even that closed later in the year on 29 October. Tolcarn Junction signalbox closed on 23 November 1964 and all of the area has now been covered by housing and an industrial estate. The Western National Omnibus Company Limited provided the replacement bus service after closure.

One curious fact concerning the Chacewater to Newquay branch is that it was the last passenger branch to be opened in the county of Cornwall, yet was the first to close entirely, lasting only 60 years (58 throughout its length). The main line junction station of Chacewater closed on 5 October 1964 but long after closure the old goods yard continued to be used as a depot for cement, which arrived sometimes daily in block loads from Blue Circle's Plymstock depot. Sadly the rail contract was lost in May 1987 and the traffic was subsequently carried by road. There is now very little left of the branch, but as can be seen from these photographs it had a charm all of its own.

22. Hayle Railway (Tresavean, Portreath, North Crofty, Roskear and Hayle Wharves Branches)

The rich pickings from the various mines in Cornwall would have been worth nothing without their output being accessible to world markets. In the early days there were no railway lines or canals in West Cornwall and everything exported or imported needed to be carried between the mines and ships at the nearest port. This would not have been a problem for many commodities, but with heavy copper and tin ore being exported and coal being imported, the tonnages involved were great. Also many of the mines were in the Camborne, Redruth and Carn Brea areas and this resulted in quite a trek to the nearest port. The problem was compounded by many of these ports being in shallow, tidal waters, or in areas where little protection was offered in times of gales and rough seas.

There was also the problem mentioned in many other chapters about the practice of mules, horses and wagons working over rough and rutted roads not being conducive to an efficient and effective transportation system for the mines. The coming of the industrial age changed all that when steam power began to make an impact, with pumping engines and railway locomotives. Prior to that, wooden 'rayle-ways' had been in use by the mid-17th century and a century later the 'rails' were made of cast iron and later wrought iron. The steam pumping engine goes back to about 1720 when one was working at Ludgvanluz in Cornwall. These machines used huge quantities of coal, which had to be carried by packhorse from port to mine, although they gradually developed and became more efficient. Richard Trevithick (Senior) was an engineer, manager and 'Captain' of several mines, and mineral agent for Lord de Dunstanville for 20 years, and he played an important role in this development. He was helped by John Harvey of Hayle, who also became famous.

The Trevithicks lived in a cottage at Illogan, near Carn Brea, and in 1797 the more famous Richard Trevithick (Junior) married the daughter of John Harvey. About this time Trevithick (Jnr) had designed a small high-pressure steam engine of a revolutionary design that was seen as a great technical advance. He built two steam railway locomotives near Camborne that saw service in South Wales, but he later left Cornwall to seek fame and fortune elsewhere. At about this time two companies sprang to prominence in the Hayle area: Harvey's foundry at Hayle and a large copper smelter at nearby Copperhouse. They were instrumental in greatly increasing the import and export trade at Hayle and both were keen to improve facilities at the port and to see an increase in the efficiency of goods handling. Both firms acquired property and built warehouses, but the basic transportation problem remained.

In 1801 there was a plan to build a canal of 7 miles 5 furlongs from Hayle to Carwinin Bridge, via Angarrack, to serve the mines in the Camborne area but the scheme was abandoned. Another prospectus called for a tramline to link Hayle and Helston but it

too failed. The roads were getting so bad in the area that in October 1819 it was stipulated that only wagons with at least 6in-wide tyres would be allowed to use them. In the meantime the Poldice Tramway was running well and making money, and this was followed in 1826 by the Redruth & Chasewater Railway, which transformed the transportation of ores from the Gwennap district. Accordingly a company was formed to construct a railway from Hayle to Tresavean Mine, with a branch from Angarrack to Helston. A Bill was presented to Parliament and received Royal Assent on 27 June 1834. The 'Hayle Railway Company' had an authorised capital of £64,000 with power to borrow on mortgage a further £16,000.

In 1836 a further Act was passed empowering the company to make certain deviations to the original plan and to substitute branches to Redruth and Portreath; the Helston branch was not proceeded with. The line was to run from Hayle Foundry to Copperhouse via a drawbridge, then to Phillack, Angarrack to Tresavean. Some of the mines passed included Stray Park, the mighty Dalcoath, Cook's Kitchen, Tin Croft, Wheal Fanny, Tregajorran, Wheal Druid and Wheal Buller. Branch lines were to include Towans (Sandhills), Roskear, Wheal Crofty, Wheal Tolgus, Portreath and Redruth. There would be steep inclines at Angarrack (1 in 10) and at Portreath (1 in 7) and other inclines at Penponds (1 in 22) and Tresavean (1 in 15). The first two would be worked by wire rope and the others by wire rope and engine, the latter on a counterbalance principle.

Good progress was made with the construction of the line and by 1837 it was almost complete, the exception being the drawbridge over a narrow strip of water that connected Harvey's foundry with the rest of the system. The line could have been opened earlier had it not been for this drawbridge, but Harvey insisted that the line should be complete in all respects. It finally opened to Pool and on to Portreath on 23 December 1837, just in

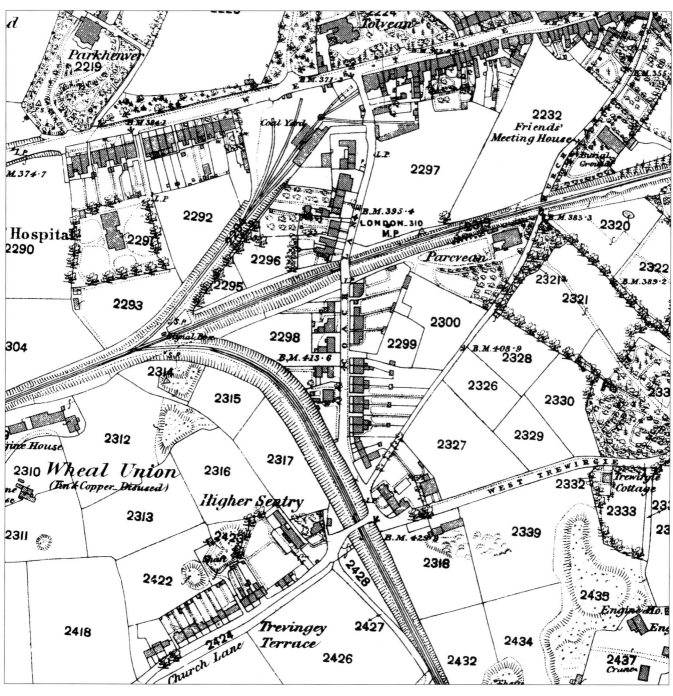

Right:
This photograph of Redruth Junction dates from the 1920s, after the doubling of the line. On the left is the line to Redruth West Yard, the former HR terminus, in the centre is the main line to Truro and Plymouth, and on the right is the line to Tresavean Mine. The signalbox did not close until October 1966.
JV collection

time for Christmas, while the line from Portreath Junction to Redruth was officially opened on 31 May 1838, and the line to Tresavean on 23 June 1838. The distance from Hayle to Redruth on the original 'main line' (via the inclines) was 9 miles 44 chains, and total mileages were as follows (mileages of some branches changed over the years due to various minor extensions):

Hayle to Redruth Junction	9 miles 44 chains
Tresavean branch	2 miles 55 chains
Portreath branch	3 miles 4 chains
Redruth branch	14 chains
Roskear branch	77 chains
Crofty branch	48 chains
Hayle branch	55 chains
Total	17 miles 57 chains

At Redruth Junction, after 1852, there was a three-way split, with the northern spur going to the original Hayle Railway Redruth terminus, the main line going on to what was to become the West Cornwall Railway's Redruth station on its route to Truro, and the southern spur to Tresavean Mine. The latter line ascended by a double-track incline of 1 in 15 then continued as a single line branch in a southeasterly direction for about 2 miles. The Portreath line commenced at Carn Brea and continued in a northwesterly direction to the top of the hill above Portreath, where an incline of 1 in 7 took it down to the harbour. The mostly single-track HR system was built to standard gauge, and the rails were attached to stone blocks.

The conveyance of passengers had been authorised by the Act but until 1841 none were carried. From that date, and in common with many other minor mineral lines, passengers were sometimes carried in the mineral wagons. Since 1831 Hayle had been served by steam packet services, which ran to Bristol and were a great improvement over the stagecoach services of the time. However, the real bonus came in June 1841 when the GWR opened its line between London and Bristol, greatly improving the West Cornwall to London journey time. The directors of the HR showed great enterprise in capitalising on this service by ordering two 20/30-seat railway carriages, or 'omnibuses' as they were known. Passenger stations were opened at Hayle, Copperhouse, Angarrack, Gwinear, Penponds, Camborne, Pool (later Carn Brea) and Redruth, and services commenced to great local celebration on 22 May 1843. Furthermore the railway provided connecting horse omnibuses from Redruth to Truro, Redruth to Falmouth and Hayle to Penzance.

The first train was free for passengers and there was much overloading; even after three goods wagons were added, many passengers were left behind at Redruth. The last two fairly flat miles of track from the foot of the Angarrack incline to Hayle were worked by horse until sometime in 1843 when braking on the locomotives improved, allowing engines to actually descend the incline with their train in tow. Speeds of up to 30mph were attained on some sections but with the inclines the 9½-mile journey took about 45 minutes to complete. There were two trains per day between Redruth and Hayle but by July 1844 this had increased to three. In 1844 there was an alarming runaway on Angarrack incline when the wire rope broke while the second part of a train was halfway up. The passenger-carrying wagons ran back slowly but gradually picked up speed. Some passengers leaped for safety but were in fact injured whereas those who endured the frightening journey ended up safely, but shaken, back at Hayle!

There were no signals on the line, other than hand signals, and trains were dispatched under the time interval system. By 1846, when the Hayle Railway was taken over by the West Cornwall Railway, the Hayle line had no fewer than five locomotives, six coaches and 119 goods wagons. The locomotives carried the names *Pendarves*, *Cornubia* (built at Copperhouse Foundry in 1838), *Carn Brea*, *Coryndon* (a 2-2-2, withdrawn by the WCR in 1851) and *Chanter* (which from 1851 ran with *Coryndon*'s nameplate).

The West Cornwall Railway was formed in September 1844 for the purpose of linking Truro and Penzance by rail. The subsequently discredited atmospheric system was proposed for Truro to Redruth and steam locomotives from Redruth to Penzance, and the line was to be leased to the HR to operate. A Bill was presented to Parliament in 1845 but it was thrown out on the grounds that the inclines were unsatisfactory for passenger traffic, especially in view of the potential number of passengers. It was therefore back to the drawing-board, and subsequently deviations were proposed to avoid the two inclines on the main line and an agreement was made with the directors of the HR to purchase the line. The second Bill had the support of the GWR and received the Royal Assent on 3 August 1846. The GWR's interest arose from its broad gauge aspirations, and part of the deal was that the WCR's track between Penzance and Truro would be laid to broad gauge when requested by the Cornwall Railway/GWR.

This chapter is of course concerned with the branches and byways of the HR, which includes Tresavean, Portreath, North Crofty and Dalcoath, Roskear and Hayle Wharves, and not the main line. However, while this is certainly not a history of the WCR main line, a brief outline of that history and the takeover by the GWR is relevant. The WCR's financial position was not strong and for some time it worked only the existing Hayle to Redruth section. A fresh Act in 1850 gave authority to build the line to standard gauge but to dimensions that could permit broad gauge track to be laid at a later date, in accordance with the original Act. The contract for construction was let in 1851, and by 1852 the permanent way had been laid throughout from Redruth to Penzance, the first passenger train running on 11 March 1852. On 25 August 1852 the entire 25-mile 12-chain line from Truro (Road) to Penzance was opened, and there were celebrations all the way along the line, especially at Penzance. Although hard to believe, the first train to arrive was, reputedly, comprised of three locomotives and 32 carriages!

The WCR sought powers to extend its line to the riverside at Truro and the line to Newham was opened on 16 April 1855, the original WCR Truro Road terminus then being closed. As mentioned in Chapter 20, the Cornwall Railway reached Truro from Plymouth in 1859 and the CR and the WCR were later linked. The WCR passenger trains were then mostly transferred from Newham to the CR station (on the present site) in 1859 and entirely in 1863. The WCR had problems in that traffic receipts were not as high as anticipated. By 1856 many miles of rail had had to be replaced following a series of derailments, but there was insufficient finance for a major capital programme and replacement of the old 'Barlow' rails took years. Furthermore in 1864 the CR, fed up with the inconvenience of transferring passengers and freight at Truro due to the change of gauge, invoked the clause in the original WCR Act which stipulated that dual gauge track should be laid from Truro to Penzance. There was no money available for the work and consequently, from 1 July 1865, the WCR was leased to the Great Western, Bristol & Exeter and South Devon Railways and transferred absolutely to them in January 1866.

The conversion of the main line was completed in 1866 but it was 1 March 1867 before the first broad gauge passenger train ran through from Plymouth to Penzance. Curiously the standard ('narrow') gauge was retained and dual gauge running was the norm. All of the mineral traffic carried over the branches (except Hayle Wharves) that are our primary focus was of course in standard gauge wagons. Until 1892 mixed gauged freights on the main line with standard gauge wagons at the front and broad gauge wagons at the rear were a regular feature. The GWR took over all of the ex-WCR lines lock, stock and barrel from 1 February 1876, and opened the broad gauge St Ives branch on 1 June 1877. The conversion from broad to standard gauge took

Above:
The 2-mile 55-chain Tresavean branch was hugely under-photographed. From Redruth Junction the line
became double track and ascended by a half-mile 1 in 15 incline, before reverting to single track to the mines.
The incline was operated by a cable, which can be seen running on rollers in this June 1933 shot. A maximum of
four loaded wagons could be handled in a single movement. Locomotives worked 'light engine' to the top of the
incline to shunt the sidings, but beyond that point all wagons were horse-drawn. *JV collection*

Right:
This wonderful view of Tresavean
Mine was captured on film on
10 June 1933, and although the
line did not close until 1 January
1936 it is clear from the severed
rail and general dereliction that
the only traffic at this time was to
and from intermediate sidings
nearer the top of the incline. The
line crossed the Redruth &
Chasewater Railway on the level
but the railways were competitors
and ran on different gauge tracks,
and there was never an exchange
of traffic. The decline in traffic to
and from Portreath, the use of
horses and inclines, and small
payloads resulted in the little
remaining traffic successfully
being carried by road lorry. The
line was operative for 98 years,
with the track being ripped up in
1938. *JV collection*

place in 1892 when the entire line from Plymouth to Penzance and the relevant branches were converted, and parts of the main line were doubled. The GWR continued to operate the main line and the surviving branches featured herein until nationalisation in 1948, when the Western Region of British Railways took over.

Tresavean Branch

The line from Portreath Junction to the original HR Redruth terminus officially opened for goods traffic on 31 May 1838. The Redruth terminus was just 14 chains east of Tresavean Junction, where the Tresavean branch turned sharply southwards. Passenger trains served the terminus from 22 May 1843 until, under the auspices of the WCR, the 'main line' was extended and opened to Truro in August 1852. The old terminus line was then merely a small depot on the up side of the through main line. For the next 115 years the line down to the old terminus was known as Redruth West Yard and was used for mixed goods. In later years coal was the mainstay of traffic but on 30 September 1967 the small yard closed, and was taken out of use on 14 February 1968.

For a while the junction down to the old terminus was called West Yard Junction but when the main line was doubled in 1894 a new signalbox was provided and the three-way divergence became Redruth Junction. The new box was located on the north side of the line just east of West Yard Junction (see the accompanying photograph). The year before the yard closed the signalbox was closed and replaced by a ground frame, which was in turn taken out of use in February 1968.

This section deals with the Tresavean branch, opened on 23 June 1838 to serve the large complex of copper and tin mines in the parish of Gwennap. At their peak these mines were the largest producers of copper in the world (see Chapter 2). The single track left the main line at the 310-mile 34-chain point, then just 3 chains from the junction the single track doubled and ran up a half-mile 1 in 15 incline. The incline was worked by a wire rope that ran over rollers placed between the tracks and attached to about every eighth sleeper. At the top of the incline the rope passed from one line to the other by means of a spreading pulley and a crown pulley, in a figure of eight.

As with the Portreath line, traffic for the Tresavean branch was put off main line trains at Carn Brea yard then worked to Redruth West End Yard. Up to four wagons, usually full of coal but sometimes with cattle food, fertilizers and lime, were then propelled out of that yard across the main line before being pulled by the locomotive on to the Tresavean branch and left at the foot of the incline. The locomotive then proceeded 'light' to the top of the incline, performed shunting activities, then changed roads ready for the descent and proceeded to the top of the incline with loaded or empty wagons. This formation was then attached to the wire rope and, as it descended, the four loaded wagons on the other line ascended. When the latter wagons had reached the top of the incline (and, by implication, the locomotive and wagons the bottom) a shunter at the top would signal to a man at the bottom, by needle signalling instrument, that detachment from the cable could be made.

The maximum pull permitted was 84 tons, although 48 tons was the norm, and wagons travelled up the incline at about 15mph. There were two sidings at the top of the incline for shunting purposes and three sidings for berthing traffic. At the 60-chain mark there was a reverse siding on the up side that was primarily used for coal supplies to Wheal Buller, although in the early days this handled minerals for both Wheal Buller and the Bassett Mines. There was a ballast siding at 64 chains, and beyond 70 chains horses always worked the branch. Approximately 1½ miles from the junction the branch crossed the Redruth & Chasewater Railway (R&CR) on the level at Wheal Beauchamp Siding, 1 mile 41 chains, near the top of Lanner Hill. A branch of the R&CR served the Basset Mines complex but there was never any interchange of traffic between the lines. The R&CR viewed the Tresavean branch as a serious rival because although

Tresavean Mine was about a mile from the nearest R&CR railhead, its owners were still valuable customers. A little over 1 mile further along the line was Tresavean Mines Yard, with terminal buffer stops at 2 miles 55 chains from the junction with the main line.

In 1840 the HR offered to carry all of the ore from the huge Consols Mine at a discount compared with the R&CR, even though the mine was a mile away from the Tresavean Yard. In order to retain the valuable traffic the R&CR lowered its rates and won the day, but at a price, for in 1840 the HR branch had directly caused a 20% reduction in R&CR profits. The Tresavean branch prospered and traffic was very encouraging until the great copper crisis of 1866, when over-production caused world copper prices to plummet and mine closures all over the Gwennap area. There was a mass migration of miners and their families to the Americas and Australia, their only alternative being severe hardship in Cornwall. The mines in this area and around Camborne turned to the tin that lay beneath the worked-out copper but such activities were barely viable. As was the case with the R&CR, coal was still a very important commodity as the steam-driven pumping engines were worked harder because the mines were being mined deeper, resulting in even more water ingress.

In 1844 the HR proposed an amalgamation with the R&CR but the latter was still the more prosperous concern and no decision was taken at its half-yearly meeting that year. However, at the end of 1914 a real body-blow was delivered to the R&CR when the colliery supplying the massive Basset Mines (the R&CR's largest customer) started transporting its coal to the mine via the HR's (by then the GWR's) branch from Portreath, then to Lanner Hill via the Tresavean branch at a saving of 6d per ton. This resulted in the closure of the R&CR just months later, in September 1915.

In later years traffic on the Tresavean line comprised pure ingot tin from the Cornish Tin Smelting Company Ltd and the Redruth Tin Smelting Company Ltd, and black tin ore for these firms, imported through Liverpool. However, mining was still in decline and, as with Portreath, working with wagonloads, horses and inclines was not particularly slick. Lorry traffic increased and the last vestiges of activity at Tresavean ceased, resulting in the inevitable closure. The entire branch closed on 1 January 1936, the same day as the Portreath to North Pool section of that branch. Although the track was lifted in March 1938, the majority of the trackbed survives and it is still possible to walk to Tresavean, where amenity landscaping works are proposed. Just for the record there was never a passenger service on the line, which was not signalled. For a line that served the community for nearly 98 years it does seem a shame that there were not more lineside photographers in the 19th century!

Portreath Branch

Portreath is an ancient fishing port that was later developed to serve the mining industry. As detailed in Chapter 1 on the Poldice Tramway, a link was provided between Portreath and the mines of the St Day and Gwennap mining districts during the 1809-10 period. This facilitated the transportation of coal to the mines for their steam-powered pumping engines and transportation of, particularly, copper and tin ore from the mines to the port for shipment to the smelters in South Wales. Although the fishing industry remained important with, for example, one company alone having 16 fishing schooners at Portreath in 1880, it was mining that had the greatest impact.

Portreath was not an easy harbour to enter or leave, particularly in poor weather. During the winter gales many days could elapse without a single ship entering the port. However, small ports on Cornwall's north coast, like Portreath, Newquay and Hayle, had the great advantage of a shorter distance to the South Wales suppliers/customers than the south coast ports, whose ships had to navigate around Lizard Point and Land's End, which could be time-consuming and hazardous in the days of sail. The activity of the mines was so great that in 1846 an inner basin was constructed at Portreath and this significantly improved cargo handling. Often

Above:
The HR's (later GWR's) standard gauge
3-mile 4-chain Portreath branch opened in 1837.
The half-mile 1 in 7 incline above the harbour at
Portreath was much steeper than the Tresavean
example. At the foot of the double-track incline were
two wagon turntables that turned single wagons
through 90° to reach the harbour sidings. After the
lines tapered into a single line beyond a road crossing
gate, there was yet another wagon turntable. In this
old scene two men have just attached a single wagon
to the cable. This picture shows to advantage the
extent and gradient of the incline. *JV collection*

Above:
The privately owned harbour of Portreath had been
connected with the Poldice Tramway as early as 1812,
effectively the county's first railway (see Chapter 1).
The ports on Cornwall's north coast were much
nearer to South Wales, where most of the mineral ore
was shipped and from where most of the coal was
imported. Thus a link to the HR and the mines
beyond became a vital part of the HR's plans. This
view shows the crossing gates and the third wagon
turntable in 1937, after the line had closed.
BR, JV collection

Left:
The old motorcycle and sidecar
(RL 9772) stand beside the not
insubstantial engine house at the
top of the Portreath incline in
1933. As stated on page 219, on
the Tresavean branch, with
mining again in decline, coal
increasingly being conveyed via
the main line in block loads and
with Portreath only being able to
take ships up to 200 tons, which
were dwindling in number, the
end was nigh. Although the line
closed on the same day as
Tresavean, this picture shows that
there was little, if any, traffic by
the early 1930s. *JV collection*

Right:
There are three quite large steam ships (for Portreath) in this fine maritime study, which, judging by the clothing of the boy on the left, shows the scene just before World War 1. The tracks beside the wharf are for mobile cranes but on the sidings there are two wagons in the coal yard on the left, and two more on the north sidings. A wagon clearly marked 'GW' stands at the foot of the incline in front of the crossing gates (lower centre).
P. Q. Treloar collection

Left:
Another interesting scene at Portreath Harbour that seems to be devoid of ships but full of wagons. The four box vans belong to the LMS and NE companies, while behind them three coal wagons are in the coal yard. On the north side of the harbour four coupled open wagons are of GWR and LMS ownership. Horses were used for harbour and quay shunting. The date is estimated at 1926, and despite the presence of wagons the level of activity seems to be low. A map of Portreath Harbour appears on page 229.
JV collection

Right:
Although 'before and after' scenes are fascinating, they are also rather sad. To think that the old order at Portreath has gone for ever is sobering. In 1990 modern housing has covered the old yards and sidings, although the row of cottages across the harbour with a larger building at their west end are common to both views. Only small fishing vessels and a few pleasure craft now use the harbour. *JV*

there would be 20 vessels loading and unloading at the same time. In the meantime, from 23 December 1837, the HR had constructed a standard gauge branch line from its main line between Hayle and Truro to Portreath, and this added to the frenetic activity at the harbour.

While the new branch was more efficient that the old Poldice Tramway, which was in fact a horse-powered plateway, its final approach to Portreath was far more difficult than the Poldice line. The HR branch descended to the harbour area via a 1 in 7 inclined plane of just under half a mile. At the foot of the incline three turntables were provided at various points to direct wagons from the incline to the sidings both to the north and south of the inner basin. As already mentioned, there was a significant crash in the world price of copper in the early to mid-1860s and this caused many mines to close; after success in the early years this recession was to be the end of the Poldice Tramway, which seemed to die a slow death around 1865. This was only one of Cornwall's many mining recessions; another depression, but this time in the tin industry, hit Cornwall in the 1890s. However, even by the turn of the century there were still some 200 vessels per annum using the port despite this significant decline in the mining industry.

Although as mentioned above, the HR main line opened on 23 December 1837, it was 31 May 1838 before the line from Portreath Junction to Redruth opened and 1852 before it was extended to Truro (Road). The main line beyond Redruth Junction was doubled in 1896, at which time Portreath Junction signalbox was opened. The Portreath branch left the up main line by a trailing junction at Portreath Junction at the 311-mile 30-chain point, some 10 chains east of the WCR's Carn Brea Works, while just beyond the junction on the up side was a ballast siding, opened in 1910. The line then headed due north and crossed the Illogan Highway, which between 1902 and 1927 (1934 for freight) carried the Camborne & Redruth Tramway. At about the 312-mile 11-chain point North Pool Siding, serving North Pool mine, made a loop on the down side of the line. Four further minor road crossings were passed before reaching Fairfield Timber Siding at 313 miles 70 chains, a single-line stub on the down side opened in 1919. Shortly after Fairfield the branch went from single to double track at the head of the incline.

The entire incline was double track, and at the foot there were two turntables (one on each line) for use by both incoming and outgoing wagons, where single vehicles were turned through 90º on to the south-side harbour sidings. The double-track incline then tapered to a single line, which ended on yet another turntable to feed the north-side sidings. Until the Poldice Tramway closed in about 1865 there was a mixture of both 4ft and standard gauge sidings all over the harbour area feeding both the inner and outer basins (or 'docks'). One standard gauge line led to a limekiln, another to substantial coal dumps, another for stabling wagons and

Below:
Nothing is now left of the North Crofty branch, which was little more than a half-mile siding. The branch left the main line at North Crofty Junction and served, amongst others, part of the extensive Dalcoath Mine complex, while a tramway from South Crofty Mine ended in a loading dock adjacent to the branch. The line closed on 1 December 1948 and was lifted shortly afterwards. Passing the site of the junction at Tuckingmill on 18 August 1990, with plenty of Cornwall's mining history as a backdrop, are Class 47 No 47808 and driving trailer No 82123 with the 07.31 Wolverhampton to Penzance train. *JV*

Above:
Dalcoath was the deepest mine in the whole of Cornwall and in its heyday it sported a very extensive internal tramway network. The HR built sidings to serve the mine and this siding was originally known as Treveor Siding; by 1898 it was used as a coal siding. Dalcoath Halt was opened in 1905 but closed during May 1908. From 1946 the Milk Marketing Board used the siding for London-bound milk trains but traffic petered out in 1980 and it closed in 1983. With Carn Brea and Lord de Dunstanville's monument dominating the right background, Class 50 No 50009 *Conqueror* speeds its Mk 1 coaches towards Penzance on 12 June 1981. *JV*

Right:
The Roskear branch of the HR was just less than a mile long. It was built to serve mines at Roskear, Dalcoath and South Crofty but more specifically to bring coal to the mines to feed the steam-driven pumping engines. The branch left the main line at Roskear Junction and several sidings were served, as described in the text. In more recent years the line served as a siding to Holman's Works, and a little traffic continued until 1983 when the line closed. It was permanently taken out of use in 1987, having survived all of the other original HR branches. On 30 August 1986, not long before final abandonment, No 50013 *Agincourt* passes the branch junction and its protecting semaphore signal with the 08.30 Brighton to Penzance service. *JV*

Above:
When photographed from a down main line train on 23 April 1983 the Hayle Wharves branch had already been lifted. The branch had been closed on 7 July 1982 and the signalbox, seen in the centre, closed the same day and would soon be demolished. It had been necessary to build this branch in 1852 to connect with the then 'new' main line from Penzance to Truro. A wagon lift from Hayle Viaduct to the quays had originally been proposed but a fixed line was preferred, even though the link would have to be steeply graded. In addition to being used for general merchandise and coal, over the years the line also served an oil depot, a power station and a gunpowder works. *JV*

for shunting purposes, and others for the direct loading/unloading of vessels. The ex-Poldice sidings were removed from 1882. A stationary engine worked the incline with two drums, one to coil the wire rope (cable) and the other to uncoil, lifting and lowering a single wagon in each direction at one time. There were metal rollers between both the up and down tracks for the cables to run on, and crossing gates were located across a road at the foot of the incline.

Traffic to and from the Portreath branch worked into and out of Carn Brea Yard on the main line. Steam locomotives worked from Carn Brea to the top of the incline, while horses were used for shunting in the harbour area. Photographs show both open ore and coal wagons in the harbour as well as box wagons. As the mines petered out the export of ore and, more importantly, the import of coal slowed. In later years demand for coal was better supplied via the WCR/GWR main line and this had a negative impact on Portreath. Furthermore the port could handle only relatively small ships, which over time had become the exception rather than the rule. Working a single wagon at a time on the incline was slow and it was perhaps no surprise to some that part of the branch

from North Pool to Portreath closed from 1 January 1936, the track being removed about 1940. The line from the junction to North Pool closed from 1 April 1938, except for a stub from the junction, which was used as a short siding until taken out of use in August 1967.

The Portreath line served a useful purpose for just under a century but once the Cornish mining industry virtually collapsed its fate was sealed. Now most of the land has been returned to the landowners and a housing estate covers the area around the harbour that was once the home of the railway and tramway sidings. The trackbed of the inclined plane can still be seen and a short section of trackbed is now a footpath, but little else remains of this rather different little branch line.

North Crofty Siding

This branch was just 48 chains long and was built by the HR to serve the mining industry. It left the main line at North Crofty Junction via a down facing point on the up side of the originally single-track main line. North Crofty Junction signalbox was a small cabin with a ground frame and a single block instrument and bell. Authority was given in 1907 to adapt the ground frame as a block post for the up main line only.

Just 17 chains along the branch was Cook's Kitchen Siding, forming a reverse junction on the up side. This once busy siding actually served part of Dalcoath Mine, but closed in 1928 and was finally removed in December 1937. At 37 chains was Tuckingmill Mileage Siding. At various times there were sidings on the up and down side. A private tramway from South Crofty Mine crossed the branch and made a connection with a loading dock adjacent to the main branch, one road being used as a coal wharf. The branch then crossed the Camborne to Redruth road (and from 1902 the Camborne & Redruth Tramway) to reach North Crofty Tin Mine, where there was a coal shed and store on the up side, near the end of the line. The branch was adjacent to the Climax Works at the top of East Hill, Tuckingmill.

The branch was cut back to just beyond Tuckingmill in 1937. Traffic dwindled and the line only just survived World War 2, being closed on 1 December 1948 and lifted on 7 November 1949. One textbook claims that 'shunting was carried out by an 0-6-0 saddle tank' but despite research no photographs of trains on the branch were unearthed. Today just about the entire line has been buried by the operations of South Crofty Mine and developments

in Pool village, although the alignment of the junction with the main line can just be detected. Thus the little line has been lost to history and the camera failed to do it justice.

Roskear Branch and Dalcoath Siding
The Roskear branch was built to serve the mines at Roskear and later Dalcoath and South Crofty. This original HR branch was 77 chains long and was effectively a single-track siding with sidings! It was controlled by Roskear Junction signalbox on the main line, which was doubled between Camborne and Carn Brea in August 1898. Until the 1980s there was still a lower quadrant semaphore signal at the end of the branch protecting the main line.

Over the years various sidings were opened and closed but the first small siding on the branch was Weighbridge Siding, opened in 1943. Next on the down side about 23 chains from the junction was Holman's No 3 Siding. The configuration was changed in 1906 but after 1963 the siding was the sole reason for the retention of the branch. The line later crossed the Camborne & Redruth Tramway, then a few chains beyond Holman's, making a reverse connection on the down side, was Harvey & Co's New Yard. About three-quarters of a mile out was South Roskear Mines Siding on the down side, while almost opposite on the up

Right:
The standard gauge Hayle Wharves branch from the main line descended at 1 in 30, and surprisingly it was made available to broad gauge trains by dual gauging in 1877. A small marshalling yard was provided adjacent to the main line, which an 0-6-0 pannier tank is seen shunting on 10 April 1959. The line then descended to the original HR terminus and the complex matrix of lines that surrounded the wharves of the once busy port. Hayle was always an important north coast port but it became particularly prominent in 1779 when Harvey opened his famous foundry in the town. As the output from the mines grew, large volumes of coal were imported and the quays were much enlarged in 1819. *Hugh Davies*

Left:
This old photograph from the historic records of BR shows the original 1837 HR terminus at Hayle. Although it was abandoned in 1852 when the WCR opened the current main line, it survived for many years until demolished for a road widening scheme.
BR, JV collection

Above:
With so many of the HR branches having closed in the 1930s and 1940s the Hayle Wharves branch became a 'must' on the Cornish railway photographer's list. Until its final years the train ran daily and was propelled down the branch with a brake-van at the rear. The motive power was latterly one of the Bo-Bo Class 25 diesels, as seen here. With the branch goods waiting to return to the main line, a railman crosses the main pre-bypass A30 prior to activating the crossing barriers. No 25223 has a good load of tanks and box vans in tow on 16 July 1978. *JV*

Above:
Back in 1959 the A30 crossing gates were manually operated and a protecting semaphore signal was in place; note that the two right-hand buildings on the hill behind are common to this and the previous picture. The driver of No 4571 is looking backwards, suggesting that he is engaged in shunting operations. To the left of the smokebox can be seen a pile of dockside coal and some coal wagons. The roof of Hayle Wharves signalbox, which closed in 1964, can just be seen above the locomotive cab roof. *P. Q. Treloar*

side, from 1925 until about 1946, was a siding that divided into two roads. Service agreements to operate the sidings were made with Dalcoath Mine Ltd in 1924 and South Crofty Ltd in 1926. Just before the end of the line at North Roskear Siding, on the down side, was a reverse branch to Holman's No 1 Boiler Works, and coal was the important import at this point. In 1910 there was a short extension of the branch to North Roskear Treatment Plant. North Roskear mine was a prolific producer of copper and tin ore. There were a total of six level crossings on the branch.

The primary commodity on the branch was coal destined for the boilers and pumping engines of the mines, but over the years traffic diminished, particularly after World War 2. The line beyond Holman's No 3 Foundry was closed in 1963, then in 1966 a short run-round loop was laid on the junction side of No 3 Foundry Sidings. In 1970 the entire branch (except the first couple of chains from the junction) was sold to Messrs Holman Bros (later Compare Construction & Mining). The surviving siding at No 3 Works received general traffic and machine parts and dispatched compressors and mining machinery, but by the late 1970s traffic was very spasmodic and the branch was taken out of use in July 1983. This was made permanent in September 1987, the track having been a deep rust colour since the early 1980s, indicating that the last train had run some years earlier.

In the early days there was merely a crossing hut at Roskear Crossing, near the junction, and no gates were provided; the crossing keeper merely put a rope across the road when a train was due! The hut contained a small ground frame that controlled the branch. However, after a crossing keeper was killed in an accident, a signalbox was provided from about 1895. The junction layout changed in March 1975 with access being only from the up main line. Level crossing gates on the main line were replaced by lifting barriers in October 1970. The signalbox survives, to

control colour light signals on the main line and the adjacent crossing; all semaphore signals in the area have long since been removed. The Roskear branch was the very last piece of non-main line track left in the Camborne area. The route through Holman's Works is now inaccessible and some of the line has been built upon. Near Roskear the trackbed is in use as a litter-strewn and overgrown path between houses. However, it may become part of a local walkway called the 'Red River Trail'.

About half a mile to the east from Roskear Junction on the main line was Dalcoath Siding. Just to the west on the north side of the line the abandoned Wheal Harriet shaft of the famous Dalcoath Mine can still be seen. Dalcoath Mine was the deepest in Cornwall and it covered a vast area with its own internal tramway system. Originally the siding was known as Treveor Siding, but in 1897 a new one was built, Dalcoath Siding, primarily for coal traffic. An adjacent halt opened in August 1905 but closed as early as May 1908. After World War 2 and long after the mine closed the siding was used for milk traffic but this too ceased in 1980 when the Milk Marketing Board turned to road transport. The siding was finally taken out of use on 12 December 1983 (see the accompanying photograph).

Hayle Wharves

When the new WCR main line alignment was built in 1852 and parts of the old line abandoned, a branch had to be constructed from the new main line to a point near the old drawbridge over Copperhouse Creek, in place of a wagon lift from Hayle Viaduct that had originally been proposed. In addition, a 25-chain length of the 'old' main line, north of Copperhouse Creek, to Sandhills continued in use as a siding. The 55-chain Hayle Wharves branch left the main line on the up side at the east end of Hayle Viaduct, adjacent to Hayle station, and descended from the main line at

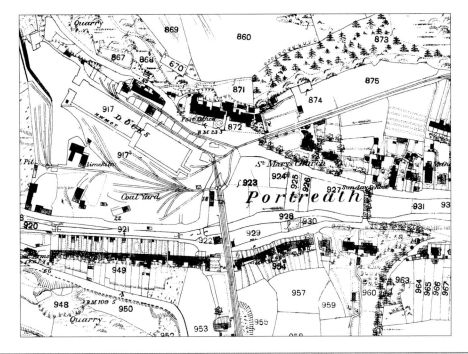

Left:
This map dated 1878 shows the track layout at Portreath, with sidings surrounding the privately owned harbour. To the south is the incline section of the 1837 standard gauge Hayle Railway (GWR) branch. Note the wagon turntables at the foot of the incline and elsewhere. Of particular interest is the very rare appearance on a map of the then dormant (and subsequently abandoned) Poldice Tramway, coming in from Scorrier (right). Closed in the mid-1860s, the track was finally removed in 1882.
Crown Copyright

Centre left:
The line that traced the alignment of the estuary back along Hayle's east quay towards the town and underneath the main line to the west quay and the foundry was the Penpol Terrace low-level line. It was always shunted by horses and this delightful practice continued until about 1964.
In this outstanding view double-headed horses haul two box vans away from Harvey's Penpol Sidings and make their way along the east quay towards the town. An Austin A30 (and an Austin A55) can be seen on the A30, while cranes by the power station coal wharf are visible in the left background. *P. Q. Treloar*

Lower left:
This old postcard was well worth the £2.50 that I paid for it at a postcard show. Posted from Hayle in February 1905 and sent to Henley-on-Thames, it shows some youngsters in front of Penpol Terrace and the line to the west wharf, gasworks and foundry. It is perhaps surprising that even in those far-off days the line looks so little used. Mr Blewett seems to be a prominent businessman running a dispensing chemist and a cycle agency. I wonder how much his Singer cycles were. Penpol Terrace can be seen on the map on page 230. *JV collection*

Overleaf:
This 1880 map shows the remarkable network of tracks around Hayle and the harbour. The line top right was once the original Hayle Railway line to Redruth that closed in 1852 but which was later used as a siding to a gunpowder works. Horses performed shunting on many of the wharf lines. The last siding that ran down from the main line to Hayle Wharves closed in 1981. Hayle's famous iron foundry is at the foot of the map.
Crown Copyright

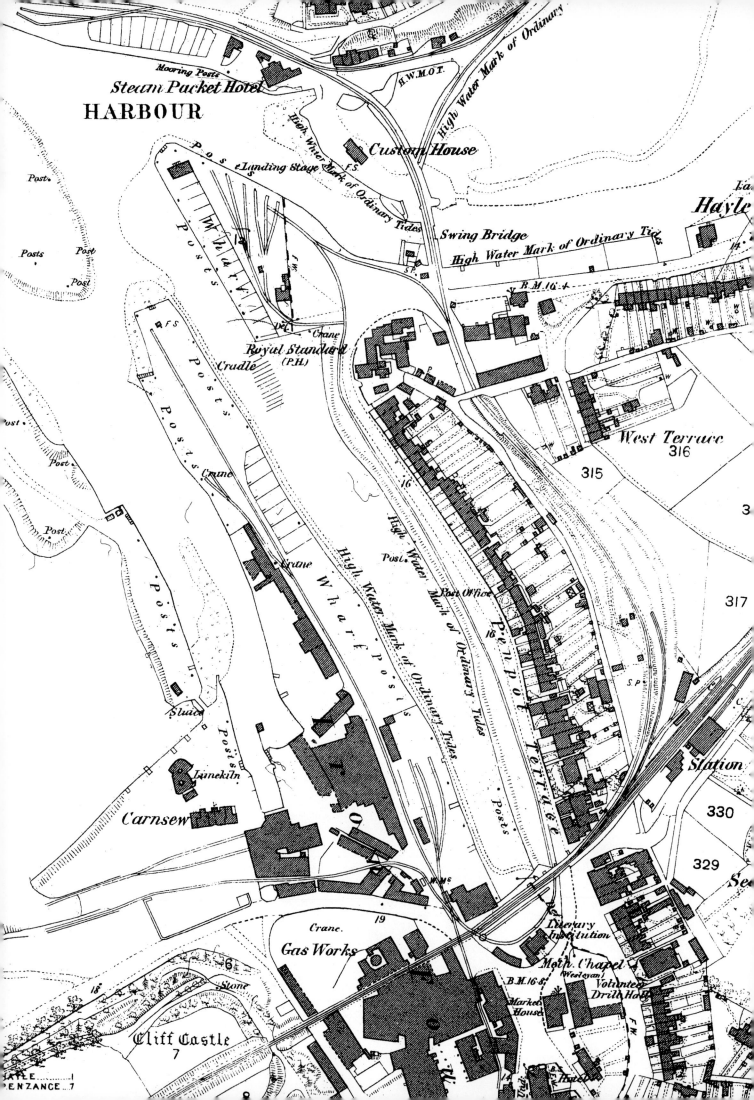

1 in 30, an incline that justified a catch point with a sand drag for safety. The only WCR branch line made available to the broad gauge, it opened on 11 March 1852, but the broad gauge track was not added until 3 October 1877. A signalbox controlled the entrance to the wharves complex.

To the west of the branch were a number of quays where commercial vessels using the tidal harbour were berthed. Back in 1779 Harvey had established his foundry at the water's edge and built some coal quays, and in 1819 these were extended and a new 450yd-long wharf constructed. This impressive quarter-mile installation was primarily for incoming coal from South Wales, used to power the foundry's engines. Not to be outdone, the Copperhouse company built its own Copperhouse Quay adjoining Harvey's. Sidings to these quays left the branch and curved westward to Penpol Sidings, from where a long siding ran along east quay past Penpol Terrace (see the accompanying photograph) and under the main line. It then curved sharply to serve sidings on the west quay, latterly used by scrap merchant Thomas Ward.

There was also a siding to the south serving the local gasworks. Locomotives were not allowed along the Penpol line and until 27 April 1961 horses were still used to shunt and haul wagons (see further picture). An adapted tractor took their place until the sidings closed between 1962 and 1965.

The branch crossed Copperhouse Creek and to the northeast a line went to Sandhills using the remains of the old main HR line. At the time of World War 1 a 2-mile 26-chain branch (mileage from the Wharves branch) was opened to the National Explosive Company's works, and part of the Sandhills/former main line formed part of the alignment. At the 2-mile point there were exchange sidings, engine shed, goods shed, other company sidings and a tramway. Beyond Copperhouse Creek on the main branch there were numerous sidings on both the up and down sides serving a fuel depot, a power station, power station coal wharf plus general merchandise. There was total sidings accommodation for 250-300 goods wagons plus 40-50 tank wagons. A small three-road goods yard was at the main line end of the branch, on the up

or east side of the branch, for storage and marshalling, and at one time there was a small shed. The Wharves branch was busy and the normal motive power was either a 0-6-0 pannier or 2-6-2 Prairie tank locomotive.

Harvey's foundry closed in 1904. For years it had produced mining engines, parts and ironwork of all descriptions, and for some decades the company also built ships, but gradually business declined, resulting in losses and closure. The loss of the mining industry in the last years of the 19th century was an enormous blow to Hayle Harbour, but although it continued to be very difficult to operate, with dredging being necessary whenever one of the heavier ships called, it remained busy through the first half of the 20th century. The lifeboat station closed in 1920, and some of the former HR branches closed in the 1930s, but on Hayle Wharves there was still a reasonable mix of traffic.

As with all freight traffic in the days of British Railways, there was a steady decline. Steam was replaced by diesel but by then a single daily train, Mondays to Fridays, was more than sufficient for the traffic. The crossing gates across the main A30 road through the town were replaced by lifting barriers in 1964 and the Wharves signalbox closed. It was normal practice in later years for the freight to be propelled from St Erth on its outward journey and hauled back.

It was announced that the coal-fired power station would close at the end of the 1970s and in the summer of 1981 a small child pressed the plunger detonating the charge that felled the chimneys. The last train ran in January 1981, and the line was taken out of use the following year and lifted.

Hayle Wharves was an interesting backwater. I vividly recall the sound of a Class 25's Sulzer engine chugging away down the track built into the roadway as it toyed with some oil tankers in 1980, but I had missed the days of steam and the horses! At the end the branch working had become an anachronism, not commensurate with the modern scene but one that was refreshingly different and for that it was memorable. Whether this was because of the brake-van being propelled down the branch, the train crew taking an hour off to enjoy their lunchtime pasty, or me waiting 55 minutes to photograph the return working, not anticipating the lunch break, I am not sure!

Above:
Adjacent to Hayle Power Station was a siding that opened in 1942 for the British Ethyl Corporation Ltd. Over the years there had been corporate changes via Associated Ethyl, Associated Octel and Esso, but oil was one of the last sources of traffic. The power station chimneys in the background were blown up in the summer of 1981, after the installation closed. I photographed the Hayle goods in 1978 and 1980, and on both occasions No 25223 provided the motive power, seen here shunting the siding in 1978. *JV*

23. Helston Branch

Although Helston's geographical position was strategic in terms of being something of a focal point for the Lizard peninsula, it was by no means a large town, with a population in 1901 of just over 3,000. However, in years gone by it had been the centre of population for a fairly extensive, if scattered, mining area, which was at its peak in the late 18th and early 19th centuries when the population was about 3,500. Over 100 tin mines were working in Wendron, Godolphin, Cober Valley and many other areas near Helston, but by the mid-1930s mining had all but petered out and the population had fallen to a little over 2,500 as locals travelled elsewhere in search of employment and a better standard of living. The town is an ancient one with a history that goes back some 1,000 years, but curiously it was to be the terminus of a branch line that was one of the last additions to the passenger rail network in the South West.

Arguably Helston was the victim of the most protracted series of deliberations concerning the provision of a railway line in the South West of England. As early as 1819 a prospectus had been issued for linking Helston with Hayle on the north Cornwall coast. This made much sense in that Hayle had a satisfactory commercial harbour of which the mining industry could usefully have taken advantage. In 1825 a scheme to link Penryn on the Fal estuary with Redruth was lodged and this also provided for a branch to Helston via Wendron. Then the original plans for the HR included the possibility of a 12-mile 30-chain branch line from Hayle to Helston, although this section was not proceeded with on cost grounds. A further scheme was deposited in 1846 to link Helston and Penryn by rail, but again insufficient capital was forthcoming.

The CR/WCR route through Cornwall became a reality, with a change of gauge at Truro, in 1859, and this renewed interest in connecting Helston to the main line. Other more complicated schemes emerged, such as the Cornwall Union Railway plan of the early 1860s, which was to link Penryn with Helston, Penzance, Lelant and the north Cornwall coast in the St Just area, plus many mining areas in between! As mentioned in other chapters, the Cornish mining industry really took a hit in the mid-1860s and the

The Helston branch timetable for July 1938 (top) and the summer of 1958 (bottom).

GWINEAR ROAD and HELSTON

Miles	Down — HOUR	7	8	10	11		1	2	T 4	6	E 7	S 7	9	
—	Gwinear Road .....dep.	10	55	45	27	.	5	40	45	15	40	50	35	.
3	Praze	18	3	53	35	.	13	48	53	23	48	58	43	.
½	Nancegollan	24	9	59	40	.	19	55	59	29	54	4	49	.
7	Truthall Platform.......	.	15	.	.	.	25	0	.	35	0	10	55	.
9	Helston D..........arr.	35	20	9	50	.	30	6	10	40	5	15	0	.

Miles	Up — HOUR	6	7	9		12	1	1	4	E 5	S 5	7	8	
—	Helston.............dep.	30	50	50	.	5	5	40	0	20	35	5	35	.
2	Truthall Platform.......	.	57	.	.	12	12	.	7	26	42	12	42	.
3½	Nancegollan	41	4	1	.	20	20	52	14	33	49	19	49	.
6	Praze	47	10	7	.	28	26	58	20	39	55	25	55	.
9	Gwinear Road 22, 27arr	54	17	14	.	37	33	5	27	46	2	32	2	.

A Service of Road Motors runs between Helston Station and Porthleven and between Helston Station and The Lizard

Table 102 GWINEAR ROAD and HELSTON
WEEK DAYS ONLY

Mls		am S	am	am	am S	am E	am S		pm	pm S	pm	pm S	pm E	pm S	pm E		pm S	pm S	pm	pm	
—	Gwinear Road . .. dep	6 15	7 30	8 35	10 15	10 50	11 5	..	12 37	1 48	2 25	3 55	4 12	4B30	5 0	..	5 24	6 55	7 50	9 30	..
2¾	Praze	6 23	7 40	8 42	10 23	10 58	11 13	....	12 44	1 56	2 32	4 2	4 19	4B40	5 8	....	5 32	7 3	7 58	9 38	....
5¼	Nancegollan	6 29	8 0	8 48	10 30	11 4	11 19	..	12 50	2 2	2 39	4 8	4 26	4 50	5 15	..	5 39	7 13	8 4	9 44	..
7	Truthall Platform	....	....	8 54	10 36	11 10	11 25	....	12 56	....	2 45	4 14	4 32	....	5 21	....	5 45	....	....	9 50	....
8¾	Helston .. .. .. arr	6 40	8 20	9 0	10 44	11 15	11 30	..	1 2	2 12	2 51	4 20	4 38	5 1	5 27	..	5 50	7 25	8 14	9 55	..
—	The Lizard ¶ .... arr	7 47	....	10 22	12T12	12K12	1 20	....	....	4T12	5 5	....	6 20	6 20	7 35	....	7 35	....	9D55	11S35	....

Miles		am S		am		am		am S	am E	am S		pm		pm		pm E	pm S		pm		pm	
	The Lizard ¶ .. dep	..	..	..	..	8 3	..	..	1025	10 25	..	12T15	..	1 23	..	..	..	..	5 10	..	7 38	..
—	Helston............. dep	5▮45	....	7▮45	....	9▮45	....	10▮20	11 48	11▮50	....	1▮15	....	3 20	....	4 10	4 35	....	7 0	....	8 37	....
1¾	Truthall Platform	..	..	..	..	..	..	..	1155	..	..	..	..	3 27	..	4 17	4 41	..	7 6	..	8 43	..
3½	Nancegollan	....	....	7▮58	....	9▮56	....	10▮31	12 1	12▮ 4	....	1▮25	....	3 34	....	4 25	4 48	....	7 12	....	8 49	....
6	Praze	..	..	8▮ 4	..	10▮ 2	..	10▮37	12 7	12▮11	..	1▮31	..	3 40	..	4 31	4 54	..	7 19	..	8 56	..
8¾	Gwinear Road ..... arr	6 10	....	8 12	....	10 10	....	10 45	1215	12 20	....	1 40	....	3 47	....	4 38	5 5	....	7 27	....	9 4	....

B 5 minutes later on 6th and 13th September D Applies Saturdays, also Mondays to Fridays 16th June to 5th September inclusive
E Except Saturdays ▮ Passengers travelling by this train on Saturdays beyond Plymouth are required to hold Regulation Tickets (see pages 31, 32 and 33) K Arr 1 20 pm until 13th June and commencing 8th September S or S Saturdays only
T Runs 16th June to 6th September inclusive
¶ By "Western National" Omnibus. Heavy luggage not conveyed. Connecting services are also run between Helston Station and Mullion Cove, etc.

Left:
There can be few finer sights than a gleaming 'Castle' class 4-6-0. Looking resplendent in the sunshine on 29 April 1961 is No 5053 *Earl Cairns* at Gwinear Road, junction for Helston, with an up working. The road must be set for departure as the crossing gates are closed against the road traffic. The main line curves to the left while the Helston branch can be seen straight ahead, on the right of the scene. The first attempts to bring the railway to Helston were made in 1819, but after procrastination by many individuals and organisations over many decades it was not until May 1887 that Helston was connected by rail to the outside world. *R. C. Riley, The Transport Treasury*

Above:
The classic country junction scene at Gwinear Road on 19 September 1959. On the down main line is 'County' class 4-6-0 No 1007 *County of Brecknock* with a down parcels train comprising examples of both bogie and four-wheeled Southern utility vans. Prairie 2-6-2T No 4588 pauses in the branch island platform while indulging in a little shunting.
P. Q. Treloar

Below:
Pounding through the remains of Gwinear Road station at 17.28 on 13 August 1983 is Class 50 No 50027 *Lion* with the 09.20 Liverpool to Penzance train. These impressive locomotives made a tremendous sound when on full power and were part of the Cornish railway scene from about 1975 until 1990. The old down island platform can be seen beside the first coach but the branch road is covered in undergrowth. The station closed on 5 October 1964, the same time as freight traffic over the Helston branch ended. *JV*

Above:
The first station down the standard gauge branch, just under 3 miles from Gwinear Road, was Praze. There was once a goods passing loop here but following track modifications in 1950 it became a single siding with the points at the up end of the platform. Beyond the substantial stone station building is a small hut that contained a ground frame. A 'mushroom' water tank is also part of the infrastructure. On 11 July 1961 a couple of goods wagons and a lorry are the only signs of life. *Peter Gray*

Left:
There are an amazing 37 goods wagons in this view of the sidings at Nancegollan. These sidings on the up side were added in 1937 when the entire station layout and platforms were remodelled. Further sidings were built in the 1938 to 1944 period, partly to handle airfield construction traffic during World War 2. There was also a holiday camping coach in the yard for many years. Performing shunting duties is No 4552 with two shunters engaged in making up the outgoing train.
P. Q. Treloar

Right:
Nancegollan was located in the middle of a tin mining area and if the line had been built some 40 years earlier the site would have been of far greater importance. Nevertheless much agricultural produce was loaded here during the season. With passenger accommodation weighted in favour of Helston-bound passengers, No 4571 clanks into the down platform with the 2.20pm Gwinear Road to Helston service on 14 April 1960. The flower tubs are a nice touch. The goods yard is on the left.
P. Q. Treloar

Left:
In this 'before and after' comparison the road bridge and the top of the old engine house chimney are common to both views. Beyond the bridge the trackbed is heavily overgrown but the grass in the old station area is well manicured. The bridge was widened on the western side and a new signalbox built when the new goods yard was constructed and a new passing loop provided in 1937. This picture is dated 1997, 33 years after the closure of the line. *JV*

Right:
Some 7 miles down the branch was Truthall Halt, shown in most timetables and for sometime known as 'Truthall Platform'. In common with the halts on many GWR Cornish branch lines (particularly the Chacewater to Newquay branch) it opened in 1905. There was not a building in sight of the halt but it was built to serve Trannack village and Truthall Manor. The only features to grace the wooden-faced platform were an oil lamp, a corrugated tin 'pagoda' hut and a huge, out of proportion, nameboard. Passengers alighting at the halt were advised to travel in the rear coach. *JV collection*

extravagant scheme was modified to become the broad gauge Helston & Penryn Junction Railway of 1864, a 9-mile 60-chain line that would merely link the two towns named in the title. The Bill received Royal Assent on 14 July with an authorised capital of £120,000, a fortune in those days. Great claims were made about the potential profitability of the line but there was a major bank failure in 1866, which, combined with the mining collapse, put people off dipping into their pockets to the degree required, and the scheme was abandoned. A broadly similar plan in 1874 also failed, and the mining collapse meant that it would be some years before the matter of a branch line to Helston was again considered.

In 1879 the Helston Railway Company was formed to provide a branch by the shortest and cheapest route available, from Gwinear Road station on the main line to Helston. The location of the proposed Helston station was selected with a view to eventually extending the line to Lizard Town. The line would be about 8 miles 67 chains in length and cost £70,000 to build; the GWR, which approved of the proposals, agreed to work the line for 50% of the receipts. The associated Bill received Royal Assent on 9 July 1880, 61 years after the early 1819 scheme! To the surprise of many the money was raised and a first sod was cut on 22 March 1882 to truly enormous local celebrations with the town 'beflagged' with special 'triumphal arches' across the streets. Great numbers invaded the town, bands played the National Anthem, and the day was rounded off by a fireworks display.

The route chosen was perhaps designed more to woo landowners than for out and out cheapness and progress was not rapid. A major viaduct was necessary across the Cober Valley and there were some 30 overbridges, underbridges and underline culverts. Soon the construction contract was suspended and the directors' meeting in February 1883 was a sombre affair. It would be three years before a new contractor was appointed, but by 1886 works were making good progress again. There was much discussion about the precise location of Helston station, and the GWR assisted in making recommendations regarding the size of the engine shed and signal interlocking. By October 1886 the directors were able to travel over a section of line in a contractor's wagon, and soon the finishing touches were completed and the agreement with the GWR, relating to everything from locomotives and rolling stock to dividend rates, was finalised.

Following an inspection by the Board of Trade, one or two very minor modifications had to be made but generally the contractors were complimented on the standard of their work. The report confirmed that the branch was built to standard gauge, with a ruling gradient of 1 in 60 and a sharpest curve of just over 9 chains. The minor changes having been made, the line opened

on 9 May 1887. As with the cutting of the first sod many years before, there was a sense of public holiday with much merriment. The first train was decorated with flags and evergreens and the two intermediate stations of Nancegollan and Praze were similarly decorated. The day was concluded with a dinner and rousing speeches.

When the branch was opened from the junction with the main line at Gwinear Road, itself some way from the village of Gwinear, a signalbox was installed on the up end of the up platform. Until then Gwinear Road had a small platform and had been a passing loop on the single-track main line between Plymouth and Penzance, but from 1887 a single-faced up platform and an island down platform were provided, extensive sidings laid and a goods transfer shed built on the down side of the main line in the 'V' of the junction. The Helston branch trailed in to face the down direction at the junction. From 1892 the main line was converted to standard gauge and the transfer of goods was no longer necessary. In 1900 the main line was doubled, a large number of sidings on the down side east of the station were laid and a Gwinear Road East signalbox opened. The old signalbox was renamed Gwinear Road West, but in 1915 it was replaced by a more modern version, which was located at the up end of the down platform. Over the years there were numerous detailed changes to the track layout.

After leaving Gwinear Road the branch ran straight for a short distance and under a minor road bridge. It then climbed at about 1 in 60 in a southeasterly direction and at 2 miles 68 chains entered Praze station, its single platform serving the nearby villages of Praze-an-Beeble and Crowan. The platform was on the up side and there was a single siding on the down side, which, until 1950, formed a loop with the branch. There was a water tower at one end of the station and a small ground frame in a hut on the platform. Although a minor station, it once boasted a stationmaster. Heading south the branch continued to climb until the 4-mile 54-chain point was reached. From 1908 until 1937 Nancegollan passing place and a down-side signalbox were located here, the loop ending at 4 miles 71 chains. Nancegollan station itself was located at 5 miles 9 chains from the junction. Originally it had a single up-side platform and a down-side siding/loop, as well as an up-side siding that formed a bay behind the platform. A signalbox was opened in 1897 but demoted to a ground frame in 1908.

In 1937 the entire layout at Nancegollan was remodelled by the GWR, with up and down platforms forming a proper passing loop, a new signalbox at the up end of the up platform and a small goods yard on the up side. There was an up goods loop behind the

Above:
**When the line opened the very old town of Helston
had a population of only about 3,000, but in
administrative and shopping terms it was the centre
of a large rural community. In the early 19th century
some 100 tin mines had been in operation in the
broad vicinity of Helston, which had contributed
to its wealth. Early plans proposed a railway from
Helston to Hayle, where the port was thriving, but the
12-mile 30-chain line was not proceeded with on cost
grounds. Closure looms despite the busy-looking
scene on 3 March 1962, as clean green-liveried
No 4570 waits to depart with the 3.30pm to Gwinear
Road.** *Peter Gray*

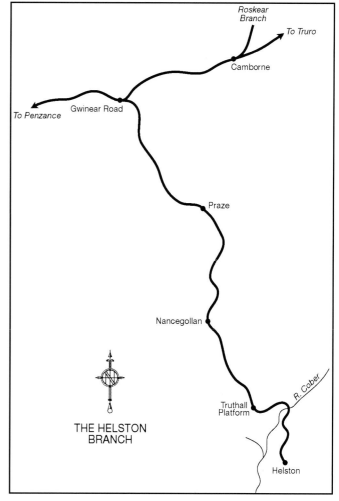

Right:
The Helston branch, from Gwinear Road station

up platform and a substantial loading dock for agricultural produce. Additional sidings were installed during World War 2 to deal with airfield construction traffic. A camping coach was kept in one of the sidings for many years, which was normally in use between April and October. There were many abandoned tin mines in the area and even today their remains can be seen.

After leaving Nancegollan the line entered a valley and ran through a succession of curves, mostly in quite deep cuttings, and these can still be traced on a modern 1:50,000 Ordnance Survey map. Running downhill at 1 in 60, the line entered the Cober Valley and at 7 miles reached Truthall Halt. This tiny single platform on the down side had a 'pagoda' hut on the cinder and sleeper platform and a single oil lamp. The GWR must have had halt mania at this time because 1905 was the same year when the many halts between Chacewater and Newquay were opened. In 1906 the name was changed to Truthall Platform and the word 'Platform' was shown in timetables for many years, although, as illustrated, the large running-in board showed the name as Truthall 'Halt'. There was not a building in sight of this halt but it was allegedly built to serve the villagers of Trannack and the residents of Truthall Manor.

From Truthall Platform the line ran due east at 1 in 60 downhill, and at 7 miles 64 chains ran on to the curved six-arch 121yd Lowertown or Cober Viaduct, the most imposing structure on the line, which crossed the river at a maximum height of 90ft. After crossing the viaduct the line climbed steeply at 1 in 60/77, then curved through a further series of cuttings to reach Helston from a northerly direction at 8 miles 67 chains. In terms of lines of latitude Helston was the most southerly railway terminus on the whole of the British mainland. The station was laid out as a through station because there were long-term plans for the line to continue to Lizard Town. However, for the whole of its working life Helston had just a single platform on the up side of the line with a stone-built station (with awning) containing the usual facilities and offices, very similar in design to that at St Ives. At the very end of the line were a two-coach carriage shed, opened in 1903, and an adjacent engine release road. There were two long goods sidings, a loading dock, cattle pen, crane and a handsome stone-built goods shed. At the north end of the station on the up side was a small engine shed and on the down side a stone chute siding, which was removed in 1932 but reinstated in 1958. The signalbox at the up end of the platform was built for the opening of the line in 1887 but was reframed in 1958, one year after the carriage shed was removed. Overall the track layout at Helston was compact but functional.

There was a large corrugated iron building near the goods shed and until 1933 this was used to house the GWR's omnibus fleet that ran from Helston to Lizard Town. The fleet was later moved to other accommodation when the building was used for the railway-owned delivery vehicles. The GWR commenced its bus service to Mullion and the Lizard on 17 August 1903 but a fire in the garage in 1904, which destroyed two vehicles, resulted in a suspension of services for over six months. The buses carried passengers, luggage and mail, and within 20 years the GWR was running bus services all over the peninsula, serving most villages, especially (from 1909) picturesque Porthleven. The two types of buses used between 1900 and World War 1 were from Milnes-Daimler and Dennis, all with 20hp engines. These famous bus services were at their peak in about 1920, and some of the bus stops had shelters with delightful names, such as 'GWR Coverack Road Motor Halt'! More modern buses were later used but by 1933 all Great Western motorbus services had been taken over by the newly created Western National Omnibus Company. The bus services were so successful that the £80,000 railway to Lizard Town was never built.

The Helston branch enjoyed a good service for a rural area, with six or seven trains per day in each direction by the 1890s; two of the seven trains in each direction were mixed but they were timed to take only about 5 minutes longer than dedicated passenger trains. The total journey time for the 8-mile 67-chain run was about 25 minutes. After 1905 journey times were 3 minutes longer for the 50% of trains that stopped at Truthall Platform. By the 1920s there were eight trains per day in each direction between the hours of 6.30am and 8.26pm. The only passing loop on the line was at Nancegollan, which was used once or twice per day.

During World War 2 there were but six trains in each direction. It was during this period that the Royal Naval Air Station at Culdrose was being built, and this installation was to produce a valuable source of traffic. In the 1950s there were nine trains per day in each direction Mondays to Fridays, but on summer Saturdays the service was an unbelievable 10 up trains and 14 down trains with five 'crossings' at Nancegollan! Journey times remained at 25 minutes, probably due to similar motive power being used over many decades and the fact that the line speed limit was 35mph from Gwinear Road to Milepost 5 and 25mph thereafter. In the 1930s, for example, there were still mixed trains but there was a dedicated goods train that was timed at 1hr 33min in the down direction and 1hr 19min on the up run.

The line received holiday traffic but Helston was not of course located on the coastline and its appeal was therefore limited, although there were bus connections to many resorts from the Helston terminus, of which many holidaymakers availed themselves. Certainly things livened up on summer Saturdays when the enhanced services were very busy, especially in the up direction in the morning and in the down in the afternoon. However, there were never any through trains from London or the North, due to difficulties in such workings reversing at Gwinear Road, a limited-length loop at Nancegollan and the limited trackwork at Helston. Although branch trains normally comprised two or three coaches on summer Saturdays, they were sometimes strengthened to six-coach formations.

There was very little variety of motive power on the Helston branch. In the early days 0-4-4Ts appeared but later small 0-4-2 and 2-4-0 tank locomotives of the '517' and 'Metro' classes normally worked the branch. Occasionally a saddle tank was seen but for some 40 years Churchward's '4500' class 2-6-2 Prairie tanks were the mainstay, one might almost say the 'Kings', of the line, with characteristics ideally suited to the Helston branch. There were normally three engines in steam on the line but the engine shed could accommodate only one. There was no turntable and locomotives normally worked chimney-first to Gwinear Road. Although the line closed to passengers just after the end of steam in 1962, once steam in Cornwall had finished the unsuccessful North British Class 22 diesel-hydraulic Bo-Bos worked the branch, but their tenure would prove to be very short indeed. They hauled the same type of maroon-coloured 'B'-set rolling stock that was working at the end of steam, but sadly they had arrived too late to produce economies, which might have deferred closure. The Class 22s also worked the freight train service from 1962 to 1964.

The freight traffic reflected the pattern and commodities of other Cornish branches with coal and fertilizer inbound and minerals, especially granite, and agricultural produce outbound. There was a thriving general goods service and a comprehensive delivery system by railway-owned commercial vehicles throughout the peninsula. Of particular note was the outgoing broccoli traffic, which amounted to 30,000 tons in 1936. However, the motor lorry made serious inroads into BR's freight traffic after World War 2 and slowly but surely wagon-load traffic declined. Small yards and minor customers were out of fashion and with the relative inflexibility of the railway, where in most cases a road interface was still necessary, it was concluded by many businesses that their traffic was far better dealt with by road transport throughout. The post-Beeching era saw no future for small freight and sundries traffic, such as that handled on the Helston branch, because it was uneconomic. Large freight concentration yards were deemed to be the way forward.

Right:
A delightful plate camera view of '517' class 0-4-2T No 1467, which has just arrived at Helston from Gwinear Road in the early 1920s; one has to admire the gleaming copper dome. In 1903 the GWR introduced a bus service between the Helston terminus and the Lizard and the service was at its peak at about the time of this photograph. The service was so successful that a once-proposed rail extension from Helston was never built. *IAL*

Left:
No 4570 was a regular performer on the branch in the late 1950s and on this day the 1.15pm service from Helston to Gwinear Road needed strengthening from three to six coaches. Having taken the spare stock from a siding, the Prairie propels the coaches back into the platform road. On the left hopper wagons are on the stone chute siding, while the goods yard seems well stocked.
P. Q. Treloar

Right:
During the last few months of service on the branch steam traction was being dispensed with throughout Cornwall and Class 22 diesel-hydraulics were drafted into service. They also worked all freight services between November 1962 and October 1964, but were photographed far less often than their Prairie predecessors. On 24 July 1962 there were two Class 22s at Helston, No D6317 on goods on the left and No D6311 on passenger duties on the right. However, these locomotives were a failure, many lasting less than 10 years. *David Hall, Butterley Photo Archives, M. Dart collection*

The 1950s were perhaps the heyday of the branch. Thereafter, with the rapidly increasing rate of car ownership and the emerging affluent society, which saw the majority of the population holidaying abroad with the advent of the package holiday, train loadings decreased. There was no doubt that the BR's network needed modernising, especially as there had been little investment in railway infrastructure since before World War 2. However, as a result of the exercise headed by Dr Beeching the primary consideration became a matter of profit or loss and at that time very few branch or cross-country lines were 'in the black'. He recommended closure of 5,000 miles of railway and 2,500 stations, and most Cornish branch lines and minor intermediate stations on the main line were vulnerable. Late in 1961, even before Beeching had reported, rumours started circulating that the Helston branch was scheduled for closure. Despite all the efforts of local pressure groups and representations by local Members of Parliament, the then Minister of Transport confirmed that the line would be closed to passenger traffic from Monday 5 November 1962, the last services being on the preceding Saturday.

Few locals believed that the line would actually close, but this possibility became a reality only when large crowds gathered at Helston station on the last day of service to actually witness the passing. Many travelled on last-day trains and there was a roaring trade in sales of tickets to keep as souvenirs. About 150 sightseers gathered on the platform in the gloom of a November evening to witness the departure of the last train to Gwinear Road, which was comprised of six non-corridor coaches. It was estimated that about 120 souls travelled on the train, certainly not a full house. Class 22 No D6312, carrying a farewell wreath, hauled the last train back to Helston, which arrived just before 10pm. Detonators heralded the arrival, fireworks were let off and cameras flashed, then the train worked back off the branch as empty coaching stock. It must have been a strange sensation to have participated in the revelry only to watch the tail lamp flickering into the darkness for the very last time, followed by total silence.

The freight service lingered on for another two years but it too succumbed on 4 October 1964. As if to rub salt into the wounds, the junction station of Gwinear Road closed from the following day, 5 October, and the whole Helston branch scene was consigned to history. The tracks were ripped up with indecent haste the following spring, and the entire line had been dismantled by the end of the year. Goods facilities were withdrawn from Gwinear Road in 1965, and on 31 October of that year the signalbox was closed and automatic barriers replaced the crossing gates. Now only a trace of the down island platform remains. The old goods shed at Helston and Cober Viaduct have survived, but all stations have been demolished, some cuttings filled, sites razed and trackbed ploughed up, joining so many other branches and byways of Cornwall.

24. St Ives Branch

The wording from old guidebooks always offers a fascinating insight into how transportation was viewed in the past. As far as St Ives and West Cornwall were concerned the 1948 view was as follows: 'A century ago [ie 1840s] the journey from London to West Cornwall occupied something like 40 hours. Nowadays, Penzance is easier of approach than Bath was then, for the Cornish expresses operating in the Western Region system of [the new] British Railways cover the distance in about seven hours, while the excellence of the roads enables an ever-increasing number of motorists to do the whole distance in one day. And though these times relate to the journey from London, equally good services are provided between Cornwall and other parts of Britain. For obvious reasons,

the run from the Midlands and the North cannot be performed quite so quickly, but through trains or through coaches make the journey very convenient, and one can breakfast in Birmingham and dine in Western Cornwall without undue sense of fatigue.'

Particularly relating to the St Ives branch the same book goes on: 'For St Ives and Carbis Bay passengers change at St Erth junction, 5 miles east of Penzance. The branch line to Lelant, Carbis Bay and St Ives is only four or five miles long and is most picturesque, running along the edge of the cliff for most of the way.' A monthly return to St Ives from London in 1948 was £6 3s 3d 1st Class and £4 2s 2d 3rd Class. Reservations could be made for 1 shilling per seat and luggage in advance could be sent for 1s 7d collected and conveyed, or 3s 1d adding delivery as well.

Above:

The St Ives branch has a claim to fame in being the furthest west of the Cornish branch lines (as distinct from mineral tramways) and the last to be built to broad gauge dimensions. The main line had become exclusively GWR owned and run in 1876 and thus it was that company that opened and operated the branch, from 1 July 1877. The junction station was at St Erth, which had previously been known as St Ives Road. In this hugely busy scene at the junction on 2 August 1958 'Hall' class 4-6-0 No 6913 *Levens Hall* heads for Penzance with the empty stock of the down 'Cornish Riviera Express' while 'Grange' class No 6824 *Ashley Grange* is halted in the up main line platform with the up milk. The train appears to have the road for the St Ives branch but it will in fact reverse into the up goods sidings to collect more milk wagons. On the right the 6.50pm branch train is headed by No 4547, while another 2-6-2T slumbers at the short bay platform on the right. *P. Q. Treloar*

Left:
On 9 November 1985 an extremely rare locomotive made a unique visit to the Royal Duchy, when Class 40 No 40122 (D200) headed 'The Penzance Fryer' tour from Manchester to Penzance. Yet another overnight one-day visit from Sussex to Cornwall on the 'Night Riviera' was therefore necessary to photograph the event, and in appalling weather the 2,000hp machine is seen storming through St Erth. The photograph shows the modern track layout, with access to the St Ives branch, on the left, being via a single set of points. The junction signalbox can be seen in the background, and at the time of writing the semaphore signals are still in operation. *JV*

St Ives, which sprang to importance in the 15th century, has a long and interesting history and it has always been quaint. In 1558 it boasted two Members of Parliament! Fishing was, historically, the main business, and even today the small boats in the harbour are a focal point. Centuries ago an Ambassador at the Court of St James's said, 'At the bottom of this high and steep hill is the quaintest little town I ever saw. There are some streets so narrow that when a donkey and cart comes along the urchins all have to run to the next corner or into doorways.' The attractive town has always been a Mecca for artists and the small harbour and adjacent sandy beaches were an enormous attraction to holidaymakers, once tourism became established. The railway had a significant contribution to make in this respect and over the past 125 years it has brought millions of visitors to the town. From a population of about 6,700 at the beginning of the 20th century the population is now around 9,000, which more than doubles in the summer months.

There was a focus on St Ives as a potential branch line destination back in the 1840s, a time when it was 'all happening' just down the road at Hayle (see Chapter 22). The WCR had obtained an Act to provide a broad gauge line through western Cornwall in 1846, but insufficient funds were available, so a further Act was obtained allowing a cheaper standard gauge line to be built. Local business people and landowners were keen to take advantage of the anticipated potential of a railway, but although two sets of plans for a main line through Cornwall had been approved in the 1840s it was to be March 1852 before the first WCR standard gauge passenger train ran from Redruth through to Penzance. Then Penzance folk had to wait until 1859 before the WCR became linked with the outside world, albeit with a change of gauge at Truro. Broad gauge rails were added to the main line in 1866 and dual gauge running for freight commenced that year and for passenger trains the following year. However, the WCR could not afford the capital costs of the conversion and a consortium of the GWR, South Devon and Bristol & Exeter companies leased the line. The whole line became exclusively GWR owned and run in 1876.

In the meantime, in WCR days the St Ives Junction Railway Company was formed with the objective of building a short branch to the town. Although the company was stymied by the

Right:
St Erth has always had a goods yard and over the years a range of commodities have been handled. For many years the up sidings were famous for milk traffic and in 1956 the Milk Marketing Board dispatched some 19 million gallons to the capital. This traffic ended in 1980 but after a long period of disuse the sidings were again used by freight wagons in the late 1990s when a local scrap metal dealer chose rail to transport his output. On 31 May 1976 one of the lamented Class 52 'Western' 2,700hp diesel-hydraulics, No D1009 *Western Invader*, was in charge of a heavy milk train. Note the loading gauge and the box van on the right. *JV*

main line delays, it was encouraging that once the main line came into operation a station rejoicing in the name of St Ives Road was opened. It was obvious that the road connection from this point, later St Erth, had limited possibilities and the finite answer to reaching the town of St Ives was to build the branch line that had been mooted earlier, and accordingly in 1873 an Act was passed to construct it. This was to be the very last branch to be built to the GWR's pre-1892 broad gauge, and construction of the 4-mile 24-chain line commenced in 1874.

Some substantial earthworks were necessary to take the line along the rugged north Cornwall coastline, and with deep cuttings along the cliffs and viaducts across the glen at Carbis Bay and near St Ives, construction took almost three years to complete. Also, what was to become St Erth station needed a substantial yard and a new complex now that it had gained junction status. The usual pre-opening inspection by the Board of Trade on 16 May 1877 found that some modifications would be required before the line could be opened to the public, including fencing, clocks at stations and a number of facing points at the terminus. The line was broad gauge and single track throughout with

sidings. Narrow gauge track was provided for the first 21 chains of the line from St Ives Road and in 1888 this was extended to the old quay at Lelant.

The line opened on 1 July 1877 and the first train, comprising six coaches and a saloon headed by an Avonside six-coupled tank locomotive called *Elephant*, left Penzance at 11am. The train was suitably decorated with flags and, as seems customary at the time, a band, that of the 11th & 13th Duke of Cornwall Volunteers, met it at St Ives, watched by cheering crowds. The line was not intended to be purely for passengers, and freight traffic was catered for. In the early days of the line fish traffic, particularly barrels of pilchards, was important, as well as, like the Helston branch, broccoli. However, by the 1890s the pilchard traffic was finished and the collapse of the mining industry generally depressed the area. Tourism was to some extent the saviour; the attractiveness of the line and the town of St Ives drew crowds and the hotel business blossomed. The GWR itself was not going to be left behind and leased the Tregenna Castle Hotel in 1878, purchasing it outright in 1895. Eventually the town of St Ives grew up around the surrounding hillsides and

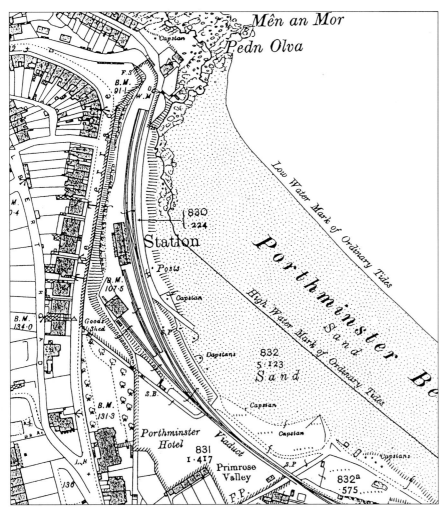

Left:
St Ives station track layout in 1908. The station area and the small goods yard on the left are now a car park and the new 1971 station is just beyond the west end of the viaduct. The tiny engine shed, which closed in 1961, is just visible at the foot of the map, centre right. *Crown Copyright*

Below:
A spirited departure from St Erth of a through ten-coach Paddington to St Ives working, on a summer Saturday in 1958. The 10.30am departure from London was scheduled to arrive in St Ives about 7 hours later. The main line locomotive handed over responsibility to a pair of the tough little '4500' class 2-6-2Ts at St Erth for the final 4¼-mile leg of the journey. Nos 4540 and 4566 take to the branch in an era when the package holiday trade to 'Costa Lotta' had yet to develop and the Cornish Riviera still attracted holidaymakers in their thousands. *P. Q. Treloar*

Right and Below:
The St Ives branch timetable for November 1888 (upper) and the summer of 1958 (lower). Again there is through traffic to and from London on summer Saturdays.

ST. ERTH and ST. IVES. — Great Western.

Mls	Down.	Week Days.									Sundays.			
		mrn	gov	mrn	aft	aft	aft	gov	gov		mrn	gov	gov	gov
	St. Erth .... dep	7 30	10 33	11 32	12 30	2 43	5 18	6 55	8 50	....	7 30	9 40	10 45	6 18
1	Lelant	7 33	10 36	11 35	12 33	2 47	5 18	6 58	8 53	....	7 33	9 43	10 49	6 18
3	Carbis Bay	7 41	10 44	11 42	12 41	2 55	5 26	7 9	9 1	....	7 41	9 51	10 56	6 26
4½	St. Ives .... arr	7 45	10 48	11 45	12 45	2 59	5 30	7 11	9 5	....	7 45	9 55	11 0	6 30

Mls	Up.	gov	gov	mrn	mrn	aft	aft	gov	gov		mrn	gov	gov	aft
—	St. Ives .... dep	6 20	9 50	11 5	11 58	2 0	4 40	5 50	8 12	....	7 0	9 15	10 20	4 50
1½	Carbis Bay	6 24	9 54	11 9	12 1	2 4	4 54	5 54	8 16	....	7 4	9 19	10 24	4 54
3½	Lelant	6 32	10 2	11 17	12 9	2 12	5 2	6 2	8 24	....	7 12	9 27	10 32	5 2
4½	St. Erth 10, 15	6 35	10 6	11 20	12 13	2 16	5 6	6 6	8 27	....	7 15	9 30	10 35	5 6

Table 103   ST. ERTH and ST. IVES

MONDAYS TO FRIDAYS

Miles		am	am	am	am	am	am	noon	pm	pm	pm	pm	pm	pm	pm	pm	pm	pm
81	Penzance .. .. dep	6 25	7 30	7A55	8 55	10F30	11 0	12 0	1 20	1 55	3 35	4 20	4 50	5 45	6 0	7 20	8 45	9 30
—	St. Erth .... dep	7 0	7 45	8 45	9 55	11 0	11 50	12 35	1 30	2 15	4 12	4 55	5 10	6 0	6 20	7 35	9 0	9 45
1	Lelant	7 3	7 48	8 48	9 58	11 3	11 53	12 38	1 33	2 18	4 15	5 13	3	6 23	7 38	9 3	9 48
3	Carbis Bay	7 10	7 55	8 55	10 5	11 10	12 0	12 45	1 40	2 25	4 22	5 3	5 20	6 10	6 30	7 45	9 10	9 55
4½	St. Ives .. .. arr	7 15	8 0	9 0	10 10	11 15	12 5	12 50	1 45	2 30	4 27	5 10	5 25	6 15	6 35	7 50	9 15	10 0

SATURDAYS

		am	am	am	am	am	am	am	am	pm	pm	pm	pm	pm	pm	pm	pm	pm	pm	pm	pm
81	Penzance .. .. dep		7 30	8 20		10 5	10 45	11 50	11 20	1 55	3 35	4 20	4 50	6 10	7 20	8 45	10 10
	St. Erth .... dep	6 35	7 48	8 40	9 36	10 20	11 17	12 5	1 30	2 15	2 45	3 55	4 40	5 15	6 25	6 50	7 35	8 15	9 0	9 45	10 40
	Lelant	6 33	7 51	8 43		11 20	12 8	1 33	2 18	2 48	3 58	4 43	5 18	6 28	6 53	7 38	8 18	9 3	9 48	10 43
	Carbis Bay	6 13	6 45	7 58	8 50	9 44	10 28	11 27	12 15	1 40	2 25	2 55	4 5	4 50	5 25	6 35	7 0	7 45	8 25	9 10	9 55	10 50
	St. Ives .. .. arr	6 20	6 53	8 3	8 57	9 50	10 34	11 32	12 20	1 45	2 30	3 0	4 10	4 55	5 35	6 40	7 5	7 50	8 30	9 15	10 0	10 55

SUNDAYS

		am	am	am	am	pm	pm	pm	pm	pm	pm	pm	pm	pm	pm
81	Penzance .. .. dep		8 40		9 45	11 0		1 10	3 0	4 0	4 45		6 45	8 0	8 45	
	St. Erth .... dep	8 0	9 0		10 0	11 15	12 35	1 35	3 15	4 15	5 5	5 55	7 0	8 11	9 0	9 40
	Lelant	8 3	9 3		10 3	11 18	12 38	1 38	3 18		5 8	5 58	7 3	8 14	9 3	9 43
	Carbis Bay	8 10	9 10		10 10	11 25	12 45	1 45	3 25	4 23	5 15	6 5	7 10	8 21	9 10	9 50
	St. Ives .. .. arr	8 15	9 15		10 15	11 30	12 50	1 50	3 30	4 28	5 20	6 10	7 15	8 26	9 15	9 55

MONDAYS TO FRIDAYS

Miles		am	am	am	am	am	am	pm	pm	pm	pm	pm	pm	pm	pm	pm
—	St. Ives .. .. .. dep	6 15	7 25	8 10	9 35	10 20	11 20	12 10	1 5	1 50	3 30	4 32	5 32	7 0	7 13	8 35	9 20
1½	Carbis Bay	6 20	7 30	8 15	9 40	10 25	11 25	12 15	1 10	1 55	3 35	4 37	5 37	5 7	7 5	7 18	8 40	9 25
3½	Lelant	6 26	7 36	8 21	9 46	10 31	11 31	12 21	1 16	2 1	3 41	4 43	5 43	7 25	8 46	9 31
4½	St. Erth .... arr	6 30	7 40	8 25	9 50	10 35	11 35	12 25	1 20	2 5	3 45	4 47	5 47	7 13	7 29	8 50	9 35
10	81 Penzance .. .. arr	7 45		8 45		11 10	11 50	12 47	1 45	2 25	4 25	5 18	6 26	7 40	8 30	9 10	9 50

SATURDAYS

		am	am	am	am	am	am	am	am	pm	pm	pm	pm	pm	pm	pm	pm	pm	pm
	St. Ives .. .. .. dep	5H45	7H25	8H10	9H20	9H55	10H40	10H55	11H40	1H 5	1 50	3 30	4 20	5 45	7 10	7 55	8 35	9 20
	Carbis Bay	5H50	7H30	8H15	9H25	10H 0	10H45	11H 0	11H45	1H10	1 55	3 35	4 25	5 50	7 15	8 0	8 40	9 25
	Lelant	7H36	8H21	9H31	10H 6	11H 6	11H51	1H16	2 1	3 41	4 31	5 56	7 21	8 6	8 46	9 31
	St. Erth .... arr	6 0	7 40	8 25	9 35	10 10	10 53	11 10	11 55	1H20	2 5	3 45	4 35	6 0	7 25	8 10	8 50	9 35
81	Penzance .. .. arr	6 25	8H25	8 50	9 50	11 10	11Z30	1 55	2 30	4 0	5 0	6 35	7 45	9 0	9 30	9 55

SUNDAYS

		am	am	am	am	pm	pm	pm	pm	pm	pm	pm	pm	pm
	St. Ives .. .. .. dep	8 30		9 35	10 25	11 50	1 0	2 10	3 50	4 35	5 30	6 25	7 20	8 35	9 20
	Carbis Bay	8 35		9 40	10 30	11 55	1 5	2 15	3 55	4 40	5 35	6 30	7 25	3 40	9 25
	Lelant	8 41		9 46	10 36	12 1	1 11	2 21	4 1	4 46	5 41	6 36	7 31	8 46	9 31
	St. Erth .... arr	8 45		9 50	10 40	12 5	1 15	2 25	4 5	4 50	5 45	6 40	7 35	8 50	9 35
81	Penzance .. .. arr			11 0		12 40		2 40	4 20		6 0		7 0	7 50		9 50

A Until 30th July dep 8 30 am   **B** Through Train from or to Penzance   **C** Through Train to Par (Table 81)
D Runs 12th July to 9th August inclusive. Through Carriages from London (Pad) dep 10 12 pm Friday nights 11th July to 8th August inclusive (Table 81)   **F** From 30th June dep 10 45 am   **G** On Fridays dep 4 40 pm   **H** Passengers travelling by this train beyond Plymouth are required to hold Regulation Tickets (see pages 31, 32 and 33)   **K** Applies until 6th September inclusive   **L** Through Train to London (Pad) arr 4 40 pm (Table 81)   **N** Through Carriages from London (Pad.) dep 10 30 am (Table 81)   **Z** On 13th September arr 11 50 am

many hotels and guesthouses became established to accommodate the increasing numbers of holidaymakers. The same development occurred at Carbis Bay where the sandy beach and the proximity of the railway station made it an ideal destination for the annual holiday of the upper middle classes.

At the time of opening there were five round trip workings on the branch on weekdays and two on Sundays. The journey time was 15 minutes, a figure determined to some extent by the overall 30mph speed limit. By 1888 there were eight weekday and four Sunday trains — obviously traffic was booming! In 1909 there were no fewer than 13 trains each way, three of which were mixed,

Left:
With Lelant station in the background the branch train runs beside the estuary of the Hayle River on its way to St Ives, the bark of the Prairie no doubt echoing against the hillside as No 4566 passes the site of the old siding to Lelant Quay on 14 April 1960. The quay line was opened in 1888 but closed in about 1914. The quay sported a large warehouse, a crane and a weighbridge, but the large volumes of traffic anticipated never materialised. *P. Q. Treloar*

Right:
This charming study of Lelant is probably Edwardian and it shows the moustached stationmaster with waistcoat and pocket-watch plus his faithful four-legged friend. The station building contained a booking hall, ladies' waiting room, gentlemen's lavatory and store. The building survives in private ownership and has now been extended (see the title page illustration). *JV collection*

Left:
Neither the shelter nor the station lighting of the 21st century have the charm or aesthetic appeal of the Edwardian scene, but at least the trains are still running. This shot shows the current scene with a two-car Class 150/2 arriving at Lelant from St Ives. The overall journey times of between 11 and 15 minutes have not changed much over the years due mainly to speed restrictions. Timetables show that a handful of branch trains have always worked through to and from Penzance. *JV*

Above:
Photographs on the headland by Lelant golf course are far less common than in the station areas but the short walk to this vantage point is very rewarding. The town and quays of Hayle can be seen on the left, and centre top is the main line Hayle Viaduct. Skirting the estuary is single 'bubble car' unit P103, No 55003, forming the 17.07 St Erth to St Ives service on 5 April 1991. *JV*

Right:
The single-car diesel-mechanical Class 121 and 122 units were regular performers on all of the Cornish branches over a period of 30 years. Although they did not have the longevity of the Churchward-designed '4500' class steam locomotives, they deserve a place in the Cornish railway 'hall of fame'. They were attractive vehicles and in the right surroundings very photogenic, the large numbers of doors and the roof ventilators somehow making them look older than they were.

With a 200mm Nikkor lens providing some 'punch', unit P103 runs along the north coast headland east of Carbis Bay and makes for Lelant with the 17.21 St Ives to St Erth service. *JV*

Left:
This is the scene at Carbis Bay about 100 years ago with an outside-framed 0-6-0 saddle tank and crew posing for the photographer, who no doubt had his plate camera on a large tripod. There seems to be a six-wheeled carriage amongst the three St Ives-bound bogie coaches. The main station building is located top right, well above platform level. *JV collection*

Below:
The branch train seems to be doing a roaring trade at Carbis Bay on 30 July 1960. No 4571 is heading an augmented 'B'-set, with both 1st and 2nd Class accommodation. Carbis Bay, just under 3 miles from St Erth, attracted large holiday crowds who lodged in the many hotels and guesthouses in the area and enjoyed the splendid sandy beach. The 4.20pm would be one of 16 departures from Carbis Bay in each direction on this day.
Peter Gray

although Sunday travellers still had the choice of only four trains. St Ives loadings were truly in the ascendant and by 1929 there was an almost unbelievable 16 trains per day each way, and by then four of them worked through to (and from) Penzance. By the summer of 1938 the signalman at St Erth must have had a tough job because there were 19 return workings on weekdays and nine on Sundays, as well as main line traffic. For a line with no passing loop this number of trains was a significant achievement. Even during World War 2 there were a dozen trains each way. In the late 1950s there were again 19 trains on summer Saturdays but with the notable addition of a 20th train, the 'Cornish Riviera Express'! A pair of Prairie tanks normally worked the ten-coach Restaurant Car express from St Erth. There had been through coach workings to and from Paddington since the 1920s. During the 1990s and through to 2001 there were still between 16 and 22 round trip workings, five of which worked to and from Penzance. In recent years a Sunday service has been provided only in the summer months.

The volume of traffic was of course reflected in the receipts for the line. For example, in 1903 the total revenues at St Ives from passenger and freight amounted to £20,887, and in 1923 it had grown to £46,862. The ratio for the same years at Lelant was similar: £784 and £1,997. The main goods traffic was coal, road stone and broccoli; there were also tens of thousands of parcels sent annually. Some 95,000 tickets were sold at St Ives in 1923, and incoming passengers, who already had tickets, almost certainly exceeded that number. By 1937 just over 60,000 tickets were issued at St Ives, plus 1,391 season tickets. On the up side, in the summer of 1978, the year when Lelant Saltings opened, some 136,000 passengers took advantage of the Park and Ride scheme.

Other than the aforementioned Avonside 0-6-0 tank *Elephant* and a 4-4-0T called *Magpie*, GWR (ex-South Devon Railway) 4-4-0ST *Stag* was also noted on the line in the 1880s and it continued in use until the broad gauge was abandoned in 1892. Early postcards show that after 1892 0-6-0STs of the '850' class worked the branch as well as '517' class 0-4-2Ts, 'Metro' 2-4-0Ts and a pair of 0-4-4Ts, Nos 34 and 35. In 1906 the earlier series of '4400' class 2-6-2 Prairie tanks arrived on the scene and from the 1930s their larger-wheeled cousins, the '4500' class Prairies, started to appear. As with so many Cornish branches the latter were to dominate the motive power scene on the St Ives line for over 30 years; the heavier '4575' series did not work the branch. Normally two locomotives in steam were necessary to work the line, although occasionally three were employed. In 1961 the first diesels, in the shape of North British Class 22s, started to appear on the branch. However, within a short space of time the ubiquitous DMUs took over and in various formations and from a number of different sub-classes they dominated services until the 1990s, when modern diesel-hydraulic units finally ousted the 30-year-old-plus units.

St Erth still has a stone L-shaped building on the up side built in traditional GWR style, and a stone-built shelter has survived on the down platform. The single-track broad gauge main line was converted to standard gauge in 1892, and from that date an additional platform was constructed giving up and down main line platforms plus a bay platform for the St Ives branch. An attractive covered overbridge was the only exit for down passengers, while for up passengers there was an across-platform connection for St Ives, but the platform surface was at two levels and even today travellers have to step down for the branch train. The main line to Hayle was doubled in 1899 and to Marazion in 1929. The signalbox, located beyond the St Ives junction on the up side, was reframed in 1929, when the westbound line was being doubled. New refuge sidings were added to the trackwork in 1936, two opposite the signalbox on the down side and one on the up side at the Penzance end of the up platform. The goods yard was on the up side, north of the branch bay platform. In addition to general goods, for many years a siding served the adjacent creamery and for decades large volumes of milk left St Erth for London every day. Except for the milk, goods facilities were withdrawn from St Erth in 1967, and for many years there was no freight handled here, but in 2000 English, Welsh & Scottish Railways started to haul loads of scrap metal from the up sidings. At the time of writing the old manually controlled lower quadrant semaphore signals survive.

From St Erth the branch curves to the north and enters a cutting under the main A30 road before curving towards the Hayle estuary. From the late 1960s road traffic was so heavy in St Ives during the summer months that in 1971 much of the town's station site was redeveloped as a car park, but more of that later. By the late 1970s BR had come up with the clever idea of introducing a 'park and ride' scheme, whereby motorists left their cars nearly 4 miles from St Ives and travelled into the town, with its narrow streets, by train. As a result, on 27 May 1978 Lelant Saltings station, 52 chains from the junction, was opened, an exposed location with a single concrete platform on the down side and a large adjacent car park. The single line then continues to Lelant, 1 mile 8 chains from St Erth, one of the original stations on the line with a single platform face on the down side. The attractive wooden building has survived the passage of time and teas are available in season. Just beyond Lelant on the estuary side of the track was a dual gauge spur to Lelant Quay; opened in 1888 it closed in about 1914, the large volume of anticipated traffic never having materialised. The quay was 600ft long, with a warehouse on the quayside together with a crane and a weighbridge. Otherwise there was never a goods yard or siding at Lelant, although it did handle small packages.

Right:
The DMUs ended their West Country days on the St Ives branch, and it seems somehow fitting that they eked out their days in such pleasant surroundings. The summer months always saw the branch trains strengthened and this was particularly the case after 27 May 1978 when Lelant Saltings station opened and the successful 'park and ride' scheme commenced. A chocolate and cream two-car unit leads another, Network SouthEast-liveried, two-car unit up the 1 in 60 away from Carbis Bay towards St Erth in 1993. *John Hicks*

Above:
Arriving at St Ives with the six-coach 2.15pm train from St Erth on 4 August 1961 is No 4549. There is no economy in the provision of motive power as No 4570 waits to attach itself to the rear of the train for the return journey. The goods yard on the right closed in September 1963 and together with the run-round loop was removed in 1964. The small locomotive shed can be seen above the last coach of the train; it closed in September 1961. The beach tents seem to be busy, probably because the crowds are sheltering from the dull weather. *Peter Gray*

Left:
This postcard was published by a St Ives photographer and shows the very end of the branch, with St Ives station and branch train in the background. Corridor coaches such as this were still working in the 1950s, but looking at the vintage bus the photograph probably dates back to the 1920s. The bay at Porthminster sands can be seen to advantage.
JV collection

Right:
In 1971 there were radical changes at the St Ives terminus when the line was significantly cut back, the delightful old GWR granite station demolished and the space given over to the lucrative car parking business. A small cheap and nasty station office building was constructed, a glorified bus shelter was built on a featureless concrete platform, and the line became a single-track siding from St Erth. In this July 1999 view a Class 150/2 unit pauses at the new platform, with car park revenues probably exceeding the takings on the train. The two buildings just above the leading coach can be seen in the previous, older, view. *JV*

The line then twists north and northwest along the banks of the estuary with sand dunes peppering the landscape. Hayle Wharves can be seen across the water and in the distance Hayle Viaduct is just visible. The line crosses a golf course while climbing at 1 in 60 in a northwesterly direction, with passengers being afforded tremendous views of the coastline on the up side. After the long and deep Carrack Gladden cutting the line descends at 1 in 60 to reach Carbis Bay at 2 miles 78 chains. Carbis also comprises a single platform on the down side of the line. Most of the platforms at stations on the St Ives branch have been extended at some time and at Carbis Bay it was lengthened from 300ft to 430ft in 1900. The stone-built station building, now demolished, was at a high level and passengers descended to platform level on a sloping footpath. The line then crosses the 78yd-long Carbis Bay Viaduct comprising four 40ft arches and curves northward, again with spectacular views along the cliffs to Porthminster Head. The line then descends steeply to St Ives.

Just outside St Ives there were points on the down side that led to a small single-locomotive engine shed. Opened with the line in 1877, it closed in September 1961. The line then curves north and crosses St Ives Viaduct, and at this point there have been significant changes over the years. The pre-1971 alignment continued on the curve to the end of the single-faced St Ives station platform, and on the down side there was a bay platform, a goods shed and siding. The bay platform was used mostly for freight traffic, with coal being unloaded on the 'off' side. From 1958 a camping coach was located on the goods shed road and another was added in 1960; they survived until the summer of 1964. On the south side of the goods shed was the signalbox, which was reframed in 1903. On the outside of the platform line was another track, which provided a run-round loop and a refuge for berthing three or four carriages. The station, 4 miles 24 chains from St Erth, was in a magnificent setting ensuring that there was no anticlimax after such a scenic and memorable journey.

Freight traffic was withdrawn in September 1963 and the engine shed siding was lifted. The signalbox was reduced to ground frame status on 9 September 1963 and closed completely on 10 March 1965. On 28 October 1963 the run-round loop was taken out of use followed by the entire goods yard in August 1964. Then in 1971 there were radical changes at St Ives. By then the line was effectively already a single-line stub worked by shuttling DMUs, completely devoid of signals or sidings.

To accommodate a very lucrative traffic in car parking revenues the line was substantially cut back to 4 miles 20 chains and a new, featureless concrete terminus platform was built, approximately where the old goods shed once stood. Although all of this rationalisation was depressing, nothing could change the beauty of the journey itself.

Nevertheless in the early 1960s it was not guaranteed that the line would survive. The 1950s had seen a revitalisation of the branch as the lingering memories of wartime gradually diminished and life and finances returned to normal. However, as with so many other branch lines, the combination of rapidly increasing car ownership, package holidays and the jet plane plus increasing affluence resulted in railway finances coming under scrutiny. This particularly applied to loss-making branch and cross-country lines. Dr Beeching was commissioned to report on the subject and he made radical 'restructuring' proposals to eliminate at a stroke all loss-making routes. The government wanted a reduction in its huge subsidies and it was impossible to defend the financial viability of many West Country branches, although many questioned the entire ethos of the exercise. Locals were shocked when the St Ives branch was included in the 'for closure' list and even more shocked when a closure date of 5 October 1965 was announced. However, in the case of St Ives the results from the recent rationalisation of station staff, the employment of diesels and an overall reduction in costs had yet to filter through. There was a reprieve for the branch, and a change of government slowed down the closure programme. Traffic levels were still high on the branch, especially in the summer months, and the branch miraculously escaped closure.

Although happily the line has survived, the trains are not very inspiring these days. From time to time locomotives, either on enthusiasts' specials or on the annual weedkilling train, visit the line, but without a run-round loop all locomotive-worked trains need to be 'topped and tailed'. Over the years loadings have varied from between two and six coaches on local trains and 10 coaches when the 'Cornish Riviera' ran from St Ives to Paddington and vice versa. In DMU days anything from six-car DMU formations in summer to a single 'bubble car' in winter worked the line. In railway infrastructure terms St Erth is the jewel on the line and as a junction station it retains much of its atmosphere, helped by the surviving station buildings, trackwork, signalbox and signals. The little line has survived for 125 years — long may it continue!

Bibliography

Anthony, G. H., *The Hayle, West Cornwall & Helston Railways* (Oakwood, 1968)
  The Tavistock, Launceston & Princetown Railway (Oakwood, 1983)
Barker, Oswald J., 'The St Ives Branch' in *Railway Bylines*, July 1999
Barton, D. B., *The Redruth and Chasewater Railway 1824–1915* (Bradford Barton, 1978)
Barton, R. M., *A History of the Cornish China Clay Industry* (Bradford Barton, 1966)
Bennett, Alan, *The GWR in East Cornwall* (Kingfisher Railway Publications, 1990)
  The GWR in Mid Cornwall (Kingfisher Railway Publications, 1988)
  The GWR in West Cornwall (Kingfisher Railway Publications, 1988)
Binding, John, *Brunel's Cornish Viaducts* (Atlantic/Pendragon Books, 1993)
Cooke, R. A., *Track layouts and Diagrams of the GWR and BR (WR), East and West Cornwall* (1995)
Cornwall Archaeological Unit, *The Luxulyan Valley* (Cornwall CC, 1988)
  Minerals Tramway Project (Cornwall CC, 1990)
Dart, Maurice, *Cornish China Clay Trains in Colour* (Ian Allan, 2000)
  Last Days of Steam, Plymouth and Cornwall (Alan Sutton, 1990)
  'The Goonbarrow Branch' in *Archive* Issue 24 (Lightmoor Press)
Drew, J. H. and Lewis, M. J. T., *Rail & Sea to Pentewan* (Twelveheads Press, 1986)
Fairclough, A., *Cornwall's Railways, A Pictorial Survey* (Bradford Barton, 1972)
Fairclough, A. and Shepherd, B., *Mineral Railways of the West Country* (Bradford Barton, 1975)
Fairclough, A. and Wills, A., *Bodmin & Wadebridge 1834 to 1978* (Bradford Barton, 1979)
Ford, H. L., *Diesels on Cornwall's Main Line* (Bradford Barton, 1974)
Gray, Peter, *Steam in Cornwall* (Ian Allan, 1993)
Jenkins, Stanley C., *The Helston Branch* (Oakwood, 1992)
  'The Helston Branch' in *Back Track*, November/December 1989
  'The St. Ives Branch' in *The Great Western Railway Journal*, Late Summer 1992
Kittridge, Alan, *Cornwall's Maritime Heritage* (Twelveheads Press, 1989)
Larn, Richard and Bridget, *Charlestown* (Tor Mark Press, 1994)
Lewis, M. J. T., *The Pentewan Railway* (Twelveheads Press, 1981)
Messenger, M., *Caradon & Looe, the Canal/Railways/Mines* (Twelveheads Press, 1978)
Mills, B., *The Branch, Plymouth to Launceston* (Plym Valley Railway Company, 1983)
Mitchell, David, *British Railways Past and Present, No 17 Cornwall* (Past & Present Publishing, 1993)
Popplewell, L., *The Railways, Canals and Mines of Looe & Liskeard* (Oakwood, 1977)
Reade, Lewis, *Branch Lines of Cornwall* (Atlantic Books, 1984)
Riley, R. C., 'Beattie Well Tanks' in *British Railways Journal*, Winter 1984
Smith, Keith and Mitchell, Vic, *Branch Line to Bude* (Middleton Press, 1994)
Smith, Martin, 'Liskeard & Looe' in *British Railways Illustrated*, December 1992/January 1993
Stengelhofen, John, *Cornwall's Railway Heritage* (Twelveheads Press, 1983)
Thomas, D. St John, *A Regional History of the Railways of Great Britain, The West Country* (David & Charles, 1981)
Tolson, J. M., Roose, G. and Whetmath, C. F. D., *Railways of Looe and Caradon* (Forge Books, 1974)
Vaughan, John, *An Illustrated History of China Clay Trains* (OPC, 1987; 2nd ed, OPC, 1999)
  'Bugle's Railways Remembered' in *Steam Railway*, August 1997
  Diesels in the Duchy (Ian Allan, 1983)
  The Newquay Branch and Its Branches (OPC, 1991)
Whetmath, C. F. D., *The Bodmin & Wadebridge Railway* (Forge Books, 1994)
Whetmath, C. F. D., Crombleholme, R., Stuckey, D. and Gibson, B. *Callington Railways* (Forge Books, 1985)
Woodfin, R. J., *The Cornwall Railway* (Bradford Barton, 1972)

Right:
The preparation of this book has evoked a number of pleasant memories. For over 30 years I have actively pursued the branch trains of Cornwall, but sadly so many of the lines and sidings illustrated herein have closed, railway infrastructure has been removed, many classes of motive power have become extinct and many railwaymen friends have 'gone on'. Fortunately there are still a handful of branches in operation in Cornwall for either passenger and/or freight, but views such as this can never be repeated. On 25 March 1992 No 08955 leaves the Ponts Mill works and makes for St Blazey with two 'Tiger' wagons and a brake-van; this would be the last time I would see the little branch freight as the works closed a month later and was subsequently demolished. This evocative picture ends our comprehensive tour of the 'Branches and Byways of Cornwall'. *JV*

Acknowledgements

In order to include in this unique volume every standard gauge Cornish branch line that was connected to the erstwhile British Railways (GWR/SR) system, plus three notable early Cornish narrow gauge lines, it has been necessary to rely on a large number of individuals and organisations for information and illustrations.

In particular I must thank the authors of all the books and magazine articles contained in the Bibliography. From personal experience I know what a 'labour of love' such literary projects can be and how much effort goes into research. I also want to record my thanks to the staff at the Cornwall Records Office at Truro, the Local Studies Library at Redruth, and the British Library in London.

In terms of geographical and chronological coverage many fellow photographers, past and present, have played an important part in illustrating this book. In particular I want to express my sincere gratitude to Peter Gray, Dick Riley, Peter Treloar and Maurice Dart, all of whom made special efforts to meet my requirements. The many other photographic contributors are mentioned in the photo credits within the book. Thanks must also go to my publishers for the freedom afforded in terms of content, design and layout but also for access to the Ian Allan and SLS Libraries.

My old friend and colleague John Frith, in casting his experienced eye over nearly 120,000 words and many hundreds of facts contained within the text, undertook an onerous task. However, any errors that do survive proof-reading are the responsibility of the author. In more than 100 visits to the Royal Duchy over 33 years I have travelled with many friends and former friends who have enriched my travels. They include John Frith, John Hicks, Keith Freak, Maurice Dart, Steve Chandler, Richard Cossey, John Chalcraft, Steve Turner, Brian Morrison, Ian Scales, Bill Walker, Steve Taylor, Mike Collins, Les Nixon and my family!

I would like to acknowledge the help and friendship of many Cornwall-based railwaymen who, in the more carefree days of old, provided shelter and information, in offices, signalboxes and on motive power. They provided privileged opportunities to view the working railway at first hand. In no particular order they include Ivor Trudgeon, Peter Hamley, Gordon Rosevear, Geoff Pengelly, Ian Blackburn, Roy Stockman, Signalman Monk, Phil Hancock, Gladys Sleeman, Albert Hooper, Driver Prophet, Don Tregaskes, Percy Wherry, John Hiscott-Walsh, Bill Richards, Fernie Phelp, Little Albert, Vernon Collins, Eric Rowe, Carey Batchelor, Herbert May, Billie Johns and many others.

The St Blazey Managers and Supervisors were the epitome of patience and provided much valuable information. They operated under British Railways, British Rail, Transrail (Railfreight) and English, Welsh & Scottish Railways, and include Norman Searle, Freeman Walsh, George Hemmett, Alan Butler, Adrian Cannon, Phil Menear, Peter Bennett, John Williams and Hugh Phillips. They all treated me as a friendly pain-in-the-neck over many decades! In the capacity of photographer/author/journalist a more than amicable professional relationship was developed and sometimes special requirements were generously arranged. This could never be achieved in today's world of corporate pressures, Health and Safety issues, the risk of public liability insurance claims, CCTV, terrorists and vandals, even with a lineside photographic pass!

The management of the English China Clay Company and the Goonvean & Rostowrack China Clay Company (now Imerys and Goonvean respectively) helped with earlier but related books and I recognise their contribution. Over the years I have been well accommodated by David and Mary Harris of Trevelyan and later Trengoffe Farms near Mount, Ted and Barbara Ellway (now retired) of the Stag Inn at Liskeard station, and Eva Mitchell (now retired) at Courtlands, Lamellion Cross. On occasions very early breakfasts were required!

Finally I want to mention the special support and encouragement given to me by my wife, Maureen, whose social life suffered somewhat during the year or so that *Branches and Byways: Cornwall* was in the course of preparation. I dedicate this book to her and the other three ladies in my life, daughters Caroline and Joanna and my faithful dog Ella!

Geographical Index By Chapter